American State and Local Politics

American State and Local Politics: Directions for the 21st Century

Edited by

Ronald E. Weber
University of Wisconsin–Milwaukee

and

Paul Brace
Rice University

CHATHAM HOUSE PUBLISHERS

SEVEN BRIDGES PRESS, LLC

NEW YORK • LONDON

Seven Bridges Press, LLC
135 Fifth Avenue, 9th Floor
New York, NY 10010-7101

Publisher: Robert J. Gormley
Managing Editor: Katharine Miller
Production Supervisor: Melissa A. Martin
Cover Design: Inari Information Services, Inc.
Composition: ediType
Printing and Binding: Versa Press, Inc.

Library of Congress Cataloging-in-Publication Data

American state and local politics : directions for the 21st century
    / edited by Ronald E. Weber and Paul Brace.
        p.   cm.
    ISBN 1-56643-071-2
    1. State governments – United States. 2. Local government – United
States. I. Weber, Ronald E., 1938-   II. Brace, Paul, 1954-
JK2408 .A683   1999
351.73 – dc21   99-6050

Manufactured in the United States of America
10   9   8   7   6   5   4   3   2   1

In the memory of the late Edward Artinian
Founder of Chatham House Publishers

Contents

Tables and Figures

Preface and Acknowledgments

Editing a book on state-local politics which involves the caliber of authors we included was truly a daunting task. The idea for this book germinated a long time ago, and Edward Artinian played a principal role in making the project happen. It grew out of a frustration by one of the editors with the books available to adopt for use in supplementing core state-local politics texts. The range of options in supplementary texts are limited, and what an instructor faces is a tradeoff between volumes that focus too much on current events in the states and localities and those which do not have a sufficient range of topics providing a challenge to the students. Since state-local politics is usually taught in the state university context and much less so in the private university context, we decided to team up in the hope of stimulating some teaching of this topic in universities that have no tradition of dealing with state-local politics. One of us has spent his whole teaching career in state universities, while the other has taught in both public and private universities (and is currently teaching at a private university).

The theme of this book is political and policy change in the states and localities over the past three decades or so, with an explicit attempt to focus on institutional change. We have observed that such changes have occurred rapidly and that it is important for today's students to understand how much change has taken place that affects their current lives. To teach contemporary state and local politics and policymaking without reference to the recent past seems fruitless. This book is designed to overcome the myopia of current generations of students and to be relevant to the issues facing students in their contemporary lives. A number of our current students expect to focus on jobs in the public sector and need knowledge about the current operations of state-local politics. Whether we like it or not, the national public sector is not growing in employment opportunities, and it is to the state-local sector that current students must look for future employment. Future teachers, law enforcement officials, and social workers are among those who regularly enroll in state-local politics courses at state universities.

In planning this book we strove to find the most expert persons available to contribute each chapter. That meant we had to accommodate the busy schedules of active scholars. In almost all cases, we knew personally who we wanted to include as authors of the chapters. In a couple of cases, we did not know personally the particular person who would author the chapter and had to rely on recommendations made by other contributors.

We are most pleased with the work of the scholars who were recommended to us. We wanted a mixture of senior scholars with well-developed reputations in their respective subfields as well as those whose careers are just taking off and who could bring in new data and ideas to the book. We believe that we have achieved both a suitable mix of topics and an excellent team of scholars who are experts on the subjects.

We suspect it is unusual to dedicate a book to a person who was not a member of the immediate family of either editor. Edward Artinian was an extraordinary man, and many books should be dedicated to him. Ed was a constant presence at national and regional political science meetings. His early career ranged from traveling book salesman to editor for large publishing houses owned by conglomerates. His dream was to be independent and establish his own publishing house. This he achieved with Chatham House and he spent the rest of his career developing a first-rate, independent outlet for political science work. We in political science owe much to him for the vision he brought to Chatham House. His death caused many of us to worry about the future of Chatham House as an independent publisher. Fortunately, two investors — Robert Gormley and Ted Bolen — convinced Pat Artinian to let them take over Chatham House and keep it independent. We are honored to be among the first authors to bring out a book under the imprint of Chatham House and Seven Bridges Press.

In addition to the large debt of gratitude we owe Edward Artinian for shepherding this project along, we want to thank several other persons at Chatham House and Seven Bridges Press for their assistance with this project: Robert Gormley, Ted Bolen, Pat Artinian, Katharine Miller, Melissa Martin, Chris Kelaher, and the project manager John Eagleson at ediType. At the University of Milwaukee–Wisconsin, we thank Robert J. Krueger, Kim Zagorski, Teresa Campbell, and Wendy Martinek, current and past project assistants to the Wilder Crane Professor. A special debt of gratitude is owed to the state legislative leadership in Wisconsin for creating the Wilder Crane Professorship about a decade ago to remember the late Wilder Crane Jr. in terms of his leadership of the University of Wisconsin–Milwaukee department of political science and for his service in the Wisconsin General Assembly. At Rice University we thank Kellie Martin for exceptional help in completing this project. In addition, Professor Laura Langer of the University of Arizona made numerous contributions that aided in the completion of this project. Finally, we thank Christopher Z. Mooney at West Virginia University for reading the manuscript in draft and helping us make improvements in it.

CHAPTER ONE
States and Localities Transformed
Ronald E. Weber and Paul Brace

OVER THE PAST three decades, states and localities in the United States have changed dramatically in function and performance. State and local government power in the U.S. federal system was at a low ebb in the 1960s. Elites as well as average Americans were confident then that most domestic problems required national rather than state or local attention, and the push for uniform solutions had strong momentum. Congress passed many pieces of landmark domestic legislation during the Great Society period (1965–66) of the Johnson administration, including major reforms of welfare, health, and education programs that deeply affected state and local delivery of public services. For example, the Social Security Act was amended to create new categories of cash assistance programs that were to be administered by the states on a matching basis. The Medicaid program, which provided funding to the states to entitle welfare recipients and other poor persons to government-paid medical care, was established to replace the old state-based medical assistance for the poor program. And the national Elementary and Secondary Education Act offered federal government funds to the localities to upgrade educational services to poor children. All of these new programs, while providing new national government funding, also placed significant strings on how the funds could be administered by the states and localities. States lacking in institutional capacity in the bureaucracies that would run these programs were required to undertake broad-scale reforms in order to meet the national government mandates.

Partly as a reaction to the nationalization of domestic policy problems during that period and partly due to internal demands to deal with the challenges of state and local economic development, the states and localities have responded by reforming their governing capabilities on a broad scale during the past three decades. A variety of external and internal forces seeking to make those governments more efficient and better able to deal with the challenges of the latter part of the twentieth century have truly transformed state and local governments into modern institutions capable of dealing routinely with myriad domestic policy problems created by societal tensions and global challenges. The broad purpose of this book is to document and describe those institutional changes as they have occurred over the past three decades, a period of growing emphasis on decentralization of power and devolution in functional responsibilities within the U.S. federal system. The basic themes developed here are (1) change from a period of centralized federalism in the 1960s to the contemporary period of New Federalism; (2) change in state and local governmental institutions such as executives, legislatures, and courts; (3) strengthened finances of state and local governments; and (4) increased interest and participation by citizens, organized groups, and the media in state and local politics.

The Fluid Nature of American Federalism

The Constitution created a federal government with limited and enumerated powers, and much of the genius of that document was the means employed for ensuring that the federal government did not overwhelm the state and local governments.[1] A system of checks and balances, whereby the three branches of the federal government restrained one another, was an important aspect of this plan. Of equal importance to the constitutional plan, however, was the basic notion that the federal government was not to intrude on the domestic matters that had traditionally been the prerogative of state and local governments.[2] Many states, fearful that the federal government might still overwhelm them, qualified their ratification of the new Constitution with the insistence that it needed to be amended by a Bill of Rights to further ensure that the federal government would be limited in scope. A key feature in this context was the Tenth Amendment, which provided that "The powers not delegated to the United States by the Constitution, nor prohibited by it to the States, are reserved to the States respectively, or to the people." This basic provision of the Bill of Rights has served as the constitutional foundation for state government over the course of American history and has been the subject of widespread legal controversy over time.

Centralized Federalism

The precise powers of the federal government vis-à-vis the states would be worked out in practice, and in the courts, as legislation and court interpretation gave meaning to the operational characteristics of federalism over the course of American political development. The proponents of a strengthened national government often carried the day in legal disputes heard by the U.S. Supreme Court. Arguably the most important case regarding federalism, *McCulloch* v. *Maryland* (1819), established that the Constitution granted certain implied powers to Congress — in this case, the power to create a U.S. bank. Another critical case, *Gibbons* v. *Ogden* (1824), confirmed congressional control over foreign and interstate commerce. These cases and others during Chief Justice John Marshall's tenure made up a body of judicial rulings that generally favored federal power as opposed to states' rights.

The federal government through Congress induced the states to adopt certain uniform policies by providing grants-in-aid to the states. The first of many acts to follow, the Morrill Act of 1862, donated federally held public lands to the states to provide Colleges for the Benefit of Agriculture and Mechanic Arts and was responsible for land-grant universities still in operation throughout the nation today. This initial donation would expand revenue grants, by which, in general, Congress provides funds to the states on the condition that they be spent in accordance with federal priorities. From the first annual cash grant under the Hatch Act of 1887, the number of grant programs rose to more than 600 in 1995, with outlays of $225 billion, or about 15 percent of total federal spending.[3] The greatest acceleration in these grants occurred during the Johnson administration of 1963–69, with more programs being enacted during those five years than had been authorized since the inception of categorical grants.[4] The Johnson Great Society period is often characterized by scholars as the height of an era of Centralized Federalism.

Typically, such conditional grants involve a two-step process. The first step concerns the original design of the grant: Congress enacts legislation defining the purposes of the grant and establishing the criteria for receiving the money, any matching requirements, and so on. During this initial stage, nonfederal government entities and their various intergovernmental lobbying organizations may lobby for federal money with little or no conditions on how the funds are spent. State and local governments often seek either relatively unconditional grants (e.g., so-called block grants and general revenue sharing) or grants with conditions that, as a practical matter, are already consistent with the states' own spending priorities (e.g., "developmental programs" that promote the states' economic welfare and do not redistribute wealth). For instance, the Community Development Block Grant program (CDBG) is intended principally to serve low- and moderate-income communities and those with relatively greater community development needs. The CDBG formula uses poverty, age-of-housing, and community population growth rate statistical factors to allocate funds to meet those needs. But while Greenwich, Connecticut, and Camden, New Jersey, are comparable with respect to the age of their housing stock, Greenwich was allocated CDBG funds of $0.69 per person in poverty in 1995 — over five times more than Camden's $0.13. Greenwich, with a per capita income of $46,070, could more easily afford to fund its own community-development needs than could Camden, with its per capita income of $7,276 (about half the national average).[5]

In contrast to these pressures by state and local governments, private nonprofit groups sometimes urge more careful restrictions to prevent states from diverting federal funds to nonfederal purposes. In response to such pressures, Congress may impose various substantive conditions on both the federal grant money and preexisting state funds to ensure that the federal grant is spent for specified classes of beneficiaries or specified federal purposes. Congress may also demand that state agencies responsible for spending the federal revenue comply with various structural or procedural requirements such as "public participation" requirements, "single agency" requirements, and merit selection of state personnel.

In the second stage of the grant process, individual states have to decide whether to accept the conditions and apply for the funds. Typically, the rewards for participation vastly outweigh the benefits that might accrue from nonparticipation. In addition, this second stage provides another opportunity for one-on-one bargaining between state and local officials and the national government. Even if the grant system consists of "formula grants" with specifically defined criteria for eligibility, the states and localities can bargain over how stringently the national government will enforce the conditions ostensibly attached to the federal funds. State and local officials may induce individual members of Congress to pressure federal agencies to relax their oversight of state and local expenditures of nonsource revenue.

The New Federalism and the Devolution of Federal Authority

Conditional grants have been a dominant feature of twentieth-century federalism. While this arrangement has been ubiquitous, it has had many detractors. A common complaint is that the reach of the federal government has become excessive and that the strings attached to federal dollars make for inefficient and ineffective programs in the field. Opponents of federal power believe that government is too centralized and too large to address contemporary needs efficiently and effectively. Those who support the movement toward decentralization contend that more effective solutions to problems can be designed at the local level. Those less supportive of the shift of responsibility to the states, however, express concern that ending federal programs that support the most vulnerable members of our society will leave many without critical services. Whether or not states can and will design and finance adequate local programs in a period of reduced federal spending is in question.

New Federalism and devolution were terms first heard around Washington in the early 1970s as the Nixon administration proposed using general revenue sharing and block grants to allow states and localities to determine how they would deal with the problems facing their communities. A small general revenue-sharing program was passed, as were several major block-grant programs. Many of these block grants were welcomed by recipient governments, but they still only constituted a relatively small portion of the total grants given to states and localities and most

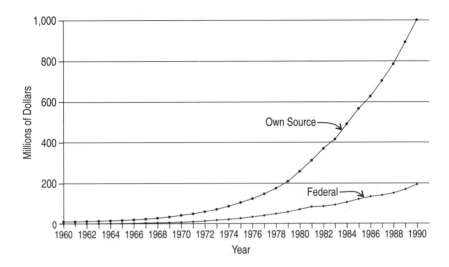

**FIGURE 1.1. AVERAGE ANNUAL STATE REVENUES BY SOURCE, 1960–90
(1982 DOLLARS)**

Source: Paul Brace, "Taxes and Economic Development in the American States: Persistent Issues and Notes for a Model," *Significant Issues in Urban Economic Development*, ed. Richard D. Bingham and Robert Mier (Sage Publications, 1997).

still contained a number of restrictions that limited how the money could be used.

During the Reagan administration, there seemed to be a consensus that federal-state-local relations needed to be reexamined and significantly changed, but there was no agreement as to what that meant. Many state leaders hoped that devolution and the New Federalism would allow states and localities greater control over the design and implementation of federally funded programs. Federal funding for many programs was reduced, however, and in many instances devolution would come to mean shifting funding responsibilities to the states.

Figure 1.1 illustrates the magnitude of some of these fiscal changes. Where in the 1960s state and federal contributions to state revenues were, on average, nearly equal, by the 1970s there was a pronounced growth in the reliance of states on their own revenues. By 1990, state contributions vastly outpaced federal contributions to average state revenues.

Figure 1.2 (p. 6) illustrates that devolution has not been strictly limited to the states. Local shares of domestic expenditures have grown as well, although state levels are at a record high. Thus, while localities are resurgent, they are a pale shadow of their once dominant position. Prior to the Depression, local expenditures made up 60 percent of total domestic outlays, while states contributed 23 percent. After the Depression

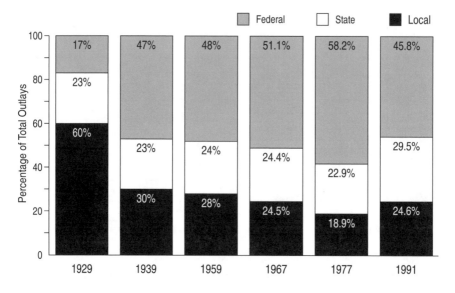

FIGURE 1.2. DOMESTIC GOVERNMENTAL EXPENDITURES:
FEDERAL, STATE, AND LOCAL SHARES FROM OWN FUNDS

Source: Figures for 1929, 1939, and 1959 are from Advisory Commission on Intergovernmental Relations, *Significant Features of Fiscal Federalism,* 1978–79 (Washington, D.C., May
1979). Figures for 1967, 1977, and 1991 are from Advisory Commission on Intergovernmental Relations, *Significant Features of Fiscal Federalism,* vol. 2, Revenues and Expenditures,
1993 (Washington, D.C., September 1993).

stimulated an enormous rise in federal expenditures, state and local contributions dropped throughout the 1960s and 1970s. As they entered the
1990s, however, states and localities combined once again accounted for
over half of domestic expenditures. Clearly, subnational governments have
risen in importance in the midst of federal devolution.

Devolution seems to embody several agendas. For some, it is an opportunity to gain greater control over federal funds allocated to the states.
Recently, many state leaders supported a welfare-reform program that
would consolidate all the funds that were being spent on social programs
such as Aid to Families with Dependent Children (AFDC), Medicaid, and
food stamps and then distribute them as massive block grants to the states,
which would then determine how best to serve the needs of those currently
receiving support. Former Governor Zell Miller of Georgia was representative of this crowd: "I want more flexibility, I want to run these programs
without federal strings."[6]

Alternatively, some seemed to view devolution as a means for cutting
back on the welfare state. Several governors saw the calls for devolution as
a back-door means for terminating support programs. Some advocates of

the devolutionary strategy nevertheless expressed fears related to the potential elimination of all standards, or the imposition of new ones. Reflecting the attitude of many Democratic governors as well as President Clinton, Governor Howard Dean of Vermont said he believed "there is a national interest in making sure that children don't starve." Democratic Governor Mel Carnahan of Missouri similarly expressed concern that Republicans in Congress would impose requirements on the states to achieve conservative policy goals. "We're not any more interested in conservative mandates than in liberal mandates," he told reporters.[7]

Calls for devolution continue. The process of turning over responsibility to the states has been carried out on a program-by-program basis and in measures that typically have been compromised to some degree. To date, devolution, like other efforts at governmental reform in the United States, has turned out to be a piecemeal, gradual process rather than a revolutionary or radical transformation. Some recent rulings by the U.S. Supreme Court, however, may prove revolutionary in charting new directions in this area.

In the past decade or so, the Supreme Court and the lower courts have become more dedicated to protecting federalism and returning power to the states and localities. The courts have stepped in to challenge the common assumption that every domestic policy problem is deserving of national legislation providing uniform policy solutions. In a media age in which political actors are constantly attempting to hog the national stage, every policy problem that arises is greeted with cries for national attention and passage of some new national legislation. This political affliction seems to be bipartisan, as both Democrats and Republicans seek to preempt state and local authority to deal with domestic policy problems. Fortunately for the states and localities, the courts do not share the exclusively national perspective of the president, Congress, and the federal bureaucracy.

In many cases involving the states and localities during the past decade, the Supreme Court has gradually formulated a new interpretation of federalism, one that has expanded and strengthened the role of the states vis-à-vis the national government. The emerging doctrine appears to reaffirm forcefully the basic axiom of federalism, whereby the states and the national government are dual sovereigns, with each having authority independent of one another. Several examples from recent U.S. Supreme Court cases illustrate the point.

In a 1991 case in which the State of Missouri challenged the national government's authority to mandate the retirement of state judges, the Court emphasized in *Gregory* v. *Ashcroft* that the "Constitution established a system of dual sovereignty between the States and the Federal government."[8] The Court held, therefore, that the national government could not mandate a retirement age for state judges. This case was followed up in 1992 by the landmark *New York* v. *United States* decision, which restored substance to the long-neglected Tenth Amendment to the Constitution. The Court invalidated provisions of the national Low-Level Radioactive Waste Policy Amendments Act of 1985, which required the states either to implement national legislative mandates or to acquiesce in "taking title" to the waste, thereby becoming subject to liability for waste generators' damages. Holding that the "take title" provisions of the act were beyond the reach of Congress's enumerated powers and violated the Tenth Amendment, the Court articulated the following clear constitutional standard: "state governments are neither regional offices nor administrative agencies of the United States," and Congress may not "simply 'commandeer' the legislative processes of the States by directly compelling them to enact and enforce a federal regulatory program."[9]

In 1995, in another landmark case, *United States* v. *Lopez,* the Court restrained Congress from relying on its constitutional power to regulate interstate commerce to ban the simple possession of a gun near a school zone, unless it could clearly show that such conduct involved commercial channels or interstate economic activity. In *Lopez,* the Court expressed concern about Congress's regulatory intervention in all education matters, an area "where States historically have been sovereign."[10] This was the first time in sixty years or so that the Court had enforced constitutional limits on the ability of Congress to enact generally applicable legislation under its Article I power to regulate interstate commerce.

In two cases in its 1996–97 term, the Supreme Court sided with the states and localities in disputes about the national government's power to regulate local authority. First, in *Printz* v. *United States,* the Court revisited the Tenth Amendment issues addressed in *New York* v. *United States,* here invalidating the provisions of the Brady Handgun Violence Prevention Act, which required local law enforcement officers to conduct background checks on gun purchasers. In its opinion, the Court stated that these provisions violated "the very principle of separate state sovereignty," which it characterized as "one of the Constitution's structural protections of liberty." Pronouncing that "such commands are fundamentally incompatible with our constitutional system of dual sovereignty," the Court reaffirmed that the "federal government may neither issue directives requiring the States to address particular problems, nor command the States' officers, or those of their political subdivisions, to administer or enforce a federal regulatory program."[11] The Court's opinion did recognize, however, that the states can voluntarily enlist in federal enforcement programs and that Congress may entice the states with federal funds to administer such programs. Second, in *City of Boerne* v. *Flores,* the Court placed limits on Congress's power under Section 5 of the Fourteenth Amendment by striking down the Religious Freedom Restoration Act, which required state and local officials to give special deference to legal claims involving religion. The Court held that Congress had usurped the judiciary's power to define the scope of constitutionally protected freedom of religion and that the act constituted a "considerable congressional intrusion into the States' traditional prerogatives and general authority to regulate for the health and welfare of their citizens."[12] While state and local officials may give special exemptions in law for religious claims, Congress cannot force them to do so.

Thus, the Rehnquist Court has supported states and localities by giving careful scrutiny to national legislative or bureaucratic attempts to force them and their officials to undertake actions that are not consistent with current understandings of the dual sovereignty of American federalism. National government action must be clearly constitutionally sanctioned and taken in a manner that recognizes the sovereignty of states and localities as well as that of the national government. The days are over when advocates of national power and authority could expect the Supreme Court to defer routinely to congressional will; the contemporary Court is not unwilling to overturn acts of Congress that violate the Tenth Amendment.

Political Reform and the Rise of State Capacity

State and local government policymaking is assuming increasing importance because of changing relationships among the national, state, and local governments and because of the increased autonomy of states and localities in designing policy and delivery of public services that is emerging from the reshaped federalism of the late twentieth century.[13] States and localities follow policy paths that are independent of the national government, their actions at times diverging widely from those pursued in Washington.[14] Proposals to reform various aspects of government or public policy are under discussion in many statehouses and city halls; one would be hard-pressed to find a state or locality where some type of reform is not at least under discussion or where policy reform is not a major instrument for political change.

U.S. state and local governments are responsible for a number of decisions that have far-ranging consequences for the interests and citizens who live under the jurisdiction of those governments. They have primary responsibility for delivering a wide variety of important services, and they provide a venue for "testing" policies that may subsequently be enacted by other states or at the national level, as well as a training ground for the recruitment of national government officeholders.[15]

U.S. politics has long been organized around demands for reform, some confined to single issues and others more far-reaching, and calls for reform play central roles in political party and interest-group strategies. Progressive movement reform groups (e.g., the New York Bureau of Municipal Reform) were active at the state and local levels during the late-nineteenth and early twentieth centuries. The prototypical conflict pitted partisan political organizations against nonpartisan good-government groups calling for reforms. A hallmark of this reform era was the creation of merit-based, semiautonomous bureaucracies at all levels of American government, which produced a fundamental weakening of American political parties. This was especially pronounced in the states, where a twentieth-century spate of state constitutional changes institutionalized professionalized bureaucracies and strengthened executive branches, largely as a response to perceptions that greater centralization was needed to manage state governments.[16] Since then, political parties have shared influence over the provision of public goods and services to the citizenry with the professional bureaucracies of the states. A similar pattern of institutional change at the local level of government led to the demise of local political parties as service providers.

At the same time that political influences were losing control to state and local bureaucracies, the states and localities were fighting back by reforming legislative bodies. Whereas three decades ago most states and large cities and counties had weak and ineffectual legislative bodies, many of today's states and localities have professional legislatures staffed by well-trained, expert individuals. In states with large populations and complex policymaking processes, the legislatures are full-time and adequately staffed. Likewise, large cities and counties expect council members and county commissioners to treat government service as a full-time job, and they provide both personal and professional staff to assist those local legislators with their tasks. These reforms in the legislative process have strengthened the hand of state and local politicians to control the independence and autonomy of the bureaucracies.

State and local executive branches have also been reformed in the effort to increase the capacity of elected officials to control bureaucracies. At the state level, governors have been given greater control over the state budget process in terms of budget formulation and implementation. State budget agencies now work largely under the political control of the governor. Governors also have been given enhanced powers to appoint and dismiss at will high-level state bureaucrats with policymaking powers, making it harder to create the cozy triangles of state bureaucrats, influential interest groups, and prominent senior state legislators that were once common. At the local level, many more large cities are run by strong mayors today than in the past, and many smaller cities are now governed by city managers hired by city councils. Large counties tend to be presided over by elected county executives, and fewer examples are found today of multiheaded county commissions running complex county governments. Thus, enhancement of gubernatorial power has brought some further control of state bureaucracies, while the presence of strong mayors in large cities and elected county executives in large counties has worked to control the independence and autonomy of local bureaucracies.

In a similar vein, states and localities have been examining how to improve the operation of state and local courts. As litigation has increased, so has the number of judges, lawyers, and parties involved in the judicial process. Lawyers, spurred by the American Judicature Society and the American Bar Association, have pushed for the professionalization of both the civil and criminal judicial processes. States have reformed the selection of judges, mostly abolished local courts presided over by nonlawyers, and hired professional administrators to manage the court dockets. States with large populations have created integrated court systems, enabling litigants and lawyers to follow a process whereby they begin at the trial-court level and proceed through up to two levels of appellate review. Today's state and local judges generally have long tenure on the bench and hence the independence necessary to make objective, nonpolitical decisions based on the law and the facts of a case.

State and local reform in its most recent incarnation involves operating in an increasingly resource-constrained environment in which national government transfers are being reduced, state responsibilities are increasing, and the political costs of state tax increases appear to be high. This places legislative parties and bureaucracies squarely in the policymaking process: parties wish to promote policies that further their political ends, while bureaucracies seek to maintain turf and programs. This tension is characteristic of the modern, transformed state and local arena of politics and government.

The Strengthened Finances
of State and Local Governments

Two things have become abundantly clear as the United States enters the twenty-first century. Power is shifting from Washington to the states, and the states have developed an enhanced institutional capacity to deal with their new responsibilities. Luckily, this shift is occurring at a time when state coffers are generally full, allowing states to address new programmatic demands without forcing them to adopt new taxes.

Fiscal Conditions of States Are Strong for Now

In a manner reminiscent of the fiscal surpluses generated in the mid- and late 1980s, many states that were forced to tighten budgets or raise taxes (or both) during the early 1990s economic doldrums once again have healthy state treasuries. The strong national economy resulted in higher than anticipated revenues for many states in fiscal years 1997 and 1998, and the states responded by enacting relatively modest tax reductions, building increased reserves for the next economic downturn, and maintaining moderate spending growth.

End-of-year balances as a percentage of state expenditures for fiscal years 1996 and 1997 were at the highest levels since 1980. Balances in fifteen states were projected to exceed 10 percent of expenditures in fiscal

1997, a healthy cushion for economic and other uncertainties in the future. States continue to build up reserves to combat future economic downturns and to guard against other unseen circumstances. Stung by the recession of the late 1980s and early 1990s, states today remain cautious in making new spending commitments; many are employing one-time revenues for nonrecurring costs and making investments in important new areas. In addition, the current surpluses have led many states to cut some taxes rather than simply to increase spending.[17] In the 1998 state legislative sessions, thirty-six states cut taxes, with some twenty-one undertaking significant reductions — more than 1 percent of the previous tax collections.[18]

With the continuation of steady economic growth during the past several years, few states have been forced to make midyear budget reductions. Where it was once routine for states to make supplemental budget allocations each spring for programs such as corrections, welfare, and Medicaid, the robustness of current state treasuries allows budgetmakers to be more realistic when the initial budgets are formulated. Also, recent reforms in programs such as welfare and Medicaid have eased the states' financial burden of operating these programs. As part of the implementation of the national Temporary Assistance for Needy Families (TANF) block-grant program, many states are targeting the working poor by structuring programs to address the barriers that hinder employment for low-income workers. Most of the activity in state welfare programs centers around restructuring programs rather than adjusting cash assistance payments. For fiscal year 1998, forty-two states maintained the same cash assistance benefit levels that were in effect in fiscal year 1997, while nine states increased their cash assistance benefit levels. Almost all states granted pay raises to state employees for fiscal year 1998, with the increase averaging about 3.7 percent. States also estimated a slight increase from fiscal year 1997 to fiscal year 1998 in the number of positions filled. About half of the states enacted changes affecting levels of aid to local governments. The most significant changes include increased property tax relief, increases in aid for schools, and the restructuring of elementary and secondary education.

States are continuing to hold down spending, an effect that is largely attributable to increased efficiencies in the administration of the Medicaid program. According to the 1997 edition of *The Fiscal Survey of the States,* states estimated an increase in their general fund spending of about 5 percent in fiscal year 1997 and about 5.5 percent in fiscal year 1998. For most states, the formulation of new welfare policy is coupled with substantial decreases in caseloads and higher funding levels. With spending for direct cash assistance declining because of caseload decreases, states have the flexibility to shift funds around and invest savings to provide additional services, such as child care, training, and other job preparation services.

Prosperity and spending restraint have been stimulating tax cutting in the states. In fiscal year 1997 — for the fourth consecutive year — state legislative actions resulted in a net decrease in state revenues. Thirty-one states enacted tax reductions, with the most significant reductions in state personal income taxes. Fiscal year 1997 revenue collections were about 2.7 percent higher than estimates states originally had used in adopting their budgets. Fiscal year 1998 budgets included an increase of about 3.9 percent over fiscal year 1997 tax collections, representing revenues from sales, personal income, and corporate income taxes.

Once the amount of projected state revenues to come from the state-negotiated tobacco settlement became known, states participating in the settlement began allocating these funds in their budgets under review in the spring of 1999. A large amount of revenue was provided in all individual state settlements for the next twenty-five years, with some of the money earmarked for programs to prevent teen smoking. The struggle in many of the states is now to protect the tobacco tax settlement from being raided by governors and state legislatures eager to spend on other activities than public health initiatives.

Basic patterns of state expenditure and revenue actions make it clear that the states are very healthy fiscally and well prepared for the next economic downturn. In the meantime, the states have been also restructuring. With the goal of improving the performance and reputation of government services, states are streamlining agencies and improving management, particularly by merging departments, using outcome measures to assess performance, and selectively reviewing privatization options. Even with a strong national economy generating ample state revenues, states are emphasizing efficiency changes rather than the expansion of services.[19]

Economic Development Efforts Persist

Despite the prosperity of the late 1990s, economic development persists as a prominent or even preeminent item in many state and local agendas. The demand for jobs and revenues places subnational governments under continuing pressure to enhance economic development by luring new employers or enhancing the quality of jobs. Many state and local leaders continue to worry that traditional approaches to economic development are self-defeating in the long-run. Many jobs secured by predatory economic competition between the states and their localities are of the low-wage and low-skill variety. While this approach may provide short-term fixes to a state or local economy, in the long run it creates a potentially vulnerable workforce, subject to the vicissitudes of a rapidly changing economic landscape. Too often, low-skill jobs gained by lavish tax concessions or financial inducements to industry do not end up producing commensurate revenues. Employers, furthermore, bemoan the lack of skills that is common in many of today's labor markets.[20]

While governors and other policymakers lament the consequences of predatory competition for employers, these contests have continued. Fairly recent efforts by the states to attract firms have been high visibility bidding contests that have left deep gouges in the revenues of the victorious contestants. Only time will tell if the high bids will be repaid over the long haul with sufficient growth to offset these generous outpourings of revenues and tax inducements.

Government efforts to lure employers with incentives is an old practice, although the modern experience with this practice has witnessed a dramatic increase in the stakes involved. In the 1980s Japanese automakers obtained then-record subsidies for new plants in Ohio, Tennessee, and Kentucky. More recently, the bidding wars have expanded to include domestic and European firms, and the subsidies have grown astronomically. For example, when United Airlines announced its intention to locate a maintenance facility, a high-stakes auction among the states ensued. The "winner," the City of Indianapolis, hooked the prize with a bid of $291 million worth of subsidies; the cost per job worked out to almost $50,000. Northwest Airlines secured $270 million in loans from the State of Minnesota to prop up the company's shaky finances. South Carolina scored big by luring automaker BMW, but not without a large price tag — the state offered Bayerische Motoren Werke AG at least $130 million in incentives to build its factory there and also paid to move 100 families so that the company could have the exact site it wanted; the state then offered to lease the reclaimed land to the prestigious automaker for one dollar a year.

Mercedes Benz and Alabama then took the bidding to a new plateau. The $253 million in incentives initially disclosed to attract the 1,500 jobs offered by Mercedes was later revealed to be a $325 million package. Some of the incentives were symbolic and almost comical, but they reveal the lengths to which states have been driven to capture these plums: for example, Alabama officials agreed to place the Mercedes Benz emblem atop a local scoreboard in time for the nationally televised Tennessee-Alabama football game at no charge to the company. Mercedes, furthermore, was designated the official automobile of the State of Alabama, which agreed to purchase not less than 100 of the company's new sport-utility vehicles, with a ten-year commitment to purchase 2,500 vehicles. The financial core of the deal was very serious business, however. Among the incentives were commitments by the state to spend $1.5 million per year for five years on image advertising and public relations promoting Mercedes's decision to locate in Alabama, to contribute $5 million to Mercedes if it should decide to build a proposed visitor's center, to make the U.S. Navy port at the Alabama State Docks available to Mercedes if it should decide to ship cars through the port of Mobile, to build a $30 million permanent training center at the plant site as well as $5 million a year toward the center's operation, a tax credit available in advance in the form of an interest-free loan, and an additional $60 million to educate and train Mercedes employees, including sending them to Germany to study at the company's headquarters. In all, Alabama would spend approximately $216,000 per direct job. What is truly remarkable is that Alabama's bid for Mercedes is not a record — through a combination of job-training grants, local site improvements, and income tax credits, Kentucky provided a steel firm with a $140 million package to secure 400 direct jobs, for a $350,000-per-job subsidy.[21]

When it comes to economic development, the states are in many ways trapped in a classic prisoners' dilemma.[22] Collectively they would be better off if they resisted temptation to engage in predatory competition over jobs, but it is very hard if not impossible to enforce collective agreements among the states, for one or more states will almost certainly find it to their advantage to capitalize on opportunities left open when other states practice restraint.

There are promising signs, however, that states are making some progress in this area. Both the National Governors' Association and the International City Managers Association have had task forces working on how to spur state and local economic development activities. The National Governors' Association task force on Jobs for the Future and Regional Training Strategies in 1997 developed a proposal to help build state-based workforce development systems to ensure that the systems' goals for employers and for individuals are inextricably linked. Rather than job placement, this program seeks ways to sustain high value-added jobs to increase productivity and to adapt to rapid economic change. It also aims to develop systems that focus on assisting individuals to acquire sustainable employment and economic independence, which is to be accomplished by providing employees with opportunities for ongoing skill development and career progression. Special efforts are to be undertaken to assure access, retention, and advancement of those most disadvantaged in the labor market.

There is thus a certain duality in current economic development efforts in the states. State leaders often profess disdain for economic competition and engage in various efforts to pursue alternative routes to development. Yet in the new era of "go-it-alone," or "fend-for-yourself" federalism — with pressing federal mandates, diminished federal dollars, increased concern about jobs, and heightened animosity among voters about increased taxes — state politicians are threading their way through these often conflicting cues and developing policy proposals that strike at the heart of taxation and development. Many states remain poised to engage in predatory competition to lure employers and placate voters' antitax sentiments, and in the emerging global economy, firms appear well-suited to capitalize on this probusiness climate. From automobile manufacturers to theme parks to sports franchises, many firms are succeeding in obtaining extremely favorable deals from governments eager for jobs and income.

Participatory Democracy in States and Localities

A final theme of this book is the emergence of increased opportunities for participation and involvement in state and local government processes. Reforms have taken place in the rules that govern voter registration and voting in state and local elections. Very few legal restrictions remain to affect the franchise; the United States has become a society with universal adult suffrage. The National Voter Registration Act of 1993 now makes it possible to register to vote in most states when renewing a driver's license or when applying for welfare or unemployment compensation. Restrictions have been placed on the ability of states and localities to remove (purge) voters from the rolls for nonvoting. State and local governments no longer can be blamed for an individual's decision not to vote.

The interest-group arena is wide open to the creation of new groups representing every varied interest. Single-issue groups abound, with generally free access to raise and spend money on issue agendas. Campaign finance regulations have been struck down when a group argues that it is engaged in free speech through the spending of money in political campaigns. In almost half the states, citizens who cannot get the state legislature to adopt political reforms have the option of wording a proposition and collecting the required signatures to get it on the ballot for a vote — many a state constitutional provision owes its origin to this initiative-and-referendum process. Elected officials who offend the sensibility of the electorate are subject to recall in many states and localities. These methods of achieving accountability from elected officials engaged in policymaking are working in a large number of states to demonstrate that meaningful public participation has an effect on elected officials.

The work of state and local governments today is under the continuing scrutiny of the mass media. Open meetings and record laws have been welcomed by the media, and media representatives are vigilant in ensuring that state and local governments follow these dictates. For example, campaign finance regulation in the states today is based on the premise that the mass media will examine the disclosure reports of the candidates and report on patterns of fund raising and spending that appear to be abnormal. The expectation in a period of investigative journalism is that the local mass media will expose abuses in the administration of government and highlight extraordinary practices. State and local elected officials recognize the important role of the mass media, and some hire public relations specialists to manage the flow of information to the media.

State and local governments are thus subject to many more democratic and participatory forces than they were thirty years ago. In the end, the citizenry are better off with the accessibility of the current scene; the genie of openness is out of the bottle and is never again likely to be capped.

The Transformation of States and Localities

The chapters that follow address and evaluate how the states and localities have dealt with the changes in institutional power and authority over the past three decades or so. We invited a number of scholars of state and local governments and politics to give their learned and scholarly attention to important changes in state and local government institutions and policies since the early 1960s. Collectively they provide an array of viewpoints on the impact of the major institutional changes that have been taking place during that era. They also examine the current status of state and local governmental practices and point out some of the challenges facing state and local officials as they enter the new millennium.

In chapter 2, "Devolution and Challenge for State and Local Governance," Robert M. Stein of Rice University outlines the political and economic features of federalism and discusses the various phases of federalism the states and localities have experienced. Stein also presents a market theory of public policy and uses it to explain how governments decide what functions to perform and what level of government is best attuned to carry out each function. He then goes on to highlight empirical studies that illustrate both the policy and behavioral consequences of the market theory of policy. Stein concludes by discussing the linkage between studies of state and local institutional change and the operation of market models of politics and public policy.

In chapter 3, "Governors: Their Heritage and Future," Nelson C. Dometrius of Texas Tech University charts the development of the gubernatorial institution and the growth in the formal powers of the governorship. He next examines gubernatorial policy roles, emphasizing the need for leadership skills, and then focuses on the increasing role that governors play in acquiring and managing grants-in-aid from the national government. Dometrius also discusses the changing role of governors in new issue areas and demonstrates how the public's perception of problems affects the emphasis governors give to them. Dometrius concludes by examining how recent institutional and demographic changes have shaped the governorship.

In chapter 4, "The Institutionalized Legislature and the Rise of the Antipolitics Era," Paul Brace and Daniel S. Ward of Rice University trace the institutionalization and professionalization of state legislatures over the past forty years, discovering both predictable and unanticipated consequences for the states. They then examine the contemporary efforts to limit terms of state legislative office and to turn back the professionalization of those bodies. Brace and Ward conclude by considering the implications for state legislative capability in the contemporary antipolitics era.

In chapter 5, "Statehouse Bureaucracy: Institutional Consistency in a Changing Environment," Charles Barrilleaux of Florida State University first discusses the role of bureaucracies in democratic governance and then considers the scope of bureaucracy in the states, focusing on how many persons are employed by state governments and how large a portion of state economies are devoted to administration. Barrilleaux then examines the idea of bureaucratic quality and the problems involved in measuring bureaucratic quality in the states. He concludes by outlining current and ongoing attempts to reform state administrations.

In chapter 6, "State Judicial Politics: Rules, Structures, and the Political Game," Melinda Gann Hall of Michigan State University examines the major institutional changes in state courts over the past forty years, focusing particularly on the consolidation of trial courts, the centralization of financing of the courts, and professionalizing the management of the courts. Hall then discusses two basic institutional changes — the addition of intermediate trial courts and further adoptions of the "merit" or Missouri plan for judicial selection — exploring both the intended and unintended consequences of those reforms and explaining how those reforms altered the operating environments of the states' courts of last resort. Hall concludes by considering how these reforms have increased the power of state supreme courts and the individual justices who sit on those courts, but without affecting the characteristics of those recruited for state judicial office.

In chapter 7, "The Embattled Mayors and Local Executives," James H. Svara of North Carolina State University first considers the context and conditions of elected mayors and appointed city managers, noting the basic features of the mayor-council and council-manager forms of city government. Then he examines two aspects of local government leadership: function of leadership and approach to leadership. Svara next contrasts how mayors act in mayor-council cities versus how they act in council-manager cities, concluding that city managers and not mayors typically are the executives in council-manager cities. Finally, Svara evaluates the challenges facing mayors and city managers as a result of the severely restrained resources they have available to deal with policy problems.

In chapter 8, "The Resurgent City Councils," Susan MacManus of the University of South Florida outlines how the institutional structure of city councils has changed over the past three decades and how the job of a city councilor has become more complex. MacManus also considers how the personal attributes of those running for and winning the office have changed and how evolving campaign strategies have affected contesting for the city council office. MacManus concludes by examining changes in the types of problems dealt with by city councilors and in the ways in which city councilors communicate with the public.

In chapter 9, "State and Local Parties in a Candidate-Centered Age," John F. Bibby of the University of Wisconsin-Milwaukee discusses the changing role of state parties during a period in which politics in the states and localities has become increasingly candidate-centered rather than party-centered. Bibby also looks at the changing political environment of the 1990s, focusing on the development of new campaign techniques and the use of political consultants by candidates and parties, the rise of political action committees (PACs), the increased competition for statewide office, and the court decisions reducing the use of patronage in staffing state and local offices. Portraying the modern state party organization as a service agency to candidates and local parties, Bibby examines the changes in how governors interact with state parties and how legislative campaign committees have emerged as the principal source of party support to state legislative candidates. Bibby concludes by considering how local parties have changed in the new environment of candidate-centered politics and documenting how party nationalization has led to the integration of national and state party organizations.

In chapter 10, "The Opening Up of State and Local Election Processes," Charles S. Bullock III of the University of Georgia examines the myriad changes that have occurred in state and local election processes over the past forty years, emphasizing the efforts taken to make mass voter participation easier and the structural changes made to increase diversity in the ranks of state and local officeholders. Bullock discusses extensively the steps taken to reduce the barriers of mass political participation and examines a variety of structural options that exist to guide the conditions under which candidates run for state and local political bodies. He also assesses the degree to which these structural options are related empirically to the success of individuals such as political minorities running for those bodies. Bullock concludes with data on the degree to which there have been increases in minority and female officeholding in the states and localities.

In chapter 11, "Interest Representation in the States," Virginia Gray of the University of Minnesota and David Lowery of the University of North Carolina at Chapel Hill first discuss the origins and maintenance of interest organizations in the states, arguing for a niche theory of organizational maintenance. Gray and Lowery next consider a number of factors that foster interest-organization communities, including community density and diversity, and they continue by focusing on the work of organized interests, emphasizing the role of lobbying regulations, how lobbying has changed, and the emerging role of political action committees. Gray and Lowery conclude by considering the overall influence of organized interests, focusing on the triumph of many interests over single interests and how influence varies with the strength of interest systems across the states.

In chapter 12, "Policy Change in the American States," Evan J. Ringquist of Florida State University and James C. Garand of Louisiana State University examine the profound changes that have taken place in state policymaking since World War II. Ringquist and Garand begin by focusing on how and why public policy has changed in the states in recent years, developing a general framework for assessing these changes across variety of policy areas. They then document how the size of the public sector has changed since the end of World War II and how priorities for government spending have changed over that time frame. Ringquist and Garand conclude by examining the literature on patterns of state policy change in several specific policy areas, including welfare, environmental regulation, education, and economic development.

In chapter 13, "Policy Change in American Cities and Counties," Elaine B. Sharp of the University of Kansas explores the topic of changing patterns of public policymaking at the local government level. Sharp begins by adopting several perspectives on policy change to guide her assessment, then she examines the various spheres of local policymaking, focusing on Paul Peterson's influential categorization of local governing activity into three types: developmental, allocational, and redistributional. Sharp then addresses specific policies within each sphere, looking at local economic development policies in the developmental sphere, local service delivery policies in the allocational sphere, and local policies toward the homeless in the redistributional sphere. She concludes by suggesting that local policy changes are a function of policy learning, as filtered through the imperatives of local politics.

The chapters in this volume provide a summation of the recent developments in state and local governmental politics and governance. The focus on institutional change facilitates the authors' ability to document a number of major changes in state and local government and to grapple with how institutional reforms have altered the politics and policies of the jurisdictions under study. This collection of essays demonstrates dramatically that institutions do matter in affecting the policy choices made by subnational governments in the United States. These findings should give heart to reformers who continue to question the efficacy of governmental institutions and encourage them to propose further institutional innovations to improve the quality of politics and policymaking in state and local governments.

CHAPTER TWO
Devolution and Challenge
for State and Local Governance
Robert M. Stein

SINCE THE 1980s there has been a growing effort to devolve more federal powers and responsibilities to state and local governments. "The intent of devolution is to enhance the responsiveness and efficiency of the federal system, based on the theory that state and local governments can do a better job of providing services for citizens."[1] Several different political agendas are served by devolution, accounting for its popularity among the public and elected officials. Public attitudes about local government have changed dramatically over the last two decades. In 1972 local governments evoked the least amount of public trust and confidence among the American public, but 1992 reversed American public opinion about local government. When asked which level of government "responds best to your needs, 40 percent chose local government; 21 percent state government and only 18 percent cited the federal government."[2]

Those concerned with growing federal budget deficits perceive devolution as a means of reducing the size and growth of the federal government. Advocates of devolution argue that the superior efficiency of state and local governments will enable the nation to maintain service levels at a lower cost. Other advocates of devolution believe government closest to the people will be more effective and responsive to its citizens. These advocates reason that the diversity of our national population limits the federal government from effectively servicing the policy needs and preferences of 275 million persons.

Devolution has come in several forms. The Personal Responsibility and Work Opportunity Reconciliation Act (PRWORA) passed in 1996 was the culmination of nearly two decades of effort to reduce the federal government's responsibility for social policy; it shifted to the states responsibility for setting standards and funding levels for assistance to indigent and low-income families. States are now free to set their own guidelines for determining eligibility and payment levels for emergency assistance, job training, and aid to families with dependent children. More than changing "welfare as we know it," the act was "hailed by many as a defining moment in the nation's progress toward devolving responsibility from the federal government to the states."[3]

De facto devolution has occurred since the mid-1980s,[4] as is reflected in the relatively slow rates of growth and, in some instances, reversals in the flow of federal aid moneys to state and local governments. State and local governments have been forced to choose between raising new moneys or diverting resources from other activities to make up for diminished federal revenues. De facto devolution has restored considerable power and policy discretion to state and local governments, but at the price of diminished federal revenues.

Another side of devolution is the shifting relationship between state and local governments. Most attention has been paid to the transfer of authority and responsibilities from the national government to the states. Local governments (i.e., cities, towns, special districts, etc.) have largely been ignored in studies and analyses of devolution. Unmentioned in the Constitution, and thought to be a creature of state government, local government has rarely figured in any of the major debates on American federalism. This trend, however, appears to have changed. One common state-level response has been to engage in what Richard Nathan referred to as "Second-Order" devolution between states and their substate units of government.[5]

Watson and Gold reported that a significant number of states have substantially reorganized their own policy responsibilities in relation to local governments.[6] Since 1995 twelve states have enacted or proposed changes in state-local responsibilities for social services, public assistance, and workforce development. Interestingly, nine of these states have assigned more responsibility to local governments. Only three states have enacted or proposed legislation that retrieves local responsibility.

Local governments are the workhorses of American federalism. The sheer number of cities, counties, and special districts (80,000+) makes this form of government the most common of American political institutions. Moreover, few national or state policies can be effectively implemented without the direct involvement of a local government. What then is the proper role of local government in the American federal system? Who should be responsible for welfare, housing, health, education, highways, and the myriad of other public sector responsibilities? In this chapter, I review the rationales for local governance in the American federal system and compare constitutional prescriptions with a market theory of local governance. The latter suggests a more expanded role for local government, grounded in arguments marshaled to support the devolution revolution. The balance of the chapter reviews current research on local government's role and its capacity to respond to the challenge of devolution, and then suggests new avenues for research.

Why Different Levels of Government
Do Different Things

Why do different levels of government perform different functions? One approach to answering this question directs our attention to the U.S. Constitution for a compendium of functional responsibilities that are assigned to national and state governments. The Constitution stipulates that the national government is obligated to provide a range of goods and services, such as providing for the national defense, the coining and printing of money, and myriad other vital and sometimes outdated activities (e.g., granting letters of marque). Supreme Court decisions have greatly expanded the scope and content of the national government's responsibilities to include all goods and services "necessary and sufficient" to fulfill its constitutionally prescribed responsibilities. In addition, interpretations of the commerce clause and the privileges and immunities clause of the Constitution have produced significant variation over time in the scope and content of the national government's powers and responsibilities. The Tenth Amendment states that "the powers not delegated to the United States by the Constitution, nor prohibited by it to the States, are reserved to the states respectively or to the people." Like some other sections of the Constitution, this amendment has been the subject of much debate over time in the Supreme Court.

Unfortunately, neither the Constitution nor a significant number of Supreme Court decisions provide a clear, unambiguous, and empirically testable rationale for why different responsibilities might be assigned to different levels and units of government. Thus, we have a Chinese menu of functional responsibilities for the American federal system, but no permanent decision rule or rules by which to make these assignments.

Another approach to answering this question comes from the market theory of public policy. A market theory of the proper role of government starts with the assumption that the most efficient and effective means of providing for individual preferences in society is a competition, in which buyers and sellers are free to engage in exchange relationships. Buyers reveal their preferences for goods and services, and sellers produce these at an agreed-upon price per unit. In some instances, markets fail to generate the goods and services demanded at the desired price or quantity. Here the government intervenes either to produce those goods or services, or to take other action to assure their production.

Two important sources of market failure — public goods and externalities — are particularly relevant in assigning functional responsibilities in the American federal system.[7] Each of these provides a set of criteria for determining which level of government is best suited to correcting the market failure.

Public goods are those goods and services that are available for consumption by all; one person's consumption does not diminish their amount or availability to anyone else. Under these circumstances there is little incentive to produce public goods, and thus private vendors do not offer them. National defense and some environmental policies (i.e., clean air and water) are examples of public goods. Because it is infeasible for the private sector to provide public goods, government often assumes responsibility for them.

By examining another source of market failure, externalities, we can determine which level of government is most appropriate for the provision of public goods. An *externality* is either a cost or a benefit resulting from an action experienced by someone not fully consenting to it. Common examples of negative externalities are air and water pollution generated by manufacturing firms and the cigarette smoke nonsmokers must breathe in public places. There are, of course, positive externalities. The suburban resident who works in a central city receives significant benefits (i.e., public safety services) without paying in full for them. Correctives for externalities include property rights (i.e., the right to recover damages from firms that pollute the air), intergovernmental aid transfers that compensate one unit or level of government for the costs (or benefits) resulting from the actions of another, and voluntary private agreements to correct inefficiencies resulting from externalities.

The externalities associated with publicly provided goods and services furnish an explicit criterion for assigning functional responsibilities across levels and units of government. Governments should be responsible for those goods and services for which the costs and benefits are wholly contained within their jurisdictional boundaries. This rule has some face validity when we consider the Constitution's assignment of functional responsibilities. National defense provides benefits to the nation's entire population; consequently, the national government should be responsible for the provision of defense forces and weapons systems. The benefits associated with public safety, roads, and public schools have defined geographic boundaries and populations of beneficiaries. These boundaries identify the level and unit of government that should assume responsibility for providing these goods and services.

Several economists, most notably Musgrave and Samuelson, have argued that repairing market failures with publicly provided goods and services is inefficient.[8] The key problem is the absence of any pricing mechanism that reveals individual preferences. Without some way of compelling consumers to express their preferences, governments cannot determine the optimal level of production.[9] In his seminal work, Charles Tiebout acknowledges that this condition holds for national-level expenditures, but he argues that a market exists and operates for the optimal provision of local expenditures because individual mobility allows preference revelation.[10] Elaborations of Tiebout's model by Buchanan, Peterson, and Miller provide the basis for examining how local governments might meet the challenge of devolution.[11]

Tiebout maintains that individuals select states and communities that accord with their preferences for publicly provided goods and services; that is, they "vote with their feet." The content and level of municipal service bundles is defined by the preferences of the median voter in each community. For Tiebout, an efficient market mechanism for the production of goods and services exists by virtue of (1) the number and diversity of states and communities, and (2) the ability of voters to choose from among these communities that which best approximates their preferences. From these simplified assumptions a number of testable propositions have been derived:[12]

1. The larger the number of competing jurisdictions, the greater the satisfaction level of consumer-voters.

2. The larger the number of jurisdictions in the same metropolitan area, the greater the competition among them for consumer-voters.

3. The larger the number of competing jurisdictions, the more homogeneous each jurisdiction will be.

4. Taxes as well as services influence residential mobility.

5. The higher the quality of the services, the higher the property values in the jurisdiction; the higher the tax levels, the lower the property values in the jurisdiction.

Tiebout's model of local expenditures is neutral regarding the content of governmental functional responsibility and similarly agnostic about what functions the states and the national government should assume. Since the content of functional responsibilities is limited only by the median voter's preferences, Tiebout has no strong theoretical reason to believe that the sorting of individuals among governments — local, state, or national — should produce a hierarchical differentiation in the functional content of different levels of government. Tiebout provides an engine, namely the market, for the assignment of service responsibilities. Others have used this market engine to deduce a set of hypotheses for assigning functional responsibilities across different levels of government.

Contemporary conditions in the United States may be optimal for the operation of Tiebout's market theory of public policy. There are approximately 80,000 governmental jurisdictions in the United States, each producing a different repertoire of goods and services. Citizens should be able to maximize their preferences for publicly provided goods and services at desired levels of taxation within the current governmental market. A significant qualification to the Tiebout model, however, may account for discrepancy between the market theory of public expenditures and the actual practice of subnational governments.

Buchanan, Peterson, and Miller introduce important qualifications to Tiebout's theory of local expenditures that significantly inform the debate on devolution.[13] Each author notes that the mobility of consumer-voters in a metropolitan area produces a significant bias affecting the retention of wealthier residents. Buchanan demonstrates that collective decision making under majority rule, with equality of consumption and taxation, will advantage low-income citizens at the expense of high-income residents. The result is income redistribution, an externality that middle- and high-income citizens can avoid by out-migration. Peterson further explores this bias, theorizing that "local politics is not like national politics" because "there are crucial kinds of public policies that local governments simply cannot execute."[14] By inference, Peterson claims that there are policies that only the national government can perform efficiently.

Peterson maintains that the scope and level of a community's functional responsibilities are constrained by the inability of cities and, to a lesser extent, of states, to control the mobility of capital and labor across their borders. Though national governments can control the flow of capital and labor across their borders, states and cities are less effective at preventing their citizens, businesses, and capital base from migrating to other locales with better tax-to-benefit ratios. Consequently, governments seek to maximize their economic well-being by pursuing policies and activities that enhance the economic base of the community, while avoiding those that threaten the community with the loss of productive capital and labor. Cities, states, and other subnational units of government pursue developmental policies (roads and highways) that generate economic resources (i.e., a tax base) that can be used for the community's collective welfare. Conversely, these units of government are expected to avoid redistributive public policies that benefit dependent and nonproductive persons (e.g., welfare, housing, and health care), while drawing resources away from productive citizens without providing them commensurate benefits. Again, by implication, the responsibility for redistributive policies is less harmful to states and national governments because of the significant transaction costs associated with migration between states and nations.

For Buchanan, Miller, and Peterson, the hypotheses derived from Tiebout's work provide the theoretical foundation for their own empirical expectations about the assignment of functional responsibility in a federal system. These hypotheses include

1. Expenditures on redistributive services are functions of fiscal capacity (i.e., wealth), not demand.

2. Expenditures on developmental services are a function of demand (i.e., population size).

3. Tax rates and tax burden (i.e., local taxes as a percentage of personal income) will tend toward uniformity among communities competing in the same market for consumer-voters.

The thesis advanced by Buchanan, Miller, and Peterson is orthogonal to the assignment of functional responsibilities recommended by advocates of devolution. Moreover, a number of other significant implications that bear on the future success of devolution flow from the theoretical work of these authors. First, politics, at least at the subnational level, is marginalized. Demand does not drive spending policies for redistributive social services. Spending for redistributive policies at the subnational level is largely a function of wealth. Politics in the form of public preference is not important to the formation of most municipal public policies, at least not those associated with significant redistributive effects. Finally, by implication, subnational units of government are more efficacious when they engage in development policies and less so when they pursue redistributive social policies. The delivery of redistributive social services is more efficiently handled by the national government.

This view seriously challenges the claims of proponents of devolution who believe that state and local governments can efficiently provide many redistributive social services. Is the scope of local functional responsibility limited by externalities associated with different goods and services? What, if anything, can state and local governments do to overcome these constraints and fulfill the expectations of devolution? Though politics may not be a significant determinant of some public policies, there remains some expectation that voters' behavior is influenced by the assignment of different functional responsibilities to different units of government. Are voters aware of the distribution of functional responsibilities among national, state and local governments? Do they tailor their political behaviors accordingly? Do voters punish only national leaders when the performance of the economy, foreign policy, and social welfare are unsatisfactory, reserving their political judgment on schools, crime, and roads for state and local officials? These are questions about the political consequences of functional assignment.

Empirical Findings

I have organized my review of the empirical literature on a local public goods market around macro- and micro-level research. Macro-level studies address the question of what local governments do — specifically, whether they can assume responsibilities for redistributive social services without suffering the loss of productive capital and labor. Micro-level research is concerned with the behavioral expectations of a public-goods market. At this level of analysis, research focuses on how public opinion and preferences shape local public policy.

Macro-level Research: Patterns of Functional Assignment

Peterson's own analysis of spending patterns among state and local governments confirms his hypotheses about the assignment of functional responsibilities in a federal system.[15] Peterson found that the aggregated spending and taxing policies of state and local governments reflect a minimal range of responsibility for redistributive social services and a predominant concern with developmental and allocational goods and services. Consistent with Peterson's tax competition hypothesis, state and local taxing policies exhibit only limited variation across the fifty states.

The ability of states to promote economic development is called into serious question by Brace's research.[16] Contrary to Peterson's expectations, Brace finds that "lateral competition could render states ineffectual in promoting development goals,"[17] and that when states succeed at stimulating income growth, job growth is significantly diminished.

Gramlich and Rubinfeld provide supporting evidence for the operation of a local public-goods market.[18] The authors discover "substantial public service variety" within metropolitan areas. Moreover, they find that "actual spending conforms substantially to desired levels in urban areas, but less so in rural areas with little public sector choice.[19]

Miller's study of municipal incorporation in the Los Angeles metropolitan area provides strong support for Peterson's thesis.[20] Examining the formation of new municipalities in Los Angeles County, Miller finds that the proliferation of new local governments was motivated less by a demand for efficiency in government than by "a revolt of the rich against the poor, carried out by exit rather than voice."[21] The mechanism of avoidance was movement to other metropolitan communities. The mobility of metropolitan populations drives the demand for new governmental entities, placing competitive pressures on existing local governments to restrict the scope of functional responsibilities to developmental and allocational policies.

Evidence for the migration hypothesis has been mixed and "not entirely convincing."[22] The data for most of these studies were collected prior to 1970. Studies conducted since 1970 have found evidence to support the migration hypothesis.[23] Peterson and Rom found that "when benefit levels become high, the size of the poverty population increases. Conversely, when poverty rates become high, benefit levels are cut. The findings are consistent with the claim that state-determined benefit levels distort policy and residential choices."[24] This finding represents the most serious challenge to the hypothesized benefits of devolution.

I have found that although spending for redistributive services is a small proportion of total municipal spending, the variation in municipal spending for redistributive services is six times greater than that for developmental and allocational goods and services.[25] Similarly, variations in the tax rates and tax burdens among municipal governments in the same metropolitan area are substantially larger than those reported by Peterson.[26] The variation in taxing and spending for redistributive services among communities in the same metropolitan area is inconsistent with Peterson's thesis. Moreover, it should covary with the flight of productive capital and labor from communities with above-average spending for redistributive programs. This finding is not reported in the literature.

How do cities continue to pursue policies antithetical to their economic interests? The answer rests with the institutional arrangements used for the provision and production of municipal services. The use of service contracts and other nontraditional modes of service delivery mitigate, through efficiency gains, the negative effects associated with redistributive services. The constraints on the municipal provision of redistributive services can be avoided by adopting institutional arrangements that minimize the negative externalities middle- and upper-class citizens experience when taxed for these services.

Another way local governments may meet the challenge of devolution is to control their size and jurisdictional boundaries. A core hypothesis in the literature on subnational public policy is that size of government matters. How size matters, however, is the subject of considerable debate. Consolidationalists have argued that large, centralized governments are associated with greater efficiency.[27] Citing economies of scale, consolidationalists claim that decentralized, fragmented, and polycentric governance is inefficient and ineffective, and they recommend that "as far as possible in each major urban area there should be only one local government.[28] Polycentrists, in contrast, argue that centralized, hierarchical government is inefficient and that it suffers from the inherent problem of bureaucratic budget-maximizing behavior.[29] They claim that a large number of metropolitan-area governments create a competitive market for new residential homeowners and businesses, and that the competition among these metropolitan-area governments constrains their taxing and spending levels and maximizes their efficiency.

The empirical evidence on budget-maximizing behavior and scale economies among larger and centralized metropolitan governments is mixed, but it generally favors the polycentrists. Oates failed to detect a significant relationship between the size of government (i.e., total expenditures) and governmental fragmentation.[30] Nelson detects a significant and positive relationship between fragmentation and government size, but only when limited to the study of multipurpose governments and not special districts.[31] Marlow and Raimondo have reported similar findings.[32]

Zax and Forbes and Zampelli extend Nelson's findings but again identify an important limit to the scope of market models for local government.[33] Forbes and Zampelli argue that population mobility is limited to the substate level; therefore, the market forces, which constrain budget-maximizing behavior, are also limited to substate-level governments. National, and to a lesser extent, state governments are more susceptible to bureaucratic budget-maximizing behavior because entry to their markets is constrained by significant transaction costs. One conclusion to be drawn from the work of Forbes and Zampelli and that of Zax is that the efficiency gains of markets are not available to higher-level (i.e., state and national) governments because of entry problems. Simply stated, the cost of moving (i.e., voting with one's feet) often exceeds the benefits associated with relocating to another state or region with superior goods and services.

Burns' study of the formation of American local governments offers an alternative to Tiebout's and Peterson's market model.[34] Burns joins market theorists in viewing local governments as public means for fulfilling private ends. For Burns, however, private actors in the local government market face a collective-action problem. Each actor would be better off if someone else assumed the burden of forming the government. Burns explains the polycentric structure, which others see as market-driven, as a small-group solution to the collective-action problem.[35] Small groups of individuals (sometimes a single person) use existing state laws to solve the collective-action problem associated with mobilizing public support for the formation of a new government. Burns finds that demand for new government services is a weaker determinant of new government formation than are flexible laws regulating the creation of new governments. Demand as a determinant of government formation abated in states that afforded their residents liberal opportunities for municipal incorporation.

The efficiency gains local governments achieve under devolution require significant institutional support. The form of service provision (e.g., service contracting) and the state laws regulating the formation and operation of local governments significantly impact the ability of local governments to overcome the inefficiencies associated with the provision of some goods and services.

Micro-level Research: Behavioral Expectations of Public-Goods Markets

The behavioral implications of a market model of subnational politics produce two distinct hypotheses. The "sorting hypothesis" simply states that competition among a relatively large number of jurisdictions for productive capital and labor will produce the homogeneous sorting of residential populations. The "rational consumer" hypothesis states that the homogeneous sorting of residential populations among governmental units is achieved by households deliberately moving to jurisdictions that best satisfy their preferences for local goods and services.

Aggregate studies of the sorting hypothesis have produced supporting evidence. Stein, Grubb, Miller, and Pack and Pack all find evidence of the homogeneous sorting of residential populations in metropolitan areas.[36] These studies, however, examine only the homogeneity of residential populations, not the relationship between homogeneity and municipal taxing and service bundles. My cross-sectional analysis identifies only a modest relationship between the racial homogeneity of municipal populations and the variation in common service activities.[37]

Closely related to the sorting hypothesis is the behavioral mechanism that is assumed to produce a homogeneous sorting of residential populations among metropolitan governments. The search for a connection between the actions of municipal governments and household moving decisions has been the focus of a significant debate.[38] The empirical evidence to support this theory has been mixed. Macro-level studies have identified a significant relationship between aggregate tax-service bundles and the location decisions of movers.[39] Substantial evidence to support the micro-level assumptions of this relationship has been lacking, however. Most citizens are ill-informed about the taxing and spending policies of their own communities. Even fewer have knowledge of the taxing and spending policies of neighboring jurisdictions.

Most who have studied this question have held that complete information, or at least widespread knowledge, about the tax-service bundles of different jurisdictions is essential to the operation of a public-goods market. This view has been articulated forcefully by Lowery and Lyons and by Lyons, Lowery, and DeHoog,[40] who find a lack of consumer knowledge about the content of government policies. A public-goods market cannot operate efficiently without significant consumer knowledge about local tax-service bundles.

Schneider et al. challenges the need for such a strong micro-level assumption for the operation of a local public-goods market.[41] Their basic thesis is that high-income movers have the inclination to become informed about local tax-service bundles, as well as the capacity to bear the costs of becoming informed. High-income movers serve as the engine for a local public-goods market. Schneider et al. argue that not all citizens need to be informed about government tax-service bundles in order for a public-goods market to be competitive. These authors claim that a subset of citizens — higher-income movers — can significantly influence the competitiveness of markets for public goods. Only movers have a need to acquire information about the different tax-service bundles, since only these individuals are making decisions based on the different bundles offered by jurisdictions in a metropolitan area. Key to this thesis is the hypothesis that these marginal consumers, not the average citizen or even the average mover, influence the demand for and supply of public goods and services.

The empirical findings generated by Schneider et al. confirm that high-income movers are much more likely than lower-income movers to hold accurate information about tax-service bundles. They also find, however, that nonmovers, regardless of income levels, are able to acquire information about tax-service bundles that rivals the information of all but the highest-income movers. They explain this finding in terms of the costs of becoming informed and the nature of search-versus-experience goods. Movers acquire information before a home purchase, while nonmovers acquire information about tax-service packages over time through direct exposure to the quality and costs of locally-provided public goods.

Peterson also argues that organized political demand, as opposed to the preferences of consumer-voters, has little to do with the formation of core local policy outputs. He finds that political variables (percentage of population that is black and percentage that is poor) were weakly related or unrelated to spending for development and redistributive public policies, which confirms his conclusion that a city's position within a larger federal system constrains the influence that local politics will have on municipal policy decisions. Peterson provides more than empirical evidence that local politics does not significantly shape local policies; he offers a theoretically grounded explanation for this finding that has not been well received by many students of subnational politics.[42] This group of scholars have endeavored to show that competing political and economic interests significantly shape local development policy.[43] Again, this literature tends to demonstrate that the policy preferences of specific constituencies (e.g., blacks, developers, etc.) have been instrumental in shaping core local policies.

A number of researchers have examined the linkage between the assignment of functional responsibility among different levels of government and the conduct of politics and content of individual political behavior. Tidmarch, Hyman, and Sorkin's study of press coverage in congressional and gubernatorial elections provides supporting evidence for a federalist interpretation of political behavior: "It is obvious that the national policy agenda, while visible, is a demonstrably smaller presence in the gubernatorial campaign coverage than in House and Senate coverage. Several issues, chiefly in the realm of state power (education, crime, and public works) make up a proportionally greater share of gubernatorial news agenda. This is, in our view, best comprehended as a product of the federal arrangement."[44]

Chubb finds that state legislative and gubernatorial elections are not significantly influenced by state economic conditions.[45] Consistent with constitutional provisions that give the national government significantly greater power to regulate the economy, he shows that gubernatorial elections turn on the performance of the president in managing the national economy. Similarly, I find that voters hold congressional and presidential incumbents more accountable than their subnational counterparts for managing the economy — evidence that voters assign the federal government a predominant role in this area.[46]

Neither Chubb nor I conclude that state-level economic and political attributes have an insignificant effect on gubernatorial or other subnational voting.[47] To the contrary, we and other researchers have shown that state-level political attributes do influence political behavior, but not to the exclusion of national influences.[48] The influence of national economic forces on subnational elections suggests that voters may assign a greater degree of responsibility for their own economic well-being to the level of government that they perceive to be most responsible for regulating the economy.

What Have We Learned?

Scholars of subnational politics have hypothesized and confirmed a pattern of functional assignment that matches the attributes of different goods and services with the level of government that optimally provides each function. The expectation is that subnational governments will assume responsibility for goods and services with minimal externalities, while the national government will assume a predominant responsibility for goods and services susceptible to externalities. For the most part, this empirical expectation has been confirmed. Exceptions have been observed, but they can be accounted for without resorting to ad hoc explanations. Moreover, researchers have shown that the hypothesized pattern of functional assignment has significant implications both for individual behavior and for the way in which politics is conducted.

The attributes of individual goods and services and their provision by different units of government influences the attitudes, perceptions, and behavior of individuals. There is evidence, albeit nascent, that voters are implicitly aware of the pattern of functional assignment among national and subnational governments. We have strong evidence that some consumer-voters respond to the different tax-service bundles provided by governments in metropolitan areas. Furthermore, there is evidence that the functional scope and content of a contested office will modulate the relative importance of state and national forces on voter behavior.

Avenues for Future Study

The field of state and local government is uniquely positioned to extend our understanding of what government does, and why. The rich comparative setting of 80,000 subnational units of governments provides ample opportunity for the most sophisticated tests of market theories of politics and public policy. Three avenues for new research are (1) an extended examination of the consequences of changing functional assignment patterns for the conduct of politics and political behavior; (2) the development of new theory on the micro foundations of market models of politics and public policy; and (3) examinations of the role political institutions play in the operation of market models of politics and public policy.

Changing Functional Assignment Patterns

What are the consequences for politics and political behavior of changing functional assignments? Past research has focused almost exclusively
on economic voting, seeking to determine whether and to what degree federal or state-level economic variables have an influence on the candidate
choices of voters at the state and federal levels. Unfortunately, the assignment of functional responsibility for economic policy is ambiguous and
produces mixed findings. Other functions provide a clearer test. We might
expect that preferences for public education would influence vote choices
in state and local elections; the same policy preferences, however, should be
less influential in balloting for judicial, congressional, and presidential elections. Abortion policy provides a critical test of consequences for changing
functional assignment patterns.

Since the 1973 *Roe* v. *Wade* decision, abortion policy has been the responsibility of the federal government, specifically the Supreme Court.[49]
Consequently, we have seen little evidence since 1974 of issue-voting on
abortion rights at either the national or subnational level.[50] With the *Webster* v. *Reproductive Health Services* decision in 1989, the Supreme Court
opened to the door to state regulation of abortion services.[51] Since 1989
a number of states have moved aggressively to regulate women's access
to abortion services, signaling state lawmakers and voters that the abortion issue has returned to the states. Consequently, we might expect more
issue-voting on the abortion question in those states covered by *Webster*
and similar lower-court decisions.[52] That is, the candidate preferences of
voters with salient attitudes on abortion policy should be correlated with
their perception of the candidates' positions on abortion. There is a strong
expectation that Congress will continue to devolve other national policy
responsibilities to the states and local governments, which will create new
opportunities to test the political content and consequences of changing
functional assignment patterns.

The Micro Foundations of a Market Model

Central to the operation of a market model of local policy and politics is
the acquisition of information by both residents and movers.[53] Correct information about choices in the marketplace is necessary to the operation
of a market model of local public policy. Schneider et al. maintain that
asymmetry in the acquisition of information does not hinder the operation
of a market for local public policy. Such research relies on survey research
methods to identify whether people can answer questions accurately about
tax-service bundles.[54] The problem with such an approach is that it pre-
sumes that information elicited by surveys is the same information that
citizens rationally need to acquire in order to make appropriate decisions
about jurisdictions that are compatible with their preferences.

It is possible that individuals acquire information relevant to their preferences without ever knowing the right answers to the questions posed by survey researchers. Examples abound. James Q. Wilson explains that people avoid high-crime neighborhoods not by knowing crime rates but by visually recognizing deteriorating housing and litter-strewn streets.[55] Similarly, parents seeking to find the best school for their child need not know the relative test scores of children in the various schools within a geographic area. They can identify schools with populations of families that are known to value quality education by relying on informational heuristics — proxies that provide cues correlated with the type of information that survey questions might probe. The characteristics of neighborhoods are generally acquired not by learning statistics from the Census Bureau, but by the casual sighting of children's bicycles and toys lining driveways or by informally rating the expense and newness of the cars parked there. Using these heuristics can, in many respects, be efficient because the costs of acquiring them are likely to be low. Heuristics can be used and adapted to the situations that consumers actually face when they need to make a decision.[56]

More important, informational heuristics permit people to link their preferences to their choices, and they may thereby serve the informational function needed to drive a local public-goods market. Researchers who have relied on survey responses to factual questions about collective goods find, not surprisingly, that most people have little information about tax-service packages. Such research is misplaced. It leads to a faulty conclusion that the majority of people lack appropriate knowledge to make decisions that link their preferences to government policies. It also has led to an overemphasis on high-income citizens, since these people tend to fare somewhat better on survey questions that test direct knowledge of government tax rates and expenditure levels.

A more appropriate methodology would seek to identify the ability of individual citizens to match their preferences to the tax-service packages that local jurisdictions provide. This requires measuring the correlation, if any, between the preferences of individuals and the collective goods that they choose to consume. Survey research is ill-suited to identifying the types of information proxies and shortcuts that people bring to bear on their decision-making processes. The relevant question for the micro-level foundations of the Tiebout model is not whether citizens generally, or high-income movers specifically, are able to report accurately to survey researchers the relative costs or qualities of collective goods.[57] The important question is whether citizens can identify and locate themselves in jurisdictions that are compatible with their preferences.

A different set of empirical conditions must be established to verify the micro-level foundations for a public-goods market. We do not need to verify that people have direct factual information about tax-service packages to maximize their preferences on collective goods. Instead, what must be determined is, first, that citizens have preference sets concerning collective goods, and, second, that they are able to connect those preferences to tax-service packages. These connections are assumed to occur via the decisions that people make about the consumption of the collective goods offered by particular jurisdictions within a geographic area. One of the key opportunities for citizens to establish such a connection is when they move from one location to another. It is not altogether clear why we should expect high-income movers to be especially competent in making a connection between their preferences and tax-service packages. While it certainly is a possibility that high-income, well-educated movers may employ better informational heuristics in their consumption decisions, it is also possible that the capacity to use such shortcuts successfully is randomly distributed across the population. It is more likely that income and education levels have an impact on the preferences that factor into people's decisions about the consumption of collective goods. Likewise, other personal traits, such as religion, ethnic origin, age, and gender, shape the choices that people make about the collective goods that they want governments to provide. New research should test for the link between preferences and tax-service packages, and then explain how this nexus is achieved.

The Institutional Setting of Market Models

There is increasing evidence that market explanations of subnational politics and policy rely on institutional factors. Burns' collective action explanation of government formation relies heavily on a set of institutional mechanisms (i.e., liberal incorporation laws) to explain how demand affects the proliferation of new municipal governments and special districts. I have demonstrated that the pernicious effects of redistributive service responsibilities could be mitigated through the use of different arrangements for the provision and production of redistributive goods and services.

It is not altogether clear from this body of research how institutional arrangements remedy free-rider problems, externalities, and other market problems associated with the public provision of certain goods and services. A thorough conceptualization of how different institutional arrangements interact with the policy attributes and market forces to produce specific policies is needed. Rules and structures matter, and the field of subnational politics and government provides an enormously rich setting in which to test theories of how institutions affect policy, politics, and political behavior.

To date, institutional research has examined how rules and different governance structures interact with the attributes of goods and services to produce efficient and effective local policy outputs. The prevailing view in the literature is that an optimal institutional arrangement exists for the efficient and effective provision of each good and service. This view holds that the attributes of different policies are mutually exclusive, and that public goods are uniquely distinguished from private goods. This thinking may be in error, however. Some goods and services possess attributes of both public and private goods. The provision of national defense is a public good, delivering to every citizen a nonexclusive and jointly consumed benefit. The production of national defense, however, requires the siting of military bases, the awarding of contracts, and other highly particularistic goods that are exclusively and nonjointly consumed. Similarly, the provision of environmental policy (i.e., clean air and water) may have public-goods attributes. The production of these public goods, however, requires the distribution of private benefits (e.g., water-treatment plants, Superfund cleanup). Other policies that may possess both public- and private-goods attributes include public transportation and federally-funded research and development.

The possibility that some goods and services possess attributes of both public and private goods raises a number of intriguing research questions. What are the consequences of this condition for politics? Are legislative coalitions for policies possessing hybrid attributes different from those that support pure public or private goods and services? What are the optimal arrangements for the provision of goods and services having both public- and private-goods attributes?

At present the evidence is mixed regarding the capacity of local governments to fulfill the expectations associated with devolution. Moreover, there is reason to believe that the ability of local governments to assume long-term federal responsibilities (e.g., social welfare) is enhanced by several institutional arrangements. Alternative modes of service provision, including contracting and regional service arrangements and flexible jurisdictional boundaries, greatly enhance local governments' capacity to avoid the negative externalities associated with the local provision of many goods and services. Interestingly, the states, not the federal government, hold the key to successful devolution of federal responsibilities to local government. The states directly determine whether these entities have the authority and flexibility to meet the challenge of devolution.

The multiple and variegated research setting that defines local government provides an ideal locus for studying the consequences of devolution. Subnational scholars have developed a rich and well-tested theory about what governments do and why. Further refinements, extensions, and tests of this theoretical model promise to help local governments meet the challenge of devolution.

CHAPTER THREE
Governors: Their Heritage and Future

Nelson C. Dometrius

THE GOVERNORSHIP IS one of the earliest of American public offices. It virtually crossed the ocean with the early colonists on sailing ships, and took root in American soil long before the federal government — with its presidency, Congress, and judiciary — was even dreamt of.[1]

The governorship continues today, though not in its original form. Consider but a few of the vast changes that have taken place since colonial times: from the buggy whip to the space shuttle; from horse shoes to fuel injectors; from family farming to today's predominantly service occupations; from a predominance of extended families, with three to four generations living in the same home, to today's polyglot of nuclear, blended, and single-parent families; and from writing on slate tablets to surfing the Internet. For any political system to continue working across such enormously different environments, it must be alive; changing, adapting, and growing to continue meeting the disparate needs of populations separated by hundreds of years of history and change. The American governorship has undergone such a change, and governors have gone from being little fish in little ponds to today's big fish in big ponds.

At the opening of a new millennium, we find contemporary governors serving multiple roles, including managing state administrative structures,[2] acting as policy leaders,[3] and even assuming "foreign policy" roles within the intergovernmental system.[4] Affecting policy is clearly at the heart of both what governors do and what citizens want them to do — securing changes in governmental practices to better the lives of the state's citizens. But governors have not always been effective managers of state policy. Many analysts have suggested that governors have truly come into their own as state policy leaders only within the past twenty-five years. It would be reckless to assume that such a recent hold on state leadership has produced changes that are now a permanent fixture of state politics. Trends point that way, but trends have a nasty habit of changing in unforeseen ways. To understand the future role of contemporary governors, we must look backwards into history. Where governors are at present is a product of their past, of how the office began and then changed over the years. Where the governorship will go in the future is partly a function of the continuity of patterns that sometimes are obscured by these changes.

Three themes reappear with regularity throughout the governorship's history. First, the office is but one element of the American political system. The term "system" implies a network of interrelated components, and our political system is such a network. Consider the human body as a biological system. It is often said that if a person were to lose one sense, such as vision, the remaining senses would become more acute in order to compensate, and the entire system would continue to function well despite its disabled element. Thus, to say that the American political system has grown to meet current needs does not mean that all parts of the system work smoothly at all times. The American governorship has changed neither in a linear progression nor in isolation. Changes in the governorship have occurred through periods of fits and starts; sometimes the office has been seen as the shining light of politics progressing toward a better future; at other times it has been viewed as a backwater on the American political scene or simply ignored as insignificant. In addition, the governorship's status and role during any particular time period is always a function both of changes in the office itself and of changes in other parts of the system to which it is inextricably connected.

Second, more than that of most offices, the history of the governorship starkly illustrates the contradictions in the American political psyche. On one hand, Americans distrust political power. We yield it to our public officials only grudgingly, and even then tie it up with a host of checks and balances. On the other hand, we are quick to despise our governments when they appear so stymied by ineffectiveness and inefficiency that major social needs go unanswered. This is the unresolvable dilemma of American governance, for power can be allocated only to political offices, not political motives. If we restrict the power of an office so that its occupants find it difficult to do bad, we may also restrict them from doing good. Alternatively, if we give an office sufficient power for its occupants to accomplish good things, they can also accomplish bad things.

These two themes come together to form a third, the formal and informal powers of the governor. Formal power is authority vested in an office, usually by the state's constitution, to affect certain state activities.[5] The power to appoint agency heads or veto legislation are examples. Informal power consists of the resources a particular individual brings to the office: popularity, experience, the ability to negotiate agreements with the legislature, and cleverness in finding ways to get things accomplished.[6] The theme of formal and informal power often makes the other two themes concrete. A state's citizenry that at one point rejects a constitutional amendment to allocate greater formal power to the governor may, a short time later, applaud its governor for drawing on other parts of the system, or using personality to get around the very formal limitations it has imposed on the office, in order to accomplish needed state innovations.

If we are to understand our governors, therefore, we must understand ourselves: the kinds of political structures we have created, the expectations we place on those structures, and how we react to individuals who live within, or get around, our political structures. This is the history of the governorship.

The Gubernatorial Heritage

During the colonial and early constitutional periods, the governorship suffered from America's distrust of centralized power. The governorship was an imported institution, with most governors serving as agents of the British crown. They exercised extensive powers granted by a king and were charged with taking care of the king's possessions and citizens. Included among these powers were: command of the armed forces, enforcing the law, granting pardons, and appointing judges and other governing officials.

Of central concern to many colonists was the governor's control over the legislature. Most colonists were of British descent, bringing the experiences and values of their homeland with them to the colonies and passing them on as a cultural heritage to their children. Part of that cultural heritage was faith in the legislature to represent popular interests and limit the power of the crown. In 1215, a defeated King John was forced to sign the Magna Carta, recognizing certain rights of the nobility that the king could not violate. From this beginning, power drained in fits and starts from the crown to other segments of British government, most noticeably its Parliament.

Given this history, it was natural for American colonists to want their own legislatures as their voice in colonial governments. The colonial governor, however, had the authority to veto legislative acts and even dissolve the legislature entirely should it become too unruly. During the years leading up to the Revolutionary War, many of those leading the call for independence were doing so from within colonial legislatures that became platforms for their views. The condemnation of British policy often became so loud and annoying that the governors used their power of legislative dissolution, hoping to silence the revolutionaries. This experience cemented even further in the colonists' minds the view that executives were to be feared and legislatures to be trusted.

Early State Constitutions

This distrust of centralized executives carried over after the Revolutionary War, and can readily be seen in early attempts to develop both a national government and state constitutions. The first basis for a national government, the Articles of Confederation, created no national chief executive and gave the national legislature very little power, reserving almost all governing power to the states. The first constitutions of the new states continued the office of the governorship but did not define the governor as a chief executive. Many states began with a plural executive, that is, a committee of officials responsible for carrying out state policy, with the governor acting merely as the chairperson. Other states created a single executive but made it predominantly an honorary office with little power. Leslie Lipson aptly represented the tenor of the times by citing a North Carolina delegate returning from that state's constitutional convention. Asked how much power the constitution would give to the state's governor, the delegate replied, "Just enough to sign the receipt for his salary."[7] While there were exceptions, this was the colonial standard; substantial power lodged in the state legislature and little in the governorship. The early governorship was an office with "many checks and few balances."[8]

One way to examine the status of early governors, and change in the governorship across time, is to look at a governor's formal power.[9] Throughout most years of the American governorship, formal power involved four key components: veto power, tenure power, budget authority, and appointment power.

Veto power consists of the governor's ability to veto acts of the legislature and protect that veto from legislative override — that is, can the governor's veto be overridden by a simple majority of the legislature, or does it require some more difficult-to-achieve "super majority," such as a two-thirds or three-fourths vote of each legislative house? The power to veto legislative acts allows the governor to be a key player in state policy development. The desires of a governor with a weighty veto power must be considered when the legislature seeks to adopt or change policy.[10] If the governor lacks veto power, or has a veto that can be overridden easily by the same simple legislative majority that originally passed a bill, the governor can readily become a nonplayer in the formation of state policy. In the early state constitutions, only Massachusetts and New York provided their governors with some veto authority. The other states, probably still remembering the oft-used and distasteful vetoes of colonial governors, denied their chief executives any veto power.

A second formal power resides in the nature of the governor's tenure. This consists of the length of the governor's term of office, now usually four years, and restrictions on the governor's ability to run for reelection. Governors with influence are those who know their job, know the other key actors in the political process, and make sure other actors know that the governor, who may well be around for a while, needs to be taken into account. A governor who can serve only two to three years in office barely has time to learn the job before it comes to an end. Worse is a lame-duck governor, whose term is nearing its end and who is barred from reelection. Legislators and interest groups know they need but wait a few months and the lame duck will be out of the picture. Many original state constitutions limited their governors to a one-year term, and most of those allowed a governor to serve no more than two consecutive terms, or a total of two years in office.

When it comes to budget authority, it is important to understand that a budget is not just dollars and cents, it is policy. Nearly every governmental activity requires funding, and the amount of money a state puts into building roads versus building schools reflects the priorities of that state. Thus the ability to influence the state budget is an important component of a governor's ability to influence state policy. Early state practices had little in the way of any budget strategy. State agencies were often funded on an as-needed basis; whenever a particular agency ran out of money, it would come back to the legislature asking for more. Budgeting was a predominantly legislative function, with gubernatorial involvement depending far more on informal influence with the legislature than on any formal grant of authority.

Appointment power is central to the notion of a chief executive. The governor, at least in the popular mind, should direct the administration of state government and be accountable to the public when inefficiency and corruption in state administration occurs. Governors are expected to oversee the actions of their subordinates to ensure competence and correct wrongdoing. This can be done if "subordinates" are truly subordinates — the governor can screen and hire individuals to direct key state functions and replace them if they perform poorly. History clearly illustrates that many early governors were anything but *chief* executives, for although they did have the power to appoint some state officials — judges, surveyors, port administrators, and the like — nearly all of these appointments were subject to legislative confirmation. In some states, the governors were themselves appointed by the legislature, not popularly elected, and they often had to share their appointment and other powers with an executive council that could, and often did, overrule them on many matters.

Of course, this weakness in formal authority looks worse today than it actually was, in part because early state government was not yet terribly complex. The number of state activities were limited, budgets were relatively simple, and overseeing the behavior of the executive branch was not too arduous a task. Many governors also had informal sources of influence, and it was not uncommon for governors to come from legislative leadership positions, spend a year or two in the governorship, and then return to the legislature. Today it is almost unheard of for a governor to return to the legislature after completing his or her executive service. Being a lame-duck governor was less of a problem when other actors knew the governor might end up back in the legislature and still be a force to be reckoned with, even if not an executive force. Unfortunately, this sort of informal musical chairs did not last much beyond the immediate post-Revolutionary period, and the weaknesses of the gubernatorial office became a more pronounced hindrance to later governors.

Power is always relative to the environment in which it is exercised.[11] A powerful corporation president can almost dictate the behavior of employees, but if the business's sole activity is to operate a carwash in a small town, the company president has far less impact on public life than does the middle manager of a major corporation such as IBM or General Motors. Conversely, the simpler the organization's activity, the easier it is to manage, and the more complex the activity, the more difficult it becomes to oversee it successfully. If a large organization makes only one product, say, brooms, it is fairly easy for the company leader to have a solid grasp of all that takes place in the organization. Steering a multifaceted organization producing everything from radios to automobiles, with manufacturing plants spread over the globe, however, is inordinately complex and requires far more in both personal skills and levers of influence if it is to be successfully accomplished by the corporation president.

So it is with governors and their states. Despite the weaknesses in their formal power, early governors had advantages their contemporary counterparts do not. The states were the key level of government within the new republic; at the same time, governing a small, predominantly rural, society was reasonably achievable. Both conditions were to change.

The Early 1800s

The governorship has undergone a number of periods of surge and decline over the years of the republic. The first set of changes came prior to the Civil War. Following Lord Acton's dictum — power tends to corrupt; absolute power corrupts absolutely — many power-heavy state legislatures began abusing their power. There were numerous, well-publicized examples of legislative corruption, and also a shift from the envisioned roles of executives and legislatures. In many ways, the American Revolution had a strong middle- and upper-class character, with propertied classes seeking to protect their wealth from British taxation. It was natural for many of these well-off citizens to take leading roles in the new state governments, and state policies were often directed toward the needs of commerce while paying little attention to those of the average citizen. This was best symbolized at the national level by the economic elite's apparent hold on the presidency, with four of the first six presidents coming from Virginia's "aristocracy" of large-scale farmers, and the other two coming from Massachusetts.

Over the early years of the 1800s, many states strengthened their gubernatorial offices as counterpoints to legislative corruption and insensitivity. Governors became popularly elected instead of selected by the legislature, and the office was provided both with more extensive power to veto legislative acts and the authority to appoint more state officials. This swing towards placing greater trust and authority in chief executives was represented nationally by the election of Andrew Jackson as president. This "barbarian" (i.e., not a member of the civilized aristocracy) was strongly supported by the small farmers and people on the frontier, and broke the back of the original eastern colonies' hold on the presidency. Jackson's presidency helped to solidify in the public mind the view of a chief executive — president or governor — as an important representative of the popular will. The colonial perception that executives were to be distrusted and only legislatures represented the people was disappearing. At the same time that the governorship was being strengthened, the states remained centers of governmental activity, with the national government only beginning to flex its muscles and discover the extent of its authority.

The Late 1800s

The Civil War changed much. First, it solidly established the role of the national government as the ultimate possessor of public authority, with the states as secondary partners. This was not just a legal shift, but a practical one as well. The cost of prosecuting the Civil War drove federal spending dramatically upward, where it remained thereafter, rising from about $2 to $3 per capita in 1860 to $12 to $13 per capita in 1870.[12] It also brought about an eventual shift in the distribution of political power within the states. During the Reconstruction period, the national government, especially Congress, took control of the secessionist states, appointing many state officials and "reforming" their governments and policies before allowing them back into the Union.

To control the defeated southern states, Reconstruction leaders centralized power in the state capitols so that a handful of Union sympathizers could control all state activities. Fearing the secessionists might regain control of county governments (the key local governments of the time), they denied former Confederates the right to hold office and decreed that many local positions were to be appointed by the Union-controlled governor. The governor also wielded strong veto power over the acts of the legislature, though the legislatures were often also under the domination of the national government.

The experience of the southern states was like a return to the pre-Revolutionary War period, with the hated central government, particularly the chief executive, beyond popular control and often imposing disliked policies.[13] Following the end of Reconstruction, when the former Confederate states rewrote their state constitutions, the concern foremost in their minds was to develop government structures that would make the perceived evils of Reconstruction unlikely ever to happen again. Consequently, they diluted the power of their state governments and their governors through such devices as the long ballot and statutory constitutions.

The long ballot is so called for a simple reason: it is long. In contrast to the simplified national form — electing only legislators and a president, who then select all other government officials — long-ballot states have numerous state and local elected officials: governor, lieutenant governor, state treasurer, state comptroller, attorney general, county district attorney, county sheriff, county treasurer, and more. In addition, numerous state functions are put under the control of boards and commissions whose members are either elected directly by the people or selected by the governor and legislature (for fixed terms so that they cannot be fired). For example, the public might elect a state board of education with five to ten members, who then set the state's educational policies and select a superintendent to run the state's education agency. The multiplicity of elected officials, each with independent sources of power and authority, ranging from the state capital down to the local level, make it unlikely that a small handful of reconstructionists or other demagogues would be able to consolidate power.

The long ballot first became popular during Andrew Jackson's presidency. Jackson avowed that the business of government was so simple and straightforward that it could easily be conducted by the average citizen. This belief justified the replacement of many long-time federal government workers with new people (who happened to be Jackson's supporters), and thus began a long period of patronage appointments to federal jobs. It also instituted the division of governmental activities at the state level into a variety of functions, each with its own separately elected or appointed leadership — an arrangement that provided both expanded patronage at the state and local levels and, at least theoretically, greater opportunities for average citizens to govern themselves. Though initiated before the Civil War, the long ballot appealed to many southern states as a way to avoid the evils of centralized power they had experienced during Reconstruction.

Another post-Reconstruction change was the move of many states to statutory state constitutions. The federal constitution is a "brief-basic" type: a fairly short document of only a few pages specifying the power of the federal government; the distribution of that power among the legislative, executive, and judicial branches; and the process by which individuals are to be selected to serve in each of those branches. A statutory constitution contains this minimum, but also far more, including precise descriptions of administrative offices, the powers of those offices, and a number of characteristics of state policy. For example, a statutory constitution might set the salaries of state officials, limit how a particular revenue might be spent (e.g., gasoline taxes could only be spent on roads), and stipulate the qualifications for and the benefit limits of public assistance. Terry Sanford, former governor of North Carolina, illustrated the character of statutory constitutions:

> The South Carolina Constitution defines what constitutes a durable hard-surface road in Greenville. South Dakota's Constitution sets the state's debt

limit at $100,000 unless the state is invaded. The Oklahoma Constitution requires the teaching of home economics in all public schools. Texas provides for the election of the inspector of hides and animals. Kansas and Nevada require election of the state printer.[14]

It is said of statutory constitutions that they confuse *what ought to be* with *what ought to be in the constitution.* Specific policies or administrative practices included in a constitution are very difficult to change. Rather than being able to change policies or administrative structures to meet modern needs by approval of the legislature and governor, the state must pass a constitutional amendment, which needs approval by a two-thirds or three-fifths vote of both houses of the legislature followed by a majority vote of the citizens. Special interests, observing how hard it is to obtain constitutional changes, have vied to get policies or favorable tax breaks locked into the constitution, reasoning correctly that there is a good chance of convincing one-third to one-quarter of state legislators to oppose any future constitutional change removing these special benefits. Thus policy set in the constitution rather than by legislative action becomes, in effect, policy removed from gubernatorial and legislative spheres of activity. While the long ballot and statutory constitutions became most popular in post–Civil War southern states, the composition of the Union was not static. New western states joined the Union, while older states regularly revised their constitutions, and the features of weak state government crept into both the new and the reworked constitutions.

The Early 1900s

After the Civil War, there was a long period of legislative dominance at both the national and state levels. This has been described as the period of weak presidents, and few governors were leading figures in their states either. The next major change came in the period between 1890 and 1920, with the beginning of the government reform movement. The reform movement had its impetus in the industrial revolution of the late 1800s, which brought enormous growth to cities, as immigrants poured in and others moved off the farms to take the more lucrative factory jobs available in urban areas. This urban concentration created demands for increased government services. The cities were fertile ground for political machines, and the growing list of government services provided equally fertile ground for graft and corruption.

The move for reform at this time went in two directions. At the beginning, the movement sought to strip legislators of their power by expanding even further the long ballot, believing that independent boards and commissions would be less corruption-prone than legislatures in providing government services. Later during this period, a number of governors — including Teddy Roosevelt and Woodrow Wilson — campaigned against the power of political machines, business trusts, and special interests. People began to look to the governorship as a possible tool to break the cozy and corrupt connection between legislatures and special interests.[15]

This rise in governors championing reform coincided with the reform movement's shift from seeking to disperse power to seeking to centralize it. It is a fair generalization that the first 100 years of American politics was devoted to cementing its democracy. This thing called democracy was, after all, a novel experiment on the world scene, and the public, its frontier mentality continuing through the late 1800s, was primarily interested in avoiding an overcentralization of power that might interfere with individual freedoms. About the turn of the century, public attention shifted from governing democratically to governing well — to making sure that public policies, once democratically adopted, were carried out efficiently and effectively. The attention shifted from policymaking to policy implementation, which, being the responsibility of the executive branch, created increased attention on the governorship. Scholars and reformers began to ask how government practices could be at all coherent when a number of separately elected individuals and boards were heading off in separate directions. The growth in government services exacerbated the problem by making the administration of state governments even more complex. For example, New York State had only 10 state agencies in 1800, a number that had grown to 81 by 1900 and to 170 by 1925.[16]

The agenda of reform turned towards strengthening the executive branch at all levels — city, state, and national. Chief executives, reformists argued, should be given greater power to hire and fire key officials, thus making those offices part of the governor's team and bringing coordination to the multiplicity of state agencies. Gubernatorial tenure should be expanded so that governors would not have to leave office after only two years, and could engage instead in long-term efforts to improve the operations of the executive branch. State constitutions should be simplified. Finally, the reformers called for governors to prepare unified budgets. Instead of agencies coming to the legislature for funds at sporadic times whenever their money ran out, all requests would be put into a single state budget where expenditures could be matched against expected revenues.

This agenda, loosely called either the government reform movement or the state reorganization movement, grew in popularity during the early 1900s. At the national level it included expanding the budget authority and staff resources of the president, while at the local level it emphasized either expanding mayoral powers or adopting the city-manager form of government. It borrowed many principles from the private sector, where authority typically was concentrated in a corporation president, and also from the administrative practices of European governments.

This movement had some early successes, beginning with the State of Illinois in 1917, and, over ensuing years, adding some twenty-five other states that reorganized at least some aspects of their executive branches. Soon, however, the reform movement ran into a roadblock of entrenched interests at the state level. State economic elites were understandably leery about creating a powerful state government that might challenge their interests. Only a few states cut back significantly on the long ballot, with a few more states expanding their governors' terms of office. Probably the most notable success was in the field of budgetary authority, where states that had not already adopted a unified budget proceeded to do so, and many, though not all, established the right to prepare the budget with the governor. Legislatures, of course, still had to approve any budget prepared by the executive branch, but a variety of large and small decisions went into the preparation of a budget package, and legislatures seldom had time to review all of these decisions. The governor's ability to propose a comprehensive budget, even if the legislature later made numerous changes, was no small matter.[17]

Along with preparing the budget, a new budget authority was increasingly adopted by the states — the item veto. A typical veto, such as that wielded by the president and early governors, applied to a legislative bill in its entirety. When the legislatively approved budget came to the governor, he had to either sign it or veto the entire package and start budget deliberations with the legislature all over again. An item veto allowed a governor to delete selected expenditures while approving the rest of the package.[18] A governor with an item veto could, for example, delete just the one new highway project he or she felt was unnecessary without having to veto the entire budget for the state's department of transportation. Though limited almost exclusively to budgets (versus substantive legislation), an item veto allowed a governor to influence significantly the final contours of state spending, which most governors used to push their policy preferences as well.[19]

The Mid-1900s

After the early successes of the state reform movement, there followed a long period during which the influence of governors in particular, and the states in general, declined. A number of forces in the first half of the twentieth century relegated the states and their governors to the backwaters of political activity. To begin with, what one can do depends on the resources available. Early in the century, the federal government adopted the graduated income tax, an exceptional generator of revenue, but only a few states followed suit. Toward the end of the 1920s, the Great Depression began pushing the country, including the states, into financial austerity. Consequently, many states did little because they could afford little.

When Franklin Roosevelt assumed the presidency in the 1930s, he made federal programs designed to lead the country out of the Depression the cornerstone of his activities. Buoyed by income-tax revenues, which were damaged less by the Depression than were other revenue sources, along with the ability to deficit-spend, which was banned by the constitutions of many states, the federal government became the center of the country's political activities. To cap off this period, the country was drawn into World War II, further cementing the public's focus on national government activities.

The agenda of the state reform movement was not totally forgotten. During the 1930s and 1940s, a few of the larger states of the Midwest and Northeast attempted to keep up with modern demands by adopting the income tax or other new revenue sources and by strengthening their state legislative and executive institutions. These were, however, relatively sparse exceptions to the decline of the states' role in national policy innovation and implementation.

The end of the war, and the less activist national climate during Dwight Eisenhower's presidency, might have allowed the states to recapture a more significant role in the political life of the country, but this was not to be. Federal government domestic activity declined little in the postwar period; it merely slowed down. Conversely, America's international role increased dramatically with the development of the Cold War, keeping public attention focused on Washington. The states, meanwhile, were still hampered by unwieldy governmental structures, inadequate sources of revenue, and a disinclination to change with the times.

A good part of the states' refusal to modernize was due to malapportionment in their legislative branches. From post-Revolutionary times on, most states followed the national government's model of two legislative houses, with seats in the lower house distributed on the basis of population — electoral regions drawn to contain roughly equal numbers of citizens — and upper-house seats distributed by region, commonly with one upper-house seat for each county. In early times this was reasonable, for counties contained roughly equal numbers of citizens, but the population shift to the cities begun in the late 1800s had continued apace during the 1900s. By the 1950s, many states had from one-half to two-thirds of their populations living in urban areas, and this produced a phenomenal disparity between the distribution of citizens and the distribution of votes in state legislatures. For example, in the early 1960s Los Angeles County, California, contained well over 1 million residents, while that state's rural Alpine County had only 15,000 residents. Nonetheless, the state's legislative structure gave each county one vote in the state senate. Nor were the lower houses of many state legislatures much better off, for although their election districts might have originally been created on the basis of population, many of those districts had not been revised for fifty to one hundred years, and they no longer even roughly mirrored the population distribution.

The result was that many states in the 1950s and 1960s had legislatures dominated by rural areas. Residents of rural counties had little interest in expanding state services, except some agricultural services, and were primarily concerned about keeping taxes low. The burgeoning cities, on the other hand, were screaming for help in such areas as mass transit, renovation of dilapidated buildings, housing assistance, public health, pollution control, and assistance for low-income citizens. Faced with insensitive state governments, urban citizens turned to where their votes did make a difference, the federal government. Seats in the U.S. House of Representatives more closely reflected the actual population distribution, and both presidential and U.S. Senate candidates garnered sizable proportions of their votes from a state's urban areas. During this period, states often complained about federal encroachment into areas traditionally left to the states to handle, but it was less a matter of federal encroachment than that the states had simply ignored the needs of their cities, and the federal government, best exemplified by President Lyndon Johnson's Great Society programs, had simply walked in unopposed.

From the 1930s through the 1960s, the states, in the view of many observers, had degenerated into largely administrative appendages to national government policy, and not very good appendages at that. With the long ballot still common in many states, there were numerous examples of bickering among state officials, sometimes breaking out into outright warfare. State legislatures, some meeting for only 60 to 120 days every two years, were trying to govern a modern society with tools adapted to the rural environment of a by-gone era. With the states themselves having comparatively little power to do anything, governors were often relegated to being "good time Charlies,"[20] performing the ceremonial roles of the office, but seldom being instrumental in developing policy to meet public needs. A number of governors did try to do more, using the club of reforming state government that governors had often wielded in the past. Though some succeeded, most failed in the face of continued intransigence from rural- and special-interest-dominated legislatures. Times were not good either for states or for governors.

The Current Era

The most recent, and perhaps the most successful, wave of state reform began in about 1965 and continued through the 1970s and 1980s. A number of social and political forces came together to produce this latest wave of reform. One was a series of U.S. Supreme Court decisions, beginning with *Baker* v. *Carr,* banning the malapportionment of state legislatures and mandating that both legislative houses had to be apportioned on the basis of population. By the end of the 1960s this began to produce state legislatures considerably more attuned to the needs of urban areas than their earlier, rural-dominated predecessors. In consequence, governors, elected by a statewide constituency and therefore sensitive to urban needs, were able to get more of their programs through the legislature.

This moving together of the interests of the executive and legislative branches also made the legislature more sympathetic to proposing constitutional changes to implement some of the leftover agenda of the state reform movement. At the beginning of the 1960s, about one-third of the states still restricted their governors to two-year terms of office, whereas only two, Vermont and New Hampshire, still did so by the mid-1990s. Veto powers, particularly the item veto, and the governor's role in overseeing the state budget were also considerably enhanced. A relatively recent — and spreading — innovation is the amendatory veto.[21] Legislatures had grown adept at muting the item veto's impact by lumping many categories of expenditures together into a single "item," once again forcing the governor into the all-or-nothing approach of either vetoing or approving the entire item. An amendatory veto allows a governor to revise the language and expenditure amounts in an appropriations bill before returning it to the legislature with his veto message.

Eliminating the long ballot, with its numerous elected state administrative positions, and streamlining statutory constitutions proved to be difficult changes to make, and both are still common in many states. Over the years, however, they have grown to be lesser problems. The growing demand for services from the increasingly important urban areas has created a sizable number of new state functions and agencies to implement them. These newer agencies, created by legislative action instead of constitutional provision, and typically headed by gubernatorial appointees, now dominate most of the states' important activities, while the old elective positions, such as state treasurer, have declined in importance.

Three other forces have enhanced the governorship over the past thirty years. The first is the growing importance of television and televised news programs, from which most citizens now get their information. Because it is a visual medium, televised news requires more pictures than do the older print media, and the governor is the clear symbolic representative of the state. Just as television has served to enhance the role and prestige of the presidency, it has had a similar effect on the governorship. The more the governor is sought after by the media for interviews, pronouncements, comments, or photo opportunities created to illustrate a state news story, the more he or she becomes prominent in the public eye and is able to lead public opinion.

Second, for both political and financial reasons, the federal government has cut back considerably on a number of domestic programs in recent years. Sometimes the programs just disappear, but just as frequently they disappear only from the federal budget by being passed down to the states, which then must assume a more active policy role. An example is the change in federal support for welfare programs, mandating both work requirements and an absolute limit on how long a person may receive assistance. The federal government merely set the goals for this budget reduction and then told the states: "you figure out how to achieve these goals." States must create programs to move people off welfare and into jobs, or they risk losing federal subsidies.

Finally, the governors themselves have changed. Larry Sabato has demonstrated that governors by the early 1980s had become younger, better educated, and more activist and energetic than their predecessors. An interplay of forces occurred as the growing prestige of the office attracted more ambitious people and those individuals then pushed for greater authority after obtaining the office.

Gubernatorial Policy Roles

In the last half of the twentieth century, governors obtained the status of potent political figures both within their states and in the nation. At least some aspects of the state reform movement's agenda, now over one hundred years old, have been largely implemented. Power, however, is a moving target. The governing structures that might have made a governor near-omnipotent in the 1940s barely allow him or her to keep up with state policies in the 1990s. Just as governors and the governorships have changed dramatically over the past thirty-five years, so have other agents of state government and the responsibilities the governors need to tackle. Though far more influential than their predecessors of earlier times, modern governors' policy responsibilities are also far greater. If we take a look at the policy roles and arenas of current governors, we will observe, as well, the persistence of three themes in current state governance.

Agenda Setting

State policy does not appear out of a vacuum or as a result of natural forces. At any given moment, there may be dozens, even hundreds, of *potential* issues, such as the quality of public education, expanding public transportation, crime control, environmental quality, insurance rates, or the state of the economy. For a potential issue to become a public problem, some entity needs to both articulate the problem — Is student performance too low? Are there not enough colleges to meet student demand? Is the cost of higher education too high for the average citizen? — and identify what the state government can do about it — raise teacher salaries, impose testing on public-school teachers, build new colleges, increase state funding, set common standards for high-school graduation, or provide vouchers for private-school tuition. It is the development of public awareness about a particular problem and its potential solutions that makes an issue one that state leaders must address. This is the agenda-setting function — identifying a short list of concerns that state policymakers must tackle.

Governors have always had a role in policymaking, sometimes substantial and sometimes marginal. A long-standing authority used by even weak governors was "message power," delivering an annual state-of-the-state message to highlight particular issues.[22] In the past, this may have been nothing more than a brief note or speech observed only by legislators and lobbyists. The modern governor, however, can use the mass media to address the state's citizens directly via speeches and press conferences. Few other state political leaders draw comparable media attention, and this special access provides the governor an exceptionally valuable platform to shape public opinion and set the state's agenda.

A governor comes to office after a lengthy and well-publicized campaign during which he or she has identified a policy agenda for the term of office. A number of state-related issues are generated elsewhere, however, and they may also become part of the governor's agenda. Natural disasters, court decisions, or actions by other governments can create situations that the state must address, and the public expects the governor to identify an appropriate response.[23] In other cases, citizens or interest groups generate policy proposals and hope to persuade the governor to put them on the agenda, capitalizing on the governor's ability to energize and focus public opinion on an issue.

Policy Development

Once some sort of public concern has been established, an appropriate governmental response must also be developed. If public-school students are not performing well, what are possible solutions and how might they be implemented? If a test is needed before high-school students can obtain their diplomas, what will the test cover, who will develop and administer it, evaluate the results, and pay for the process? Developing legislative proposals that address all these details requires a significant amount of expertise.

In the past, gubernatorial policy-development resources were sparse, and the same could be said of state legislatures. Legislative proposals were often developed by those who already had the expertise, such as lobbyists and state agency leaders. Thus, for example, a state teachers' association, far fonder of pay raises and smaller classes than of teacher testing, or the state education agency, often interested in protecting its turf and expanding its budget, would be where governors and legislators would turn for ideas on solving education problems. Political leaders seeking innovative solutions received few such proposals from established bureaucratic or lobbying interests, and the leader's ability to promote her own ideas was hampered by a lack of information on how well a novel solution might work or how much it might cost.

One source of policy development that has grown increasingly important for governors has been the National Governors' Association (NGA).[24] Begun shortly after the turn of the century as the Governors' Conference, this organization was originally used by presidents to garner public support for their policies. Around 1960 the National Governors' Conference (changed to the National Governors' Association in 1977) began to take a more active role in assisting governors, and the governors found they frequently had more in common with each other than with their own state legislatures. Training sessions for new governors were held to smooth the transition to office, with experienced governors providing advice, and more, to their newly-elected counterparts. There was at least one instance of an established governor lending his budget officer to a first-term colleague to help him get a start in office.

With the expanding role of the federal government during President Johnson's Great Society era, the NGA became more active. The rapid growth of federal grants and mandates was accompanied by an equally rapid growth in paperwork and regulations restricting how states administered the funds. Governors began pushing the federal government to ease these rules, seeking freedom to establish alternative procedures and administrative arrangements to accomplish the intended goals. Having gained experience with how governors of different parties could work together for common purposes, the NGA expanded its role in seeking common ground among the governors. A key change was the adoption of the Center for Policy Research and Analysis in 1974, which provided governors with significant policy-development assistance — studies of educational reform, environmental legislation, and a host of other issues facing the states.

Many governors did not rely solely on NGA assistance but expanded the policy-development tools of their offices. From the term of Franklin Roosevelt on, the presidency expanded its policy leadership by, at least in part, expanding the size of the presidential staff — close advisers to the president who monitor political developments and seek out policy initiatives. A number of governors lately have followed suit.[25] Many have instituted offices devoted to policy development, while others have transformed their state budget offices to include management and policy. A 1988 survey by the NGA reported that one quarter of the governors had staffs of over one hundred.[26] Through a variety of strategies, governors have added the resources they need to develop policy initiatives.

Policy Achievement

A third role of the governor is to make policy. Regardless of how an issue gets on the state's agenda, it must be resolved, and the public expects the governor to take the lead in problem resolution. The governor is often blamed for major unresolved state problems, regardless of how the problems developed. Knowing this, a governor will use every weapon in his or her arsenal to obtain agreement on a solution. Consider the cases of three governors, Mark White of Texas (1983–87) and Bill Clinton of Arkansas (1978–80, 1982–90), who dealt with education reform, and Lowell Weicker of Connecticut (1991–95), who dealt with that state's budget. Each case demonstrates aspects of the agenda-setting, policy-development, and policy-achievement functions.

Texas: informal power. Mark White campaigned for the Texas governorship by promising an array of initiatives to improve public education. On taking office, however, he learned that the budget surplus he had thought existed was instead a deficit of several billion dollars. Nonetheless, he proposed a 24-percent increase in teacher's salaries and began a media campaign to sell the public and the legislature on his package and the taxes needed to fund it. The sales effort fell short, and the legislature refused to pass a salary increase.

The Texas governorship is not a strong office. The state's budget is developed by the Legislative Budget Board, not the governor, and it is hamstrung by a statutory constitution dedicating selected taxes to particular expenditures. State administration contains many elected agency heads and over two hundred boards, with members serving fixed terms, who control a sizable portion of the state's administrative structure. The Texas governorship is not impotent, but the governor has to rely heavily on building coalitions to get things done.

After his first defeat, coalition-building was the approach Governor White took to obtaining education reform. He worked with two other key state leaders, Lieutenant Governor Bill Hobby (leader of the state senate), and Speaker of the House Gib Lewis. The trio created a select committee to study public education, and White appointed business leader H. Ross Perot to chair the committee. At first glance, the result did not look promising. Among other things, the committee recommended that the state spend $1 billion to improve the educational system, an amount sure to give legislators and the public some pause; that teachers undergo competency testing, a requirement that the teachers' associations opposed; and that students be required to obtain grades of "C" or better in their courses in order to participate in extracurricular activities — a near-sacrilege in a state where high-school football was the leading entertainment for many communities.

Despite these obstacles, the package of recommendations was adopted. Perot, never lacking in flamboyance, was able to keep media attention focused on the benefits of the package, and he also managed to corral the support of the business community for the proposal. Governor White kept public attention on education reform by calling a special session of the legislature to deal with the education proposal, and Lieutenant Governor Hobby and Speaker Lewis pushed their colleagues toward adoption. The glare of publicity during the special session restrained legislators from bowing to the opposition from interest groups. Governor White thus was able to accomplish what became the centerpiece of his administration by marshaling and energizing the efforts of others in areas where his own formal authority was lacking.[27]

Arkansas: formal and informal power interact. In Arkansas, the topic was also education, and the governor, Bill Clinton, also had made educational improvement a theme of his campaign. Arkansas had a similarly weak governorship, but it also had a history of gubernatorial leadership in setting the state's agenda despite the office's structural deficiencies.[28] Instead of proposing major reforms immediately, however, Governor Clinton appointed a study committee chaired by his wife, Hillary Rodham Clinton. This gave the governor time to work with many legislators and interest groups to identify concerns and develop compromises for inclusion in the legislative proposal. Before any of this work was completed, the Arkansas Supreme Court declared the state's system of financing public education unconstitutional, warning that a solution had to be found or the courts would step in and take over.

Though Clinton began by working with key state leaders, a major object of his later efforts was public support instead of, or at least along with, elite support. The governor and his staff developed a campaign for his legislative proposal that included speeches across the state, television, radio, and newspaper advertisements, and direct mailings to citizens. As in the Texas case, Governor Clinton called a special session to deal with education reform, keeping the spotlight on legislators. The Arkansas governor, however, had a much weightier veto power than that of his Texas counterpart.[29] When the legislative session did not go well, Clinton threatened to veto any legislation that did not include teacher testing, and he finally obtained a package that contained most of his original proposals.[30]

The examples of White and Clinton show that successful governors always build on the full use of their powers, both formal and informal. Though neither state had a strong governorship, each governor was able to employ the informal tools of office — building coalitions and using the media to garner public attention — to achieve legislative success. Even so, Clinton would not have been as successful without his ability to threaten a veto at a crucial juncture of legislative deliberations.

Connecticut: strong formal power. A far blunter use of a governor's formal powers was undertaken by Lowell Weicker. Faced with a substantial deficit after assuming the governorship of Connecticut, Weicker proposed laying off a number of state workers, limiting Medicaid allowances for nursing homes, and instituting a state income tax.

Weicker was able to accomplish much through his budgetary powers, including proposing an austere budget to the state legislature and defending it with the governor's potent item veto. The starkest use of his formal power, however, came when Weicker refused to accept from the state legislature any budget that did not include a state income tax. Adoption of an income tax is always a politically controversial step, one that political leaders are not fond of taking. Twice the legislature sent a budget to the governor without including an income tax, and twice Weicker vetoed the budget and sent it back to the legislature. The third time around, the legislature added the income tax and the governor signed the measure. Substantial bargaining with the legislature also was involved, but it was the firm use of the veto that accomplished Governor Weicker's objective.

In all three cases, governors were under the gun to solve their state's problems. Those problems might have been put on the state agenda in the first place by a gubernatorial campaign promise, as was the case in Texas, or by a court decision, a prime motivation in Arkansas, or by financial conditions, as in Connecticut. But however they got on the state's agenda, the public expected the governor to be a key player in solving the state's problems, and each of these governors rose to that challenge.

Gubernatorial Policy Arenas

Modern governors are expected to fulfill the roles of agenda setter, policy developer, and policy achiever much more than were earlier governors. They also fulfill these roles in broader and increasingly complex arenas. The increased role of the federal government provided a strong impetus for this in the 1960s. President Johnson's Great Society programs brought the federal government into areas traditionally reserved to the states but, in so doing, did not completely ignore the states. Some federal programs established mandates that the states had to follow, while others enticed them to follow federal policy guidelines via the use of grants. Both practices led to the growth of state agencies and the recruitment of more highly trained employees. In addition, the increasing entanglement of federal and state employees, policies, and funds, in carrying out policy has led governors over the past quarter century to play a far larger intergovernmental role than they had previously.

Manager of Federal Grants

One new development in the gubernatorial role was the operation of programs funded primarily through federal grants, for which governors had to compete against other states, and sometimes their own local governments. In this intergovernmental role, governors encountered a situation that presidents had been familiar with for decades: it is often easier to achieve things with other governments than with your own legislature. Governors began going to Washington to seek federal grants that might enable them to promote programs in areas their own state legislatures were unwilling to fund.[31]

Governors also began searching for ways to relieve themselves of unwanted federal mandates and the restrictions that accompanied grants. Recall that the federal government stepped in at the beginning because many states lacked the institutional ability, or will, to meet the needs of rapidly expanding urban and suburban areas. Some federal officials, not fully trusting the states, attached considerable restrictions on how federal grant funds could be spent. Some grants even went directly to local governments, bypassing the states entirely; this led governors to feel left out with regard to policies affecting their states. Such federal practices were understandable, for this also was the time of the civil rights revolution, and some states were less than sympathetic to the demands of their black citizens to provide jobs, integrate schools, and combat housing and employment discrimination.

Over time, the states developed a far greater capacity to deal with the myriad of modern problems. State executive and legislative branches became more professionalized. State revenue sources expanded from a primary reliance on property taxes and special fees in the 1950s, to include income taxes, sales and receipts taxes, and income from such governmental activities as utilities and insurance trusts. Between 1960 and 1980, state and local government employment increased over 120 percent, compared to a considerably smaller 22-percent increase at the federal level, and many of the new state and local employees were considerably more professional and better trained than earlier employees had been.[32]

The federal government became more sympathetic to state complaints. In the early 1970s President Nixon presented his New Federalism program, designed to return some control of federally-funded programs to the states. A keystone of the program was revenue sharing: federal revenues provided to state and local governments for purposes of their choosing, within broad guidelines. Revenue sharing was later sacrificed by President Jimmy Carter in his attempts to curtail federal spending, but returning some control to the states has continued. A more enduring tool has been to use federal block, instead of categorical, grants. Categorical grants are very specific in their intended use and include substantial restrictions and documentation to ensure that federal funds are spent as Congress intended. Block grants are more general. In the field of education, for example, there may be different categorical grants for establishing reading programs, removing asbestos from school buildings, providing access for disabled students, or improving science training, each with its own grant program that allows funds to be spent only for that specific purpose. Block grants, on the other hand, may contain general rules that specify the funds go for education, but leave the specific expenditure items for the states to decide. Early in President Ronald Reagan's term of office he proposed folding a number of categorical grants into far fewer block grants, and Congress, while not agreeing completely, did condense seventy-seven categorical grants into nine new block grants.

Federal Policy Involvement

Governors are also quite active in contributing to the making of federal policy. The Reagan administration proposed a substantial restructuring of federalism, with some joint federal-state activities — food stamps, child nutrition, handicapped education, and Aid to Families with Dependent Children — turned over entirely to the states while the federal government would assume total financial and administrative responsibility for the Medicare program.[33] As details of these proposals became clear, many governors began lobbying Congress against them, fearing that states would be burdened with program responsibility while receiving insufficient federal resources to pay for the programs. Governors feared the proposals would result in the federal government's cutting its budget at the expense of the states, which would have to raise their taxes.

Although this aspect of President Reagan's New Federalism did not pass, the idea of some federal-state program restructuring continues to be considered regularly and keeps the governors consistently involved in federal policy. The health-care program presented early in the Clinton presidency envisioned a significant role for the states. Though not all governors were enthusiastic about it, President Clinton had worked closely with governors in developing his health-care plan and had made sure to include a substantial role for the states and their governors.[34]

A strong role for governors in the Clinton administration should not be surprising, since President Clinton was both a former governor and a former leader of the NGA. During his term as one of NGA's leaders — NGA leadership is shared between a Democratic and a Republican governor — he and his Republican counterpart, Michael Castle of Delaware, worked closely with Congress during a 1988 welfare-reform effort. At that time, Clinton's involvement in the federal policymaking process was so intense that he was even considered "an honorary member" of the House-Senate conference committee on the welfare bill.[35]

This close cooperation between federal leaders and the governors has, if anything, expanded recently. When the Republicans captured control of the U.S. House and Senate in the 1994 elections, they also ended up with thirty Republican governors, their first majority of governorships since the late 1970s. During the early days of deliberations over the Republican "Contract with America," many Republican governors cautioned their congressional colleagues about going too far too fast, fearing, again, the possible imposition of billions of dollars of program responsibilities on the states as congressional leaders pushed toward balancing the federal budget.[36] Later, congressional Republican leaders began reaching out to their gubernatorial counterparts to include them in their strategy sessions and incorporated many of the governors' ideas in proposed legislation. The close working relationship between the governors and Congress was described as the opposite of previous years, "when governors came to Washington as supplicants, not role models. Today, they almost swagger with their newfound celebrity, forming what has been called a 'new branch' of government and appearing regularly on TV talk shows that once ignored them."[37] The governors' newfound fame in Washington may be transitory, but their close involvement in federal policy is likely to continue.

New Issues

The governors' federal role, either affecting policy in Washington or managing federal grants in their home states, also has moved them into new policy areas. The perennial state issues — those likely to show up consistently on the agendas of governors — have been crime, education, highways, and, to a lesser extent, health and welfare. Now governors are expanding their attention to these latter areas, adding, as well, such issue concerns as environmental needs and economic development.

Health and welfare. The states have historically been concerned only with meeting minimal needs: providing emergency medical treatment and some basic medical services to the indigent; orphanages and foster homes for children; limited support for those at the lowest end of the economic ladder; and regulation of hospitals, nursing homes, and other medical-care providers. Federal grant programs of the 1960s and 1970s raised the salience of health and welfare issues, involving the states as partners in such areas as Medicare, maternal and child health, family planning, increased regulation of hospitals, and job training.

When federal regulations loosened, the governors gained maneuvering room to seek out more creative solutions to state needs. Some initiated cost-containment measures in the health field, with governors like Richard Celeste of Ohio, Bruce Babbitt of Arizona, and Martha Layne Collins of Kentucky reorganizing their state health-care structures to provide more coherent planning and implementation. Others moved beyond cleaning up state administrative structures to seeking alternative solutions to state health-care needs. Governors John Evans of Idaho and William Janklow of South Dakota pressed for transferring the traditional institutionalized care for the mentally ill to community-based programs. Governor Lee Dreyfus of Wisconsin sought similar deinstitutionalization from nursing homes to community programs for the elderly, and Governor Michael Dukakis of Massachusetts proposed a universal medical-insurance program for his state's citizens.[38] As an example of the increased role health-care issues play in gubernatorial policy concerns, in 1984 a coalition of southern governors established the Southern Regional Task Force on Infant Mortality to draw attention to the problem of infant mortality and to seek state strategies to deal with it. Contemporary governors "exert a tremendous impact on the

American health care system, at the national level as well as within their own states."[39]

Environment. Environmental issues have historically been of interest to only a few states and governors, though these few have sometimes been policy leaders. California's clean-air regulations, for example, have always been more stringent then federal rules on auto emissions, and the enormous size of the California market has forced automobile manufacturers to change their products accordingly. Governor Tom McCall of Oregon developed a strong environmental program based on what he termed the "Oregon Story," the ability of that state both to protect its environment and to generate economic health.[40]

Most states, however, were nudged into greater environmental involvement by such federal actions as the 1972 Coastal Zone Management Act, requiring states to develop preservation plans for their coastal resources; the Resource Conservation and Recovery Act of 1976, requiring states to track hazardous wastes and develop safe procedures for their treatment, storage, and disposal; and the Superfund program of 1980, whereby the state and federal governments collaborate in the cleanup of hazardous waste sites. Some states have been particularly zealous in environmental protection and cleanup, particularly those with severe environmental problems, while others have resisted environmental efforts, seeing them as threats to economic development.

The nature of the state — its economic and political environment — has affected gubernatorial response to environmental issues, particularly hazardous-waste disposal. In Texas, weak political institutions — a weak governorship and a still largely amateur legislature — allow special interests great influence over state policy. Though we saw earlier that Governor White could marshal informal resources to promote an education program, a lack of formal power still limits Texas governors. To date, Texas environmental policy remains relatively weak and palatable to state economic interests, for the probusiness culture of the state has made environmental concerns a primarily vote-losing strategy that governors have opted to avoid. In contrast, California's stronger governorship, professional legislature, and environmentally-conscious political culture often lead its governors to place environmental issues high on the agenda.[41]

Hazardous-waste issues can force governors into the thick of intergovernmental politics. Governors both encounter and utilize the NIMBY syndrome: Not In My Backyard. Locating waste-disposal sites within a state is a no-win proposition, and governors and legislatures alike are apt to keep the issue at arm's length by delegating the decision making to a state agency or commission. In some cases, however, governors must play the role of state defender when it comes to apparent or real encroachments on their jurisdiction either by other states or by the federal government. This defense may involve political posturing for vote-getting purposes —

as when the occasional governor of the 1950s or 1960s would "stand in the schoolhouse door" to prevent the integration of schools — but it can also grow out of real concern about preventing one's own state from becoming a dumping ground for the hazardous or nuclear wastes of others. In the mid-1980s, governors Richard Riley of South Carolina, Dixie Lee Ray of Washington, and Robert List of Nevada pressured the federal government and their fellow governors to revise national nuclear-waste policy. These states took unilateral actions to prevent overuse of facilities within their boundaries — South Carolina by increasing the disposal fee charged, Nevada by shutting down the disposal site for packaging and shipping violations, and Washington by a near-total ban on out-of-state wastes.[42]

Later in the 1980s, three states created a crisis in federal nuclear-waste management. The source of the crisis was the Western Isolation Pilot Project (WIPP) in New Mexico, a new facility for the long-term storage of nuclear waste supported by New Mexico Governor Garry Carruthers but opposed by many New Mexico legislators who feared that the facility was not yet (nor ever would be) safe. In 1988, Governor Cecil Andrus of Idaho wrote to the Department of Energy (DOE) closing Idaho borders to new shipments of nuclear waste. Idaho's facility was supposed to provide temporary storage only, though this "temporary storage" had been going on for two decades, and Andrus wanted to spur the opening of the WIPP plant in New Mexico as an alternative site. Much of the waste reaching Idaho came from Colorado's Rocky Flats nuclear-generating facility, and the closing of Idaho's borders led the DOE to consider temporarily retaining the waste in Colorado. Enter Colorado Governor Roy Romer, who wrote to DOE that Rocky Flats was not an appropriate location for long-term storage of nuclear wastes. In what appears to have been a coordinated effort, governors Andrus and Romer whipsawed the federal government to illustrate the weakness of federal policy on nuclear-waste disposal. Later involving the NGA, senators from the affected states, and New Mexico's Governor Carruthers, they obtained agreement on a restructuring of federal policy to make it more sensitive to the needs of the states on waste-disposal issues.[43]

Economic development. Another role governors have recently assumed is responsibility for the state's economy. Major economic policies — growth rates, interest rates, full-employment targets, and others — are produced by actions of the private sector and decisions of the national government. There is little the states or governors can do about them. Nonetheless, some 90 percent of governors believe that they are responsible for their state's economic health[44] and that they will be held accountable by the voters for the condition of the state's economy. Governors have responded by involving themselves in state economic development, seeking to generate new businesses and new jobs. Most states have added agencies or offices of economic development in attempts to secure economic growth. Many of these efforts revolve around seeking to encourage industries to build new plants in the state or even move to the state from their current locations.[45] Governors take a natural role in these efforts since business leaders want the governor, as spokesperson for the state, to be present at any negotiations. Nor is this faith misplaced, for studies show that most governors are highly influential over their state's economic development agencies.[46]

Given that policies affecting the overall economic climate are largely outside the governor's and the state's control, state economic development focuses on appropriating existing economic resources, mostly from other states. Economic development policies revolve around tax breaks or benefits that might lure a business to relocate from state A to state B, which obviously encourages state B to offer counterincentives for a business to stay where it is. The result has been zealous competition among the states for economic resources, competition that has grown so fierce at times that *Business Week* ran a special report in the mid-1970s on the "new war between the states."[47]

Recently, governors have moved their competition outside U.S. boundaries, searching the international marketplace for foreign investment — a less conflict-laden activity, since in that arena one state's gain does not automatically lead to another state's loss.[48] Major trading states, particularly those on the East and West coasts, have long sought investment by foreign firms, but this has spread to the interior states as well. The recent North American Free Trade Agreement, for example, opened up significant opportunities for states bordering Canada and Mexico to seek cooperative economic arrangements. This has created the interesting phenomenon of some states developing what amounts to their own foreign policies. In so doing, governors have discovered what presidents have long known, that economic and domestic policies are linked. Governor Pete Wilson of California, for example, energized his reelection campaign by pushing for the denial of state benefits to illegal aliens, most of whom were from Latin American countries. Though this helped him win reelection, it did little for California's relationship with bordering Mexico, who saw Wilson's campaign statements as denigrating its citizens. That made it difficult for Governor Wilson to lead trade missions to Mexico in search of economic opportunities. Meanwhile, Governor George W. Bush of Texas avoided the illegal alien controversy in his own election campaign and later attended the inauguration of Mexico's new president, free of any political baggage and eager to develop friendships with Mexico's political leaders that might prove useful in building closer economic ties.

The Governorship into the Future

Given that governors have labored over recent decades, often with considerable success, to make their offices effective agents for meeting public needs, it would be understandable to feel complacent about the office. Understandable, but a mistake. Gubernatorial failures, as well as successes, do occur, and many of the successes are achieved in spite of, not because of, the structure of the office.

The Office

Governors have gained a great deal of formal authority in recent decades. States have increased gubernatorial terms to a near-universal four years; in at least forty-seven of the fifty states, the governor is clearly the key budgetary official;[49] the public is looking more to state executives to provide strong leadership; and the increased quality of the governors and their ability to utilize the mass media feeds into that leadership role. Recall, however, that the governorship started from a very low point. Despite enhancements to the office, many governors continue to have less authority over their executive branches than the president does over his. In contrast, the problems being dealt with in the state capitals are increasing in number and complexity, fast approaching the caliber of problems faced by the president. Furthermore, our review of the heritage of the governorship has shown that enhancement of the office is not constant. There have been peaks and valleys over our two-hundred-year history, with each peak rising higher than the last, but none guaranteeing that a drop into a valley would not occur again in the future. Indeed, though some scholars proclaim the success of modern governorships, it is helpful to recall that Lipson declared that governors had moved "from Figurehead to Leader" in 1939,[50] while Sabato declared over thirty years later that governors had remained good-time Charlies until the 1970s.[51] The picture is not clear, and some scholars suggest that the phenomenon of gubernatorial prominence may be illusory.[52]

Many governors continue to face severe restrictions on their authority especially through the long ballot and statutory constitutions. In the 1990s, there remain over 500 statewide elected officials, excluding the governor and legislature. In this number are 43 attorneys general, 42 lieutenant governors, 38 state treasurers, 36 secretaries of state, 25 state auditors, 16 state comptrollers, 12 commissioners of agriculture, 5 land commissioners, 4 labor commissioners, 1 commissioner of mines, 11 public utility boards or commissions, 11 state boards of education, 15 state superintendents of education, and others.[53]

When governors cannot control their own executive branches, problems are bound to develop. Lesser state offices frequently serve as platforms for aspiring governors, and it remains the rule more than the exception for governors to face their own attorneys general, state treasurers, or other "subordinates" as candidates opposing them for reelection. Even outside of election times, a governor sometimes must preside over, and even be in-

volved in, civil wars paralyzing the executive branch. Governor J[
of Kansas tried to work with her state's Indian tribes to promote the ̮
nomic development. To this end, Finney issued a decree foregoing state
taxes on tribal sales, only to have her own attorney general file suit against
her to block the action. This instigated other suits and legislative battles,
which deadlocked much of Governor Finney's program for the remainder
of her term.[54] Turning the tables, Governor Bush of Texas initiated legal
proceedings in 1998 against his attorney general when, after obtaining a
multi-billion-dollar legal settlement from tobacco companies, the attorney
general proceeded to allocate some of the settlement money without prior
agreement from the governor or legislature.

While any elected administrative official can interfere with a governor's ability to direct the executive branch, lieutenant governors are
probably the most problematic of the group. Unlike the U.S. president and
vice-president, many governors and lieutenant governors run for office separately, not as a team. The lieutenant governor also is typically a legislative
official, head of the state senate, not a member of the executive branch. The
result is that a lieutenant governor of a different party or ideology than
the governor may even use his or her legislative position to work against
the governor's program. Usually governors and lieutenant governors are
responsible enough to develop an acceptable working arrangement, but occasionally an ambitious lieutenant governor may take steps to embarrass
the governor for personal or partisan reasons.

In many instances, whenever the governor leaves the boundaries of
the state, the lieutenant governor becomes the acting governor, and this
provides ample opportunity for mischief. One example was Lieutenant
Governor Evelyn Murphy of Massachusetts, who, while Governor Dukakis
was in Germany on a trade mission, used her role as acting governor to an-
nounce her own plan to resolve the state's ailing finances, a plan different
from the governor's proposal. California has faced two similar situations
in recent years. Democratic Governor Edmund Brown Jr. twice left the
state on trips only to have his Republican lieutenant governor take over
gubernatorial authority each time and proceed to make key government
appointments that Brown had to rush back to the state to cancel. The same
problem later plagued Governor Pete Wilson, who found his campaign
for the Republican presidential nomination in 1992 effectively crippled
when Democratic Lieutenant Governor Guy Davis took over the governor's
powers whenever Wilson ventured outside the state on a campaign trip.

The NGA — an effective instrument used by governors in the past
to demand federal responsiveness to their concerns — has recently been
under attack. In the 1994 elections, Republicans were swept into numerous
governorships and state legislatures that had previously been dominated
by Democrats. Some of the new Republican governors tried to move the
NGA to a more conservative position, leading some Democratic governors

to complain that the bipartisanship of the organization was being under-mined; a few Democrats even threatened to leave. Three years later, it was Republican governors who were threatening to leave, claiming the NGA policy-development staff was still leaning too much toward policies favor-ing Democrats.[55] These battles within an organization that historically tried to find common ground among the governors has led to some weakening of its influence on national policy and a lessening of its effectiveness in assisting governors.[56]

The rising importance of the gubernatorial office places growing de-mands on its occupants as well. As state responsibilities expand, governors need larger and more skilled staffs to deal effectively with the increasingly complex problems landing on their desks. The state media that provide governors an effective platform to influence public opinion can also turn a searchlight back on the governor and his administration. Human beings make mistakes, and, as presidents have found to their dismay, the media's quest for stories can turn even minor errors into highly visible failures that are quickly communicated to voters. Change is the constant, and governors must adapt to change or be swallowed up by it.

The State

Along with the powers of their specific offices, governors have been and will continue to be affected by the political systems within which they operate. The era of weak state governments seems to be at an end, at least for the present. Not only have most states modernized their political structures — legislatures have become more professional and state administrative person-nel better trained — but all have become involved in a variety of new issues and programs. Republicans and Democrats alike serving in the national government agree that state capacity has improved over the past quarter-century, and that the states should be given greater responsibility for and latitude in implementing joint state-federal programs.

Nonetheless, factors that have recently pushed the states and their gov-ernors toward a greater sharing of policy responsibility with the federal government could retreat again. The devolution of policy responsibilities from the federal government to the states also cannot be counted on as necessarily permanent. Differences over which level of government can best deal with a particular problem area seldom derive from a pure debate over the principles of federalism. Inevitably, the question of which level of gov-ernment is more likely to adopt a particular preferred policy is a motivating factor. During the 1950s and 1960s a number of states' rights advocates wanted the states to deal with issues of integration, health, education, and welfare because the states were dominated by individuals with policy opin-ions similar to theirs — for example, that poverty represented a lack of individual responsibility and government's job was to protect the "good folks" (i.e., the economically successful), not the poor. On the other side of the issue, the poor, blacks, and urban residents often did not support states' rights because they found the leaders in Washington to be much more sympathetic to their wishes than those in their state capitals or city halls. Nor was this unusual. In the 1980s President Reagan, a strong advocate of returning authority to the states, often was willing to sacrifice state authority and retain federal prerogatives if it appeared that state actions might interfere with the business community, a favored Reagan constituency.[57]

Thus, the role of the states in the intergovernmental policy mix will depend, at least in part, on the president's and Congress's perceptions of what the states will do with this authority. In the late 1990s, moving more programs to the state level appeared likely, with a former governor as president and a Republican-controlled Congress looking out at a sea of Republican-controlled governorships. But two state government scholars, Ann O'M. Bowman and Richard C. Kearney, warned that any resurgence of state retrenchment (taxpayer revolts cutting state fiscal capacity), interstate conflict over economic or natural resource policies, or political corruption, which historically has been a more common problem at the state and local levels than at the national level, could sidetrack the growth of state responsibilities.[58]

Recent events suggest Bowman and Kearney's fears may be well-founded. Ability is always determined by comparing the resources available to the challenges faced. The states and their governors have accepted new challenges, but the resources widely used to address these challenges may not always be there. The current battleground is taxes. During the recession times of the 1980s and early 1990s, a number of states raised taxes to keep state services from being cut drastically. The healthy economy of the later 1990s has produced surpluses in many states, along with calls to reduce taxes. Some are campaigning to go further, eliminating selected types of taxes, particularly the income tax, or placing severe restrictions on future tax increases. Governors Fife Symington of Arizona and John Rowland of Connecticut, for example, made proposals in early 1995 to eliminate the income tax in their states, and movements either to ban certain taxes or to require super-majorities for tax increases have also appeared in other states.

There is a considerable difference between mere tax cuts and the latter proposals — differences that hearken back to our earlier discussion of the cumbersome restrictions imposed by statutory constitutions. Everyone knows the healthy state enjoyed by the American economy in the late 1990s will not continue forever. Economies go through surges and declines, and some economic weakening is bound to recur. When it does, states that have merely cut their taxes can raise them again to keep vital state programs going, but a state that has eliminated its income tax will find it much tougher to reinstitute a tax that has been eliminated. Indeed, this is the goal of some tax-elimination movements. Knowing that weaker economic times will recur at some future point, they hope to make it so difficult for their state governments to raise taxes that they will be forced instead to cut programs.

Obstacles to tax increases serve a similar purpose. Some seek super-majorities for tax increases, constitutional requirements that tax increases have to be approved by something greater than a simple majority — say a two-thirds legislative vote of approval — before they can go into effect. The term *super-majority* can be misleading, for it sounds highly democratic; no new taxes without widespread popular support. True in a sense, but it also means minority rule. Even if 65 percent or more of the public favors a tax increase to protect programs they see as important, a small minority need only garner one-third of the votes in *either* legislative house (not both) to block the majority from doing what it wants. This could easily be similar to the pre-reapportionment era when a rural-dominated state legislature could prevent the state from meeting majority demands, forcing citizens to turn instead to the federal government.

This is not to argue for never cutting taxes. Cuts are often desirable, and limiting the scope of government has been a core American value since the Revolution. But some of the more far-reaching proposals may have unintended consequences. Were similar tax restrictions to be imposed on all levels of government — federal, state, and local — the relative positions of the states would be unchanged. However, as is more likely, should tax restriction measures apply only to the states, their role within the system would decline compared to other governmental levels.

The People

The most important factor in the governorship's future is the complex and ever-changing relationship between the individuals sitting in governors' chairs and the citizens who put them there. The governorship is a near-unique office in that it allows outsiders access to visible and important roles in the governmental process. Newcomers are common in lower elective offices, those at the city or county level, and in state or federal legislative seats representing only portions of a state. We also see that occasionally newcomers obtain other statewide offices, such as state treasurer, attorney general, or one of the state's U.S. Senate seats, but these positions are all limited in authority, roles, and public attention, while the governorship is the chief state office.

Women and minorities increasingly have been able to capture the governor's chair and establish their credentials as successful political leaders. Earlier, the only successful women candidates were those succeeding their husbands, with Nellie Taylor Ross of Wyoming and Miriam "Ma" Ferguson of Texas both following their husbands into office in 1924. More recently, women have succeeded in obtaining governorships on their own, with the earliest such women being Ella Grasso of Connecticut and Dixie

Lee Ray of Washington, both taking office in the 1970s. The gender expansion of the governorship continued through the 1980s, with such governors as Kentucky's Martha Layne Collins and Vermont's Madeleine Kunin, and the early 1990s produced four women governors: Joan Finney of Kansas, Barbara Roberts of Oregon, Ann Richards of Texas, and Christine Todd Whitman of New Jersey. The governorship seems to be a particularly favorable office for women, for, between 1970 and 1988, 40 percent of female candidates for governorships were elected, while only 11 percent of female candidates for U.S. Senate seats were successful in their campaigns.[59]

Minorities have improved their political standing through the governorship as well. The 1970s and early 1980s saw the election of three Hispanic governors: Jerry Apodaca of New Mexico, Raul Castro of Arizona, and Toney Anaya of New Mexico. In 1982, Los Angeles Mayor Thomas Bradley ran for governor of California and lost by less than 1 percent of the vote, the first black candidate to be so nearly successful. Bradley paved the way for other black candidates, and L. Douglas Wilder of Virginia eventually became the country's first elected black governor.[60] In the 1994 gubernatorial elections, Idaho candidate Larry EchoHawk was expected by many to be the nation's first Native American governor, but the Republican surge during that year swept his opponent into office instead.

The term *outsiders* refers not only to women and minorities, but also to political novices who decide to make a first run for elective office at the top position instead of an entry-level position. Seeking to jump into politics at the top has long been a tradition for the governorship. Many national leaders entered politics this way, including Woodrow Wilson, taking over the governorship of New Jersey from his prior position as a university president, and Ronald Reagan, who had served previously only as president of the Screen Actors Guild before becoming governor of California. Both used their experience as governors later to win the presidency. President Bill Clinton followed a similar path. He did serve time in the Arkansas legislature before running for governor, but he also became a very youthful governor, first winning the office at the age of thirty-two, and garnering significant experience as governor before becoming one of the country's younger presidents.

While most governors have obtained experience in other offices before assuming the governorship, the openness of the office to political novices continues. In the early 1990s, four "outsider" governors were elected: Bruce Sundlun of Rhode Island, Fife Symington of Arizona, David Walters of Oklahoma, and Kirk Fordice of Mississippi. Outsiders provide a breath of change into American politics, bringing new policy proposals and new ways of doing things into traditional governing structures. The 1998 elections produced a much-talked-about outsider, Jesse "the Body" Ventura, elected governor of Minnesota in a three-way split of the vote with candidates from the two traditional parties. It is too early to tell how this outsider will perform. Governor Ventura — a former professional wrestler, high-school assistant football coach, and mayor or a Minneapolis suburb — may introduce a number of important changes in how his state operates. Alternatively, he may find his background prepares him poorly for governing a complex major state.

Change, of course, is just change, which can be bad as well as good. In Louisiana, David Duke, former neo-Nazi and Ku Klux Klan leader, spent a very brief period in the state legislature before mounting a nearly successful campaign for the governorship in 1991. In Arizona, Evan Mecham ran for governor four times between 1964 and 1982 before being elected in 1986, with 40 percent of the vote in a three-way race. As a perennial outsider, Mecham did not court the advice of experienced political leaders, and he made a number of errors in his appointments: three of his nominees had criminal convictions or allegations of violent crimes facing them, while his nominee to head the Department of Revenue had failed to file tax returns, and his choice to review the state's self-insurance program had earlier had his insurance license revoked and was currently under criminal investigation. With Arizona's strong governorship, Mecham took many actions on his own that prompted state turmoil, including rescinding the Martin Luther King holiday and creating a deadlock with the legislature on budget items. By the end of his first year in office, Governor Mecham faced recall, impeachment, and criminal investigation for campaign finance irregularities, and he was finally removed from office.[61] Arizona had a brief period of respite, but another "outsider" governor, Fife Symington, resigned after being convicted of bank fraud in late 1997, and was later sentenced to two and one-half years in prison. It would be quite understandable for the citizens of any state, after suffering under one or more controversial governors, to withdraw their trust from the office and decide to hamper future officeholders with added restrictions on its authority.

So we return to the perennial tension that seems to affect the American governorship more than most political offices. Citizens want effective government, but at the same time they are leery of the political power this requires. Yes, a strong chief executive means greater problems if the current officeholder abuses his power, but it also means quick and effective action if the officeholder is seeking to address state needs. Weakness in the office prevents the former and the latter alike — little opportunity for abuses of power but also little opportunity to meet citizen demands aggressively. It is the citizens of each state who must determine the sort of governorship they want, deciding if the federal government's checks-and-balances system is sufficient, or if their governorship still needs more checks and fewer balances.

CHAPTER FOUR
The Institutionalized Legislature and the Rise of the Antipolitics Era
Paul Brace and Daniel S. Ward

AS THE 104th Congress debated with President Clinton about the future of policymaking in the United States late in 1995, the states stood ready to reap the benefits or bear the costs of the debate's outcome. Already relieved of unfunded federal mandates in the early days of the first Republican-controlled Congress in more than forty years, state governments were at the brink of the greatest shift of power since the New Deal. Rather than centralization in Washington, however, Republicans sought to pass on increasing fiscal responsibility and administration of welfare, education, health, and other policies to the statehouses, under the assumption that those closest to the problems would be best able to provide innovative and efficient solutions. Although many governors and state legislators welcomed the new responsibilities, others questioned the fiscal and institutional readiness of state governments for these new tasks. This chapter focuses on the latter topic, the institutional properties of state governments, particularly their legislatures. Based on the best available information regarding the performance of state legislatures, how might we expect them to respond should national Republicans succeed in divesting the federal government of policymaking authority?

This question must be addressed in the context of an important irony, namely that the move toward state-based policymaking is occurring simultaneously with efforts in the states to "deinstitutionalize" their legislatures. The past generation has seen a dramatic rise in the professionalism of state legislatures, marked by longer sessions, increases in pay and benefits, enlarged staffing, and modernized facilities. Prior to these changes, according to one close observer of state government, a substantial proportion of state legislatures could have been described as "racist, sexist, secretive, boss-ruled, malapportioned and uninformed."[1] The most visible, but not only, reversal is that associated with the term-limits movement. By the end of 1995, twenty-one states had imposed term limits for state legislators. At the same time, efforts are underway to reduce legislative staff size and to rein in the operating expenditures of some state governments. In other states, efforts to reduce the role of government more generally have found support.

The case of Louisiana is instructive. By constitutional amendment that state reduced the length of the legislative session every two years by having a "fiscal" session in one year, and a regular session every other year. In many capitols, moves like these are afoot that can make the political vocation less attractive.

In the following sections we first explore the related concepts of "institutionalization" and "professionalization" as they have developed in the scholarly and reform literatures. A substantial body of research has focused on questions concerning the interplay of resources, incentives and operating characteristics in representative assemblies. Following this discussion of the causes and ostensible benefits of institutional maturation, we consider several facets of institutional change at the state level over the past four decades. As we shall see, most state legislatures have undergone massive changes in their incentives for service, resources for legislating, and operating characteristics and career patterns. Yet while change has been pervasive, it has not spread uniformly to all legislatures, nor has it occurred evenly over the course of the past forty years. Remarkably, on some levels the process of institutionalization, as reflected in the salaries paid legislators, has been relatively static for the past twenty years. Alternatively, however, the financial resources other than salary devoted to the legislative process have increased uniformly for four decades. As the following discussion makes clear, institutionalization of state legislatures over the past four decades has been a multifaceted phenomenon.

We then turn our attention to contemporary efforts to limit terms of office and otherwise diminish the professionalization of state legislatures. Since the 1980s, reform efforts throughout the country have sought to turn back the tide on careerism in state legislatures, by limiting terms of office and cutting back on salary or other perquisites of office. With the benefit of data from over forty years we may ask, as we approach the late 1990s in the midst of the term-limits revolution, if we are on the eve of a new era of citizen legislators, or simply returning to the amateurism that stimulated the call for professional reforms decades ago. Given the ongoing devolution of federal policies to the states, it is a particularly apt time to ponder the implications of the changing institutional characteristics of state legislatures.

What Is Legislative Institutionalization?

Professionalization in legislatures (or other institutions) normally is studied by political scientists in the context of "institutionalization." That is to say, the former is a subset of the latter; thus, it makes sense to begin with a clear understanding of the broader concept. The most influential study of legislative institutionalization was conducted by Nelson Polsby, whose work focused on the U.S. House of Representatives.

Polsby highlighted three primary characteristics of an institutionalized organization: boundedness, complexity, and universalistic and automatic decision-making criteria. Boundedness concerns the "channeling of career opportunities," such that an institutionalized organization will have stable membership and a clear leadership ladder. Complexity entails the nature of the working environment. Institutionalization brings about differentiation of tasks, specialization, and "the general increase in the provision of various emoluments and auxiliary aids to members."[2] Finally, universalistic and automatic decision making contrasts with particularistic and discretionary behavior. The primary example given by Polsby is the introduction of the seniority system in Congress, whereby committee chairs were chosen not arbitrarily by a Speaker or by a majority vote, but by rule: the longest-serving member on a committee from the majority party would ascend to the position.

Another prominent legislative scholar, H. Douglas Price, reached essentially the same conclusions as Polsby, though using slightly different terminology.[3] Price viewed the relationship between the elements of institutionalization (a term he does not use) identified by Polsby as part of a causal process. The development of congressional service as a career reduces membership turnover (i.e., boundedness), which, in turn, provides an incentive to establish an effective committee system (i.e., complexity), and ultimately produces the seniority system as a means of selecting committee leadership (i.e., automatic, decision making). While Polsby's work has the advantage of incorporating a broader spectrum of events and behaviors under the rubric of institutionalization, Price's more narrow approach supplied the causal mechanism missing from Polsby's seminal article. Price called this general process "professionalization," and he directly encouraged its study at the level of state legislatures.

Based on this groundwork, scholars have examined state legislative professionalization extensively in the past decade. Professionalism has been defined usefully as "the enhancement of the capacity of the legislature to perform its role in the policymaking process with an expertise, seriousness, and effort comparable to that of other actors."[4] Many alternative indices have been developed in order to study the process of professionalization, most of which borrow from the institutionalization framework by including measures of complexity, such as numbers of committees, size of staff, legislator compensation, length of session, and operating expenditures.[5] Another element of institutionalization that frequently factors into studies of professionalization is boundedness, normally measured by membership turnover rates.

Several scholars have examined the consequences of professionalization. Among the most important systematic findings regarding the effects of professionalism are the following: voters in states with more professionalized legislatures report more frequent contact with their representatives, but ironically, rate their performance lower;[6] professionalized legislatures are more autonomous in initiating policy and seeking information;[7] professionalization has decreased the occupational diversity of state legislators, with increasing numbers calling themselves full-time legislators;[8] professionalization has had a positive impact on the percentage of minorities serving in state legislatures, but women have not been advantaged;[9] professionalism (measured simply as compensation) has enhanced Democratic representation in state legislatures.[10] It should be apparent that the literature on legislative professionalization is extensive and the findings vast and complex. Attempting to relate these research efforts to the current political debate may seem to be an overwhelming task, but drawing some common principles from them may ease that task considerably.

In the following section we examine the processes of institutionalization and professionalization by focusing on many of the key factors (highlighted above) that scholars have identified as being most critical for understanding the operation of state legislatures. We link these variables through a logical framework that is premised on the notion of individual incentives for legislative service.

Dimensions of Institutional Change in State Legislatures

Institutionalization denotes a process of change. When considering institutional change in state legislatures, two questions arise. The first question is easy: Was there any? We address this by considering trends in the various dimensions of legislative professionalization (to be described later) since the 1950s and 1960s.[11] The second question is a little less simple but nonetheless important: as they changed, were the states becoming more or less alike over time? This second question is of interest because it allows us to assess the degree to which institutionalization has touched all state legislatures. To address this question we track the comparative diversity of states in their professionalization over time by examining the variance in several measures of institutionalization.

To conclude that a process of institutionalization has occurred in the states in this period, we must observe that change has occurred in at least some of the various facets of institutional development to be described here. This, however, does not tell the whole story because if we are to speak of change with any generality, we must also assess the scope or breadth of this change across the states. If change is evident and variance is growing smaller, we may conclude that institutionalization was reaching most if not all states. This would indicate that institutional maturation took place in most legislatures and that they were becoming homogenous over time. Alternatively, it may be the case that change is evident but variance has increased. This would suggest that institutional change was occurring primarily in lead states but that these changes were leaving other states

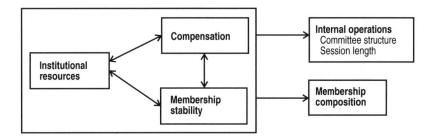

FIGURE 4.1. THE DYNAMICS OF LEGISLATIVE PROFESSIONALIZATION

behind. Such a scenario would indicate growing disparities in institutional development across the states.

Research on the professionalization of legislatures, described earlier, consistently directs our attention to three central elements: compensation, institutional resources, and membership stability. Professionalized legislatures provide greater compensation[12] and other resources.[13.] These legislatures, in turn, have a more stable membership.[14] Following the logic governing individual incentives makes it is easy to imagine how these forces reinforce each other. It is generally accepted that career ambitions drive a large proportion of elite political behavior in the United States.[15] As noted, Price has argued that the development of congressional service as a career fundamentally reshaped congressional politics early in the twentieth century. The term *career* implies the capacity for an individual to earn a livelihood at the task; in the absence of sufficient salary, it is likely that political offices will be held by "amateurs," those who either have substantial personal wealth or considerable spare time (the New Hampshire state legislature, paying just $200 per session, has long been populated by citizens in retirement). But remuneration alone does not make a political career attractive. If the position being sought is powerless, and its work conditions unappealing, then few will seek long-term service. Applying this logic to state legislatures, we see that legislators who are offered greater salary, with access to more resources to perform their jobs, are more likely to want to maintain their legislative careers than those in the opposite situation. At the same time, those who stay longer will have an incentive to boost their salaries (or other compensation) and to spend more on the internal operations of the institutions, such as staff support and technological developments. In other words, the relationships are reciprocal or reinforcing. Figure 4.1 portrays the dynamics of legislative professionalization.

In addition to displaying the relationships between compensation, internal resources, and membership stability, the figure also depicts two expected "impacts" of professionalization. The more professional a legislature, that is, the more career-oriented its membership, the more we expect it to exhibit professionalized operating procedures. Two frequently cited examples are provided in figure 4.1: length of legislative session and the structure of the committee system. Studies of legislative change have also explored the impact of professionalization on the composition of the legislative chambers, including gender, racial, and partisan characteristics.

Consider the impact that professionalization might have on these variables. According to David Mayhew, Congress is probably the most highly "professionalized" of legislatures, in the sense that it promotes careerism among its members and gives them salaries, staff, and other resources to sustain a career.[16] To Mayhew, the organization of Congress met the reelection goals of its members remarkably well.[17] It is likely that the desire for a continued career in a legislature influences the manner in which most legislatures organize themselves. The pattern is a reinforcing one, as we would expect legislatures that are organized to facilitate member reelection needs could also stimulate greater career commitment. In sum, resources, structure, and career incentives may all evolve to be mutually reinforcing, promoting the process of institutionalization.

But how might this affect the politics of legislatures? In his classic study of congressional politics, Richard Fenno argued that members of Congress have multiple goals, including reelection, making good public policy, and gaining positions of leadership in the institution.[18] In order to achieve these goals, however, they must continually be reelected; hence, we expect them to structure the body to enhance all of these goals, including reelection. Lengthening legislative sessions and expanding the committee system are two methods for doing so. Longer sessions provide opportunities both to work on legislative interests and to serve constituency needs, which allow members to work on their policymaking goals and enhance reelection chances. The expansion and decentralization of committee systems reflect growing specialization in legislatures. Specialization allows legislators to work on issues of special interest to them and/or their constituencies, while also providing additional leadership positions within the overall body. It would be difficult to imagine legislators with avocational or part-time commitments to political service promoting an elaborate committee system or a full-time legislative session. Institutionalization thus changes legislator incentives and the structure and operating characteristics of legislatures, promoting more extensive activity and decentralized decision making. This is not to argue that these chambers are necessarily more effective, but that they should exhibit distinctive organizational and operational characteristics, which can be expected to affect the politics and policies of these bodies.

The process of institutionalization may not be politically neutral. Morris Fiorina has argued that "legislative service has an asymmetric impact on people from different occupational and income strata."[19] In other words, when service becomes a career, individuals without alternative sources of income are more likely to serve. To turn the issue around, when legislatures pay little to their members, they are likely to attract individuals of independent means who can adjust their schedules to fit the legislative session. Because it is well known that Republicans and Democrats traditionally have drawn their officeholders (and voters) from different social strata (Republicans are generally wealthier and Democrats more working-class), a reasonable hypothesis is that a full-time, career-oriented legislature would attract Democrats who otherwise could not abandon jobs to serve in part-time assemblies. Alternatively, a part-time, amateur assembly could benefit the many Republicans who are self-employed or financially independent. For them, a legislative salary is a less critical consideration. If this partisan pattern is evident, we would expect the process of institutionalization to promote greater proportions of Democrats in institutionalizing legislatures.

To examine the process of institutionalization, and the critical differences in institutional development among states, we first focus on the three central variables portrayed in figure 4.1; we then turn to the internal structure of the state legislatures that result from those dynamics and explore four separate issues relating to these dimensions of institutionalization: (1) change over time, (2) differences between states, (3) change in the variance over time, and (4) comparison of leading and lagging states.

Institutional Resources

Looking first at institutional resources, we examine the annual average operating budget per legislator. We would expect a more professionalized body to spend more on its own operations than would an amateur body. Naturally, we need to control for the size of the legislature because these bodies vary widely in their size (and presumably this affects operating expenses to some degree). Table 4.1 (p. 78) displays these data in constant (1982–84) dollars since 1956, and it makes clear that there indeed has been a revolution in at least one dimension of legislative institutionalization over the past four decades. In 1956 legislatures inside and outside the South appropriated less than $30,000 per legislator in operating expenses on average; by 1990, this figure had grown to almost $147,000. Recalling that this change is evident in constant dollars, we can note that operating expenditures increased by *400 to 500 percent* over the course of this period. Of course, we became a wealthier, more populous nation over this period, but this change in operating expenditures vastly outpaces population and income growth over the course of the entire postwar era. In the postwar era (1945 to 1994) population and income grew by roughly 200 and 230 percent, respectively.[20] To appreciate the magnitude of this change, consider that if the postwar population and income had grown at a rate comparable to legislative operating budgets in just the 1956 to 1990 period, we would have been a nation of over 660 million people with a per capita income of over $32,000 per year by 1990!

TABLE 4.1. AVERAGE LEGISLATIVE OPERATING BUDGET PER LEGISLATOR
(IN 1982–84 DOLLARS)

	LOB/Leg			LOB/Leg	
Year	Mean	Std. Dev.	Year	Mean	Std. Dev.
1956	24980.1	37890.0	1974	96479.7	122116.9
1958	25414.7	39291.5	1976	105689.9	135070.0
1960	29127.1	40784.3	1978	110373.6	143821.6
1962	33175.4	43717.0	1980	108901.2	137578.1
1964	35396.5	48919.2	1982	112916.4	143390.1
1966	42965.1	59812.9	1984	119773.4	155248.0
1968	58536.1	92992.0	1986	130666.0	169008.9
1970	68022.7	92423.0	1988	126498.2	177899.4
1972	81299.9	108005.4	1990	146772.8	187881.9

Source: Data computed by the authors using *State Government Finances in (year)* and
Government Finances in (year) (Washington, D.C.: Government Printing Office, various
years).

The growth depicted in table 4.1 tells only part of the story. This table
also displays the standard deviation in operating budgets by year, and this
is an indicator of the degree of variation among the states in these budgets. This measure indicates that dramatic growth in institutional resources
was not uniformly distributed across the states. The yearly variance in such
resources increased dramatically as well, indicating that there has been a
vastly unequal growth over the course of this era.

There is a notable regional difference in legislative operating budgets. Over the course of the 1956 to 1990 period, southern legislatures
on average appropriated $60,817 per legislator, per year, for internal
operations. Outside the South, the legislatures appropriated $86,178 on av-
erage. Clearly, southern state legislatures lagged substantially behind their
counterparts in other parts of the country.

Table 4.2 depicts the average resources per legislator by state over the
course of the period from 1956 to 1990. At both extremes there are some
notable standouts. At over $660,000 per legislator per year, California
stood far above the pack by a considerable margin. The next highest-
ranking state, New York, allocated more than $360,000 per legislator per
year. Although substantially smaller than California, New York towers over
the lowest-ranking state, New Hampshire, which devoted only an average
of $7,312 per legislator per year to operations. In light of these differences,
it seems that to use a single term, *state legislature,* to describe both institutions is roughly akin to describing Buckingham Palace and a suburban
three-bedroom ranch both as single-family dwellings.

Despite the wide disparity in the operating resources available in these
state legislatures, both California and New Hampshire experienced sub-

TABLE 4.2. AVERAGE LEGISLATIVE OPERATING BUDGET PER LEGISLATOR,
1956–90 (IN 1982–84 DOLLARS)

State	LOB/Leg	Rank	State	LOB/Leg	Rank
Ala.	35828.0	35	Mont.	19232.7	45
Alaska	177680.1	4	N.C.	33266.3	38
Ark.	24548.2	42	N.D.	10491.7	49
Ariz.	73958.6	16	Neb.	68938.0	18
Calif.	660811.0	1	N.H.	7312.3	50
Colo.	52305.5	23	N.J.	136413.7	7
Conn.	42794.6	32	N.M.	27433.4	39
Del.	47346.8	28	Nev.	51740.0	25
Fla.	148479.7	6	N.Y.	364522.1	2
Ga.	45207.0	30	Ohio	91794.1	14
Hawaii	106024.3	11	Okla.	50611.2	26
Iowa	39615.9	33	Ore.	73246.4	17
Idaho	19495.2	44	Pa.	169741.1	5
Ill.	114332.7	8	R.I.	25527.0	40
Ind.	45243.9	29	S.C.	50577.2	27
Kans.	34473.3	36	S.D.	15223.0	46
Ky.	60744.6	21	Tenn.	39344.0	34
La.	86467.0	15	Tex.	110199.3	10
Mass.	112086.4	9	Utah	25020.8	41
Md.	60493.6	22	Va.	60773.2	20
Maine	19617.3	43	Vt.	12111.6	48
Mich.	213801.3	3	Wash.	94629.6	13
Minn.	62775.2	19	Wisc.	102654.3	12
Mo.	52068.6	24	W.Va.	43831.2	31
Miss.	34304.9	37	Wyo.	13497.9	47

Source: Data computed by the authors using *State Government Finances in (year)* and *Government Finances in (year)* (Washington, D.C.: Government Printing Office, various years).

stantial growth in operational expenses, which increased roughly four and five times in each state respectively. Thus, while the legislative chambers at each extreme were separated by huge differences, both shared in the growth of operating budgets.

Overall, then, it is clear that operational expenditures have undergone colossal increases since the 1950s. Despite this growth, however, major differences among the states have persisted, with many states spending only a tiny fraction of what high-spending assemblies allocate. Because of the states' vast differences in population and wealth, we should not be too surprised by persistent disparities in their resources. And, even though differences are still very pronounced, notable growth in these resources has occurred at both ends of the spectrum, from New Hampshire to California, over the course of the period. Going into the 1990s, statehouses throughout the land were spending vastly more (in constant dollars) on their operations than they had in the 1950s, and clearly this is one of the most remarkable dimensions of institutional change occurring in state legislatures.

Legislator Compensation

While the resources described above have no doubt made many aspects of legislative service less arduous, for many representatives the salary for legislative service will make or break their legislative careers. Many political pundits, themselves often well paid, spin dream-like tales of institutions of high-minded individuals serving for the public good. Of course, for people not blessed with a trust who have children to feed and school, legislative compensation can determine whether they can afford to approach public service as a vocation or merely as an avocation.

Legislative compensation is often a controversial affair, and efforts to raise salaries are easily transformed into hot-button issues that arouse alienated or distrustful constituents. At the national level, efforts to raise congressional salaries have stirred virulent protests. Lawmakers at any level of government can ill afford to take the matter of pay increases lightly.

The antipolitician sentiment that characterizes so much of contemporary political discourse might lead us to believe that career-minded professional politicians had succeeded in feathering their nests with ever-increasing salaries. To a certain extent, this is true — state legislative compensation, including expenses, underwent a substantial increase from 1956 to 1990, both inside and outside the South, as is illustrated in table 4.3. At the end of that period, legislators were making approximately double what they had at the beginning. The rate of increase in the standard deviation is smaller than the average, suggesting that there was some movement toward convergence in legislative salaries across the states during this time.

The range of average compensation is displayed in table 4.4 (p. 82), and the two extremes are again anchored by California and New Hampshire. Members of the California assembly, on average, received over $46,000 per year in salary and compensation for their service. Their counterparts in New Hampshire received only slightly more than $250 per year. Once again, the diversity is striking.

To be truly appreciated, the nature of legislative compensation must be considered relative to each state's economy. Obviously, $20,000 per year goes much farther in some states than in others. It is also important to track the relative compensation over time to see if it has grown or shrunk relative to the state's economy. A simple way to combine both concerns is to construct a measure of average relative compensation — a ratio of salary with expenses to state per capita personal income, each measured in constant dollars. This ratio has the additional advantage of being very

TABLE 4.3. LEGISLATIVE SALARY WITH EXPENSES, 1956–1990
(IN 1982–83 DOLLARS)

Year	Mean	Std. Dev.	Year	Mean	Std. Dev.
1956	8721.3	8766.2	1974	17767.5	15108.4
1958	8650.8	8468.0	1976	17478.6	14897.5
1960	9442.1	8155.0	1978	17259.4	13217.0
1962	10838.5	9372.8	1980	15626.7	12034.8
1964	11860.0	10567.1	1982	14703.2	11335.0
1966	12745.2	10911.4	1984	16771.4	13384.0
1968	15114.1	14195.3	1986	17919.1	14379.5
1970	16757.8	14620.5	1988	17518.8	13761.3
1972	19373.0	16942.0	1990	17374.4	13669.6

Source: Data compiled by Michael Berkman from the *Book of the States* (Lexington, Ky.: Council of State Governments, various years).

simple to interpret. If, for example, the measure equals .5, we can conclude that legislative compensation in that year was one-half per capita personal income for that state. Alternatively, if this measure equals 2, we can see that combined salary and expenses were double per capita personal income for that state in that year.

As illustrated in table 4.5 (p. 83), it is notable that on average state legislative compensation was only a fraction of per capita personal income in the 1950s, the era of so-called amateurism in many statehouses. In the 1960s this pattern changed. Compensation began exceeding per capita income in 1960 and reached a peak in 1972. In that year, average compensation equaled better than 1.5 times per capita personal income. Southern states followed roughly the same trajectory as nonsouthern states, but these changes were delayed by several years and were not quite as pronounced as the average levels in the rest of the country. On average, southern states paid their legislators less ($10,810 versus $15,885 for the rest of the country). Their ratios of compensation to income, however, were close to those in the rest of the country (1.127 versus 1.301). Thus, the South tended to pay its legislators less, but that area of the country also had lower incomes, so the relative compensation there was, on average, nearly commensurate with that in other regions.

Given the antipolitician mood and nationwide efforts to deinstitutionalize legislatures, it is surprising to see that the high point of relative legislative compensation occurred over twenty years ago. In the ensuing decades, average relative compensation has suffered a fairly significant decrease in the South and a modest erosion elsewhere. Average relative compensation outside the South in 1990 was about on par with what it had been in 1968, and southern average relative compensation levels in 1990 had declined to about what they were in 1962.

TABLE 4.4. AVERAGE ANNUAL LEGISLATOR COMPENSATION
(SALARY PLUS EXPENSES) (IN 1982–84 DOLLARS)

State	Mean	Rank	State	Mean	Rank
Alaska	25064.8	9	Mont.	3326.0	44
Ala.	6099.3	40	N.C.	11035.2	25
Ark.	7299.0	36	N.D.	3228.1	45
Ariz.	15228.3	18	Neb.	8584.1	32
Calif.	46301.3	1	N.H.	250.6	50
Colo.	16841.4	16	N.J.	22132.9	10
Conn.	8220.7	33	N.M.	2548.3	47
Del.	14199.8	19	Nev.	7534.0	34
Fla.	16423.3	17	N.Y.	45781.2	2
Ga.	9997.7	31	Ohio	27168.4	8
Hawaii	19623.7	13	Okla.	18252.3	15
Iowa	12993.9	21	Ore.	10566.7	28
Idaho	5710.9	41	Pa.	41040.7	3
Ill.	37955.0	5	R.I.	375.9	49
Ind.	12692.9	22	S.C.	14055.7	20
Kans.	7102.4	38	S.D.	5355.7	42
Ky.	4905.7	43	Tenn.	10579.9	27
La.	10233.8	30	Tex.	10942.1	26
Mass.	30842.0	6	Utah	2624.6	46
Md.	21456.3	11	Va.	10504.5	29
Maine	6975.4	39	Vt.	7143.1	37
Mich.	38186.3	4	Wash.	11604.1	24
Minn.	18803.6	14	Wisc.	29148.4	7
Mo.	20226.0	12	W.Va.	7501.8	35
Miss.	11983.2	23	Wyo.	2021.2	48

Source: Data compiled by Michael Berkman from the *Book of the States* (Lexington, Ky.: Council of State Goverments, various years).

In many quarters, public sentiment has come to disfavor "professional politicians" and "legislative fat cats," yet, surprisingly, state legislators in 1990 were earning on average about what they were earning in the 1960s. When it comes to what legislators are earning, it is evident that public attitudes about politicians and their careers are being driven more by perception than by reality.

Quite clearly, legislative "service" means very different things in different states. As reasoned earlier, compensation levels may affect the recruitment of politicians by shaping who will and will not seek a public office, as well as the kinds of energy and resources they will expend to capture that office and to organize the chamber once elected. A low salary can effectively eliminate many from serving and may also promote "amateurish" assemblies with low levels of electoral competition (few want in)

TABLE 4.5. RATIO OF LEGISLATOR COMPENSATION TO STATE
PER CAPITA PERSONAL INCOME (IN 1982–84 DOLLARS)

Year	Mean	Std. Dev.	Year	Mean	Std. Dev.
1956	.9	.8	1974	1.4	1.1
1958	.9	.8	1976	1.4	1.1
1960	1.0	.7	1978	1.3	.9
1962	1.1	.8	1980	1.2	.9
1964	1.2	.9	1982	1.2	.9
1966	1.2	.9	1984	1.3	.9
1968	1.3	1.1	1986	1.4	1.0
1970	1.5	1.1	1988	1.4	1.0
1972	1.6	1.3	1990	1.3	.9

Sources: *U.S. Statistical Abstract* (Washington, D.C.: Government Printing Office, various years); and *Book of the States* (Lexington, Ky.: Council of State Government, various years).

and high turnover rates (few wish to stay). A high salary, however, may promote the kinds of careerism and reliance on campaign contributions for reelection that many find disturbing. There is no golden rule that will solve this issue, but it is important to realize that much of what transpires in legislative elections and reelections is shaped by the kinds of people, energy, and resources that are organized for capturing office, and compensation levels can reasonably be expected to play a vital role in this area.

Membership Stability

The average statehouse of 1990 clearly provided more resources for the legislator than it had in the 1950s, and the average legislator was paid better in absolute and relative terms in 1990 than in the 1950s and early 1960s (though not as well as in the early 1970s). It is reasonable to assume that the incentives for state legislative service improved quite substantially in many, if not most, states. We may now ask if legislators lured by more resources and better pay have been compelled to stay longer. While we cannot make a direct causal connection between the incentives we describe and the rate of turnover, reference to table 4.6 (p. 84) reveals that there has been a dramatic drop in the proportion of new members in lower houses over the 1966 to 1990 period. At the beginning of that period, slightly more than 45 percent of lower-house legislators were freshmen. By the end of the period this had dropped to less than 20 percent.

The range of values across time also helps to illustrate this transformation. In 1966 the legislature with the highest turnover had 71 percent new members, increasing to 75 percent the following year. In other words, in these chambers fewer than 30 percent of the membership had previously served a term of legislative service. By the end of the period, 55 to 60 per-

TABLE 4.6. PERCENTAGE OF NEW MEMBERS IN LOWER HOUSE, 1966–90

Year	Mean	Minimum	Maximum	Year	Mean	Minimum	Maximum
1966	45.60	18.00	71.00	1980	28.85	15.00	54.29
1968	34.17	10.00	75.00	1982	26.45	14.14	54.29
1970	32.44	15.00	57.00	1984	30.82	9.58	55.00
1972	39.60	21.00	68.00	1986	25.18	3.75	50.00
1974	34.96	10.00	73.00	1988	20.78	2.00	40.00
1976	35.22	10.20	73.33	1990	19.00	2.00	45.00
1978	30.37	13.64	73.33				

Source: Data compiled by Michael Berkman from the *Book of the States* (Lexington, Ky.: Council of State Goverments, various years).

cent of the legislators in these high-turnover states had served at least one term. At the other extreme, in some chambers approximately 98 percent of members had served at least one term by 1990. These differences illustrate the stark contrast between legislatures. In some, the chambers were (and to a certain extent still are) a bit like bus terminals, with new faces constantly scurrying through. At the other extreme, a substantial number of legislators stay for at least two terms and often more.

It is abundantly clear that a major stabilization of membership occurred in statehouses during this period. Simple analysis shows that higher operating expenditures and relative compensation are negatively correlated with turnover as measured here (r=−.25 and −.26 respectively), indicating that turnover rates went down as operating expenditures and salary went up, as we would expect. Much is left to explain, and we must be cautious in our interpretations of even these modest relationships, however. It could be either that a stable membership promotes higher salaries and greater resources for legislation, or that these incentives might induce members to stay longer. Also, compensation levels are highly correlated with operating expenditures (r=.59), and this makes it exceedingly difficult to disentangle the relative impact of these two influences. In the end, it is probably safest to conclude that a complex interplay of enhanced resources, compensation, and membership stability worked to reinforce trends toward professionalization.

The decline in legislative turnover was not limited to just a few statehouses, as table 4.6 makes clear. While there was substantial diversity in turnover rates in the 1960s and 1970s, states experienced a decline in turnover going into the 1980s. Membership stability had become a prominent feature of virtually all statehouses throughout the land. Still, however, there was a wide variety of membership turnover evident across the states throughout this period, as table 4.7 illustrates. In Massachusetts, the state with the most stable membership, on average only one in five members were new in any given year. Contrast this with Alabama where, in an av-

TABLE 4.7. PERCENTAGE OF NEW MEMBERS IN LOWER HOUSE, BY STATE

State	Average	Stability Rank	Minimum	Maximum
Alaska	42.11	48	18.00	58.00
Ala.	54.78	50	23.00	73.33
Ark.	20.08	2	7.00	35.00
Ariz.	27.79	19	15.00	45.00
Calif.	22.90	6	3.75	43.00
Colo.	36.57	39	23.00	51.00
Conn.	35.28	38	19.00	57.00
Del.	31.92	30	7.00	54.00
Fla.	32.78	32	10.83	62.00
Ga.	25.75	12	12.22	51.00
Hawaii	27.89	20	16.00	43.00
Iowa	32.69	31	12.00	63.00
Idaho	30.11	26	20.00	40.00
Ill.	23.50	7	8.00	47.00
Ind.	27.69	18	9.00	48.00
Kans.	28.49	22	13.00	57.00
Ky.	30.00	25	13.00	49.00
La.	39.30	45	7.00	68.00
Mass.	20.04	1	9.58	28.00
Md.	42.30	49	29.00	64.00
Maine	38.40	43	22.00	57.00
Mich.	23.90	9	9.00	56.00
Minn.	28.70	23	13.00	41.04
Mo.	23.75	8	15.00	44.00
Miss.	36.94	40	2.00	58.00
Mont.	37.69	41	18.00	58.00
N.C.	34.42	35	20.00	49.00
N.D.	31.03	28	18.00	54.00
Neb.	25.85	13	18.00	48.00
N.H.	38.65	44	33.00	43.75
N.J.	39.94	46	21.25	75.00
N.M.	28.47	21	13.00	50.00
Nev.	35.04	37	17.00	65.00
N.Y.	22.80	4	9.00	47.00
Ohio	22.86	5	7.00	51.00
Okla.	25.96	14	14.85	32.00
Ore.	31.54	29	18.00	47.00
Pa.	20.81	3	8.00	33.00
R.I.	27.62	17	17.00	41.00
S.C.	30.19	27	18.00	44.00
S.D.	34.71	36	26.00	57.00
Tenn.	29.64	24	14.14	58.00
Tex.	27.41	16	17.00	53.00
Utah	38.00	42	24.00	57.00
Va.	24.62	10	11.00	41.00
Vt.	33.82	34	22.00	54.00
Wash.	26.20	15	10.00	45.92
Wisc.	25.27	11	13.00	36.36
W.Va.	41.54	47	31.00	57.00
Wyo.	33.19	33	20.97	40.32

Source: Data compiled by Michael Berkman from the *Book of the States* (Lexington, Ky.: Council of State Goverments, various years).

erage year more than half of the lower house was comprised of freshmen legislators.

Ultimately, the issue of institutionalization and membership stability is complex because the characteristics that make a legislature more institutionalized make it a more desirable job and could serve to stimulate greater electoral competition. On the other hand, the resources available to legislators in more institutionalized chambers give them additional incentives to stay and may provide additional resources for enhancing their electoral prospects. In the following sections we consider some implications of this stability by examining several internal characteristics of legislatures that we would expect to be affected by the trend toward professionalization.

A Democratic Bias?

Has membership stability come to benefit one party more than the other? Morris Fiorina has argued that reforms in state legislatures helped the Democratic Party outside the South. Simple support for this thesis is provided in table 4.8. In nonsouthern states, Democrats on average went from minority status in the 1950s (i.e., comprising less than 50 percent of members) to majority status in all subsequent years except 1968 and 1970. Note that the growth in the proportion of Democrats in state legislatures roughly parallels the pattern of increased compensation described above. Outside the South, then, there is at least preliminary evidence that changes in professionalization may have contributed to improved fortunes for the Democrats. The pattern in the South is dramatically different, however, reflecting the declining fortunes of the Democratic dominance in that region, along with the ascendance of the Republican Party and the spread of two-party competition throughout the region.

Legislative Organization and Operation

By 1990 the average legislature had more resources, more salary, and more stable membership. We may ask now if these changes could have altered the operating characteristics of state legislatures. Arguments concerning professionalization might lead us to expect that a more stable, career-oriented membership would promote more decentralized decision making akin to the pattern that emerged in the U.S. Congress. This decentralization would allow more members to specialize and exercise influence in the legislative process. A key measure of such decentralization would be in the committee structure of a legislature. Alternatively, many of the reforms in the 1960s were directed at making the legislatures more efficient, and members in some legislatures were complaining about excessive committee assignments. These committee assignments would become increasingly problematic as

TABLE 4.8. AVERAGE PERCENTAGE OF DEMOCRATS IN STATE LEGISLATURES

Year	Nonsouth	South	Year	Nonsouth	South
1956	45.7	95.8	1976	62.1	87.7
1958	47.8	95.9	1978	62.1	88.2
1960	59.6	97.3	1980	59.9	86.9
1962	53.3	96.1	1982	53.2	82.3
1964	51.6	94.7	1984	55.9	82.6
1966	58.9	92.2	1986	54.7	76.5
1968	47.6	86.7	1988	56.2	73.5
1970	47.8	86.2	1990	52.7	63.6
1972	53.0	85.4	1992	53.9	68.6
1974	54.9	83.0			

Source: Data compiled by Michael Berkman from the *Book of the States* (Lexington, Ky.: Council of State Goverments, various years).

TABLE 4.9. RATIO OF LEGISLATORS TO NUMBER OF COMMITTEES
IN LOWER CHAMBER

Year	Mean	Year	Mean	Year	Mean
1966	5.09	1974	6.37	1984	6.08
1968	5.74	1976	7.11	1986	6.56
1970	6.75	1978	7.05	1988	6.23
1972	8.29	1980	6.42	1990	6.20
		1982	6.22		

Source: Data compiled by Michael Berkman from the *Book of the States* (Lexington, Ky.: Council of State Goverments, various years).

legislatures became more full-time assemblies, because they could cause scheduling conflicts that were not a problem in more amateurish eras.[21]

Growing numbers of committees would suggest that such decentralization was occurring. The average number of committees in lower houses from 1966 to 1990, controlling for the total number of members, is displayed in table 4.9. Lower values of this measure (i.e., fewer members per committee) would support the decentralization/specialization hypothesis. As can be seen, there has been a fluctuating trend that would tend to support this hypothesis both inside and outside the South. It is somewhat surprising, however, that the greatest average decentralization was evident in 1966 and 1968, with the greatest centralization occurring in 1972 outside the South and in 1976 in the South. Examination of the variance in decentralization (not displayed) indicates that there was no appreciable change in the dispersion of this dimension of institutionalization.

Another important feature of legislative operations is illustrated in

TABLE 4.10. AVERAGE SESSION LENGTH (IN DAYS)

Year	Mean	Year	Mean	Year	Mean
1968	94.4	1976	124.8	1984	155.5
1969	128.9	1977	146.6	1985	155.5
1970	121.5	1978	127.0	1986	162.4
1971	160.7	1979	149.1	1987	144.2
1972	134.1	1980	124.3	1988	146.4
1973	145.9	1981	171.3	1989	160.5
1974	128.6	1982	149.7	1990	144.2
1975	146.6	1983	170.7	1991	158.7

Source: Data compiled by Michael Berkman from the *Book of the States* (Lexington, Ky.: Council of State Goverments, various years).

table 4.10. This graph shows the average number of days in session (note that biennial legislatures are not included in the averages for the years they are not in session). In general, there has been a significant increase in the number of days in the legislative session. Beginning with an average below 100 days in 1968, and ending in 1991 with roughly 160 days in session, roughly twelve work weeks were added to the average session. When examined separately, these fluctuations were not nearly as evident in southern states, and there was no trend in that region toward increasing session length. The South did not succumb to the pressures promoting greater session length that were operating elsewhere in the country during this period. The result is that the states have manifested greater diversity in session length, which is not surprising, because many states abandoned biennial in favor of annual sessions in this period. For example, in the 1968 to 1969 period, twenty-five states met only biennially, but by 1990–91 only seven states did so.

In the end, there was tremendous variation in the number of days state legislatures spend in session. A handful of states (California, Illinois, Massachusetts, Michigan, New Jersey, New York, Ohio, Pennsylvania, and Wisconsin) met virtually year-round, while the rest worked anywhere from about 50 to less than 200 days per year. Considering the averages for the period, it is clear once again that there were (at least) two distinct tiers of state legislatures.

Turning Back the Professionalization Tide?
Antigovernment Politics in the 1990s

Going into the 1990s, state legislatures had evolved over the preceding three decades (at least) toward greater resources, more salary, and more stable (if Democratic) membership, with less-centralized decision making and longer working sessions. Statehouses had become more professional, with enhanced opportunities for politicians to make politics at the state legislative level a full-time vocation, thereby providing attractive venues for career building by ambitious politicians.[22] At the same time, reelection margins for incumbents grew substantially,[23] with membership stability tied both to this professionalization and to growing institutional rewards and incentives.[24]

According to the National Conference of State Legislatures, between 1968 and 1991 the percentage of respondents to surveys in a sample of states who rated the work of their legislators positively dropped from 50 percent to 28 percent.[25] Disenchantment with politics in general, and with political institutions in particular, led many Americans to favor political reforms that would reduce the attractiveness of political careers. This discontent seems to have fueled efforts to limit the terms for legislators in twenty-one states, beginning with Colorado and Oklahoma in 1990. Citizens in many states have begun to vent their frustration with politics by enacting laws that could likely turn back the tide of institutionalization. As of 1998, twenty-one states had enacted some form of term limits. These states are listed in table 4.11 (pp. 90–91).

The most prohibitive of these limits would restrict members of the lower house to three two-year terms (Arkansas, California, Michigan, Oregon), be they consecutive or interrupted. The most liberal restrictions are found in both houses of the Louisiana legislature and in the Wyoming Senate, all of which impose a limit only after twelve years of *consecutive* service, meaning that an individual could serve twelve years, take a one-term break, and then return to the legislature.

Many have offered opinions, both pro and con, about the likely effects of term limits in the long run. Advocates of citizen legislatures see largely positive effects, ranging from simply introducing fresh ideas into previously stagnant institutions, to term-limited legislators' greater willingness to deal with the difficult issues facing state governments. From a positive perspective, term-limit measures are expected to end "politics as usual" by opening up the assemblies to people from less conventional backgrounds.[26] Other reform advocates argue that term limits will help break the electoral connection between representatives and their constituents. With the electoral connection severed, legislator priorities will be altered, and presumably promoting a broader view of the representative's job. In this view, the legislator would be expected to become more Burkean, motivated more by conscience than by constituents, and presumably less in favor of political pork and more interested in the well-being of the state as a whole.[27] Still others believe that term limits will reduce the influence of lobbyists because once the incentive for reelection is removed, so too is the need for campaign contributions. In addition, campaigns for office should become less costly.[28]

Not surprisingly, there also have been many criticisms of term limits. Some critics are worried that the composition of the legislatures will be

TABLE 4.11. STATE TERM LIMITS AS OF 1998

Arizona: Limits state lawmakers to four consecutive two-year terms and members of the executive branch to two consecutive four-year terms. (C - Article IV, Part 2, Section 21)

Arkansas: Restricts statewide elected officials to two four-year terms, state representatives to three two-year terms and state senators to two four-year terms. (C - Amendment 73)

California: Limits state lawmakers to three two-year terms in the Assembly and two four-year terms in the Senate. Constitutional officers are limited to two four-year terms. (C - Article IV, Section 2)

Colorado: Limits state lawmakers to four consecutive two-year terms in the House and two consecutive four-year terms in the Senate. (C - Article V, Section 3)

Florida: Restricts an individual from running for reelection to the legislature, executive branch, or U.S. Congress if by the end of their current term they have served for eight consecutive years. (C - Article VI, Section 4)

Idaho: State legislators and statewide-elected officials are limited to eight years in a 15-year period. (S - ID ST 34-907)

Louisiana: Limits members of the House and Senate to three consecutive four-year terms. (C - Article III, Section 4-E)

Maine: Restricts state legislators and constitutional officers to four consecutive two-year terms in each body. The state auditor is limited to two consecutive four-year terms. Restrictions on state lawmakers become effective with the 1996 elections and apply to individuals currently holding office. Applies to time served by senators and representatives beginning 1 January 1995. (S - ME ST T. 21-A, Section 553)

Massachusetts: Limits governor, lieutenant governor, secretary, treasurer, auditor, or attorney general to two consecutive terms within an 11-year period. Limits state senators and representatives to four consecutive terms in nine years. (S - MGLA Chapter 53, Section 48) Note: A 1997 decision by the Massachusetts Supreme Court invalidated that state's term-limit statute.

Michigan: Limits state representatives to three terms, state senators and members of the executive branch to two terms. (C - Article IV, Section 54)

Source: National Council on State Legislatures.

---

drastically altered for the worse, as incentives for service reduce the eligible pool of recruits to "the old, the rich and the bought."[29] Some wonder if a shortened career view will promote specialization, as legislators strive to realize their personal policy agendas before their terms end.[30] Alternatively, others have voiced concerns that short careers may inhibit legislators' incentives for developing policy expertise because they have less time to reap the rewards of authority that normally come with such specialization.[31]

Some effects of term limits are beginning to be felt already, such as the propensity of California legislators to leave their elective posts before their

Missouri: Restricts state lawmakers to eight years in the same house and 16 years total of legislative service. (C - Article 3, Section 8)

Montana: Restricts state senators, state representatives and state officials to eight years in a 16-year period. (C - Article IV, Section 8)

Nebraska: Had limited state legislators to two consecutive terms in office (C - Article III, Section 8). Nebraska Supreme Court in February 1996 voided the provisions.

Nevada: Limits members of the Assembly to serving 12 years or six terms and members of the Senate to three terms or 12 years. Secretary of state, state treasurer, state comptroller, and attorney general are limited to eight years or two terms. Governor is already limited to two consecutive terms. (C - Article 4, Sections 3 and 4; Article 5, Section 19; Article 15, Section 3)

Ohio: Limits state senators to two consecutive terms and state representatives to four consecutive terms. Limits members of the executive branch to two consecutive terms. Terms are considered consecutive unless there is a break of four years. (C - Article II, Section 2)

Oklahoma: Restricts state lawmakers to 12 years of legislative service. (C - Article 5, Section 17-A)

Oregon: Holds state lawmakers to six years in the House and eight years in the Senate or no more than 12 years of legislative service. Statewide officeholders are limited to eight years. (C - Article II, Section 19)

South Dakota: Limits state lawmakers to four consecutive two-year terms in each house and statewide officers to two consecutive terms. (C - Article III, Section 6)

Utah: Prohibits state officers and members of the House and Senate from placing their names on the ballot if they have served more than 12 consecutive years in office. (S - UCA 20A-10-201)

Washington: Limits state senators to eight out of 14 years, representatives to six out of 12 years, and the governor and lieutenant governor to eight out of 14 years. Terms served before November 1992 will not count toward limits. (S - RC WA Section 44.04.015)

Wyoming: Limits state senators to three terms in any 24-year period, representatives to six terms in any 24-year period, and constitutional officers to two terms in any 16-year period.(S - WSA Section 22-5-103)

---

terms expire, which requires costly special elections.[32] Longer-term consequences should emerge beginning in Michigan in 1999, when no member of the House will have served more than four years.[33] At that point, the loss of seniority — and with it expertise and institutional memory — will take hold, for better or for worse.

Term limits are not the only ongoing effort to bring about state legislative change. California, once the vanguard of professionalization in the 1960s and 1970s, is now leading in its reversal. Proposition 140, passed in 1990, cut legislators' pensions and sharply reduced the size of the legislative staff.[34] Voters in other states (Texas, Massachusetts, and Nevada) have frozen legislative salaries or repealed increases.[35] Some legislatures, such as those of Arkansas, Kentucky, and Rhode Island, have turned to internal reform in response to public outcry over scandals, real and perceived.[36] Rather than the expansion that characterized the state legislatures in the 1970s, today the terms "rethinking, restructuring, and retooling" are on the minds of legislators.[37]

What will be the impact of these changes? Advocates of citizen legislatures see largely positive effects, ranging from the simple introduction of fresh ideas into previously stagnant institutions to a greater willingness of term-limited legislators to deal with the difficult issues facing state governments. Opponents contend that a short-term perspective will prevail. One legislator argues that "if you say to somebody, 'this may seem like a good idea, but in six years this may come to haunt us,' they don't care. They just look at you like you're crazy."[38] Reformers counter by pointing out that careerists respond to the ultimate short-term concern: reelection. Advocates of professionalization argue that large, well-paid staffs and senior legislators with considerable policy expertise are the best check against undue special-interest influence. Their opponents insist that it is precisely the combination of career politicians, professional staff, and lobbyists that have created pernicious "iron triangles" at the state level that rival those in Washington. Unfortunately, for every popular argument in favor of term limits or reduced professionalism, there seems to be an equally persuasive counterargument. Fortunately for the observer trying to make sense of this debate, political scientists have provided a long history of theoretical and empirical studies that consider the causes and consequences of legislative professionalization. Not only can this research help us to evaluate the veracity of arguments on either side of the issue, but it also may assist us in trying to predict the likely outcome of the reform movement in today's political context.

The preliminary evidence concerning the effects of term limits is decidedly mixed. The Council of State Governments conducted a survey of legislators, staff, and government relations professionals on term limits from July to September 1997.[39] The preponderance of those sampled felt that term limits would likely increase the influence of legislative staff and lobbyists and would make legislative leaders less effective. Ninety-one percent of government relations professionals in states without limits and 86 percent in states with limits believed staff would gain influence. Lobbyists were seen as gaining influence by 73 percent of legislators and 88 percent of staff in states without limits, and by 87 percent of legislators and 89 percent of staff in states with limits. Many of the respondents felt term limits would hamper the budgetary process by compromising the work of appropriations committees (67 percent of legislators and 65 percent of staff in states without term limits, 77 percent of legislators and 63 percent of staff in term-limit states). This survey also found partisan and gender differences regarding term limits. Democrats and female legislators tended to view the reforms more negatively than did Republicans and males.

Another survey of legislators raises doubts about the magnitude and breadth of the consequences of term limits feared by opponents. Based on a much more comprehensive survey of nearly 3,000 state legislators nationwide,[40] Carey, Niemi, and Powell found the perceived effects of term limits to be quite limited. First, they found no systematic differences in the composition of membership between term-limited and non-term-limited legislatures. They did find that term limits reduced the amount of time legislators devoted to securing "pork" for their districts, and at the same time heightened their attention to the needs of their states and the demands of their conscience relative to district interests. In terms of the institution, term limits seemed to be shifting power away from majority party leaders toward the executive and legislative staff.

The vague or varied empirical consequences of term limits thus far make it difficult to judge their ultimate impact. Complicating matters further, recent court decisions have raised doubts about their legal status in some jurisdictions and invalidated their status in other venues. In 1997, U.S. District Judge Claudia Wilken struck down the California term-limit law, ruling that it violated the constitutional rights to voting and association under the First and Fourteenth Amendments. But she put her decision on hold. In October a three-judge panel of the U.S. Court of Appeal upheld the decision, but on different grounds. It ruled 2 to 1 that Proposition 140 was unconstitutional because it did not disclose that the ban on reelection of veteran legislators lasted for life. Two months later, an eleven-judge panel overturned its colleagues with opinions written by five different judges. The court of appeal ruling held, 9 to 2, that voters knew they were imposing a lifetime ban on veteran legislators. In the fall of 1997 a U.S. District Court struck down California's legislative term. In March 1998, the U.S. Supreme Court overturned this decision without comment. In a decision handed down in May 1998, the Sixth U.S. Circuit Court of Appeals rejected complaints that Michigan's term-limits law would create "a legislature of novices." In terms of the federal constitution, it would appear that these limits are permitted. However, in January 1998 the Washington State Supreme Court ruled that a state constitutional amendment was required to limit the number of terms a legislator could serve. In addition, term limits have been successfully challenged on the basis of state law in Massachusetts and Nebraska. While the federal constitutional status of term limits on state legislators seems sound, time will tell how this matter is ultimately played out as state constitutions are applied to these provisions across the land.

Quite obviously, it is too early to tell if the effects of term limits will be as positive as their proponents expect, or as dire as their detractors fear. Inferring the consequences of term limits is made even more complicated by the substantial gains Republicans have made across the land in this period

at all levels of government. Many of these newly elected officials are publicly sympathetic with the idea of limited government, but it would seem an
exaggeration to say that the enactment of term limits is what has brought
them to government service. In the end, the impact of term limits may take
many years to emerge, as incremental changes in composition, behavior,
and institutional operating characteristics take hold. It seems safe to say
at this point that their immediate effects are not enormous, but also that
the fears of many practicing politicians and policy professionals are nonetheless very pronounced. The realities of term limits should be felt more
clearly when more legislators are term-limited. The number of term-limited
political careers was quite small through 1996, but in the 1998 elections
the tempo of term limitations picked up. Half of Arkansas' 100 House
members, 67 of Michigan's 110 members, and 32 out of 98 members in
Washington State served out their final terms. Oregon turned out 22 of its
60 members, Colorado lost 18 of 65 House members and 9 of 35 Senate members. Maine's term limits ended the House careers of 11 members,
and one Senator was kept from running. Finally, Montana's term-limit law
prohibited 10 of 50 House members from seeking reelection.

The general consequences of term limits in 1998 are difficult to as-
certain because of the highly unusual nature of this particular midterm
election. From 1942 through 1996, the president's party lost on average
382 state legislative seats at the midterm, but in a stunning reversal that
was evident in congressional contests as well, the Democrats gained 37
state legislative seats in 1998. The anomalous nature of this election makes
it most difficult to judge the general effects term limits had on campaigns
and election outcomes. No clear pattern of partisan advantage jumps out
from the results of the elections in the term-limited states mentioned earlier, with Democrats and Republicans sharing pretty equally in seat gains
and losses across these states. There were, however, some notable effects
on individual careers and party leadership in several states. In Arkansas,
Representative Charles Stuart was term-limited out of office after serving
44 years in the statehouse, and the Speaker of the House was also term-
limited. In both Maine and Michigan, term limits forced the exit of the
House Speakers, majority leaders, and minority leaders. Interestingly, three
wives of term-limited representatives were on the ballot to succeed their
husbands.

The best guess about the impact of term limits on careers in state legislatures comes from work by Gary Moncrief and his colleagues[41] and a
recent extension of their analysis by David Hedge.[42] Moncrief et al. examined the rates of retention, over a twelve-year period, of the cohort
of state legislators first elected in 1979 to 1980. Based on their fifty-state
analysis, they estimated that term limits would have the largest impact in
professional legislatures, where members were limited to the fewest years of
service, and in those legislatures with sufficient compensation to make ser-

vice in that body a career, but without sufficient opportunities to advance to "better" political offices. Extending this analysis to 1996, Hedge found the same patterns to be evident. One implication of these studies is that for many legislatures, the natural turnover rate was sufficient to limit the impact of term limits to only a small proportion of members. In addition, and not surprisingly, it is in the more professional chambers where the impact will be greatest.

Looking to the Future

At this point it would be tempting to make a bold or even obvious projection as to the likely effects of term limits in the long run. The bold projection might be that term limits will produce the kind of citizen politics their proponents envision, with Burkean legislators ignoring pork and interest groups and, acting out of noble conscience, producing a new era of political enlightenment and effective public policies. Yet even if one subscribes to this view, it remains hard to imagine how so many conscience-driven legislators can be organized and focused with any consistency on the fundamental public policy issues of the day. A disorganized polity, V.O. Key wisely observed, worked to the benefit of the haves.[43] For the have nots, political organization was and presumably is essential. One does not have to be a cynic to wonder what forces will serve to organize the term-limited polity, and whether these forces will be beneficial or malignant for the less-easily-organized interests in our society.

The more obvious forecast would be a return to amateurism, akin to the patterns in the 1950s, which have persisted in some states up to the present. We would expect to see certain occupational groups come to the fore and an increasing conservatism emerge, as career-oriented Democrats were displaced by Republicans with part-time commitments to politics. While it would seem undeniable that a change in the incentives and resources for service will alter the types of people running and their perceptions of their jobs as legislators, it is not necessarily the case that a model derived from the 1950s will best fit the new era. The 1950s was characterized by a large and expanding federal presence and by state legislatures commonly filled with notoriously unskilled and untalented individuals. Furthermore, so much of the character and tone of that bygone era was at least partly founded on malapportioned districts, with underrepresented urban interests and overrepresented rural concerns.

Clearly, the reach and scope of federal activity is a pale shadow of what it once was. Increasingly, citizens have looked to state government to deal with new and pressing issues. Reapportionment has left a lasting impact on state legislatures that is renewed by the redistricting that follows every decennial census. Where statehouses once operated under the tyrannical rule of malapportioned rural interests, there is necessarily greater balance since the reapportionment revolution of the 1960s. Thus, the character of legislative service has been transformed in many ways, some stemming from increased material rewards, others related to other dimensions of the quality of service. The caliber of state politicians has improved under these conditions, and we should bear in mind that new challenges, as well as general improvements in the operating characteristics of state legislatures, may inhibit their descent into past patterns of amateurism.

CHAPTER FIVE

Statehouse Bureaucracy: Institutional Consistency in a Changing Environment

Charles Barrilleaux

V.O. KEY JR. described state government in the 1950s as "peculiarly a politics of administration," noting that "most decisions of state governments are of matters on which public information is limited and about which only a romantic would expect many people to be informed or to have much of an opinion one way or another."[1] Contemporary state government decisions, likewise, are often of low interest or visibility to the public. Even where decisions are made initially under conditions that place them in the public eye, that attention lasts only briefly for any issue, and policymaking is then relegated to the more mundane world of state policymaking. This absence of drama and interest leads some state decisions to be made quietly and to be influenced mainly by organizations, interests, or individuals with a stake in the outcome and with information about the issue at hand rather than by public demand. Because sometimes important decisions are made outside of what typically is viewed as the political process, state governments place a premium on having relative certainty in the sorts of decisions that will be made.

Bureaucracies are an important component of states' policymaking machinery because they are a repository of information about past decisions, as well as technical and programmatic expertise, and because they represent the most stable manifestation of the state. They provide public services through the process of policy implementation and aid in determining what people will get from government through their formal and informal roles in the policymaking process. And, as state governments assume increased responsibility for designing and funding public programs that are handed down to them as one result of national government downsizing, the role of state administration will become more important. Understanding similarities and differences in the size and organization of state bureaucracies may provide insights into the paths state governments will follow in an increasingly decentralized environment.

In comparison to other state government institutions — the governor's office, legislatures, and courts — the amount of systematic comparative research on state administration is slim. Only fairly recently have researchers turned their attention to the role of institutions in policymaking and politics, so it is only natural that work that views administrative influences systematically is scant. Another explanation for this relative paucity of research lies in the scarcity of solid information about state administration. Data on administrative structures, salaries, designs, and the like are not as easily found or as readily comparable as are those on other branches of state government. These factors, as well as others, conspire to make state-level administration less often studied than it may deserve to be.

State administration is now receiving attention as a result of the movement toward reduced national government responsibility and presence in a variety of public programs. The Nixon administration, in a response to the national government's expanded role in education, welfare, and other functions traditionally provided by the state and local governments that was brought on by the Johnson administration's Great Society and other policy initiatives, began in the early 1970s to shift programs and discretion back to the states. The mechanism for this was the General Revenue Sharing program, wherein state and local governments received "block grants" to provide services. The shift to decentralization began in the early 1970s and has continued, placing a premium on state governments' abilities to manage (and fund) large programs. State governments have developed much stronger administrative capabilities over the period since 1970 and, as is discussed here, this capability may prove to be especially important as we move into a period in which state governments are expected to do much more than was the case in the recent past.

In this chapter, a brief discussion of the roles of bureaucracies in democratic governance is followed by a look at the scope of bureaucracy in the states, focusing on how many persons are employed by state governments and how large a portion of state economies is devoted to administration. Next is an examination of the notion of bureaucratic quality and the problems involved in measuring that construct in the states, and this is followed by a discussion of current and ongoing attempts to reform state administration. The final section provides an overview of the subject.

The Evolution of Bureaucracy: From Neutral Agent to Participant

Bureaucracies are expected to perform in two distinct ways: as neutral policy implementers and as institutions that are fully engaged in the process of policymaking. The first role — policy implementer — is generally seen as an appropriate function of public employees and public organizations. The second role is not so widely accepted as appropriate even though most observers view it as an empirical reality. In short, the appropriate role of bureaucracy in a democracy is open to debate; the contours of that debate are discussed in this section.

The term *policy implementation* refers to the act of putting into place the programs and actions mandated by legislation. Hence, bureaucrats are responsible for organizing, and in some cases delivering, the services provided by governments. In the course of their daily lives, individual citizens often contact state-level bureaucrats. These contacts may involve renewing a driver's license, being pulled over by a state highway patrol officer (and possibly losing that just-renewed license), applying for public assistance benefits, and so on, and these bureaucratic encounters often are citizens' most frequent points of contact with their state governments. In general, citizens want such contacts to be pleasant and efficiently handled, and the quality of these contacts in many ways establishes citizens' perceptions of the quality of governance within their states.

The second function of state administrators — policymaking — is less well accepted, given its apparent conflict with notions of representative democracy. Formal flowcharts showing the part played by state employees in the governmental process (carrying out tasks assigned by democratically elected officials) delineate acceptable bureaucratic roles in policy implementation. The involvement of administrators in making public policies conjures images of sinister bureaucrats wielding illegitimate power, in the service of either individual or organizational budget maximization.[2] Some critics argue that allowing bureaucrats to be involved in policymaking weakens democracy because it permits elective officials to shirk their responsibility to produce public policies and affords them the luxury of blaming bureaucratic scapegoats for all that goes wrong.[3]

Another view holds that bureaucratic involvement in policymaking is a practical response to an increasingly complex system. Bureaucrats are involved in policymaking by virtue of their having more information, expertise, and interest in some policy areas than do other parties. Information is critical in decision making, and some critics fear that bureaucrats, who many hope will serve as neutral observers of political processes and policy decisions, may instead present information in a manner that is most advantageous to their employer or to their own views of policymaking.[4] The majority of cases of bureaucratic involvement in policymaking, however, are considerably less dramatic than some critics suggest. Much bureaucratic influence in policymaking occurs at the "street level,"[5] where it is a simple reflection of individuals exercising discretion in doing their jobs. When a state police officer decides to give a warning rather than writing a ticket, he or she is exercising discretion and thus making a policy decision. Welfare administrators who use their judgment to make decisions when confronted with unclear legislative guidance on welfare eligibility are also making policy. From this micro-perspective, governments would be incapable of getting anything done if bureaucrats were not allowed to exercise professional discretion.

Few observers of modern governments can afford to ignore the roles played by bureaucracies. Bureaucracies, as noted earlier, are responsible for implementing policies passed by governments, and they provide stability in times of political change. Bureaus typically are long-lived, their personnel does not change rapidly, and their structures and functions are relatively constant over time. In the formal organization of American governments, national, state, and local bureaucracies are construed as a portion of the executive branch that serves under the governing unit's chief executive. In the United States, the federal bureaucracy, at least in the ideal form, serves the president; governors are the chief executives over state bureaus; and mayors, city managers, county executives, and other executive officers are responsible for administering local bureaucracies.

The earliest writings on the proper role of bureaucracy in the American system portrayed it as being distinctly subordinate to the executive. Alexander Hamilton, who, in his contributions to the *Federalist,* mentioned administration more frequently than did James Madison or John Jay, has received credit for observing,

> Though we cannot acquiesce in the political heresy of the poet who says: "For forms of government let fools conteste / That which is best administered is best," yet we may safely pronounce that the true test of a good government is its aptitude and tendency to produce a good administration.[6]

In Hamilton's view, the most difficult task was *not* administration per se, but devising a system that would allow the construction of an effective administrative apparatus that was responsive to political control by elected officials. This concern continues: complaints about bureaucracy often are tinged with a suspicion that they operate in the absence of effective political control. The mechanisms available for controlling bureaucracy, either by an executive or by a legislature, are blunt. Bureaucratic operations may be reined in, mainly through the budgetary process, by cutting bureau budgets in response to perceived failures to administer faithfully legislative or executive orders; by periodically reviewing agency outputs, through "sunset review" mechanisms that require periodic legislative evaluation of agency performance; and, in the most drastic cases, by reorganizing either agencies or entire executive branches, although the value of such reorganizations for other than political reasons is questionable.[7]

Legalistic models of institutional roles, in which the behaviors of individuals are defined by the formal structure of rules and regulations guiding their job, have long been discounted by political scientists. In the earliest days of the study of administration, there was widespread belief in a dichotomy between politics and administration. This view dates back to the scholarly writings of Woodrow Wilson. Wilson's most often-cited research, published in 1887, established the politics-administration dichotomy as the idealized model of administrative behavior.[8] Reacting to a general sense that the U.S. administrative system had become too politicized, a process put into place with the election of Andrew Jackson in 1828, Wilson (and other reformers) called for a system of government in which the executive branch exercised little policy role other than implementation, leaving responsibility for governance to the legislative branch. One requirement of this revised system of governance was the presence of a professional and apolitical bureaucracy composed of persons whose primary allegiance was not to political masters but to the service of the executive branch through administration.

Prior to the election of Jackson, the U.S. bureaucracy was staffed largely by persons of the "gentleman" class, who held their jobs irrespective of the president in power.[9] Jackson viewed the president's ability to appoint people to government jobs as a patronage opportunity too great to ignore: it provided him the opportunity to reward his supporters and attract new support with the promise of government jobs, and it ensured that he would head a government staffed by loyalists rather than by those who might support another candidate for office.

The system enacted by Jackson was called the "spoils system," after the phrase "to the victor go the spoils." The strengths of the spoils system are almost wholly political, with benefits accruing to the candidate or party that most recently gained control of the executive branch. Its weaknesses were possibly more glaring: the spoils system aided in creating a government that was too strongly influenced by partisan politics and that experienced wholesale personnel changes with each change of presidential administration. Given that one of the supposed strengths of bureaucracies, in their idealized form, is that they provide a sort of institutional "memory" for governments, this presented a problem: the national government was unnecessarily weak in its administrative capabilities as result of the spoils system.

Wilson's solution to the problem of spoils — one that was emerging simultaneously through "good government leagues" (goo-goos) in cities throughout the nation — was to implement a merit-based system of employment and management. Merit systems differed from patronage systems in that getting, keeping, and being promoted in public service jobs ostensibly was to be determined through objective assessments of merit — by "what you know" rather than "who you know." Wilson's solution to the problems of administration in the United States was to establish a civil service system wherein hiring was based on qualifications, and where administrators would be sufficiently professional to serve different political administrations and to act as neutral policy implementers who would not let personal views intrude upon their actions. These merit-based systems had diffused to all of the state governments by 1950, and the vision of neutral competence is the guiding premise of most American public administration.

This politically neutral view of administration, despite evidence to the contrary, was widely accepted in the political science literature for the first half of this century. Its logic was questioned most eloquently by Norton Long in an essay published in 1949.[10] Using a blend of traditional political theory, behavioral studies of organization, and then-new behavioral studies of politics as a basis, Long argued that it is impossible, and impractical, to assume that bureaucrats are neutral agents of the wishes of elective officials. Long's essay is in many ways a watershed piece for students of administrative politics: it placed administration squarely within the political process, providing a theoretical basis for the development of some important research on the nature of policymaking and politics in the American system.

Viewing administrators as players in politics, rather than as neutral observers of the political process, complicates our understanding of the dynamics of democratic politics. In a world in which bureaucrats may be viewed realistically as policy implementers who, if they have policy opinions, do not act on them "at the office," it is less difficult to explain how public decisions are made. The introduction of bureaucrats and bureaucracies into the policymaking process, however, produces problems for democratic theory and practical problems for empirical research, as it is difficult to observe bureaucratic influence on policymaking. One vision of bureaucratic roles in policymaking places them in policy "subsystems"[11] in which a premium is placed on expertise, information, and interest. These subsystems typically include members of organized interest groups, legislative committees, and executive bureaus, all of whom are specialists in the policy realm. In this view, bureaucrats influence policymaking by helping to define problems and solutions.

Unlike some actions that are more easily measured quantitatively, bureaucratic influences are difficult to isolate and capture in a measure. In an influential study of policymaking in the national government, John Kingdon, relying on interviews with hundreds of informants over several years, argued that political appointees within presidential administrations (i.e., the persons given the highest-level management jobs following a change of administration) have some direct influence on policymaking via their ability to steer organizational policy agendas. Civil servants' roles in policymaking, according to the Kingdon research, emerge most strongly in the definition of alternative policies given the executive expression of a particular policy direction.[12]

Studies of administrative roles in state policymaking largely concur with the model suggested by Kingdon. Glenn Abney and Thomas Lauth described the policy role of administrators in terms of tensions between professional norms and political processes. Administrators who responded to their surveys indicated that their roles in the policy process come largely through providing information and, at times, acting as policy advocates by lobbying legislators, providing testimony at legislative hearings, and interacting with clientele and organized interests.[13] Administrative roles in policymaking are especially pronounced in the area of policy design. Legislatures typically enact legislation that lacks specificity, calling for general solutions to problems and leaving the details of program design to bureaucrats. This allows considerable latitude for bureaucrats to become involved in policymaking processes, because they are able to follow the broad mandate of legislators and rely on their own expertise and ideas for constructing policies that meet those legislative goals. Richard Elling described this policy role in light of making recommendations: governors and legislators determine broad contours of policies and, consistent with Kingdon's depiction of administrators' roles, agency personnel help to define the range of plausible approaches to designing public policies.[14]

Empirical studies of policymaking in the states provide little evidence of bureaucratic roles in that process, due in large part to the failure of researchers to consider those effects. More often, the focus of research is on the policymaking effects of legislatures, with recent research suggesting that legislatures produce public policies that are consistent with the ideological positions of citizens within states.[15] Where administrative roles are evaluated in empirical research, the evidence suggests that more professionalized and larger state bureaucracies exert statistically significant independent influences on policymaking in a number of areas, including health care,[16] regulation of industries, and other specific policy areas. Overall, as theory suggests, bureaucratic influences seem to be most pronounced where policies are most technically complex. Legislatures, as is suggested in the literature, work to produce policies that are consistent with public demands and ideological leanings, but bureaucratic roles become more pronounced where policies are not salient ideologically, that is, where policymaking requires greater expertise and more precise information.

Regardless of normative desires, empirical reality establishes state bureaucracies as important components of American states' policymaking systems. How they influence policies and how their influence varies among the states is an open question. The question of the size and scope of state bureaucracies is addressed in the section that follows.

The Size of State Government Employment

State governments are among the nation's largest employers. States employed more than 4.6 million persons in 1992. In 1982, the states employed about 3.1 million people; the average rate of growth during the ten-year period was 2.3 percent. The total payroll for state government employees was $5 billion in 1982 and rose to $9.8 billion by 1992, an average annual increase of 6.9 percent. Mean salary for state employees was $2,621 per month in 1992.[17] In that year the average state employed 151 full-time equivalent (FTE) persons per 10,000 population. The state with the highest FTE/10,000 ratio was Hawaii, with 437/10,000 and the lowest ratio was seen in California (104/10,000). Alaska paid the highest average monthly salary for full-time employees ($3,324); the lowest monthly wage was paid in West Virginia ($1,969). Clearly, the ratio of employees to population is influenced by population size, with more populous states typically having lower ratios, and wages reflect cost of living differences as well as state income and employment norms.

In October 1972 the national average number of state government employees per 10,000 population was 119. The state with the highest ratio of state government employees to population was, as in 1992, Hawaii, with 376.4/10,000 and the lowest ratio was seen in Ohio (88.2/10,000). The highest average monthly wage for state government employees in 1972 was again seen in Alaska, and the lowest was in Arkansas. All told, the rankings were remarkably consistent over time: states that were low in the rankings in the early 1970s remained low in the 1990s, and high-spending states in the first period were high in the later period.

Although state employees are often criticized as prototypical bureaucrats, sitting in offices, promulgating inefficient regulations, and so on,[18] many of them are employed by colleges, universities, courts, and prisons. The single largest functional area is higher education, which accounted for about 14.15 percent of total employment in 1992. The second largest sector of state government employment in 1992 was hospitals (12.1 percent), and corrections represented the third largest single area with 7.6 percent of total employment. The largest growth area in recent years has been corrections and other activities associated with crime and punishment: the number of state government employees in corrections increased by 90 percent in the decade 1982 to 1992.

The changes in percentages of total employment in particular functional areas provide evidence of state "problem" areas in particular decades. During the period 1972 to 1982, the largest percentage of annual employment growth was in social insurance administration, reflecting the administrative buildup that was brought on by passage of social policy initiatives, such as Medicaid and Aid to Families with Dependent Children, that grew out of the Great Society programs of the 1960s. Given that the intent of these programs was to stimulate state activities in those areas, it follows that state administrative capabilities should have expanded to run them. The 1982 to 1992 period, however, saw relatively modest growth in social insurance administration (.54 percent), and massive growth in states' corrections employment, with an annual rate of growth of 6.63 percent. Each of these growth spurts illustrates the dependence and responsiveness of state administrative development to national government policy initiatives. During the 1970s, when the national government provided incentives for building state social-service capabilities, the states did so. Likewise, during the 1980s the states responded to federal policies supporting increased prison building and staffing by doing exactly that. Note, however, that the increase in corrections facilities did not result in a real decline in the size of social-insurance administrative sectors, which continued to show modest growth despite the shift in policy focus.[19] Whether the growth of state employment in these sectors is wholly dependent on federal government largess in the periods of growth, or represents an expression of states' true employment preferences, is open to question. However, coming years should provide some insights into states' responsiveness to staffing needs in particular policy areas, as the national government's withdrawal from state policy concerns will provide increasing opportunities to observe how states respond both to altered federal incentives and to problems they recognize within their borders.

One of the issues that arises from the threat or opportunity (depending on one's point of view) of reduced federal involvement in state service provision has to do with state-level administrative capability. In short, how well equipped are the states to manage the complex policies that developed during a period of increasing national government presence and assistance in state service provision? In the years 1969 to 1993, state and local governments represented a larger proportion of personal income than did the national government (the state and local data are combined because they were reported together by the U.S. Bureau of the Census, the principal source for such information). That makes sense: of the more than 80,000 governments presently operating in the United States, the national government is but one. In 1992 state government represented about 25 percent of total U.S. civilian government employment, local governments represented over 59 percent, and the national government accounted for about 16 percent of government employment. The shift of policy responsibility from the national government to the states may hasten the growth of state employment, although the concurrent push for states to streamline their governments indicates that growth may not be the means by which they manage their new policy responsibilities.

The Quality of State Administration

Good administration is like obscenity: hard to define but easy to recognize. And, as with obscenity, there is wide variation in what observers view as constituting good administration. Different people emphasize different aspects of quality, making it difficult to say with any precision which states' administrative sectors are better than others. It is possible, however, to introduce some benchmarks for comparing states. One attempt to establish a yardstick for measuring the relative quality of state administration was developed by Lee Sigelman in the mid-1970s.[20] Sigelman distinguished between professional and political standards of administration. Within the professional category, he identified four standards — expertise, information processing, innovativeness, and efficiency — against which to compare the quality of state administration. The three polit-

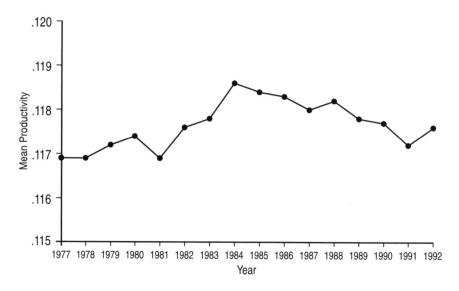

FIGURE 5.1. STATE GOVERNMENT PRODUCTIVITY, 1977–92

Source: Author's calculations based on data drawn from U.S. Department of Census, Bureau of Economic Information, *Regional Economic Information System* CD-ROM (Government Printing Office, 1996).

Note: Productivity = $\dfrac{\text{state government Gross State Product}}{\text{state government wages}} \times 100$

ical standards he identified were representativeness, partisan neutrality, and integrity.[21] In theory, a unit of government showing high scores on each of these benchmarks could be described as having achieved "quality" administration.

Establishing criteria for administrative quality has proved easier than measuring them. Using data representing the states from the 1960s and early 1970s, Sigelman was able to measure five of his seven standards. An attempt to update the Sigelman measures to capture state administrative quality during the 1980s revealed that several of the measurement items used to construct the original measures were no longer available, which lessened the authors' ability to draw comparisons between the two proximate periods.[22] Despite this, both studies reported similar conclusions about the factors that contribute to the development of relatively better state administration. States with wealthier and more urbanized citizenries tend to have more professional administrative sectors. And where legislatures are more professional, so too are administrators. More liberal publics, too, are associated with more professional bureaucracies.

Recent indicators of administrative quality in the states show simi-

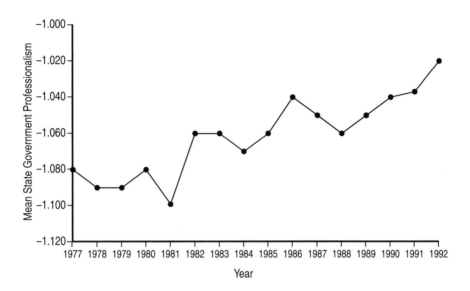

FIGURE 5.2. STATE GOVERNMENT PROFESSIONALISM, 1977–92

Source: Author's calculations based on data drawn from U.S. Department of Census, Bureau of Economic Information, *Regional Economic Information System* CD-ROM (Government Printing Office, 1996).

Note: Professionalism = $\dfrac{\text{efficiency in state government}}{\text{private sector productivity}}$

lar patterns and relationships.[23] The data problems (i.e., an inability to measure the same things at different times, which hampered prior investigations) led researchers, however, to seek measures of professionalism that were replicable over several years. Two measures that are useful for comparing the states over time capture state government productivity and state government professionalism. Productivity is defined as the ratio of state government salaries to state government gross domestic product, and professionalism is measured as the ratio of average state employee wages to average private sector wages within a state.[24]

Figure 5.1 plots state government productivity (GSP) for the years 1977 to 1992. Productivity changed very little over the period despite a reduction in the size of the public-sector labor force within the states during the same period. This in some ways illustrates the constancy of administration over time: despite changes in the composition of the state workforce and of the measure of GSP, the measure changes very little.

Data in figure 5.2 (p. 108) illustrate mean state government professionalism over the same period. The logic underlying the measure is that the greater the difference between average state government salaries and average wages in a state (state government wages tend to be greater than average wages), the more professional the state government. State governments that pay higher salaries should be more successful in attracting good employees than state governments that pay lesser salaries. As the data show, there has been a decline in the difference between state government and private pay over the years in the series, suggesting that the employment advantage enjoyed by state governments has declined over the years.

Data for individual states in 1977, 1987 and 1992 are displayed in table 5.1. The relative positions of states change little over time, indicating that states' bureaucracies are relatively "fixed" in their productivity and professionalism. This is consistent with both scholarly and popular notions of administration: bureaucracies are designed in part to provide certainty, and that design feature contributes to their representing relatively stable characteristics over time. This is often expressed, especially in the popular view, as a dysfunctional characteristic of administration inasmuch as certainty and stability may work to block change and may prove to be barriers to policy innovations; yet it also suggests that state-level bureaucracies represent a fairly consistent manifestation of each states' governing capacity. That these bureaucracies change relatively consistently indicates that no state experienced either a massive improvement or a decline in the productivity or professionalism of its bureaucracy in the years covered by these data. American democracy values consistency and certainty in its institutions, and state bureaucracies provide both.

Recent Changes in State Government Management

Widespread public distrust of government has had profound effects on administration at all levels. One of the clearest expressions of public disaffection with government "as usual" is seen in weak and deteriorating support for taxation. The political resonance of antitax statements has proved useful for gaining election to office at all levels. Tax cuts mean reduced revenues. Reduced revenues mean lessened services. But because the demands placed on governments are increasing despite reduced resources, state governments, along with the national government and the local governments, have been forced to seek ways to produce services more efficiently.

Growing out of this situation is one movement calling for government "reinvention." Reinventing government is almost certainly at least partly a fad: students and practitioners of management regularly embrace various systems that come and go and often have little discernible effect on what gets done. From another perspective, however, the rhetoric of reinvention, coupled with the changes in state politics and administration wrought by an apparent financial crisis in state government finance, may prove to be more than rhetoric. One measure of this is the use of reinvention themes in

TABLE 5.1. STATE GOVERNMENT EFFICIENCY AND PRODUCTIVITY,
1977, 1987, AND 1992

	Efficiency			Productivity		
State	1977	1987	1992	1977	1987	1992
Alabama	1.027	1.010	.965	.118	.118	.117
Alaska	1.533	2.487	2.018	.114	.109	.114
Arkansas	1.053	1.019	1.028	.116	.116	.115
Arizona	.967	.893	.843	.124	.128	.128
California	1.057	1.023	1.027	.115	.118	.115
Colorado	1.031	.974	.960	.119	.122	.119
Connecticut	.964	.978	.961	.114	.117	.114
Delaware	1.034	1.211	1.391	.120	.119	.119
Florida	.831	.836	.798	.121	.122	.123
Georgia	1.091	1.084	1.035	.117	.119	.118
Hawaii	1.031	1.044	1.027	.117	.118	.123
Idaho	1.110	1.025	1.005	.117	.115	.116
Illinois	1.082	1.044	1.007	.113	.114	.115
Indiana	1.103	1.054	1.011	.114	.115	.115
Iowa	1.098	.968	.985	.116	.117	.117
Kansas	1.039	.990	.979	.118	.120	.117
Kentucky	1.144	1.088	1.025	.117	.115	.118
Louisiana	1.476	1.322	1.274	.117	.115	.115
Maine	1.005	.969	.904	.112	.115	.117
Maryland	.835	.855	.843	.119	.120	.117
Massachusetts	1.013	1.009	.991	.111	.116	.116
Michigan	1.067	.996	.929	.117	.117	.117
Minnesota	1.088	1.058	1.052	.113	.114	.114
Mississippi	1.116	1.088	1.056	.117	.116	.114
Missouri	1.079	1.009	.968	.115	.117	.116
Montana	1.153	1.012	.968	.116	.115	.114
Nebraska	.978	.893	.941	.130	.131	.126
Nevada	1.110	1.039	1.047	.118	.123	.121
New Hampshire	.862	.905	.858	.120	.120	.121
New Jersey	.912	.961	.931	.117	.116	.117
New Mexico	1.271	1.106	1.144	.115	.117	.115
New York	1.036	1.074	1.019	.114	.113	.112
N. Carolina	1.142	1.111	1.110	.117	.119	.119
N. Dakota	1.161	1.047	1.029	.115	.115	.115
Ohio	1.064	1.008	.973	.117	.119	.118
Oklahoma	1.088	.995	.942	.120	.119	.119
Oregon	1.096	1.019	.964	.113	.115	.116
Pennsylvania	.987	.926	.902	.116	.119	.118
Rhode Island	.950	.971	.945	.113	.112	.111
S. Carolina	.982	.989	.975	.121	.124	.121
S. Dakota	1.075	1.039	1.019	.115	.118	.119
Tennessee	1.066	1.051	1.004	.121	.119	.121
Texas	1.261	1.090	1.070	.120	.122	.121
Utah	1.124	.970	.989	.117	.129	.127
Vermont	.990	1.003	.956	.115	.115	.114
Virginia	.973	1.003	.951	.118	.115	.118
Washington	.981	.896	.932	.123	.129	.123
W. Virginia	1.129	.971	.936	.116	.117	.116
Wisconsin	1.082	1.032	.996	.113	.113	.114
Wyoming	1.621	1.595	1.369	.116	.116	.114

Source: Author's calculations based on data drawn from U.S. Department of Census, Bureau of Economic Information, *Regional Economic Information System* CD-ROM (Government Printing Office, 1996).

the pronouncements of representatives from the Democratic and Republican parties, which have both embraced government reform as a goal. This may indicate either that something will be done or that each side recognizes the political value of the terminology and seeks to use it, or possibly some mixture of the two.

State government reform involves attempts to streamline government to reduce costs in a number of areas, to improve the lines of communications between citizens and government, to work better with the private sector, and otherwise to make government more efficient managerially and economically.[25] Government reinvention forces consideration of fundamental questions regarding the state's obligation to its employees versus its citizens, whether there is some inherent value in public provision of certain services,[26] and other core questions about governance. As the range of state government responsibilities increases, the ability of states to handle the increased administrative and policymaking duties that follow devolution will come under increased scrutiny. Reforming state government management systems may become a necessity rather than a political issue.

There are several barriers to reforming state government management. It is often remarked that as bureaucracies age they become less willing to accept change, implying that the organization's behavior, in the aggregate, is driven at least partly by the behavior of individuals within that organization.[27] Larger, older bureaus are more difficult to change: employees develop patterns of behavior, the agency cultivates relations with clientele groups,[28] and past decisions and protocols become "fixed" in the institutional memory. Hence, reformers seeking to change state government occasionally do so by reorganizing the executive branch. Studies of the effects of such reorganizations suggest, however, that they have no discernible effect on the costs or productivity of state governments, which leads researchers to conclude that they are motivated largely by politics.[29]

A recent study of the condition of state and local administration, conducted by a panel organized under the title National Commission on the State and Local Public Service (hereafter the Commission), suggests that states initiate management changes that streamline government and make it more responsive to political and public demands, rather than instituting constitutionally-mandated reorganizations of state government, which typically involve removing some departments, creating others, and generally effecting widespread changes in the formal, legal structure of governments.[30] The central thrust of the argument surrounding state government's needed changes, insofar as administration is concerned, hinges on strengthening executive (i.e., gubernatorial) authority over state administrative agencies. Bureaucracies, the report argues, "stifle the creativity that is so desperately needed, putting one obstacle after another in the way of new ideas and energetic leaders" and creating a system in which "innovation tends to become an accident."[31]

The Commission report points to a number of problems with state and local administration that stifles new ideas and innovations, all of which revolve around problems characteristic of large organizations. Included among them are the multiple layers of rules and regulations that grow over time and ossify decisionmaking. Commission recommendations call for flattening of bureaucracies so that the number of layers between the top and the bottom is reduced.[32] The basic message is that state administration has too many managers and not enough front-line employees: services would likely be improved if more employees were placed in the trenches, where services are delivered, and fewer were given responsibility for managing the production of those services.

The Commission also called for a widespread deregulation of state government actions, pointing to problems with civil service systems, procurement rules, and inflexibility in budgeting processes. As noted earlier, civil service systems were originally intended to distance public employees from the whims of politicians who might misuse public service appointments for political gain; they were designed to ensure hiring on the basis of merit rather than political contacts. Merit systems, however, have evolved to a point at which they introduce a number of inefficiencies in hiring, and many systems are so bound by rules and other complications that Commission analysts argue that "merit is often the last value served."[33] Merit systems have taken on lives of their own: many states have huge numbers of job classifications — for example, Louisiana, a state with fewer than 3 million residents, had more than 3,800 job classifications in 1992; Texas, with more than 12 million residents, had under 1,400; New York had more than 7,300 individual job classifications.[34] Administering civil service systems requires a battalion of employees in every state. Altering the present system of merit would enhance the ability of managers to hire the workers they view as most appropriate for the job, but would weaken both programs designed to reward veterans for their service and state programs designed to encourage diversity in the workplace. Since merit systems were designed to *improve* governance, it appears that they are in need of overhaul; Commission recommendations for decentralizing merit and removing some of the barriers to hiring the "best" employee for a position, if adopted, may improve the cadre of state workers and hasten employment decisions.

Improving state procurement systems, likewise a major component of the Commission's call for reform, seems mundane (reinforcing Key's characterization of state politics being about administration), but it represents a major activity of state government, one in which a large portion of state revenue is transferred to private vendors. Present systems are criticized as being too slow, as having too-stringent requirements for seeking multiple bids in some cases and insufficiently stringent requirements in others, and generally as an impediment to efficiency in state administration. States have attempted to loosen some purchasing requirements by raising the levels for expenditures requiring multiple bids, thereby increasing the decision-making discretion of agency employees and, presumably, lessening the time it takes to get work done.

State civil service systems, likewise, have undergone some recent changes in the attempt to redesign government, but changes in this area are difficult to bring about given the ossification introduced by some employee union contracts and by the very nature of civil service employment, which places barriers in the way of removing employees. Some states have experimented with performance pay rather than step systems. As its name implies, this system bases pay on some objective measure of performance, while step systems reward seniority and job title. Performance pay has been a source of great contention in state employment because it represents a change from past practice. While pay for performance, ideally, rewards those who are most productive and work hardest, it also introduces difficulties in the workplace (since public pay data are open records) by making distinctions among employees. Those who are rewarded less generously may become disaffected from the workplace, and some critics argue that pay for performance, particularly in times of budget scarcity, introduces more problems and contention than is necessary. Others, however, argue that state governments must offer more competitive salaries to attract and retain the most desirable employees.[35]

Trends in federal relations over the past twenty-five years point to increasing reliance upon states to provide and manage some important public programs. Because this shift to state responsibility carries with it a reduction in the amount of money states receive from the national government, a premium is placed upon management efficiency in state government. This requirement that states "do more with less," along with political forces, motivates attempts to reform state management practices. As with most reforms, it is unlikely that any single act will move state governments to a point at which they may be pronounced "reformed." Instead, reform will be a continuous process in which incremental adjustments continue over time and states change gradually rather than in a single, dramatic act.[36] Change in increments has long characterized American politics and policy-making,[37] and it is unlikely that calls for reform will result in more than symbolic rapid responses.

The problems confronting administrative change are myriad. In a recent study of a major push by Governor Lawton Chiles to effect administrative reform in Florida, Frances Stokes Berry and her coauthors portrayed administrative reform in the state as a situation in which apparent good intentions ran afoul of existing political realities.[38] In short, the Chiles reform package — designed in part by David Osborne, whose subsequent book, *Reinventing Government,* became something of a guide for would-be reformers throughout the nation — looked practical but was stymied by entrenched forces and inertia.

Aside from containing many of the gimmicks that so often characterize administrative reforms, the Florida package proposed that the state's personnel system be changed by reducing the number of classified positions, that pay flexibility be increased, and that it be made easier to hire and fire employees. Further, management was to be changed by implementing a number of currently popular management techniques, including Total Quality Management (TQM), which has been applied with considerable success in Japan and with less success in the United States. Management structures would be altered, middle management would be cut, agencies would be decentralized, and budgeting would focus on outcomes.[39] Administrative reform efforts in Florida appear to have been hamstrung by a lack of political or financial resources and by the reluctance to change that often characterizes large organizations. In some ways this is to be expected: attempts to bring about large-scale policy changes are often short-lived, with participants losing interest in whatever reform is to be wrought upon learning how difficult it is to effect change politically, how costly it is to address problems, and the like. Further, public problems have short shelf lives; policymakers and the public lose interest, and new problems emerge.[40] Restructuring and reforming government in the states is a difficult process requiring the expenditure of considerable political and economic capital, and it is difficult to envision the wholesale adoption of major changes in the near future.

Reformers are often frustrated with the difficulties they face when attempting to change bureaucracies. But in the American political context, this institutional consistency may be a blessing. In the current context of American state politics, where legislatures increasingly face term limits and other constitutional and fiscal changes that curtail their members' collective ability to develop expertise in the details of policymaking and governance, bureaucracies may prove to be important guardians of the status quo. The inherent inertia of American government that is so important to its daily operations and continued peaceful existence receives substantial support from the system of administration in place in the states.

CHAPTER SIX

State Judicial Politics: Rules, Structures, and the Political Game

Melinda Gann Hall

THE PAST FEW decades have been a period of extraordinary change for state courts. During the 1960s, state courts almost universally were condemned by court reformers as overloaded and slow. Many state court judges also were branded "unqualified or otherwise unfit for office."[1] Inefficient and confusing jurisdictional arrangements between courts, severe docket overloads, and significant delays in case processing were among the serious problems confronting state courts. "Justice delayed is justice denied" became the anthem of court reformers. Moreover, judicial elections fell into disfavor. Concerns that the rigors of electoral politics discouraged the most qualified attorneys from seeking judicial office and resulted in a bench too closely connected to partisan politics fueled a movement in the American states to redesign plans for staffing the state court bench.

In response to these damning criticisms and the obvious challenges facing state courts, the American states invested significant time and energy in reorganizing state judiciaries. Since the 1960s, many states have dramatically altered the organization of their judiciaries in an effort to alleviate a whole host of management problems and to address grave concerns about the delivery of justice. Many states also have changed the means by which judges are selected, in order to improve the quality of the bench and to strike a different balance between the politics of electoral accountability and the normative expectation of judicial independence. Through a wide variety of organizational changes, many state courts have been transformed into highly professionalized institutions that now collectively meet the extraordinary demand of processing over 100 million cases per year, or 99 percent of the nation's litigation.

This chapter explores the major institutional changes in state courts from the 1960s through the 1990s, including the consolidation of trial courts, centralized financing of all the courts within a state's judiciary, and the professional management of courts. Thereafter, this chapter focuses on two basic institutional changes — the addition of intermediate appellate courts to state judiciaries and the adoption of the Missouri Plan for judicial selection — and the consequences, intended and unintended, of these reforms on the politics of the states' highest courts. For although the institutional changes adopted by many states since the 1960s were designed to increase the capacity and efficiency of courts and to improve the quality of the bench, the creation of intermediate appellate courts and the adoption of the Missouri Plan have dramatically altered the operating environments of the states' highest courts. Most basically, these changes have increased the power of state supreme courts and the individual justices who hold office in these institutions, without significantly affecting the characteristics of those recruited for state judicial office in any measurable way.[2]

While formal structural reforms in state judiciaries have heightened the power of state supreme courts, recent changes in the nature of American federalism have had similar effects on state judiciaries. As the national government increasingly retrenches from areas of previous involvement, the vacuum is being filled by state governments. Moreover, there have been recent signals that even when Congress attempts to address pressing contemporary problems, the U.S. Supreme Court will not tolerate intrusions into areas of traditional state action, like crime and education. An excellent example is the Supreme Court's recent ruling in *United States* v. *Lopez,* in which the Court invalidated the Gun-Free School Zones Act, enacted by Congress in 1990.[3] *Lopez* was the first instance in over five decades where the Court held that Congress exceeded its authority under the Commerce Clause. In brief, as the states experience an overall resurgence, either because of congressional retrenchment or because of the Supreme Court imposing constitutional limits on national action, the power of state courts is expanding. With the power to resolve the vast proportion of the nation's legal disputes, and with recent shifts in federal-state relations, the ability of state courts to affect the distribution of wealth and power in the United States is at a zenith.

These exciting changes in the political climate render discussions of institutional reforms in the states particularly timely. Before proceeding, however, it is crucial to recognize several fundamental propositions about the nature of judicial decision making in American appellate courts and the vital importance of institutional context in shaping what judges do. First and foremost is the fact that the most divisive and important political issues facing the nation are presented to the courts in the form of lawsuits, and the judges who render judgments in these cases have significant discretion in fashioning solutions to the problems embodied in the cases. Especially at the level of state supreme courts, rarely are the problems simple or the solutions obvious, nor is the law a vice that rigidly binds judges' decisions. Often laws are ambiguous or have no obvious application to particular factual situations, and judges necessarily must rely on their personal perceptions of justice to resolve the cases immediately before their courts. Thus, judges do not merely enforce existing laws in a mechanical fashion but, instead, contribute significantly to their meaning and, in the process, make authoritative judgments about some of the most perplexing and significant problems of the day.

Further, courts are institutions composed of individuals who have well-defined preferences toward matters of public policy. Judges, like other public officials, are serious players in the political game who have their own agendas and a keen awareness of their impact on the political landscape. All things being equal, judges prefer to have their own views govern the court's treatment of an issue. However, judges are constrained in expressing and enforcing their preferences by the law relevant to the case, the socio-political environment within which the court is located, and the institutional context within which the cases are decided. Rules governing an institution are especially important because they determine, to a significant degree, the range of opportunities available to individual judges to pursue their own agendas and also the sanctions available to punish judges who fail to acquiesce to their court majorities, the electorate, or other relevant constituencies. While most ordinary citizens are not comfortable thinking of judges as political actors who rely on their personal concepts of justice or political preferences to decide cases, normative ideals obscure the complex realities of judicial decision making.

Given the discretion inherent in judicial decision making and the importance of context in shaping judicial decisions, even seemingly simple institutional changes can have a resounding impact on the politics of courts. Stated more broadly, understanding courts necessitates a fuller understanding of the effects of institutional arrangements on judicial behavior and a close examination of whether particular reforms are achieving their desired results.

State Courts in American Politics

One of the most basic questions confronting anyone interested in judicial politics is Why bother studying state courts, given the extraordinary power of the federal courts, especially the U.S. Supreme Court? The answers to this question are straightforward.[4] Perhaps most critical is that state courts have the responsibility of resolving the overwhelming majority of the nation's legal disputes. In fact, 99 percent of the litigation in the United States takes place in the state courts.[5] As mentioned, this amounts to over 100 million cases annually, in a nation of about 260 million people.

The sheer volume of cases processed by state courts and the number of people actually involved in or directly affected by this litigation, are staggering. The substantive importance of the issues presented to state courts also is notable, however. State courts resolve conflicts that span the entire spectrum of problems endemic to personal, social, economic, and political intercourse. These conflicts also involve every possible type of litigant pattern, including disputes between private citizens in their daily interactions, between citizens and the government, and between the various branches and agencies of government. Moreover, even with the tremendous expansion of federal authority during the past century, certain spheres of government action, such as the prosecution of criminal defendants and the resolution of family issues, remain largely within the purview of the states. Whether commonplace or controversial, state court decisions in the aggregate have a profound impact on the overall distribution of wealth and power in the United States and on the daily well-being of the citizenry.

William J. Brennan, a justice on the New Jersey Supreme Court prior to his appointment to the U.S. Supreme Court, commented that state courts actually are more important politically than federal courts, because state courts resolve problems most directly relevant to citizens' day-to-day lives.[6] Marriage and divorce, child support and custody, traffic incidents, tenant-landlord disputes, debt collection, and other such matters, while often relatively unexciting, are exactly the sorts of cases that the overwhelming majority of Americans are likely to be litigating.

Even the most seemingly mundane state court case can have significant political implications extending far beyond the litigants. Consider, for example, a divorce case. Divorce is quite common in the United States and, in most cases, is neither complex nor contentious. Parties in a divorce seek simply to dissolve a contractual relationship, divide property accumulated during the marriage, and arrange for the custody and support of children. But the manner in which property is divided between husband and wife, and the way in which issues of child support and custody are decided, have far-reaching consequences for the economic and political status of men and women. Among the fundamental judgments made daily in state courts are the extent to which women (and far less often, men) who forgo careers in order to be full-time caregivers for their households will be compensated beyond the assets accrued during the marriage, and whether men will be considered equal partners in the care and custody of children.

Further, not all cases brought to state courts entail such ostensibly routine matters as divorce or debt collection. State judiciaries often are asked to address the most volatile issues dominating the political agenda. In recent years, state courts have ruled on such hotly debated issues as whether local jurisdictions can refuse to prohibit discrimination based on sexual orientation, whether state legislatures can authorize harsher sentences for crimes motivated by racial prejudice, whether surrogate parenthood contracts are legitimate, and whether relatives can decide to discontinue life-sustaining medical treatment on behalf of terminally ill family members no longer capable of making such judgments themselves. State courts also have conducted a number of sensational criminal trials that inspired considerable debate about several of the most persistent problems confronting American society — racism, economic privilege, police misconduct, and spousal and child abuse.

Because of the volume of litigation and the critical issues presented in the cases, the power of state courts and the judges who interpret, apply, and develop state law is remarkable. But perhaps not widely recognized is the fact that state courts act independently of federal authority in the large majority of cases. Generally speaking, a state court decision is subject to U.S. Supreme Court review only if the case involves some provision of federal law. Matters governed exclusively by state law, where state governments are acting within the parameters established by the Constitution and other federal law, are immune to federal scrutiny.

Also not so obviously, state courts play an important role in the interpretation of federal law, including constitutional law. In a state criminal prosecution, for instance, the defendant may raise issues about jury selection, evidence admissibility, or the propriety of a given sentence, which are matters governed by the U.S. Constitution and other applicable federal and state law. Other examples of controversial issues decided recently by state courts — gay rights, hate crime, surrogate parenthood, and the right to die — also are governed by both federal and state law.

The U.S. Supreme Court has ultimate authority over interpreting the Constitution. However, in cases involving federal constitutional law, the actual application of Supreme Court rulings in state cases rests in the hands of state court judges, who retain significant discretion. Case law may, or may not, exist to cover the particular case being litigated, depending on whether the Supreme Court has been willing to address the issue and whether the specific factual situation has been presented previously. Especially when new issues or fact patterns emerge or when Supreme Court rulings are not clear, state court judges necessarily must rely on their own interpretations of the Constitution to resolve the disputes immediately before their courts. Furthermore, there is some evidence to suggest that even when rulings are relatively clear, compliance with Supreme Court mandates on some issues is neither automatic nor absolute.[7] Moreover, because the Supreme Court currently decides less than two hundred cases per term, the supervisory capacity of the nation's highest court over state supreme courts is quite limited.

Some scholars have noted an increasing tendency for state courts to distance themselves even farther from federal authority by basing state court decisions involving individual rights and liberties solely upon state constitutional grounds. In a trend described as the new judicial federalism, some state supreme courts appear to be moving in a liberal direction, while the U.S. Supreme Court has become more conservative.[8] In other words, some states are not merely conforming to the minimal requirements for protecting individual rights and liberties as dictated by the Supreme Court, but actually are exceeding federal standards. Such behavior is constitutionally permissible; states can heighten the protection of individual rights and liberties by relinquishing state power in favor of such rights. Under well-established principles of federal supremacy, however, states cannot enhance their power by subverting rights beyond what is permitted by the Supreme Court's interpretations of the Constitution.

In sum, state courts are where the action is as far as the overwhelming proportion of litigation is concerned, and the judges who decide these cases have tremendous influence over the development of state and federal law. Quite simply, state courts and those who staff the state court bench have an enormous impact on American politics across all issues of public policy. Perceptions that state courts are not important, based on naive assumptions either about the nature of state court dockets or about the power of the federal courts, are incorrect. A complete understanding of state politics, or more generally, American politics, demands an understanding of state courts — their organization, personnel, and procedures, as well as their decisions.

The Organization and Reform of State Courts

Although efforts to alter the institutional features of courts have been described as a movement, the American states differ dramatically in the types of structural changes enacted over the past several decades and the pace at which these revisions occurred. As one observer commented, "while initiating change in any institution is normally a slow and agonizing process... the legal system is perhaps the most static institution in American society and thus is particularly resistant to innovation."[9] Also, because each state has complete authority over the structure of its judiciary, the fifty states have developed systems of courts reflective of their own unique political values and political history, and the result is that no two state court systems are exactly alike.

Moreover, the politics of revising institutional arrangements, the essence of court reform, is very complex. Any discussion of court reform limited to a single chapter necessarily must oversimplify this fascinating process. Perhaps it is best simply to note that there is no universal agreement about which institutional features are most effective from a management or political perspective, nor is there uniformity in the manner in which certain types of reforms are implemented in practice. Additionally, courts responded, and continue to respond, to a number of management problems without formal structural change. By the 1960s, however, even the most casual observers agreed that substantial alterations in the operations of state judiciaries were necessary to meet the burdens of increased caseloads and to ensure the delivery of justice to the litigants involved in these cases.

As virtually every discussion in the contemporary literature notes, the basic agenda for modern court reform was established by Roscoe Pound in his address to the American Bar Association (ABA) in 1906. In a presentation about the difficulties confronting American courts, Pound produced a comprehensive set of recommendations for restructuring many features of state judiciaries. Pound's recommendations included the consolidation into a unified trial court bench of multiple lower courts having overlapping jurisdictions; the centralization of financing for all courts within a state; the professional administration of courts; and the merit selection of judges, with corresponding removal mechanisms for those not fulfilling the obligations of office. As Dubois indicated, Pound's ideas initially were not warmly received,[10] but his prescriptions for structural reform ultimately were endorsed by the ABA and other important organizations concerned with judicial administration, and they have been enacted into law in various formats in the large majority of American states.

Consolidating Trial Courts

The consolidation of state trial courts emerged as a top priority for those concerned with the quality and efficiency of justice. Throughout the 1960s, many states continued to operate systems in which multiple trial courts had jurisdiction to hear a particular case, where rules of procedure were promulgated by each institution, and where no methods were provided for state supervision of the profusion of lower courts operated by local governments.

Stemming from a strong tradition of connecting justice very closely to the local community, the states historically had authorized local governments to establish a multiplicity of specialized trial courts to resolve the host of cases relevant to municipalities, such as minor criminal offenses and civil disputes involving small amounts of money. These limited-jurisdiction trial courts greatly proliferated in the mid- to late 1800s, especially in cities.[11] As Glick and Vines observed, the creation of these courts represented an innovative response to the increased burdens of litigation being placed on state courts.[12] For instance, small-claims courts were established to provide an inexpensive and nonintimidating forum for settling the sizable population of cases involving the routine collection of debts. Limited-jurisdiction trial courts were established, however, without any attention to maintaining a coherent organizational structure for the state judiciary. Instead, the changes to state judiciaries were "sporadic and haphazard, and little attention was paid to jurisdictional boundaries."[13] And, after a time, these courts found themselves unable to meet the demands of ever-increasing caseloads.

Because limited-jurisdiction trial courts were created, operated, and financed by local governments, they essentially functioned as autonomous institutions within the state judicial system, even though they were responsible for handling the large majority of the cases being litigated at the state level. These kinds of institutional arrangements, wherein local governments have extraordinary discretion in fashioning and operating courts independent from the rest of the state judiciary, result in confusing litigation procedures, provide strategic opportunities for attorneys to engage in court- or judge-shopping, and allow lower-court judges to operate with relatively little supervision and, consequently, little accountability. Court reformers also viewed the fragmentation characteristic of state judiciaries as being largely responsible for "the persistence of archaic management techniques" that only exacerbated the problems facing these courts.[14]

Moreover, these specialized trial courts increasingly came under attack because of the manner in which they processed cases. Highly inefficient jurisdictional arrangements and other management issues aside, critics began using such derogatory labels as "sausage factories" and "assembly lines" to describe limited-jurisdiction trial courts because of the often lax procedures for conducting trials and the lightening speed at which cases were resolved. Additional concerns centered around the fact that many jurisdictions did not require the judges in these courts to be attorneys. In short, the ability of specialized trial courts to achieve substantive justice was seriously called into question.

Given these and other urgent problems, consolidating the various limited-jurisdiction trial courts into the state judicial hierarchy, which would facilitate administrative efficiency, became a priority for those involved in judicial reform. As with all other types of organizational change, however, the consolidation of state trial courts did not meet with universal enthusiasm. As Glick noted, trial attorneys and general-practice lawyers not employed by larger firms opposed consolidation.[15] Understanding the legal labyrinth at the local level was integral to these attorneys' success. And, needless to say, local governments were not willing merely to acquiesce to increased state authority, nor did the incumbents and other personnel within these courts support anything other than the status quo. Further, there was a distinct partisan dimension to court reform. Democrats in cities generally viewed court reform as a Republican political tactic to reduce the Democrats' control over patronage; consequently, urban Democrats tended to oppose changes to existing arrangements.[16]

Moreover, some scholars and practitioners fundamentally disagreed with the notion that a single model for trial court consolidation was appropriate for all state court systems. Several alternative proposals were later developed that provided for varying levels of trial court consolidation, depending upon the particular needs and resources of the state.[17]

Despite the intense controversy over the politics of consolidation, however, Illinois became the first state to consolidate its court system in 1970. Just over a decade later, the Council of State Governments observed that "state courts made remarkable progress."[18] While there still are significant variations in the extent to which trial courts are consolidated, the states have streamlined the litigation process significantly by drastically reducing the number of specialized trial courts, by sharpening jurisdictional boundaries to eliminate or reduce the mess of overlapping jurisdictions, and by bringing these courts under the supervisory jurisdiction of the state supreme court.

Wisconsin is an excellent example of a state that restructured its judiciary to fit the prototype advocated by the court reform movement. Since 1978, Wisconsin has operated only one type of limited-jurisdiction trial court, the Municipal Courts, which have original jurisdiction to hear cases arising under the laws of the municipality where the court is located. The supervision of these courts, like all others in the state, is vested in the Wisconsin Supreme Court. Wisconsin does not have any other limited-jurisdiction trial courts, even those used routinely in other states to resolve small claims cases, or civil cases involving relatively small sums of money. Instead, small-claims divisions are located in the Circuit Courts. The Circuit Courts, which are the only trial courts of general jurisdiction in Wisconsin, have original jurisdiction over all matters arising under state law within their respective geographic jurisdictions (usually counties). In larger jurisdictions, the Circuit Court is organized into separate civil and criminal divisions, to maximize efficiency in processing heavy caseloads.

Arkansas, in contrast, is a state that has chosen not to consolidate its trial courts, although the state has taken a number of other steps in recent decades to modernize its bench. Arkansas continues to operate multiple trial courts of limited jurisdiction: Municipal Courts (the principal courts of limited jurisdiction, hearing misdemeanors, preliminary stages of felonies, and civil cases not exceeding $3,000), City Courts (the main courts of limited jurisdiction for communities not having a Municipal Court, where the mayor acts as judge), Police Courts (similar to City Courts, but where judges are elected as such rather than as executive officers), County Courts (which decide county taxes and expenditures cases), Justice of the Peace Courts (which resolve misdemeanors and civil cases involving less than $300), and Courts of Common Pleas (which hear civil actions not exceeding $1,000).[19] Further, Municipal Courts have small-claims divisions for processing very minor civil matters. These various courts all are funded exclusively by local and county governments rather than under a comprehensive state budget. To some extent, however, these courts have been brought under the supervisory authority of the Arkansas Supreme Court. In addition to the limited-jurisdiction trial courts, Arkansas has two types of general-jurisdiction trial courts — the Circuit Courts and the Chancery and Probate Courts — which serve as the state's major trial courts.

To be sure, the organization of the Arkansas judiciary represents a set of political choices not endorsed by court reformers. As recently as the 1991 legislative session, however, efforts to consolidate Arkansas' general-jurisdiction trial courts and to replace the various limited-jurisdiction trial courts with only one such court per county were resoundingly defeated.

Arkansas does not stand alone on this issue. Recent statistics indicate that eight other states[20] continue to operate four or more trial courts of limited jurisdiction, although these eight states vary considerably in the extent to which they have adopted centralized financing of their lower courts and other aspects of structural reform.[21]

In essence, state trial court consolidation, like most other items on the political agenda, is an ongoing and contentious process. Controversy notwithstanding, the states have done a great deal since the 1960s to eliminate the bewildering jurisdictional arrangements that were of such concern to judicial reformers. Still, the actual consequences of these changes on the state courts' ability to manage their dockets effectively and to achieve justice remain largely unexplored scientifically. Whether, for example, Wisconsin processes cases more efficiently and achieves a higher standard of justice than does Arkansas, and whether, apart from the myriad forces that affect court performance, any differences in these important goals can be attributed directly to court unification, are open questions.

State Financing of the Judiciary

Closely associated with the goal of consolidating local specialized trial courts into the state judicial hierarchy is the transfer of funding for these institutions from local governments to the state. While inadequate funding and other fiscal problems are common to all state courts, centralized financing (and budgeting) is viewed by reformers as a highly effective means to improve the efficiency and quality of the lower courts.

The financing of the various courts within a state's judiciary was, and is, derived from a complicated combination of state, county, and municipal funding sources. Because limited-jurisdiction trial courts traditionally have been seen as within the exclusive province of local governments, however, the states not only failed to incorporate these institutions fully into the state judicial hierarchy but also refused to include them in the state budget. Funding for specialized trial courts rested entirely with city and county governments, which used court fees and fines levied in misdemeanors as revenue to support their operation. Even so, the courts remained at the mercy of local legislative bodies for actual appropriations.

There are numerous consequences to having local courts funded independently of the state budget. Perhaps the most serious repercussion is an uneven distribution of resources among these courts. Given the tremendous variations in local tax bases and lower-court caseloads (which, in turn, affect revenues), some courts within a state are left with seriously insufficient resources. Such matters as the ability to recruit qualified judges and other court personnel, to purchase supplies and equipment, and to acquire and maintain adequate facilities are affected by budgeting arrangements which, in many cases, leave the lower courts floundering. In the *1989–90 An-*

nual Report of the Arkansas Judiciary, for example, Arkansas noted that some judges in its limited-jurisdiction trial courts had no research or clerical assistance and had to answer their own phones and type their own paperwork, in addition to fulfilling their judicial responsibilities.

To assure adequate funding and a more equitable distribution of resources among courts, reformers advocate a shift from local financing to state financing of limited-jurisdiction trial courts. Such a shift is perceived by reformers as a means to achieve a more uniform delivery of services and a higher quality of justice.

The centralization of financing and budgeting for state judiciaries emerged as a distinct trend in the early 1980s. As the Council of State Governments reported, a majority of states had either adopted centralized financing by 1983 or had solid plans to accomplish the task.[22] Twenty-nine states had committed, as of 1983, to provide total or substantial funding of their court systems, while three years earlier, only twenty-two states had adopted such arrangements. Moreover, by 1983, six additional states were considering including the lower courts in their state budgets.[23]

In the 1990s, the momentum for centralized financing and budgeting has stalled. Stumpf and Culver attributed this trend largely to the elimination of federal revenue-sharing grants and increased demands overall on state budgets.[24] State financing of limited-jurisdiction trial courts, even those incorporated into the state judicial structure, therefore ranges from complete financing to absolutely none. Still, centralized financing remains a top priority for court reformers. And, as with trial court unification, the political implications of the centralized financing of a state's limited-jurisdiction trial courts as an alternative to local funding have not been fully explored.

Professional Administration of the State Judiciary

A third item on the agenda of court reform is the professional management of state judiciaries. Unlike other suggested reforms, the professional administration of state courts has received universal acclaim. Prior to 1960, twenty-two states had already created offices of state court administrator.[25] Just a decade later, thirty-seven states had established such offices, and by 1977, all of the states had joined in the movement. Every American state now has a judicial administrator, who usually works under the direction of the Chief Justice and has statewide authority.

Inspired by such serious problems as haphazard record keeping, the inability to track cases effectively, litigants and witnesses being lost in the shuffle of endless paperwork, and almost crippling backlogs, establishing a centralized office directed by a professional administrator was viewed as essential to addressing the challenges facing state courts. In a relatively short period of time, judicial administrators have become an integral part of the state judicial system. And, unlike changing basic institutional structures, adding professional management to the courts was a relatively painless and noncontroversial means to improve judicial efficiency.

State court administrators have a wide range of responsibilities that depend, in part, on the resources of the state. Judicial administrators perform the fundamental function of collecting data and preparing statistical reports. This important information is used for a variety of purposes but is especially important for designing solutions to the particular problems confronting a state's courts.

State court administrators also assist the state supreme court in designing rules of procedure that govern the conduct of trials and appeals. They supervise the process of transferring judges within the system from one court to another on a temporary basis to deal with caseload problems. Court administrators provide, and seek out, educational opportunities for judges and other court personnel (e.g., orientations for new judges, continuing legal education opportunities). They engage in grant writing to seek funds from federal programs and private agencies to support special projects, and explore ways in which the latest technological innovations can be used in courtrooms and administrative offices. In short, court administrators are involved in the entire spectrum of activities related to the judicial process and have become an indispensable part of the state judiciary.

Intermediate Appellate Courts

The trial courts were not the only state courts confronting severe problems in the 1960s. Appellate courts faced the same crises of management and conscience that plagued the rest of the state judiciary. State supreme courts, or courts of last resort,[26] were severely overburdened by massive numbers of appeals and were having substantial difficulty processing cases in anything approaching a timely fashion. Therefore, resolving the problem of overloaded appellate dockets became another essential cornerstone of the judicial reform movement.

Differences in structure and function between trial courts and appellate courts render structural solutions designed for the trial courts completely unworkable for appellate courts. For instance, simply increasing the number of judges on the states' highest courts was not a viable option for enhancing the capacity and efficiency of these institutions. Unlike trial courts where only one judge decides each case, state supreme courts generally sit *en banc,* where all of the judges on the court collectively review each case.[27] Expanding the size of a supreme court would have no effect on the ability to process more cases or to decide them more quickly. Indeed, even the most naive observers of judicial politics recognized that substantially increasing the number of judges on the states' highest courts was likely to decrease, rather than increase, the efficiency of these institutions.

TABLE 6.1. STATES BEGINNING TO OPERATE INTERMEDIATE APPELLATE COURTS

_1962–63*_	_1966–67_	_1968–69_	_1970–71_	_1974–75_
Alabama	Arizona	Maryland	Colorado	Massachusetts
California	Michigan	New Mexico	Oklahoma	
Florida		North Carolina	Oregon	
Georgia			Washington	
Illinois				
Indiana				
Louisiana				
Missouri				
New Jersey				
New York				
Ohio				
Pennsylvania				
Tennessee				
Texas				

_1978–79_	_1980–81_	_1982–83_	_1984–85_	_1986–87_
Iowa	Arkansas	Hawaii	Alaska	South Carolina
Kansas	Wisconsin	Idaho	Connecticut	Virginia
Kentucky			Minnesota	

_1988–89_	_1992–93_
Utah	Nebraska

Source: Council of State Governments, _Book of the States_ (years as indicated).
*On or before 1962–63

The structural alternative advocated by reformers for resolving the appellate court caseload crisis was the expansion of the state appellate structure from a single-tiered to a two-tiered system.[28] Under the new jurisdictional arrangements, intermediate appellate courts[29] would handle the vast majority of appeals from the trial courts, leaving supreme courts with the discretion to choose only the most important cases for their dockets. In other words, intermediate appellate courts would remove caseload pressures from supreme courts by assuming responsibility for the bulk of appeals from the trial courts. And because intermediate appellate courts usually decide cases using three-judge panels instead of sitting _en banc,_ any court composed of at least six judges could resolve different cases simultaneously. More broadly, intermediate appellate courts were part of a comprehensive plan to create unified, hierarchical systems of justice in the American states.

Table 6.1 documents the pace at which the states added intermediate appellate courts to their court systems. As the data demonstrate, only fourteen states operated intermediate appellate courts at the begin-

TABLE 6.2. THE NUMBER OF JUDGES SERVING IN STATE APPELLATE COURTS

State	Court of Last Resort	Intermediate Appellate Court	State	Court of Last Resort	Intermediate Appellate Court
Alabama	9	5	Montana	7	—
Alaska	5	3	Nebraska	7	6
Arizona	5	21	Nevada	5	—
Arkansas	7	6	New Hampshire	5	—
California	7	88	New Jersey	7	30
Colorado	7	16	New Mexico	5	10
Connecticut	7	9	New York	7	48
Delaware	5	—	North Carolina	7	12
Florida	7	57	North Dakota	5	—
Georgia	7	9	Ohio	7	65
Hawaii	5	3	Oklahoma	9a	12
Idaho	5	3	Oregon	7	10
Illinois	7	42	Pennsylvania	7	15
Indiana	5	15	Rhode Island	5	—
Iowa	9	6	South Carolina	5	6
Kansas	7	10	South Dakota	5	—
Kentucky	7	14	Tennessee	5	12
Louisiana	7	54	Texas	9b	80
Maine	7	—	Utah	5	7
Maryland	7	13	Vermont	5	—
Massachusetts	7	14	Virginia	7	10
Michigan	7	24	Washington	9	17
Minnesota	7	16	West Virginia	5	—
Mississippi	9	—	Wisconsin	7	13
Missouri	7	32	Wyoming	5	—

Source: Council of State Governments, Book of the States, 1996–97.

a. Statistic reported for the Supreme Court; 5 judges sit on the Court of Criminal Appeals.
b. 9 judges sit on the Court of Criminal Appeals.

ning of the 1960s. But by the end of the 1970s, a majority of states had established these institutions, and by the early 1990s, thirty-eight states had the two-tiered system of appellate courts recommended by judicial reformers.[30]

Although most states now have intermediate appellate courts, these courts are far from uniform. Intermediate appellate courts differ significantly from state to state in such features as size, organization, and the exact nature of their dockets.[31] Table 6.2 presents data about the number of judges currently serving in state appellate courts, including both intermediate appellate courts and supreme courts. As the table demonstrates, intermediate appellate courts currently have from three to eighty-eight judges staffing the bench. Some states have created one intermediate appellate court with a statewide jurisdiction, while others have organized circuits and operate an intermediate appellate court branch or division within each circuit. Finally, dockets vary among these courts. In some states, intermediate appellate courts receive all cases properly appealed from the trial courts;

state supreme courts then have the discretion to choose which cases they wish to review. Other states, however, have a somewhat different juris- dictional scheme: rather than going directly from the trial courts to the intermediate appellate courts, most cases go first to the supreme court, which has the authority to accept the case, reject it, or assign it to the intermediate appellate court. Within both schemes, however, intermediate appellate courts have mandatory dockets while supreme courts have largely discretionary dockets.[32]

As with all reforms, an essential question remains: Have intermedi- ate appellate courts been successful in helping to alleviate the appellate caseload crunch? The answer seems to be a definite "yes." Numerous studies have concluded uniformly that intermediate appellate courts have increased both the capacity and the efficiency of state judiciaries by reduc- ing caseload pressures on supreme courts and by providing an additional forum for the resolution of disputes at the appellate level.[33] Intermediate appellate courts have absorbed most of the increases in litigation in recent years and appear to be keeping pace with current litigation trends.[34] In- deed, a cursory examination of caseload statistics from Nebraska, the latest state to create an intermediate appellate court, demonstrates the point quite clearly. In 1991, the year preceding the inclusion of an intermediate appel- late court in the Nebraska judiciary, the Nebraska Supreme Court received 834 mandatory filings. However, with the operation of the intermediate ap- pellate court in 1992, the level of mandatory filings in Nebraska's highest court dropped precipitously to forty.[35]

As mentioned at the beginning of this chapter, adding intermediate appellate courts to state judiciaries has affected more than caseload pro- cessing. As many scholars have observed, the introduction of intermediate appellate courts has had a profound effect on the power of state supreme courts and the individuals who hold office in these institutions. Because the lower tier of appellate institutions now handles the overwhelming bulk of appellate cases, state supreme courts have been freed from the drudgery of overburdened, highly routine caseloads. By transforming the dockets of supreme courts, intermediate appellate courts have heightened the policy making role of the states' highest courts. As Glick stated so succinctly, "the more discretion, the more opportunities a court has to select cases which may have a social impact."[36] And, as the policymaking role of an institution increases, the power of individual decision makers within the institution increases.

The political impact of two-tiered appellate structures is particularly evident in three important dimensions of state supreme court decision mak- ing: (1) the extent to which supreme court justices assert their power over state legislatures through the process of judicial review, (2) the willingness of individual justices to dissent, and (3) the ability of the justices to promote their personal preferences in the cases resolved by their courts.[37]

Judicial review. State supreme courts vary in how frequently they are presented with opportunities to overturn acts of state legislatures and how often they actually do it (an action generally defined as judicial activism). A study of all fifty states documented that from 1981 through 1985, 2,660 state laws in 3,248 court cases were challenged as unconstitutional in state supreme courts.[38] There were significant variations among the states, however, in the number of laws challenged, ranging from only 14 in Texas to 165 in Georgia, with an average of about 53 laws challenged per state during the five-year period. Moreover, there were important variations among supreme courts with regard to the proportion of statutes actually invalidated. During 1981 to 1985, invalidation rates ranged from about 3 percent to 46 percent, with an overall total of about one-fourth of the challenged statutes being declared unconstitutional. More importantly, variations among supreme courts in both the opportunities for activism (i.e., the number of statutes challenged) and in the exercise of judicial activism (i.e., the invalidation of statutes being challenged) were correlated significantly with discretionary appellate dockets, or the presence of intermediate appellate courts.[39] Stated differently, intermediate appellate courts have had a substantial influence on the ability and willingness of supreme courts to become aggressive players in state politics by challenging legislatures in the lawmaking process.

Judicial dissent. Intermediate appellate courts have facilitated the expression of dissent, or higher levels of formal internal conflict, in state supreme courts. Dissent rates measure the proportion of cases in which at least one judge openly expressed disagreement with the court's decision. Countless studies have documented the correlation between a two-tiered appellate structure and the willingness of state supreme court justices to cast votes contrary to their court majorities.

One might expect dissent to result simply from ideological disagreement; a justice dissents because he or she does not agree with the majority's decision about the proper outcome of the case. However, dissent rates are determined by a variety of factors, including the court's docket type, the internal operating rules of the court, and conditions in the external environment.[40] Intermediate appellate courts, however, are a primary factor in promoting the expression of dissent. Most basically, courts with mandatory dockets (i.e., intermediate appellate courts and supreme courts in states lacking a two-tiered appellate structure) are required to review large numbers of cases that are relatively routine, where few opportunities occur for finding error or for generating disagreement among the judges. Hence, courts with mandatory dockets tend to have relatively low dissent rates. Alternatively, courts with discretionary dockets (i.e., supreme courts in states with a two-tiered appellate structure) are presented with far fewer routine cases, and they actively select cases for review that involve more important or controversial issues. Consequently, courts that enjoy docket control manifest higher levels of dissent. The most recently collected data on dissent rates in state supreme courts indicate that from 1980 to 1981, California ranked highest among states, with a dissent rate of 54.8 percent, while Hawaii ranked lowest with a dissent rate of 2.4 percent.[41]

What difference does the formal expression of dissent make politically? The answers to this question are numerous and complex. Divisiveness among the members of a state's highest court politicizes the court by shattering the myth of certainty in the law, leaving the legitimacy of the court's rulings vulnerable to attack from the public and other institutions. Dissent also makes coalition formation within the institution more challenging, which, in turn, facilitates political maneuvering to build and maintain majorities. And, from the perspective of the individual justice, dissenting clearly distinguishes the justice from the rest of the court, leaving the justice open to attack or accolade, depending on the issue. In short, dissent serves to demystify the judicial function and lift the protection of the "purple curtain" from courts and from individual officeholders.

Judicial preference. Two-tiered appellate arrangements enhance the opportunities for state supreme court justices to promote their personal preferences in the court's decisions. Discretionary dockets, which result from lower appellate courts handling first appeals, free supreme courts from the burdens of large, routine caseloads, where few opportunities arise for developing innovative solutions to the problems embodied in the cases. Docket control allows justices to select cases for review that involve the most divisive and critically important political issues, where the law is not well established and where flexibility exists in shaping law to a particular conflict. Justices who render judgments in these cases necessarily must rely upon their personal perceptions of justice, or ideological preferences, to construct workable solutions to concrete problems. Indeed, these propositions are entirely consistent with the voluminous literature on the U.S. Supreme Court, which has a discretionary docket and where the justices' political preferences are a primary factor in how they decide cases.[42]

Alternatively, mandatory dockets, which are characteristic of intermediate appellate courts and supreme courts in states lacking a two-tiered appellate structure, provide few opportunities for the judges to utilize their particular preferences about matters of public policy to fashion interesting solutions to the cases. Wold and Caldeira remarked about the California Courts of Appeals, "because of the 'routineness' of most cases, the justices...have few opportunities for legal innovation or creativity. They perceived their job chiefly as the 'processing' of a large and very repetitive caseload."[43] Accordingly, "the ideological positions of the justices are not and cannot be critical influences in the vast majority of cases."[44]

State Judicial Selection and the Promotion of the Missouri Plan

One of the most enduring issues of American politics is how to select judges for the state court bench. Because of the intense controversy necessarily associated with decisions about who controls access to political power, the subject of judicial selection has produced endless debate, replete with countless claims and counterclaims about the various alternative selection schemes. At the heart of the recent controversy is the insistence by judicial reform advocates that partisan and nonpartisan elections have detrimental effects on the operations of courts. Among other things, elections are seen as inhibiting the willingness of qualified attorneys to seek judicial office, and as interjecting improper political considerations into the judicial arena without actually ensuring the accountability expected of electoral schemes.

The selection system that has become de rigueur with court reformers and most judicial politics scholars is the "merit plan," or Missouri Plan. Introduced formally in 1937 by the American Bar Association, with the enthusiastic endorsement of such organizations as the American Judicature Society and the League of Women Voters, the "merit plan" was put into practice for the first time in Missouri in 1940.

The Missouri Plan evolved from the growing dissatisfaction with the union between electoral politics and judicial selection. While all state court judges initially were chosen by legislatures or governors (and in some states still are), the emergence of Jacksonian democracy in the 1820s triggered a movement to transfer the responsibility for selecting judges from political elites to the electorate. In 1832, Mississippi became the first state to establish a completely elected judiciary, and every state entering the Union from 1846 through 1912 mandated the selection of judges through popular election.[45] Initially the states used partisan elections to choose judges. However, concerns about the dominance of political parties quickly led to the adoption in some states of an alternative electoral scheme — nonpartisan judicial elections. The partisan election movement reached its zenith in the 1840s, while nonpartisan elections reached their peak in the latter part of the nineteenth century.[46] Despite their popularity as mechanisms for judicial selection, both partisan and nonpartisan elections were denounced by court reformers. Surprisingly, legislative selection and gubernatorial appointment have received scant attention or direct criticism from those who favor the Missouri Plan; the plan is designed primarily to replace elections rather than alternative appointment schemes.

The Missouri Plan is an interesting hybrid of appointment and election systems and is touted as capturing the best features of both. While there are significant variations from state to state in the way the Missouri Plan actually operates,[47] the basic process begins with the governor's appointment of a judicial nominating commission that has the responsibility for recommending candidates for each vacancy. As vacancies occur, the commission

TABLE 6.3. METHODS FOR SELECTING STATE COURT JUDGES:
COURTS OF LAST RESORT, 1962–63

Partisan elections	Nonpartisan elections	Missouri Plan	Gubernatorial appointment	Legislative election
Alabama	Arizona	Alaska	Connecticut	Rhode Island
Arkansas	Idaho	California	Delaware	South Carolina
Colorado	Michigan	Kansas	Hawaii	Vermont
Florida	Minnesota	Maryland	Maine	Virginia
Georgia	Montana	Missouri	Massachusetts	
Illinois	Nebraska		New Hampshire	
Indiana	Nevada		New Jersey	
Iowa	North Dakota			
Kentucky	Ohio			
Louisiana	Oregon			
Mississippi	South Dakota			
New Mexico	Washington			
New York	Wisconsin			
North Carolina	Wyoming			
Oklahoma				
Pennsylvania				
Tennessee				
Texas				
Utah				
West Virginia				

Source: Council of State Governments, *Book of the States*, 1962–63.

screens potential nominees, evaluating their qualifications for the judgeship. The commission then presents a list of three candidates to the governor, who must appoint one of the three to fill the vacancy. Upon appointment, the nominee immediately assumes office. Shortly thereafter, usually in the next general election, the candidate must win voter approval in a retention election. Retention elections ask voters to decide whether a current office-holder should continue in office; opposing candidates do not appear on the ballot, nor is the partisan affiliation of the candidate listed on the ballot. If the voters approve, the judge begins a regular term of office, facing subsequent retention elections at the end of every term. If voters disapprove, the process begins anew.

Because candidates' credentials are screened by nominating commissions, reformers argue that the Missouri Plan results in the recruitment of significantly more qualified judges than those chosen in partisan or nonpartisan elections. Additionally, Missouri Plan advocates believe that because voters have the opportunity to remove unacceptable judges in retention elections, the plan ensures continued popular control over the bench.

Tables 6.3 and 6.4 provide information about the methods the American states used in the 1960s and the 1990s to staff their highest courts. As table 6.3 demonstrates, in the early 1960s twenty states held partisan elections, fourteen states used nonpartisan elections, seven states favored

TABLE 6.4. METHODS FOR SELECTING STATE COURT JUDGES:
COURTS OF LAST RESORT, 1996–97

Partisan elections	Nonpartisan elections	Missouri Plan	Gubernatorial appointment	Legislative election
Alabama	Georgia	Alaska	Connecticut	Rhode Island
Arkansas	Idaho	Arizona	Delaware[c]	South Carolina
Illinois[a]	Kentucky	California	Hawaii[c]	Virginia
Louisiana	Michigan	Colorado	Maine	
Mississippi	Minnesota	Florida	Massachusetts[c]	
North Carolina	Montana	Indiana	New Hampshire	
Pennsylvania[a]	Nevada	Iowa	New Jersey	
Tennessee	North Dakota	Kansas	New York	
Texas	Ohio[b]	Maryland	Vermont[c]	
West Virginia	Oregon	Missouri		
	Washington	Nebraska		
	Wisconsin	New Mexico[a]		
		Oklahoma		
		South Dakota		
		Utah		
		Wyoming		

Source: Council of State Governments, *Book of the States,* 1996–97.

a. Retention elections after initial partisan election
b. Partisan primaries
c. Governor's choices limited to list provided by the Judicial Nominating
   Commission

gubernatorial appointment, and four states used legislative election. As of 1962, only five states employed the Missouri Plan to select supreme court justices.

As table 6.4 indicates, however, numerous states have altered the means by which they recruit and retain supreme court justices. Since the 1960s, fifteen states (or 30 percent) have changed plans for staffing their highest courts, with eleven of fifteen adopting the Missouri Plan.[48] The Missouri Plan now has won approval in a total of sixteen states. As table 6.4 also documents, however, some features of the Missouri Plan have been adopted in states where governors appoint justices. Four of the states using gubernatorial appointment restrict the governor's nominations to candidates recommended by judicial nominating commissions.[49] Finally, twenty-two states still use partisan elections or nonpartisan elections to staff their supreme courts.[50] Clearly, judicial elections have retained their popularity in a large proportion of states.

Contrary to formal descriptions, the politics of judicial selection is amazingly complicated. For instance, there often are substantial differences between formal selection mechanisms and informal practice. Because governors have the power to make *ad interim* appointments to replace judges who leave office before the completion of their terms, many judges in elective systems actually get their jobs initially through appointment rather than by winning an election. Moreover, as a highly effective political maneuver, judges frequently choose, quite intentionally, to resign or retire from the bench during their terms if their political party controls the governorship. Through strategic retirements and *ad interim* appointments, the political party retains control of the office and the new appointee gains the advantage of running as an incumbent in the next regular election.

In a study of elected state supreme courts, Herndon reported that 56.4 percent of the justices serving from 1948 through 1957 initially were appointed rather than elected.[51] Similarly, Dubois noted that slightly more than half (52.7 percent) of all justices serving in state supreme courts from 1948 through 1974 first obtained their positions through appointment rather than election.[52] In short, gubernatorial appointment is much more widely used than formal descriptions indicate, and seemingly straightforward selection procedures often are manipulated to achieve critical political goals. Of course, these patterns of executive influence and party loyalty are overt in appointive systems, including the Missouri Plan. Governors have a pronounced tendency to appoint members of their party to judicial nominating commissions and to judgeships.

Complexities aside, two primary empirical questions dominate the controversy over judicial selection: (1) Does the Missouri Plan improve the quality of the bench? and (2) Do retention elections guarantee continued popular control over the judiciary?[53] First, as mentioned, a fundamental argument of those favoring the Missouri Plan is that it produces a superior bench.[54] Given the importance of this contention to the controversy raging over how to choose judges, does empirical evidence support the proposition that the Missouri Plan recruits better judges? To the extent that quality can be measured objectively, the evidence accumulated to date suggests not.

In a comprehensive study of the career experiences and background characteristics of state supreme court justices, Glick and Emmert concluded that the credentials (e.g., prestige of legal education, prior legal and judicial experience) and backgrounds (e.g., gender, religion, race) of those selected for judgeships are quite similar, regardless of the method of selection.[55] Moreover, their findings are perfectly consistent with earlier studies of judicial selection.[56] Basically, the Missouri Plan does not appear to result in the recruitment of judges who differ in any obvious ways from judges chosen by other methods, including elections.[57]

A second question relevant to the debate over judicial selection is whether the Missouri Plan provides an adequate level of electoral accountability. Though this question is enormously difficult to answer, empirical research indicates that the Missouri Plan, at least by some measures, does not.[58]

Research on judicial elections (partisan, nonpartisan, and retention elections) has documented two distinct trends in these races: a pronounced incumbency advantage and low levels of voter turnout.[59] As numerous studies also have established, however, retention elections produce a level of incumbency defeat and voter participation lower than that of any other type of judicial election. In a study of supreme court elections in twenty-three states from 1948 through 1972, Dubois determined that the incumbency advantage is highest in retention races, less in nonpartisan elections, and lowest in partisan elections.[60] Dubois also reported that voter participation is lowest in retention elections and highest in partisan elections.[61] Others have documented similar patterns. Watson and Downing found that only one of 179 judges facing retention from 1942 to 1964 in Missouri was defeated.[62] Similarly, Hall and Aspin noted that there were only 22 defeats in 1,864 trial court retention elections (or 1.2 percent) in ten states from 1964 to 1984.[63] They also described voter turnout in these elections as characteristically poor.

There are a number of plausible explanations for why incumbents rarely are unseated in retention elections and why these elections fail to capture the attention of the electorate. On one hand, incumbents might win simply because there is no reason to vote them out; nominating commissions arguably choose candidates less in need of ousting than judges chosen by the electorate in partisan and nonpartisan elections. Of course, one of the primary contentions of Missouri Plan advocates is the superiority of Missouri Plan judges. As already noted, however, there is no evidence to indicate that judges in Missouri Plan states are better qualified than judges chosen by other means.

An alternative, and more plausible, explanation is that retention races fail to provide adequate voting cues to voters and do not generate sufficient campaign hoopla to stimulate voter interest. Partisan labels, the single most important voting cue in American elections, are noticeably absent in retention races. The removal of partisan labels from judicial elections is viewed as a giant step forward by judicial reformers, who prefer that voters cast their ballots on the basis of the candidates' credentials rather than their political party affiliation. Indeed, states using nonpartisan elections agree with Missouri Plan advocates on this point. Because electoral campaigns in retention elections tend not to involve opposing candidates aggressively challenging incumbents' records or raising significant issues, however, voters are presented with little information about incumbents and are not stimulated by campaign activity or controversy to pay attention or to vote. In fact, gathering information about an incumbent seeking retention can be a daunting task. The net result is that many voters simply do not bother to vote, and incumbents win by default.

Because incumbents rarely are defeated and only a small proportion of the voters actually cast ballots in retention elections, many have concluded that the Missouri Plan fails to provide for popular control of the judiciary. The rates of incumbency success and voter turnout are so reduced in retention elections relative to partisan and nonpartisan elections that the ability of retention elections to provide a meaningful degree of electoral accountability is seriously called into question.

This issue of accountability can be addressed from a somewhat different perspective. While the research just discussed uses incumbency defeat and voter turnout as indicators of popular control, other studies have suggested that accountability (whereby judges conform, at least to some extent, to constituency preferences when casting votes in the cases before their courts) is a form of judicial behavior. In other words, some scholars view accountability as a form of constituency influence in the judicial process, where judges are linked to voters by the threat of electoral defeat and therefore vote in accordance with perceived constituency preferences on highly salient issues.

There is some very interesting evidence demonstrating that, at least on the issue of the death penalty, justices chosen under competitive electoral conditions (e.g., having been challenged in previous races; winning previous elections by narrow margins) are highly unlikely to overturn death sentences in capital cases, simply because doing so would be a politically unpopular act. Citizens across the nation strongly favor capital punishment for heinous murders, and a justice who overturns death sentences in these cases is likely to face the wrath of angry voters and possible political challengers.[64] In order to retain their seats, justices acquiesce to the preferences of their constituencies.

This situation, wherein justices base their decisions, at least in part, on perceived constituency preferences and possible sanctions in the electoral process, is the ultimate dread of judicial reformers, who perceive any type of constituency influence in the judicial process as wholly illegitimate. Perhaps it is important to observe that conflicts between the principles of judicial independence and accountability are inevitable, and decisions about how to balance these competing values are normative. Moreover, while judicial independence is highly valued by Missouri Plan advocates, independence is not supposed to come at the expense of popular control. Nonetheless, if competitive elections promote accountability, then surely the Missouri Plan does not. As evidence suggests, justices who anticipate electoral challenge or possible defeat do not experience the same linkages with their constituencies as do those acting in a more competitive environment.[65]

The issue of its effectiveness as a tool for judicial accountability aside, the Missouri Plan has had a pronounced impact on the operational environments of state supreme courts. Because it removes any serious threat of electoral sanction, the Missouri Plan has enhanced the power of state supreme court justices while simultaneously reducing the power of the electorate. Justices in "merit plan" states have little to fear from voters and consequently have greater latitude in deciding cases in accordance with their own ideological preferences. Alternatively, competitive electoral conditions, more likely with partisan and nonpartisan elections, serve as an important constraint on justices deciding controversial cases. Justices who face the possibility of stiff electoral competition from opposing candidates and active voters incited by aggressive campaigns have less discretion in the way they decide such cases. These justices must take constituency preferences into account in order to survive politically, even if their personal preferences are very much to the contrary.

The Missouri Plan continues to be promoted as the most effective means for selecting judges in the American states. As with state trial court consolidation, however, not everybody is buying. In 1987 Ohio refused formally to replace nonpartisan elections with the Missouri Plan. According to Felice and Kilwein, voters essentially viewed the matter as a voting rights issue and refused, by a two-to-one margin, to relinquish any control over the composition of the state court bench.[66] Arkansas also rejected the Missouri Plan in its 1991 legislative session.[67] Every year, nonetheless, the states continue to do battle over this issue. The conflict over the selection of judges is far from resolved.

THE AMERICAN STATES have taken dramatic steps in the past few decades to address a host of serious problems burdening state courts. To confront the critical challenges facing courts at every level of the judicial hierarchy, the states significantly altered the organizational structure of their state judiciaries. State court systems of the past, characterized by bewildering and inefficient jurisdictional arrangements, inadequate financing generated at the local level, a lack of professional management, and severely overburdened dockets at both trial and appellate levels, have been replaced with much more professionalized and efficient systems of justice. State courts of the 1990s are, without a doubt, far better equipped to meet the enormous responsibility of resolving the overwhelming proportion of formal conflict in the United States. Indeed, state courts seem well positioned to address the ongoing problems common to the judicial process and to meet the new challenges of the twenty-first century.

As noted in this discussion, the effects of the various changes in institutional arrangements on judicial efficiency and other factors related to the performance of courts have not been investigated sufficiently. Many questions about the politics of judicial reform remain unanswered. There is a dire need for scholars to explore why certain states adopt particular reforms, and what ultimate effect these reforms have on the efficiency and capacity of courts.

Moreover, our understanding of the effects of institutional context on judicial behavior and of the power of courts in the political process is rather poor. As described, several institutional changes — such as the transformation from one-tiered to two-tiered appellate systems and the adoption of the Missouri Plan for choosing judges in a number of states — have had a resounding impact on the politics of the states' highest courts. By releasing supreme courts from the onerous burdens of large, repetitive caseloads, and by lessening the connection between supreme court justices and the electorate, these institutional changes have permitted supreme courts and the individuals who occupy the bench to exercise greater discretion. How other forms of institutional change influence judicial decision making has yet to be determined. Research into the consequences of institutional arrangements on the politics of courts is in its infancy.

As it stands, state courts are enormously powerful institutions whose members have a profound impact on the distribution of wealth and power in the United States. Furthermore, the power of these institutions, and those who occupy the bench, may continue to increase with future changes in the organizational features of these institutions. Overcoming ignorance of the politics of state courts is necessary for a complete understanding of American politics and the vital role played by judicial institutions in the political process. Stated simply, state courts no longer can be dismissed as inconsequential, and arguments about the advantages or disadvantages of particular reforms cannot continue to be justified solely upon normative grounds.

Astute observers of American politics ultimately must become watchful of state courts as both those institutions and the nature of federalism in the United States continue to evolve. If, in fact, the national government pursues its current course of retrenchment while the U.S. Supreme Court simultaneously enforces barriers against federal encroachment into areas of traditional state activity, the power of the states and their courts, particularly those at the apex of states judiciaries, will continue to expand well beyond already significant levels. State judicial politics, largely ignored by scholars of both judicial and state politics, will demand attention and evaluation, and studies of these institutions will serve to promote a comprehensive understanding of "who gets what, and how" in the United States.

CHAPTER SEVEN

The Embattled Mayors and Local Executives

James H. Svara

THE IMAGE OF the local executive may be one of power and control. If it is true that "you can't fight city hall," as some believe, then the person in charge of city hall must be a powerful person indeed. In actuality, these officials are embattled because they are on the front line in confronting a wide range of challenging situations. They are held accountable for their government's success despite deficiencies in power and resources to tackle the problems of their cities. Because local government is close to citizens and the most accessible level of government, local officials experience the dissatisfaction citizens have with all levels of government, whether or not their own jurisdiction is doing well. Having to meet impossible expectations with limited resources is a prescription for frustration, but it is the situation mayors and other local executives face. The fact that there are many leaders who take on this challenge with dedication and enthusiasm, and who compile records of successful action, indicates another aspect of their situation: they have the potential to make an observable difference in the quality of life in their community. The flip side of being a visible, accessible, and vulnerable official is the possibility of being a leader who can see the results of his or her efforts.

Cities have one executive and one mayor, but the two offices are not necessarily combined. Cities that use the mayor-council form of government vest executive powers in an elected official — the mayor — who is the political head of city government and in charge of the administrative organization. The executive mayor ultimately has authority of hiring and supervising staff, formulating and (after approval by the council) expending the budget, and directing the organization, subject to the city charter. In council-manager cities, it is the city manager — an executive appointed by the city council — who exercises these powers. These cities also have a mayor who is the political head of the government and presides over the city council, but usually has no powers not available to other members of the council. The overlap is shown in figure 7.1 (p. 140).

Each of these officials can make an important contribution to city government. On the surface, executive mayors in the strong mayor-council

FIGURE 7.1. DISTRIBUTION OF POWERS IN COUNCIL-MANAGER CITIES

form have the greatest potential because they can draw on two sources of leadership. As we shall see, however, there are also structural and political constraints in this form of government which can frustrate this official or limit total governmental capacity.

Context and Conditions of Mayors and City Managers

As background, it is useful to review the general constraints on leadership by local officials, the basic features of the mayor-council and council-manager forms of government, and the major dimensions of leadership. It will then be possible to profile each of these types of officials and the nature and sources of their leadership.

Constraints on Local Officials

The factors that hold back local officials are the weakness of cities in the federal system, disparity of resources in metropolitan areas, restricted resources, and rampant pluralism in the local political process. Each factor will be briefly explained. Local governments are the lowest rung in the American federal system. Cities are creatures of state government, which maintains a degree of control over how they operate. Cities can use only those revenues that have been permitted by the state and can exercise only those powers that have been authorized. Although in the past cities have received substantial federal government assistance, the amount of federal aid has been shrinking in the past since the late 1970s. In 1980 — just after the peak of federal contributions — state and federal funds accounted for 37 percent of municipal budgets. In 1992 intergovernmental revenues had dropped to 28 percent because federal funds declined from 16 to 7 percent. City governments increasingly rely on their own resources to replace lost intergovernmental revenues.

In addition to state restrictions, many cities, especially central cities and older suburbs, face an imbalance between the needs they must address and the resources they can command. Commercial centers, factories, research parks, and higher-value residential property have been moving to the outer areas of metropolitan areas. Central cities and older suburbs, geographically hemmed in by other suburban municipalities and/or precluded from expanding their boundaries because of restrictions on annexations in most states, are experiencing a loss of residents, jobs, and other resources that generate revenues. At the same time, their populations increasingly consist of the elderly, the poor, minorities, and new immigrants who have substantial need for government services. With higher incidence of poverty and fewer economic opportunities, cities experience higher levels of crime and social neglect and are less able to maintain their facilities and infrastructure. The option of consolidating central cities with their surrounding counties to pool resources has not been a politically feasible strategy. Suburban residents have long resisted being reunited with the central city, while, in the past thirty years, African Americans in the central city have tended to oppose the dilution of their voting strength by adding predominantly white suburban residents to the city electorate.

The social dynamics of cities have also presented challenges to local government officials. Cities have attracted diverse populations. A wide range of groups with divergent value systems make it difficult for officials to find common ground, and the competition among groups for opportunities strains social cohesion. Officials have difficulty sorting out and prioritizing the demands and complaints from their citizens, and they may also experience high levels of conflict in their own ranks, reflecting the divisions in the urban society as a whole. The ability to manage conflict is often essential to making decisions and delivering services. Without it, city government can be immobilized and simply react to crises rather than planning and anticipating problems.

Given the importance of delivering services in local government, how officials lead and control administrative departments and staff is critical to the effectiveness of the government. City government, some contend, is so centralized, that is, dominated by top officials at the "center" who must approve actions and make resources available, that staff flexibility and responsiveness are undermined.[1] Others argue that city government is so decentralized, that is, influence is dispersed widely in the organization, that there can be no effective control over the performance of departments and street-level staff.

All cities experience these tendencies at least to some extent, and they become more likely to occur as the size of the city and the metropolitan area increases. There can be variation, however, in the level of conflict among officials (as opposed to conflict in the population as a whole) and in the degree to which administrative departments and staff work cooperatively with elected officials, depending of the form of government used in the city.

TABLE 7.1. FORMS OF GOVERNMENT BY SIZE OF CITY

Population	Mayor-Council	Council-Manager	Other[a]	Number of cities
2,500–4,999	63.8	28.7	7.5	1968
5,000–9,999	50.1	38.4	11.6	1838
10,000–24,999	42.3	46.6	11.1	1602
25,000–49,999	35.0	59.1	5.9	682
50,000–99,999	34.9	63.0	2.1	338
100,000–249,999	35.9	61.1	3.1	131
250,000–499,999	41.0	53.8	5.1	39
500,000–999,999	82.4	17.6	0.0	17
1 million and over	75.0	25.0	0.0	8

Source: *The Municipal Yearbook,* 1995.

a. Includes commission, town meeting, and representative town meeting.

Forms of Government

In contrast to governments at the national and state levels in the United States, which are similar in their basic structure, local government organization is based on two different constitutional principles — the separation of powers found in mayor-council cities, and the unitary model (which incorporates some elements of parliamentary government) found in council-manager cities.[2] "Reformers" organized in the National Municipal League promoted the new council-manager form of government in the early decades of the twentieth century as part of a package of institutional changes designed to improve the performance and efficiency of city government and to combat corruption. It was well established by the 1930s but still limited to a small minority of cities, and few cities changed form of government during the Depression or war years. After World War II, however, the use of the form exploded in cities of all sizes, as additional cities changed their structure to handle the great expansion in infrastructure construction and growth in services to accommodate postwar development. Compared to 1945, the proportion of cities using the council-manager form had doubled by 1955 in cities between 5,000 and 50,000 population, and by 1965 in cities between 100,000 and 500,000 population. The proportion of cities using the form continued to increase, although less dramatically, in the 1990s even though the problems faced by cities had shifted from physical to social and economic needs.

The current distribution of the forms of government in cities of different sizes in the United States is summarized in table 7.1. The mayor-council form of government is more commonly used than the council-manager in small cities and in very large cities, while in cities with populations between 10,000 and 500,000, the council-manager form is used more often than other forms. In the past, all the cities over 1 million in population used the mayor-council form, and New York, Chicago, Los Angeles, and Philadelphia still do. Some growing council-manager cities in the Sunbelt, however, are at or approaching the 1 million mark: Dallas, Phoenix, San Antonio, San Diego, and San Jose. A question to which we return, after examining the kinds of leadership provided by different kinds of mayors and by city managers, is whether the council-manager form can provide strong leadership to large cities in the new century.

There is also variation in the use of forms of government across regions.[3] The percentage of cities using the council-manager form is as follows:

- Northeast   29.1%
- Midwest   47.3%
- South   29.5%
- Mountain/plains   43.6%
- West Coast   76.0%

The mayor-council form is most commonly used in the Northeast. The council-manager form has been most popular from the Midwest to the West Coast. The aggregate figures, however, mask subregional variations. For example, the council-manager form has been widely used in the southern states along the Atlantic coast, and much less commonly used than the national average in the interior southern states.

Mayor-council form. The mayor-council form of government is based on separation of powers, with authority divided between the executive and the legislature. The strong mayor-council version of this form has separation of powers between, on the one hand, a mayor with extensive powers and integrated administrative control over staff and, on the other, the elected legislative body. In strong-mayor cities, the mayor and council members are typically the only elected officials. The lines of authority for all or most departments of city government lead to the mayor's office.[4]

In approximately 39 percent of the mayor-council cities over 50,000 in population, there is a Chief Administrative Officer (CAO).[5] The scope of that position and its duties depend on what responsibilities are assigned by the officials who appoint the CAO. These usually include authority over implementation of programs, day-to-day administrative concerns, and budget formulation, as well as playing an advisory role in developing other policy recommendations. It has been common to assume that the CAO is appointed by the mayor, derives his or her influence from the mayor, and operates within the orbit of the mayor.[6] In a 1997 survey of cities with populations of 2,500 or more, however, 51 percent of the CAOs are appointed by the mayor with the approval of the city council, and another 38 percent are nominated by the city council.[7] Only 11 percent are appointed by the mayor alone, although direct mayoral appointment is found in half of the cities over 30,000 in population. When appointed by the mayor, the CAO serves at the mayor's "pleasure," and turnover is high, especially when a new mayor comes into office. When appointed or approved by the council, the CAO is similar in characteristics to the city manager.

The council, on the other hand, is confined to a more limited role in strong-mayor council cities. Even in policy making, the council is heavily dependent on the mayor for proposals and information, and it can be checked by the mayor's veto power. The mayor also occupies a favorable position for mobilizing public opinion in support of proposals. The council, however, must approve policies and can override vetoes, so there is the potential for deadlock between the executive and legislature.

The checks and balances in mayor-council cities affect both how officials relate to each other and the freedom of mayoral action. Since the purpose of offsetting powers is to permit one set of officials to hold the other in check, it is common for conflict to arise in the relationship between the mayor and the council.[8] The conflict may concern policy preferences and priorities, the prerogatives of office, or both. Conflict can be positive when it signals that important decisions are at stake and increases the attention and participation of officials and citizens. It can be harmful when contentiousness impedes the ability of officials to resolve issues and commit to long-term goals. Gridlock is a condition that has been common at all levels of government in recent years when the executive and legislature are controlled by different political parties. Conflict, and the power plays that it generates, can also interfere with accountability, as officials seek to evade control and preserve their resources and freedom of action. The "bureaucracy" can play the mayor and council off against each other and develop its own base of constituency support. Thus, separation of powers and conflictual relationships can produce the loose control of administrative activities that some contend is endemic in city government.

Council-manager form. The council-manager form is based on the unitary model of organizing government. The council possesses all governmental authority, except as it delegates authority to the manager, and, thus, there is no separation of powers or checks and balances in the system. This form provides for specialization of roles but not separation of powers. The council and mayor occupy the overtly political roles in government, set policy, and select the city manager. The manager provides policy advice and recommendations to the council and directs the administrative apparatus. Within this broad division of functions, there is considerable sharing, which the form of government promotes. The city manager also provides policy leadership in helping to frame the council's agenda and has latitude — and therefore influence — in determining how policy goals are converted into programs and services. The council, on the other hand, has the potential to oversee the administrative performance of the city by appraising how the manager is doing (and deciding whether the manager will continue in office) and by securing information about the performance of administrative staff in general.

The mayor is typically the presiding officer of the council and has no formal powers different from those of other council members, except for the veto power in 13 percent of council-manager cities. Mayors, directly elected in 62 percent of these cities, can be an important source of policy guidance and coordination of participants, although they rarely exercise any administrative authority.[9]

The manager is the executive officer with extensive authority for directing staff, formulating and (after approval by council) expending the budget, and controlling operations. Given the great scope of the manager's influence and authority, some feel that the form weakens public control. Others contend that democratic government is not jeopardized. "In this system," Newland has contended, "executive authority can safely be great, because limits on the executive are even larger, and they may be exercised swiftly and decisively."[10] The manager is appointed by the council, with no voter involvement, and serves without term at the pleasure of the council. The manager is typically the only staff member hired by the council (in some cities, the city attorney and/or clerk are selected by the council as well), and all other employees are hired under the authority of the manager. If the council is displeased with a staff member — if, for example, it would like to have the police chief removed — the council can only attempt to persuade the manager to make the change and, if unsuccessful, either accept the situation or fire the manager. The norm of the system is for elected officials to respect the insulation of staff from "political" interference.

The structure of council-manager government promotes cooperative relationships among officials. Because the ultimate control over city government lies with the council, there is less likelihood of power struggles between the council and the manager. The council and the manager do not compete for the same "rewards" from public service. Elected officials seek public support and reelection, whereas managers are concerned about how the council assesses their work and their standing and respect in their profession in order to have the option of moving to another city. Furthermore, city managers have a professional commitment to helping the council accomplish its goals, and, if they do not, they can be replaced. To be sure, tensions can emerge among elected officials, or between them and the staff. The important difference from mayor-council governments is that, with no separation of powers, officials do not have to deal with structural impediments to cooperation, and positive relationships are common. For example, in surveys of city managers in North Carolina and Ohio (see table 7.2, p. 146), over 90 percent reported that the city council and city manager have a good working relationship.[11] Considering all officials, these were the ratings given by the managers in the two states. The approach

TABLE 7.2. WORKING RELATIONSHIP RATINGS OF CITY MANAGERS
(IN PERCENTAGES)

	North Carolina	*Ohio*
Very positive	39	32
Good	30	36
OK, but could be improved	29	25
Poor	2	7
Very poor	0	0

to leadership taken by the mayor and the city manager in the council-manager form can be different than that of executive mayors operating in a separation-of-powers setting.

This discussion is not meant to argue for the superiority of one form of local government over another. Rather, it is intended to offer a perspective on the differing dynamics of the local government process, and on the factors that affect how mayors and city managers fill their positions. After discussing other aspects of leadership, we explore the philosophies that underlie these two forms of government at the end of the chapter.

Aspects of Leadership

Two aspects of leadership have a bearing on how chief executive officers perform and are assessed. One is the function performed. According to the distinction presented in figure 7.1 (p. 140), leaders can provide political and/or executive leadership. The second aspect is the approach to leadership — whether it is based on the use of power or on promoting positive relationships. With an understanding of these two aspects of leadership, it is possible to differentiate more fully among the two kinds of mayors, the mayors and the city manager, and the elected and appointed executive.

Leadership functions. All mayors can be expected to provide political leadership in their cities. City governments also require executive leadership to perform effectively, whether leadership comes from the executive mayor or the city manager. The political aspect of leadership involves distilling the demands and preferences of citizens into issues that can be addressed, articulating and fostering acceptance of goals to resolve these issues, and mobilizing support for the approval and accomplishment of these goals. Political leaders seek to win over supporters by selling their ideas, building coalitions, offering deals, and making compromises. They are accountable to voters who periodically cast judgment on the quality of their leadership by deciding whether to return them to office. Executive leaders, on the other hand, control and coordinate the use of the city government's human and physical resources to implement policies and deliver services.

They are judged by the effectiveness and efficiency of the city government, by the responsiveness of city staff to citizens, by the level of productivity and innovation, and by the ability to anticipate emerging needs and changing conditions.

The strong mayor-council form requires that voters assess executive leadership at the same time that they judge political leadership, but it is harder to get information about executive performance and, except in cases of gross failure to perform (i.e., the mayor who is blamed because streets are not cleared of snow quickly enough), issues of executive leadership are likely to be overshadowed by the political issues in the campaign. A city council is better able to focus on the executive performance issues in its ongoing assessment of whether a city manager should continue in office. Indeed, as of 1993, 84 percent of council-manager cities have a formal appraisal process that occurs at least once a year.[12]

The distinction between the two dimensions of leadership raises some interesting questions about each of the types of leaders we are considering. How do "strong" mayors combine the two dimensions? Why don't council-manager mayors seek to augment their influence by taking on certain aspects of executive leadership? How do city managers, who have influence in policy matters, keep from becoming political leaders as we define the term?

Strong mayors are able to blend the dimensions of leadership into one. They can tap organizational resources or utilize executive powers to advance their political ends. Examples of these abilities are offering government jobs or contracts in exchange for support of a mayoral project, and cutting the budget for services in the districts of council members who oppose the mayor. Since the city's chief executive gains and retains office through election, the lines are blurred between campaign resources and the resources of the city that may be used to secure backers. Furthermore, because the executive commonly faces council resistance or opposition and recalcitrance from city departments, the mayor must often use organizational resources to secure support and compliance from other officials. This does not imply corruption, but the blending of the two dimensions makes it more likely that political considerations may impinge on executive decisions.

Mayors in council-manager cities face the opposite situation: they cannot use organizational resources to support their political leadership. Most mayors understand and support the basic tenets of the council-manager form. A few, however, might wish they could exercise certain executive powers in order to advance their political agenda.[13] For example, an activist mayor might think it advantageous to appoint a few of his supporters to key positions in order to produce more rapid and complete acceptance of his ideas for change in the city. This could, however, have negative consequences. The manager's executive authority would be compromised, and his or her effectiveness would be impaired. The council members might suspect the mayor of trying to direct the administrative organization independently of the rest of the council. The council could seek to limit the mayor's power by withholding support for his ideas. In seeking a little more power by moving into the executive leadership dimension, the mayor could wind up with less influence than he had before.

City managers cannot be divorced from the political leadership dimension. Their recommendations influence the policy choices of elected officials, and they exercise discretion in choosing how to interpret and implement policy goals. According to the ethical standards city managers have established for themselves through the Code of Ethics of the International City and County Managers Association, it is the responsibility of city managers to support elected officials and help them establish and accomplish their goals. City managers are professionals when they are guided by their training and experience to base their actions on assessment of need (as opposed to weighing of demands) with objectivity, fairness, and respect for the political authority of the city council. City managers become political actors if they substitute their own preferences for those of the council, use organizational resources to help supporters and weaken opponents on the city council, or solicit support from citizens that would enable them to stand against the council and resist its control. It is impossible for the city manager not to be political, but professionally responsible managers do not seek to become political leaders or substitute political for professional considerations in guiding their actions.

We noted previously that strong mayors have certain advantages because they can combine the two dimensions of leadership, but this condition also limits the capability of the mayor because it comes with the constraints imposed by separation of powers. If we compare strong mayoral governments with council-manager governments, it might appear that the mayor is constrained by having to be a political leader without executive resources, and that the manager is hemmed in by being an executive who cannot use political tools and methods. What can overcome these limitations is the potential for partnership between the mayor and the city manager, who, while continuing to be accountable to the entire council, can complement the political leadership of the mayor with professional support.

Approaches to exercising leadership. Leaders may attempt to base their influence on the use of power or on promoting positive relationships. It is possible to combine the two, although the logic of each approach tends to preclude the other. In the *power-based approach* to leadership, leaders and followers have unequal positions. Leadership is achieved by gaining leverage over other actors. The approach is summarized by the classic question about the use of power, "how does A get B to do something B would not do otherwise?" A variant is "how does A prevent B from accomplishing something B wants?" Formal and informal resources are instrumental to the exercise of leadership in the power-based approach because it is presumed that there is a "cost" in getting other actors to do something they would not have chosen to do on their own, or in blocking their efforts. In organizations, differences in power and authority are institutionalized in superior/subordinate relationships and hierarchy. Thus, the executive has the option of using power to secure compliance.

Resources come into play in "exchanges" between actors — for example, exchanging support of the leader for a benefit to the follower. A key attribute of leaders, according to the power-oriented approach, is their ability to pyramid resources by investing their assets to get more power than they started with.

The approach to leadership based on *fostering positive relationships* emphasizes the interaction among actors rather than the differences in power between them. The key question in this approach is, "how does A get B to recognize they have a common goal and can both be better off if they work together?" The leader accomplishes this not by what he offers or threatens to do but by building trust and inviting followers to share in setting goals. In this approach, the leader shapes relationships and sets the tone, particularly through the example of the leader's own behavior. This approach stresses facilitation. The facilitative leader empowers others by drawing out their contributions and helping them accomplish their goals; promotes open and honest communication among officials; and creates a shared vision incorporating his or her own goals and the goals of others.[14]

Considering the two approaches to leadership together provides a framework for closer examination of the three kinds of officials. Strong mayors who blend the political and executive dimensions have the choice of stressing power or building relationships. The availability of formal and informal power resources, however, and the likelihood of conflict with the council and other officials, make it likely that this mayor will rely on power to establish leadership. Doing so then makes it difficult to appeal to persons who have been treated as opponents to join in stable cooperative relationships. The council-manager mayor, on the other hand, does not have formal power resources and must utilize facilitative leadership to be effective. As we have seen, seeking organizational power may produce short-run benefits, but it engenders resentment from the council and weakens the capability of the city manager. Finally, city managers as formal organizational leaders can take a power-oriented approach to the way they exert leadership in relationship to staff, although effective internal leadership is more likely to be based on enabling and empowering others rather than on authoritarian rule. The power-oriented approach will not work in dealings with the city council or the community, over whom city managers do not exercise power.

Mayors in Mayor-Council Cities

The ideal mayor in mayor-council cities is an innovator (also called an entrepreneur) who provides creative solutions to problems and pyramids resources to increase his or her ability to build coalitions and gain leverage over other actors. This mayor is effective at both initiation and implementation of policies and programs. The approach to leadership is essentially power-oriented.

Leadership is fashioned from a combination of formal and informal resources. The former are part of the governmental structure and the latter are derived from personal conditions or the political process. Formal resources available to mayors have remained fairly constant over time, but each incumbent differs in his or her ability to make the best use of these resources. Some important informal resources, for example, support from a political party, have been declining over time.

Formal Resources

The terms "strong" and "weak" mayor refer to the level of authority assigned to the mayor, but there is no "pure" strong or weak mayor form. Strong and weak mayors are arrayed along a continuum. The key formal powers, which may be assigned to the executive or divided among a number of officials, are the following:

- Appointment of department heads

- Development of the budget

- Direction of administrative departments

- Veto of council actions

The mayor's authority varies widely. Kevin White, mayor of Boston in the 1960s and 1970s, offers an example of extensive authority. He used his powers over administrative organization to shift functions he considered important from semiautonomous agencies to ones under the mayor's office. For example, the responsibility for community development programs in neighborhoods was shifted from the Boston Redevelopment Agency to the Neighborhood Development Administration in his office. Between 1967 and 1976, the staff in mayoral agencies more than doubled from 284 to 584, and the funds expended mushroomed from $378,752 to approximately $6.5 million.[15]

The absence of direct administrative authority, on the other hand, limits the mayor's ability to achieve accountability from departments in city government. A celebrated example was the inability of Los Angeles Mayor Tom Bradley (or the city council) to remove Chief of Police Daryl Gates after the riots in 1991. Despite widespread criticism of the chief, the mayor could not act. The police chief is appointed by and responsible to the Police Commission, whose five members are appointed by the mayor with approval of the council, and can be disciplined or fired only by the Board of Civil Service Commissioners. When Gates resigned in June 1992, he could claim that no one forced him out.[16] Clearly, such limitations on appointment authority hamstring the executive.

The variations in charter provisions defining the mayor's position in mayor-council cities are illustrated in table 7.3 (p. 152). Ten cities have been chosen to illustrate the variety of institutional settings in which the mayor operates. In Minneapolis and San Francisco, there is extensive fragmentation of authority. Different parts of city governments are run by different officials. San Bernardino provides integrated executive control in the hands of the mayor but limits the mayor's appointment of department heads, who must be approved by the council and cannot be removed without two-thirds approval from the council. In Atlanta, on the other hand, although the council approves appointments, it must have a two-thirds vote to block the removal of a department head. Memphis offers another variation: council approval is needed for appointment and removal, but the mayor can appoint a new complement of department heads at the beginning of a term. New Haven and Akron, on the other hand, combine unrestricted mayoral appointment power over certain officials with protected tenure for others. The mayors in Boston, Louisville, and Knoxville have extensive autonomy in choosing and/or dismissing department heads.

Beyond the organizational leadership resources derived from appointment of department heads, control of other appointments can augment the mayor's leverage, and patronage appointments can reinforce party organizational cohesion and support. Most mayors, however, do not directly control large numbers of city government jobs. Civil service protection of most positions limits the jobs a mayor can dispense. Court cases in the past twenty years have limited the ability of elected officials to remove, promote, or transfer staff for partisan reasons unless employees are directly involved in providing advice on policy strategies, as opposed to policy implementation.[17]

Mayors in Minneapolis, San Francisco, and New Haven share the budget-formulating function with others, but those in the other cities can develop executive budgets. Mayors can use this control to induce and reward support or to punish opposition.

A 1991 survey conducted by the International City Management Association measured the variation in mayoral authority within the mayor-council form of government.[18] There was a substantial difference between cities based on their population, as indicated in table 7.4 (p. 153). In cities over 100,000 in population, two-thirds of the mayors developed the budget, and approximately 90 percent appointed department heads and had veto power. In cities under 50,000, the likelihood that the mayor possessed

TABLE 7.3. AUTHORITY OF SELECTED MAYORS IN APPOINTMENTS AND BUDGET

City	Appointment Power	Limit on Budget Authority
Minneapolis	Mayor shares appointments with president of council + 3 other council members; subject to approval by council. City coordinator appoints heads of staff departments. Park and Library directors appointed by their own boards.	Prepared by mayor and approved by council. Board of Estimate sets levy, which council cannot exceed.
San Bernardino	Mayor appoints with approval of council; may be removed by mayor with approval of two-thirds of council.	None
San Francisco	Mayor appoints CAO[a] for 10-year term and Controller for life with council approval. Department heads appointed by CAO, commissions appointed by mayor, or are directly elected.	Controller prepares budget; CAO prepares requests for certain departments. Mayor and council only can decrease budget requests.
New Haven	Mayor appoints four coordinators and certain department heads; appoints others if vacancy occurs but may not remove except for cause.	Board of Finance chaired by mayor prepares budget.
Akron	Mayor appoints and may remove certain department heads except for two appointed by separate commissions. Most can be removed only for cause.	None
Memphis	Mayor appoints CAO and department heads with approval of council. Heads serve for a term concurrent to that of appointing mayor and may be removed with council approval.	None
Atlanta	Mayor appoints CAO; appoints department heads with approval of council for term of four years. May remove department heads subject to override by two-thirds vote of council.	None. Mayor has line-item veto.
Louisville	Mayor appoints department heads with approval of council. May be removed by the mayor.	None
Boston	Mayor appoints most department heads without council approval. Mayor has no formal authority over parks and roads, welfare, transportation, or schools.	None. Council only may decrease appropriations.
Knoxville	Mayor appoints and may remove department heads.	None

Source: James H. Svara, "Institutional Powers and Mayoral Leadership, *State and Local Government Review* 27, no. 1 (Winter 1995), 75. Reprinted by permission of the Carl Vinson Institute of Government, University of Georgia.

a. CAO=Chief Administrative Officer.

TABLE 7.4. FORMAL POWERS OF MAYORS IN MAYOR-COUNCIL CITIES

Population	Budget Development		Appoint Dept. Heads		Veto	
	Percent	Number	Percent	Number	Percent	Number
Over 500,000	75	6	87	7	100	8
250,000–499,999	77	10	83	10	85	11
100,000–250,000	61	19	90	27	90	28
50,000–99,999	65	55	73	58	88	75
25,000–49,999	46	77	65	98	75	123
10,000–24,999	36	149	60	216	65	265
2,500–9,999	27	339	51	532	49	616
Under 2,500	24	36	39	45	39	57
Total	32	555	55	993	56	1184

Source: International City Management Association, 1991 Form of Government Survey. Special tabulations by ICMA staff. James H. Svara, "Institutional Powers and Mayoral Leadership," *State and Local Government Review* 27, no. 1 (Winter 1995), 76. Reprinted by permission of the Carl Vinson Institute of Government, University of Georgia.

these powers decreased with declining population. The government of most moderately large to large cities generally corresponded to the strong mayor-council form — with variations in practice such as those noted in table 7.3 — while medium-sized cities were divided between strong and weak mayoralties, and small cities approximated the weak mayor-council form of government.

Mayors possess varying degrees of formal authority, but it is important in governments with separation of powers to consider how the presence of checks and balances affects both how officials relate to each other and the freedom of mayoral action. As we have noted, offsetting powers that permit one set of officials to hold the other in check commonly produce conflict between the mayor and the council. The conflict may concern policy preferences and priorities, the prerogatives of office, or both. A consequence of such tension in the relationship is widespread distrust of the mayor by the council. Negative attitudes held by council members may constrain the mayor even if he or she has superior resources. Although "strong" mayors may have a great advantage in resources over the city council, the resistance generated by seeking to manipulate the council can limit the mayor's capacity to get things done.

The results of a national survey of city council members in 1989, which included ratings of the executive's performance, illuminate the nature of the relationship between the mayor and the council.[19] The following proportions of council members rated the performance of the mayor as good or very good in the following areas:

- Accomplishing the goals established by the council — 53 percent rated performance as very good or good

- Providing council with sufficient alternatives for making policy decisions — 36 percent

- Providing council sufficient information to assess the effectiveness of programs and services — 40 percent

The mayor thus is seen by many council members as relatively independent in pursuing goals and unwilling to provide information to the council. The views of council members in the cities over 200,000 in population were especially critical. Only one quarter of the council members in these cities rated the mayor's performance as good or better in providing sufficient alternatives or sufficient information to assess program effectiveness. These ratings suggest that the mayor commonly is perceived to be distant from the council and that the council often cannot trust the mayor.

These findings indicate that the mayor is likely to encounter resistance from the council regardless of the level of formal power in the mayor's office. Kathy Whitmire, former mayor of Houston, identified micromanagement by the city council as an impediment to attracting strong leaders to head city departments.[20] Twenty years earlier, Carl Stokes, then mayor of Cleveland, also identified the city council as the cause of "negative capability" in city government; in order "for a mayor to govern, actually govern, he has to have political power over the councilmen."[21] In Cleveland, neither the mayor nor the council was in charge. The council president controlled a simple majority of votes and could hold up any program proposed by the mayor. Mayor Stokes could veto council actions, and he controlled enough votes to prevent an override of his veto, since that action required a two-thirds majority. In this situation, negative attitudes along with checks and offsetting powers produced stalemate.

Informal Resources

The formal resources of the mayor's office provide only part of the explanation of effective mayoral leadership. Even in mayor-council cities, informal resources are extremely important. Mayors such as Richard Daley in Chicago[22] and Richard Lee in New Haven[23] were noted for their ability to convert a formally weak position into one of strength. Support from a political party or community elites, strong popular backing, and a host of private backers indebted for jobs, favors, contracts, and recognition can give mayors the added political clout that can be helpful in the council and their own administration to get ideas accepted and acted upon.

Several trends in American politics have reduced these informal resources of the mayors and made it more difficult for mayors to use their influence. First, the declining strength of political parties and the increasing independence of voting behavior by citizens remove a force that mayors could use to bind together officeholders and secure support for their programs. Despite the greater likelihood that elections are partisan in mayor-council cities, parties are less helpful than before as a resource to mobilize and organize support. Second, there has been a splintering and thinning of power elites resulting from the breakup of large corporations, takeover of local firms by national and international concerns, increased competition and downsizing, and the move of companies to the suburbs. The changes have diminished the active involvement of corporations in the general political affairs of central cities and reduced the likelihood that a cohesive private interest stratum can be tapped by the mayor to influence the behavior of council members and other political actors. Third, the proliferation of interest groups and the political organization of neighborhoods has increased the range and diversity of organizations operating in local politics. All local officials find it more difficult to secure broad-based agreement for governmental ventures and to develop common goals. Fourth, council members are more diverse in their characteristics, more activist in their orientation, more frequently inclined to pursue an independent (and often narrow) political agenda, and more likely to see council membership as the start of a political career. Such councils are not likely to accept the leadership of the mayor out of deference to the mayor's power or common party loyalty. All of these changes in city politics make it more difficult for the mayor to lead effectively. The new openness of the local electoral process and the individualism of persons elected to office diffuse the concentration of power needed for governing the city.[24]

The mayor's performance is also affected by such individual characteristics as the following:

- Experience

- Personal or occupational financial and staff support

- Personal attributes: charisma, reputation, wisdom

- Commitment to the job: time, resources, and energy expended

- Effectiveness in dealing with the media

These factors determine how well and how fully the mayor fills the position and how creatively the mayor exploits resources — formal and informal. A charismatic or adroit formally weak mayor may be able to win substantial support from the community and wring more advantage from limited powers than others have done. A mayor can even capitalize on adversity. A fiscal crisis in New York in the early 1970s altered power relationships, and Mayor Edward Koch was able to expand the mayor's control over the budget and quasi-independent agencies and reduce his dependence on municipal unions and minority groups.[25] Mayor Edward Rendell in Philadelphia used a severe shortfall in revenues and a large deficit to force concessions from unionized employees and the privatization of some city services.[26] Ferman has argued that "effective political skills" are the critical factor for strong mayoral leadership.[27]

Effectiveness at achieving implementation

Effectiveness at policy initiation		Low	High
	Low	Caretaker	Broker
	High	Reformer	Innovator

FIGURE 7.2. TYPES OF MAYORS IN MAYOR-COUNCIL CITIES

The structure of the mayor-council form confers powers to mayors, and they cannot function effectively without using them well. Expanding powers will promote the potential for political leadership but will not guarantee it. As the Winter Commission recognized, "obviously, there is no way to legislate strong leadership."[28] This observation reminds us that structural change will not necessarily augment the mayor's political leadership.

Types of Mayors

Effective leadership by the mayor is critical in the mayor-council city. Without it, the offsetting powers of the mayor and council can produce policy stalemate and administrative departments can resist change. The performance of mayors can be judged by their effectiveness on two dimensions: initiating policies, on the one hand, and getting policies implemented, on the other. The various types of mayors that can be classified using this approach (see figure 7.2). If the mayor is a *caretaker* with no goals, the city will drift and be reactive when problems occur. If the mayor is a *reformer* or policy initiator but poor at getting things done, or a *broker* who can arrange compromise but has a weak policy agenda, city government will lack a key element of leadership. This form functions best when the mayor is an *innovator* who can help provide a clear direction for city government and ensure that city departments are focused on accomplishing the goals of elected officials.

Mayors in Council-Manager Cities

The ideal mayor in council-manager cities is a facilitator who promotes positive interaction and a high level of communication among officials in city government and with the public, and who also provides guidance in goal setting and policy making. This type of leadership is well-suited to the conditions of the council-manager city in which cooperative relationships among officials are common, and the city manager provides support to the elected officials to whom the manager is accountable. Effective leadership by this kind of mayor improves the working relationships among officials, makes the form of government function more smoothly, and increases the involvement of elected officials in setting policy.

Typically, the mayor in the council-manager city has been dismissed as a ribbon cutter or ceremonial head of the government. Close examination of these mayors, however, indicates that they fill a broad range of roles that fall into three broad categories.[29] The first set of roles are traditional or "automatic" in the sense that they are built into the office, and all mayors will fill them unless they are inept or make an effort to avoid them.

- Mayors perform *ceremonial tasks,* which can be used by the mayor to build public trust and support for other activities. Effective mayors are adept at linking ceremonial activities with substantive concerns and policy positions of the government.

- As a *link to the public,* the mayor announces and explains positions taken by the council, receives a large volume of comments and complaints from citizens, and has extensive dealings with the media.

- As *presiding officer,* the mayor is responsible for assuring the orderly conduct of meetings and may foster discussion and resolution of business in council meetings.

- As *representative/promoter,* the mayor has extensive contacts with other local governments and with state and federal government agencies. Mayors also devote considerable attention to promoting the jurisdiction and creating a positive image for the city.

The second set of roles involves active coordination and communication, active in the sense that the mayor must recognize and choose to fill them. In these roles, the differences between the approach and effectiveness of the activist mayor and the passive one are likely to emerge.

- As *articulator/mobilizer,* the mayor raises awareness by articulating issues and promoting understanding of problems. Effective mayors have the ability to frame, explain, and communicate an issue in a way that it is recognized by other officials and the public.

- Through the *liaison and partnership with the manager* role, the mayor can promote positive communication between the manager and the city council, although the manager must remain in contact with and accountable to the entire council. There can also be an active partnership between the mayor and the manager in which the strengths of one complement the other.

- In the *team relations and network builder* role, the mayor works to coalesce the council into a cohesive team and establishes a positive "tone."

Finally, there are three additional roles that deal with policy leadership and guiding the work of the council.

- In the *goal setter* role, mayors engage in activities to create a sense of direction or a climate for change. Goal setting is promoted by fostering acceptance of practices such as council goal-setting retreats for the council or community strategic planning efforts.

- As *delegator/organizer,* the mayor helps the council and manager understand and maintain their roles, including helping the council members understand their responsibilities.

- The final role is *policy initiator* in which the mayor develops programs and policies to address problems. If active in this role, the mayor is instrumental in shaping the policy agenda. This agenda can have the clear stamp of the mayor or chairperson but still be drawn from the council and other sources or primarily derived from the mayor or chairperson's personal preferences.

These roles are mutually reinforcing and success in one enhances success in others. Further, they go on concurrently.

Resources. Facilitative leadership does not depend on a superior power position. There are resources available in the council-manager form and within the incumbent as a person to develop leadership in the areas of coordination and policy guidance. The strategic location occupied by the mayor in the center of communication channels to the council, the city manager and staff, and the public provides the foundation for effective leadership. Mayors with a clear conception of the job — its possibilities, interdependencies, and limitations — are more likely to be able to take advantage of this resource.

Willingness and ability to commit time can give the mayor a relative advantage over other officials, but this does not mean that the amount of time per se determines effectiveness. Mayors must use time well to convert it into other resources like knowledge or networks. They also need personal qualities such as energy, resourcefulness, positive attitude, contacts and connections, ability to communicate, a clear sense of purpose, and the ability to keep sight of broad goals while making specific choices. Interpersonal skills, such as inclusiveness, ability to share responsibility, sharing of information, facilitation of the expression of divergent views, and ability to resolve differences are important traits the mayor needs to have in his or her dealings with the council and the manager.

Types of leadership. There is variation in the nature and scope of leadership depending on how well the roles that make up the office are filled. A mayor who does not fill even the traditional/automatic role — who, for example, is an ineffective presiding officer who allows the council to flounder in meetings — could be called a *caretaker,* whereas one who fills these roles well but attends to no other duties is a *symbolic head.* Both the *coordinator* and the *director* create an atmosphere that promotes cohesion and communication among officials and strengthens the capacity of the council to identify problems and make decisions. Coordinators, however, are not strongly associated with a policy agenda of their own, even though they contribute to fashioning and acting on an agenda as part of the council. Directors do have their "own" policy agendas, although they reflect to a greater or lesser extent the views of other officials. This is a subtle distinction in the sense that neither a coordinator nor a director is a solitary leader, and both have broad goals for their cities. Coordinators are effective at developing a sense of cohesion and purpose in their cities and strengthening the policymaking process, but they are not active policy initiators. They are more process-oriented than policy-oriented. Directors create an agenda in the sense that they originate it (at least in part) and put their imprint on it, and they are recognized by other officials and the public for this contribution.

In sum, although these mayors lack formal powers over other officials, they occupy a strategic location in the communication channels with the council, the manager, and the public. Such a facilitative leader must demonstrate a commitment to the full involvement of members of the governing board through inclusiveness, sharing of information, supporting expression of divergent views, and accepting the initiative of other members, as well as having respect for the authority of the city manager. The moderately effective mayor goes beyond ceremonial leadership to provide effective coordination and communication. The highly effective mayor also helps to develop a common set of goals with wide council support.

City Managers

The city manager is the executive in council-manager cities. Such an official obviously would head up the administrative organization. Do city managers provide leadership in other areas as well, and should they do so?

Is Policy Leadership Appropriate?

The well-established tendency is to think of decision making in local government as a "dichotomy": the policy realm is handled by the council, and administrators should confine themselves to administrative, that is, internal organizational, leadership. Since this "dichotomy model" is commonly attributed to the scholars and activists who created the council-manager form of government in the early twentieth century, it is important to note that the founders of this form intended for city managers to be leaders in policy formation as well as innovative administrators. The National Municipal League's endorsement of the council-manager form in its second Model City Charter in 1919 was explicit on this matter: the manager was to be a leader who formulated policies and urged their adoption by the council.[30] The reformers did not intend to simply add an administrative technician who would take charge of implementation of policies. The dichotomy model emerged in the 1920s.[31] Although it was incorporated in the code of ethics of the International City Management Association in the 1930s and 1940s, a broader view of the managers' roles has prevailed since that time. Empirical studies have consistently shown that city managers commonly influence policy choices and are community leaders.

Spheres of Leadership

City managers have unique roles and relationships, and they work under conditions that are different both from those of administrators at higher levels of government and from those of the elected executive in the mayor-council form. To an extent not found at other levels or in other forms of government, city managers, along with other local-government-appointed executives such as school superintendents and directors of public authorities, are both general policy leaders and organizational directors. City managers do not report to an elected executive or go through political appointees in developing policy recommendations for elected officials, and they report on performance directly to the governing board. Because of their close working association with the residents of the communities which they serve, they have a special obligation to value community leadership and to preserve and protect the democratic quality of the political process as a whole. Unlike elected executives, city managers are accountable to the entire governing board and are expected to provide leadership from a professional perspective. This does not mean that the city manager is not involved in politics, but that this involvement should be guided by professional considerations and standards.

Furthermore, city managers are directly responsible for the administrative performance of their government. Because they do not operate under the direction of an elected executive or a political appointee, they have more autonomy than do other administrators. The expectations for this position also are higher. The use of resources by local governments is more closely scrutinized than at other levels of government, and city managers, as experts, are expected to achieve a high level of organizational performance. They must also be adept at bridging the political world of elected officials and citizens, as well as the technical world of the specialists who work for city government: for example, planners, engineers, and law enforcement officers.[32] This entails translating the specific views and practices of specialists to elected officials and helping to clarify the demands of political superiors.

Leadership is provided in three spheres: council relations, community, and organization.

- *Council relations:* Administrators support elected officials — and thus provide facilitative leadership — and provide information and recommendations that can lead to innovation in goals and policies pursued by local government. When administrators provide such leadership, they raise the awareness of elected officials regarding conditions that require attention and offer creative solutions to community problems. Administrators also support the exercise of leadership by helping elected officials accomplish their goals.

- *Community:* Leadership consists of strengthening communication with the community, maintaining support from key groups, and involving segments of the community that do not normally participate extensively in community affairs. Administrators have taken steps in many local governments to (a) establish citizen participation councils for policy input and/or program evaluation, (b) create co-production arrangements by which citizens share in the production of a public service — for example, separation of garbage by citizens to support recycling programs — and (c) utilize citizen surveys to assess the quality of service delivery.

- *Organization:* Administrators have the choice of taking power-based or facilitative approaches to internal leadership. The former stresses hierarchy, control, and task orientation; the later emphasizes developing commitment to a shared vision, empowering employees, and flattening the organization. Most of the current studies of public- and private-sector leadership studies stress the superiority of the facilitative approach. Administrators also are challenged to be innovative and to concentrate on clarifying the ends toward which they work rather than focusing exclusively on the means of accomplishing tasks.

The ways in which these spheres interact can be illustrated by a profile of a hypothetical city manager who is active in all areas. She has a close relationship with the mayor, who helps to maintain a good flow of information between the council and the manager and staff, but she is also careful to maintain direct ties with all the members of the council and to keep them fully informed. She works at keeping the council abreast of developments and trends that will affect the future of the city in order to help them formulate the "mission" of city government — its goals and purposes. She develops policy proposals that advance the accomplishment of these goals and recommends changes in policy when needed. She also has a strong community focus, developing extensive contacts with a broad array of groups in the community while maintaining close ties with the city managers and other governmental leaders in the area. She is able to draw upon her independent knowledge of what is happening in the city to better anticipate problems and understand the pressures that her council members are experiencing. She seeks support among citizens for a community-based strategic planning process to create a shared vision for the city and develop broad understanding and support for it.

Within the organization, she is innovative, incorporating technical expertise drawn from her graduate education in public administration, her experience working in other cities, and her professional networking through the state and national programs of the International City Management Association. She devotes much of her time and attention to council and community relations and relies heavily on her two assistant managers; this approach jibes with her team approach to management. She strives to incorporate new management practices, such as Total Quality Management and citizen surveys, into the operation of the city organization. Although this hypothetical manager is unusual in the high level and scope of her leadership, the city management profession holds up performance of this kind as a model. Most managers seek to emulate it, and many do so successfully.

City council members generally give city managers high ratings on their performance. In the national survey of council members in cities over 25,000 in population (mentioned earlier, on p. 153), over 80 percent of respondents agreed that the council and city manager have a good working relationship and that the manager does a good or very good job of accomplishing the goals established by the council.[33] Over 70 percent felt that the manager was at least doing a good job in providing the council with sufficient alternatives for making policy decisions and sufficient information to assess the effectiveness of programs and services.

In conclusion, city managers are executives who bring a wide range of professional considerations to the discussion of city government policies and practices.[34] These approaches are not *better* than political considerations that receive more emphasis from elected officials and citizens; rather, they are *different*. For example, elected officials stress responding to the demands of their constituents and achieving results in time for the next election. Administrators stress responding to the needs of citizens and meeting long-term goals. By raising professional considerations in policy discussions, city managers help to ensure a balanced approach to policy decisions.[35] By acting out of commitment to this management philosophy and a set of ethical standards, city managers also promote fairness and efficiency in the delivery of services and the use of organizational resources.

The Challenges Faced by Mayors and City Managers

All city government officials need to raise the level of their performance to meet the challenges they face, and mayors and city managers have the special responsibility of providing leadership in this effort. Citizens look to local officials to solve problems, but it is getting harder for them to do so. More functions, such as public assistance, are being shifted from the federal government to state and local governments, but federal assistance is being reduced as well. In fact, part of the logic of devolution at the present time is that giving state and local governments greater flexibility will make it possible for them to accomplish, with less money, the same results achieved under federal programs. At the same time, there is more pressure on local governments to reduce taxes and downsize their organizations. Proposition 13, the tax-rollback referendum that passed in California in 1978, started a movement to shrink government at all levels. The unpopularity of the property tax — a major source of local government revenue — increases the emphasis on tax cutting in local government. It remains to be seen how much strain on governments and/or service restrictions to citizens these changes will produce, but the pressure on officials to perform will certainly increase.

There is a new awareness that government is not necessarily the best source of services.[36] Local governments increasingly contract with private profit-making or nonprofit entities to provide services. Local governments have privatized the delivery of services such as solid-waste collection, the management of municipal facilities such as water-treatment plants, and internal management activities such as purchasing office supplies. There may be savings to be gained by this approach, although experience shows that government departments, when permitted to compete with private suppliers, can match price as well as quality. Beyond the consideration of changing who supplies services, it is increasingly common for governments to "co-produce" services with citizens — for example, citizens separating their garbage to support recycling — to more actively involve nonprofit agencies and voluntary organizations in solving community problems, and to eliminate some services completely. Those who advocate shifting of functions to the private sector believe government should be permanently reduced in size.[37] Mayors such as Stephen Goldsmith of Indianapolis are taking the lead in achieving these changes. Many mayors and city managers will be responsible for developing increasingly complex arrangements with contractors, citizen groups, voluntary organizations, nonprofit agencies, and individual citizens instead of simply raising revenues (within the limits imposed by the state) and hiring city staff to carry out programs and deliver services. This community involvement strengthens the linkage between government and citizens, but at the same time, it makes the task of governing more complex.

Local officials also must promote new approaches to intergovernmental cooperation. As urban areas spread further outward, an increasing number and array of jurisdictions must work together to deal with major problems that extend across municipal and county boundaries. In the future, mayors will be judged perhaps as much for how they establish linkages for common action with their peers in other jurisdictions as for performance within their own city limits. City managers usually have professional networks in urban areas, and they must build on their communication with each other to promote elected officials' awareness of the need for common action.

Finally, there is a challenge that comes from renewed interest in comparing forms of government. Some officials will feel the need to advocate alteration, while others will want to preserve their existing form of government. There are some, particularly in larger cities, who argue that the council-manager form is inadequate to meet the pressures on local government. At the heart of this position is the contention that the leadership of the mayor and the city council and the city manager is not sufficient. A number of large cities abandoned the council-manager form in recent years — Rochester, New York, in 1985; Toledo, Ohio, in 1992; St. Petersburg, Florida, in 1993; and Fresno, California, in 1993. On the other hand, Cincinnati, Ohio, which had used the form since 1926, voted by a 64- to 36-percent margin in 1995 to retain the council-manager form of government. Furthermore, there is stability in the underlying support for, and growth in the use of, the council-manager form, as the following trends indicate:

- 1990 to 1993: 18 percent of elections resulted in abandonment (average of 2 out of 11 each year)

- 1975 to 1993: 21 percent of elections resulted in abandonment (43 out of 203)

- 1975 to 1993: 330 additional cities used the council-manager form (increase from 2,452 to 2,782)[38]

There has been no increase in abandonments, and the council-manager form continues to be attractive to most cities.

The underlying issue in the debate over form of government highlights the contrasting approaches to leadership discussed in this chapter. The mayor-council form is based on the concept of executive leadership, with one person being the driving force in the governmental process. Along with having broad powers, the mayor faces broad challenges in providing political leadership, directing the administrative organization, and preserving the position and power needed to act in the face of internal and external opposition. Professional considerations are important in this form, but political forces are pervasive and can dominate. The council-manager form combines the concept of representative leadership and accountable professional leadership. The entire council, under the guidance of the mayor, contributes to setting goals, approving policies, appointing the city manager, and overseeing administrative operation. The city manager draws on education and experience to assist the council, interact with the community, and direct the staff. When the council is able to function cohesively, as it usually does, the form blends politics and professionalism in a more balanced way than in the mayor-council form.

The central weakness in the council-manager form is the drift that can result when the council is fragmented, and this becomes more likely as district elections become more common in council-manager cities. In this form, no one in the government has the power to force the council to come to agreement. If the mayor cannot persuade the council members to work together, he or she has no leverage over them. One remedy is for voters to select different council members, and, indeed, this usually happens. Some will argue that the situation requires changing the form of government in order to have one strong leader who can be held accountable. Such a change, however, could create separation of powers, increased contentiousness, and diminished professionalism.

In cities and other local governments, officials and citizens face not only a choice of candidates, parties, and philosophies to address their needs, but they also engage in a continuing constitutional debate over how to best structure government itself.

The differences between forms of government are important, but they should not obscure the similar problems faced by all mayors. As mayors try to improve housing and education or to promote economic development, they seek to persuade individuals, groups, corporations, and other governments to act, even though they have no direct control over them. In this sense, the form of government does not make much difference. Every mayor must be able to shape a vision for his or her city and seek to enlist the support of a wide range of actors to help achieve that vision. A more important difference between cities with different forms of government is how much help the mayor will get from the council and from a professional administrative officer who also brings leadership to city government.

CHAPTER EIGHT

The Resurgent City Councils

Susan MacManus

Face it, being a public official — a policy maker, a decision-maker — is a difficult job. You're dealing frequently with problems that don't have clear answers and yet you have a large body of constituents waiting for answers — expecting you to come up with new services to meet changing needs without increasing costs. That's a tough assignment. In many cases, rewards aren't easy to measure. You don't earn a lot of money, you probably don't get consistent and reliable feedback, you can't see immediate or measurable results, and you can be abruptly bounced out of office by a group of nameless voters.... And it can all run away with you before you know what happens.
— Handbook for Newly Elected City Officials

CITY COUNCILS — bodies described as homogeneous, consensual, part-time, and deferential to mayors and city managers — have changed considerably over the past three decades. They have become more diverse, conflictual, and even more defiant of chief executives, reflecting trends in the polity at large. There have been significant changes in the structure of city councils, the complexity of the job, the personal attributes of people who successfully run for the office (age, gender, race), campaign strategies and tactics used by those seeking council posts, the types of problems to be dealt with once elected, and the ways councilors communicate with the electorate.

At the same time, the old saying that "the more things change, the more they remain the same" has some validity. Municipalities still bear the major responsibility for financing and delivering the bulk of the services that have the most direct impact on the average American's day-to-day quality of life, such as police and fire protection, water, sewage disposal, garbage pick-up, streets, parks. The motives of those who run for city council have changed little over the years. And "politics" has consistently been a driving force behind the actions of individual council members, although the specific dynamics have shifted in many communities.

Political shifts on councils have generally paralleled changes in a community's demographic and socioeconomic makeup and its political geography. Frequent reshapings of the constituency bases of many city council members have occurred for two primary reasons. One is that national constitutional law requires periodic redistricting to conform to the "one person, one vote" requirement. The second is the highly mobile nature of Americans. People moving in and out of a community can change its constituency profile rather quickly, and we *are* a nation of movers!

More Americans are choosing to leave large central cities for smaller suburban or rural municipalities. Between 1990 and 1994, nearly three in ten cities with populations of more than 100,000 lost population, and a nearly equal number grew by less than 1 percent. Of all urban dwellers, 60 percent now live in suburbs — not the nation's 522 central cities. During the same time period, three in four rural areas gained population, mostly as a consequence of out-migration from cities by Baby Boomers.

The Formal Structure of City Councils

All city councils are unicameral rather than bicameral legislative bodies, such as the U.S. Congress and all state legislatures (with the exception of Nebraska's). Beyond that basic similarity, however, periodic surveys of municipalities conducted by the International City/County Management Association (ICMA), the National League of Cities (NLC), and individual researchers have shown that there is considerable variation in how U.S. city councils are structured and operate.

Structural Variations

Structural arrangements vary *most* across population size categories and forms of government. Formal structures can affect who runs for and wins council seats, elected councilors' roles, differences in council-executive relations, and factionalism on individual councils. One should be cautioned, however, that structure is only one factor affecting council composition and behavior.

Size of council. Compared to state legislatures and the U.S. Congress, local city councils are relatively small. Five percent have fewer than three members, more than half (57 percent) have four to six members, 34 percent have seven to nine members, and 4 percent have more than nine members.[1] In general, the bigger the city, the larger the council. In cities with populations of 500,000 to 1 million, the average council has thirteen members. For cities with populations exceeding 1 million, the average is twenty-two. Some of the largest councils are in big cities like Chicago (fifty) and New York (fifty-one).

There has been a trend toward slightly larger councils. Of the cities reporting structural changes in their government over the past five years, 16 percent have enlarged their councils. Two situations have prompted council enlargement: the city-county consolidation movement and the desire to elect more racially and ethnically diverse councils.

In places approving city-county consolidation, the new "city" council is usually larger. There have been over twenty such consolidations approved by voters since 1962. The most recent ones have occurred in Athens–Clarke County, Georgia (1990), Lafayette–Lafayette Parish, Louisiana (1992), Augusta–Richmond County, Georgia (1995), and Kansas City–Wyandotte County, Kansas (1997).

A number of cities, especially in the South, have enlarged their councils by a seat or two to promote the election of more women and minorities. Advocacy groups have long maintained that larger councils yield greater representation for these groups, especially when combined with district-based elections. There is some evidence, although weak, that increasing council size independently increases female and minority, especially African-American, representation levels.[2]

In the past, some have argued that the reason women and blacks win more seats on larger councils is that the seats are less prestigious than those where there are fewer seats for which to compete.[3] There is only marginal support for this theory, however.[4] Seats on larger councils are viewed today as equally, if not more, prestigious, especially in big cities. There, nearly every council member tends to have wide media exposure, which makes council posts highly desirable, especially for those who someday may want to run for mayor or for some other local, state, or national office.

Do larger councils make it more difficult to reach consensus? Many say they do, especially in cities where each council member represents a specific geographically-defined district with distinctly different constituents. Others argue that it can be equally difficult to reach consensus on smaller councils in communities where strong personalities dominate and vie for attention. The data show that there tends to be more conflict on larger, more diverse, councils with single-member district constituency bases.[5]

Electoral constituency base. Municipalities elect their council members in a variety of ways, although most national surveys report the percentages of cities falling into three broad classifications: at-large, single-member district, or mixed (combination). There are, however, variations within these three classifications that clearly affect the campaign style of council candidates and their representational outlook once elected.

Under an *at-large* system, all council members run citywide and are voted on by all the voters in the city. Under a *pure at-large* system, if there are six seats up for election, each voter can vote for up to six candidates. The six candidates receiving the highest number of votes are duly elected. But there are other forms of at-large systems as well. In some cities, a person runs for a numerically or alphabetically labeled seat but is elected citywide (an *at-large by position* system). A candidate must decide whether he/she wants to run for Council Seat #1, or A, or Council Seat #2, or B, and so forth. The council seat, regardless of how labeled, has no geographical basis. On election day, all voters in the city can select the candidates they prefer to hold each nongeographically defined seat up for election. If there are six seats up for election, each voter may cast six votes — one for each seat.

There is yet a third type of at-large election called the *at-large from residency district* system. The city is divided into equally populated, geographically defined districts. A candidate runs to represent the district he/she lives in (for example, District 1), but all voters in the city get to vote on who shall represent that district. If there are six districts, each voter casts a ballot for a preferred candidate from each district.

A *single-member district council* election system limits each voter's choice to a single contest. A voter must choose among the candidates who have filed to represent the district in which the candidate and the voter both reside.

Voters in cities using a *combination,* or *mixed,* election system to choose council members can vote for all the at-large positions but for only one of the district-based council seats. For example, if a city has two at-large seats and four single-member district seats, each voter can cast three ballots (for the two at-large seats and for one district-based seat — the one in which he/she resides).

Proponents of mixed systems promote them precisely because they retain some council members who bring a citywide perspective to matters before the council but allow other councilors to represent more narrow neighborhood or group perspectives. Minority groups (racial or partisan) who comprise a sizable portion of the population but are not concentrated in a specific neighborhood often prefer at least some at-large seats.

In recent years, there has been a shift away from at-large elections to single-member district or mixed systems. ICMA surveys show in 1981, 66.5 percent of U.S. cities elected their council members using some type of at-large election; by 1991 the figure had slipped to 59 percent. Of the 323 cities changing electoral format, 70 percent switched to single-member districts and 30 percent moved to a mixed system. The 1996 ICMA Survey reported that 16.8 percent had single-member districts and 22.3 percent had mixed, or combination, systems to elect their members (see table 8.1, p. 170).

The desire to enhance female and minority city council representation has been the primary reason for shifting to single-member districts or mixed electoral systems. The proposition that single-member districts promote more minority and female representation is the most often-tested hypothesis relating to American city councils. In many instances, court rulings, or litigation threats, against existing at-large systems have pushed cities to change (see chapter 10).

TABLE 8.1. CHANGES IN AMERICAN CITY COUNCILS

Feature	1988	1991	1996
Election Type			
At-large	64.0	59.0	60.9
Single-member district	11.6	11.7	16.8
Mixed	24.3	29.3	22.3
Term Structure			
Staggered	80.0	81.0	82.6
Simultaneous	20.0	19.0	17.4
Term Limits			
Yes	4.2	4.2	8.6
No	95.8	95.8	91.4
Average Council Size	6.2	6.2	6.2
Average Length of Term (yrs.)	3.1	3.1	3.3
Party Affiliation on Ballot			
Yes (Partisan)	26.5	25.5	24.1
No (Nonpartisan)	73.5	74.5	75.9
Average Annual Salary			
Full-time	$2,400	$4,341	NA
Part-time	$1,800	$3,326	NA
Incumbent Reelection Rate			
Running for reelection	37.4	46.6	45.9
Reelected	84.0	86.1	88.3
Frequency of Meetings			
More than once a week	0.6	0.5	0.6
Once a week	9.2	7.0	6.5
Three times a month	NA	3.1	3.4
Twice a month	66.8	67.2	69.1
Once a month	21.4	20.2	20.4
Other	2.0	2.0	0.0
Nature of Position			
Full-time	6.0	25.3	NA
Part-time	94.0	74.7	NA
Use Standing Committees	53.1	NA	53.2
Have Council Staff	21.0	28.8	38.7
Gender Composition			
Male councilors	84.5	81.3	78.7
Female councilors	15.5	18.7	21.3
Racial Composition			
White	93.6	92.5	91.1
Black	4.1	4.8	5.5
Hispanic	1.8	2.3	2.4
Asian American	0.2	0.2	0.3
Native American	0.3	0.3	0.7
Age			
18–39	22.9	18.7	15.4
40–59	58.2	58.7	60.8
60 and over	18.8	22.6	23.8

Sources: Mary S. Schellinger, "Today's Local Policy Makers: A Council Profile," *Baseline Data Report* 20, no. 4 (Washington, D.C.: International City Management Association, July/August 1988); Evelina R. Moulder, "Profile of the City Council, 1991," *Baseline Data Report* 23, no. 6 (ICMA); Tari Renner and Victor S. DeSantis, "Contemporary Patterns and Trends in Municipal Government Structures," *The Municipal Year Book* 1993 (Washington, D.C.: ICMA, 1993); Tari Renner and Victor DeSantis, "Municipal Forms of Government: Issues and Trends," *The Municipal Year Book* 1998 (Washington, D.C.: ICMA, 1998), 30–41.

NA=not available.

Minority spokespersons frequently argue that minority candidates have a better chance of winning when they run from districts, especially when they make up less than a majority of the city's population and live in a residentially concentrated area. In such settings, switching to a district-based election system permits the drawing of a district in which minorities make up a majority of the electorate. District-based elections are also alleged to increase voter turnout rates and reduce campaign spending costs, although the data are clearly mixed on those counts. For example, in districts where competition declines once a minority incumbent becomes entrenched, turnout often declines in the district.[6]

Some feminist-group spokespersons have made the campaign-cost-reduction argument the centerpiece of their push for single-member district elections. Assuming that women would have more difficulty raising money than men would, feminists have argued that districts would permit female candidates to rely less on money and more on grassroots campaign techniques such as going door-to-door or visiting neighborhood civic associations and churches. This argument is patterned on one made by black civil rights activists who made the adoption of district-based elections a primary objective. Nevertheless, there has been no empirical evidence to support the claim that district-based elections result in the election of more women to city councils. To the contrary, national survey data show that at-large systems seem to yield more female council members.[7] And successful women candidates raise as much, and sometimes more, campaign funds than their male counterparts, regardless of their constituency base.[8]

For racial/ethnic minorities, district-based elections have been shown to promote slightly higher levels of representation depending upon the size of the group, their geographic concentration, their political cohesiveness, and their ability to coalesce with other groups.

There is considerable evidence that the *size* of the minority electorate within a community is a far more powerful predictor of a group's proportional representation on city council than the electoral system itself.[9] For example, one summary of this literature notes: "As black populations have grown, especially in large central cities, as black political participation rates (registration and turnout) have equaled or exceeded those of whites, and as successful black candidates have paved the way for others, the independent effect of electoral structure on black council representation levels has waned in certain parts of the country."[10] (Research to date has shown that the electoral system in place affects the Hispanic and Asian representational levels less than it does black representational levels.)

Even the importance of minority-group size is beginning to weaken as more minorities capture at-large posts in big cities such as Houston or win district seats with less than majority-minority populations. Some observers project that this trend will accelerate as more Americans begin to label themselves "biracial" or "multiracial" and cities become more multiethnic in composition.[11]

Not all shifts away from at-large elections have been driven by minorities. In some communities, neighborhood-based groups have pushed for district or combination systems, asserting they increase voter turnout and improve constituency service. Of these claims, there is far stronger support for the assertion that switching to districts improves constituency service than for the turnout stimulant notion. Other communities have held referendums, wherein voters have opted to keep at-large elections. Proponents assert that giving each voter a chance to affect the election of every city council member forces those elected to maintain a citywide, rather than a narrow, district perspective.

Some advocates of at-large elections view single-member districts as a return to the old, often corrupt, ward politics that characterized many big cities in the early 1900s. In those days, employment and contracts were often traded for votes.[12] Others favoring at-large elections philosophically oppose single-member districts when they are intentionally drawn for the primary purpose of advantaging certain racial/ethnic groups, thereby violating the "color-blind" language of the Fourteenth and Fifteenth Amendments to the Constitution. Supporters of district-based elections counter that they are needed to make up for past discrimination against these groups. In recent years, the Supreme Court has leaned toward the color-blind position and ruled against districting plans drawn exclusively on the basis of race (see chapter 10).

For council members elected at large, the constituency base is the entire city, while a council member elected from a single-member district serves a constituency that is limited to the residents of the district. Districts are geographically defined and drawn to ensure that each council member represents the same number of persons (one person, one vote). In cities with combination, or mixed, electoral systems, some council members have the entire city for a constituency base while others represent voters within specific geographically defined districts. Obviously, intracouncil dynamics are quite complex across councils with different constituency base mixes. Council member disagreements are far more likely to surface in communities with highly diverse racial/ethnic, income, and educational makeups.

Length of term. In most cities (81 percent), especially larger ones, council terms are four or more years long. In 22 percent, terms are two years in length, and in 7 percent, they last three years.[13] Most elected officials, along with some constituents, tend to favor longer terms. They argue that longer terms allow council members more time to focus on getting things done legislatively rather than on fund raising and running for reelection. They also believe that "longer terms are better at promoting minority council representation because they attract stronger minority candidates, that is, better educated, more affluent individuals who are willing to risk campaigning for office when they do not have to run for reelection every other year."[14]

Proponents of shorter terms argue they enable voters to "get rid of a bad apple" more quickly — an essential check and balance to nonuse or misuse of power. Some minority and women's group advocates also prefer shorter terms as a way to promote turnover, thereby increasing the number of open seats. But there is scant evidence that shorter terms increase turnover significantly. Overall, over 88 percent of all city council incumbents seeking reelection win again (see table 8.1, p. 170). Nonetheless, some studies show that exceptionally long terms (five years or longer) slightly deter the election of women and minorities, while shorter terms do not.

Proponents argue that shorter terms should reduce campaign costs, although there is little evidence to support this claim. Campaign costs are more a function of the competitiveness of the contest and the size of the jurisdiction/district than of election system or length of term. For example, in some big cities such as Los Angeles and Houston, even a district seat may require expensive media-based campaigns because of the sheer number of voters in the district or the area covered by the district.

Term limits. A relatively small proportion of all U.S. municipalities (8.6 percent) have adopted term limits for their council members (see table 8.1). There is a trend in this direction, however, especially in larger cities. For example, among cities 500,000 and over in population, 40 percent have term limits. The comparable figure for cities with populations from 2,500 to 4,999 is 2 percent.

The primary effect of adopting term limits is to open up the election system. Advocates strongly assert that term limits create open seats, thereby giving newcomers, including women and minorities, a better shot at winning. Not having to face an incumbent, they claim, reduces the amount of money that must be raised to make a serious bid for election.

Others vehemently oppose the imposition of term limits, arguing that it violates a person's right to vote for a candidate of choice who happens to have been in office for a while. Term-limit opponents argue that the *ballot box* rather than some artificial structural device is the appropriate and effective way to oust an unacceptable council member in a democracy. Opponents also question the campaign cost-reduction argument by pointing out that open seats tend to draw more candidates into the race. In a crowded open-seat race, a candidate most likely will spend the same amount or more to gain name recognition and get his/her message before the voting public. Thus, while the argument that open seats encourage many newcomers to run is sound, there is little evidence that campaign costs are reduced by adopting term limits.

In general, the voluntary retirement rate among city council members is considerably higher than for state legislators or members of Congress. Many simply choose not to run again, for reasons ranging from the time involved to undesirable media scrutiny. (Reasons for leaving office are discussed in more detail later in the chapter.)

Term structure: staggered versus simultaneous. Some cities (17 percent) set up their council election systems in a way that requires all council members to stand for election at the same time (simultaneous terms). However, the vast majority (83 percent) stagger their elections to ensure at least some continuity and experience on the council (see table 8.1, p. 170). Larger cities, with bigger councils, are the most likely to have staggered terms.

Those who prefer staggered terms argue that they make it easier for challengers (especially women and minorities) to gain name recognition and beat incumbents, particularly in smaller jurisdictions. Conversely, proponents of simultaneous elections believe that they encourage slating and group coalition-building and can reduce campaign costs if joint advertising is used.

There is data, albeit weak, showing that simultaneous elections have benefited some black candidates in the South. Staggered terms, however, have helped Hispanic candidates (mostly in the West where Hispanic populations are larger) and female office-seekers. No studies have yet tested the proposition that campaign costs are lower where simultaneous term structures are in place.

Partisan versus nonpartisan. Overall, over three-fourths of all U.S. cities elect their council members via nonpartisan elections (see table 8.1). This means that a candidate for city council runs without a party label beside his or her name. The adoption of nonpartisan elections was a popular component of the municipal reform movement that emerged after the turn of the twentieth century to combat corrupt big-city partisan-driven political machines. (Other structural changes that were part of the reform package included at-large elections and the council-manager form of government.)[15]

Proponents of nonpartisan elections argue that candidates should be judged on the basis of their issue stances, rather than simply on political party labels. Opponents claim that nonpartisan elections lower voter turnout rates and result in disproportionately high numbers of Republican, affluent, white, and male winners.[16] While this may have been true at one time, more recent data show that female and minority candidates fare as well in nonpartisan as in partisan contests, while Hispanics fare better.

Timing of elections. The date a specific election is held, usually dictated by state law, can make a difference in the voter turnout rate and in the profile of the electorate. Participation in council elections obviously is highest when they are held concurrently with high-profile (presidential or gubernatorial) general elections. Turnout is lower when elections are held "off-cycle" on dates unique to municipalities, unless, of course, there is a "hot" local contest or referendum. Most U.S. cities (around 60 percent) hold their elections separately from either the presidential or gubernatorial contests. This may partially explain why turnout rates for city elections are typically in the 25- to 35-percent range.[17]

Those who favor holding elections concurrently with high-profile national or state elections emphasize that such scheduling increases voter participation, which, in turn, makes the voters more representative of the community as a whole. In low-turnout elections, there is a tendency for older, as well as more educated and affluent, voters to show up at the polls in numbers that are disproportionately high relative to their proportion of the voting-age population.

Those who advocate holding local elections separately from presidential or gubernatorial elections say that this scheduling forces residents to focus on the specific issues facing their community. Local candidates have an easier time informing voters about their credentials and positions without having to vie with top-of-the-ballot presidential and gubernatorial candidates. Off-cycle elections also may make it easier for local candidates to raise money. In a presidential election year, many donors prefer to give to presidential candidates or their preferred political party's campaign fund rather than to a local candidate.

Full-time or part-time position? The frequency of formal council meetings, the salary attached to the position, and the average amount of time spent on council business weekly are all indicators of whether a council seat is a full-time or part-time position. The available data show that roughly three-fourths of all city council members in the United States serve in a part-time capacity. Only in cities with populations over 1 million is there a high incidence of full-time councilors.

National surveys by ICMA have found that larger cities (over 250,000) are more prone to hold weekly meetings, whereas the vast majority of communities with populations below 10,000 hold bimonthly or monthly council meetings. Council meetings also are longer in larger cities, especially those with a council-manager form of government. (This form of government typically gives more authority to council members, as noted in the previous chapter.) The typical council meeting lasts two to four hours in over half of the cities, but four to eight hours in nearly one-fourth of the cities, mostly the larger ones.

Longer and more frequent council meetings reflect the growing complexity and the contentious nature of the job. In large cities, more than half (55 percent) of council members report spending forty or more hours weekly on council matters. Even in medium-sized cities, 41 percent of the councilors report spending at least thirty hours per week, as do 17 percent of those in small cities. Thus, in spite of the fact that a council position technically may be "part-time," it is closer to a full-time job for many, and this is another reason some choose not to run for reelection.

Salary. Contrary to popular opinion, few council members run because of the salary attached to the post. For *part-time* council members (roughly three-fourths of all council members), salaries range from $1 to $39,000, with smaller cities more likely to offer salaries of $10,000 or less. Even *full-time* council members do not get paid much except in the very largest cities. Salaries for full-time councilors range from $1 to $90,680 (from $63,000 to $90,680 in cities over 1 million in population).

A survey by the NLC that did not distinguish between full-time and part-time council members found that in cities over 25,000, 59 percent earn salaries below $10,000 (5 percent receive no salary). Only 14 percent earn salaries in excess of $30,000 annually.[18]

The battle over raising elected officials' salaries is long-standing. Proponents consistently have argued that it is a way to make representation on city councils less elitist — more akin to a "citizen's legislature." If a reasonable, livable salary were offered, less affluent persons might realistically seek political office, they maintain. Those who favor minimal stipends for city councilors worry that an elected official whose salary is his or her sole income may have to rely too much on special-interest contributions in running for office and for reelection, effectively placing that official "in the pockets" of special-interest groups.

Council Operations

The number of important issues facing city council members has expanded over the years. These issues frequently have extensive, often entangled, technical, legal, and financial dimensions. To cope, many councils have stepped up their reliance on committees and professional staff support.

Council committees. An NLC survey of cities with populations over 25,000 found a sharp escalation over a ten-year span in the proportion of councils using committees to conduct hearings, propose legislation, review budgets, review existing policies, evaluate programs, and search for answers to specific questions. Large cities, with more diverse populations and problems, and larger city councils have relied most on committees to spread the council workload. Over 90 percent of cities with populations in excess of 200,000 use them, as do 81 percent of all medium-sized cities and 72 percent of all small municipalities.

Typically, there are two types of council committees, standing and ad hoc, which differ in longevity and scope. A *standing committee* is "a permanent body with jurisdiction over specific policy areas" created by charter, local ordinance, or council resolution. Standing committees also are often given quasi-judicial authority to hear disputes and render judgments in situations involving zoning, tax assessment, building permit, and civil service. An *ad hoc committee* is a "temporary committee established to address short-term problems or issues."[19]

Well over 90 percent of U.S. cities surveyed by the ICMA report that their standing committees make policy recommendations to the full council. The standard areas covered by these committees are: planning and zoning, community development, parks and recreation, cable television, civil service, budget and finance, beautification and code enforcement, and senior citizens service committees. Based on a 1996 NLC survey, we can anticipate the formation of standing committees focusing on the needs of children and families.[20] Ad hoc committees "are often used by local governments to address quickly issues that standing committees may not have the time or ability to deal with.... The temporary status and narrow mission of ad hoc committees may strengthen the ability of their members to come together, gather information, and reach consensus."[21] Typical concerns addressed by ad hoc committees include military base closures or reconfigurations, environmental concerns, sports team relocations, and natural disasters.

Staff support. Paralleling trends at the national and state levels, city councils have increasingly turned to professionals for staff support (see table 8.1, p. 170). This stepped-up reliance has been driven by a sharp increase in the number of issues requiring the attention of highly trained professionals and by rising service demands from constituents. While many council members would like even more staff support, it is often difficult for them to justify when their communities may be experiencing fiscal difficulties. In such a situation, hiring more administrators ("bureaucrats" to the public) can backfire politically. When resources are scarce, taxpayers prefer that funds be spent on services and facilities directly benefiting citizens, not on new administrators.

When resources do become available, a majority of city councilors lean toward hiring staffers who will serve the council as a whole, rather than council committees or individual councilors. In big cities, however, where more councilors are elected from single-member districts, 59 percent favor assigning new staff to individual council members, primarily to handle requests for services and assistance from people living in their respective districts.

Roles, Responsibilities, and Citizen Expectations of Council Members

The typical city council member represents, legislates, oversees city management (checks the chief executive, city departments, and employees), and judges. James Svara has written one of the best descriptions of councilor roles:

> Members of the city council...speak for and make decisions on behalf
> of the citizens of the community [their representation role], engage in

"lawmaking" — policy leadership, enactment of ordinances and resolutions, debate, criticism, and investigation [their legislative role], . . . respond to problems their constituents have with administrative agencies by seeking to bring about corrective action . . . and oversee the execution of policy in order to insure that the purpose of their lawmaking is accomplished [their executive oversight role], . . . and fill a judicial function either in the informal sense that they serve as the "court of last resort" for certain kinds of appeals from citizens who feel they have been harmed by city government, or in the more formal sense, in a few cases, of following strict procedures to adjudicate regulations or settle legal disputes.[22]

In all cities, councils bear the legal responsibility for adopting public policies (lawmaking). But they vary, according to their form of government, in the degree to which they are involved in the appointment, removal, and oversight of department heads, the structuring of departments and agencies, and budget preparation.

Form of Government: Authority and Responsibility

The three most common forms of government in U.S. cities are mayor-council (strong and weak), used by 35.2 percent; council-manager, used by 48.5 percent; and commission, used by 1.4 percent.[23]

Strong mayor-council form. The strong mayor-council form of government, usually found in cities over 250,000 in population but often in those over 100,000 as well, is characterized by a mayor (elected separately from the council) who has strong appointment, budgetary, and management powers. Thus, in a strong mayor-council city, the council members are more likely to focus most of their efforts on their representation (constituency service) and lawmaking functions.

Weak mayor-council form. The weak mayor-council form of government is most common in cities under 10,000 in population, where both the mayor and council members serve on a part-time basis. In some cities, the mayor is separately elected, but in most, the mayor is a member of the council who has been chosen mayor by his or her council peers. In both situations, the mayor is primarily an executive figurehead, which leaves to the council relatively strong appointment, budget, policy initiation, and management powers. Even so, such councils typically meet only once or twice a month because the issues they must deal with are considerably narrower in scope than those confronting big-city councilors.

City commission form. The city commission form of government, once popular, has virtually disappeared. By 1996 only 1.4 percent of all cities still used it, mostly those with populations in the 12,500 to 25,000 range. Under this form, there is very little separation of the executive and legislative functions. Commissioners (equivalent to council members) act as executives when they oversee a specific functional area (e.g., Public Safety,

Public Works, Budgeting and Finance). When they sit collectively as the city commission, they engage in legislative and representational functions — adopting budgets, passing ordinances and resolutions, and protecting the interests of city residents. One of the biggest criticisms of this form is the absence of clear lines of authority. Constituents often do not know who to call or who to blame for actions or inactions. Accountability deficiencies are a major reason why cities have abandoned the commission structure over the years.

Council-manager form. The council-manager form of government grew out of the municipal reform movement. Designed to separate politics from administration — to "put policy-making authority in the hands of an elected city council and administrative responsibilities in the hands of the manager, who was hired by and accountable to the city council"[24] — it is very popular among medium-sized cities. Over 61 percent of the cities with council-manager governments have populations between 5,000 and 50,000, but some larger cities are governed by this form as well.

City councils are generally strongest in council-manager cities, primarily because council members hire and fire the manager, set the terms of his or her employment, and constantly monitor the conduct of city departments, offices, and agencies, while continuing to engage in their legislative and judicial activities. Managers need the political support of at least a majority of the council to formally approve their budgets and management policies and procedures.

Dos and Don'ts for Council Members

Being a council member in today's complex, and often conflictual, environment is not easy. There is a real possibility that at any time a councilor may say or do something that will grab the media's attention, incite council colleagues, or prompt a lawsuit. Many professional associations now prepare, and regularly update, handbooks advising council members on the various intricacies of the position, including how to deal with the media.[25]

The public expects a lot from its elected officials (see box, p. 180). As the Kentucky *Handbook* notes, "[The public] wants everything from you.... They expect you to be infallible, invincible, omnipotent, and untiring. But they don't want you to be too powerful.... They want to know what you are doing all of the time and whether it has anything to do with public affairs or not.... The public eye is always nearby watching you."[26]

The media often serve as the public's eye. An NLC guide on how to deal with the local media advises elected officials, "If you aspire to prominence and success in local government, you must be prepared to welcome, and utilize to advantage, your inevitable exposure to the media."[27] But the same guide warns that "the agendas of the media and the government are sometimes not compatible" and hints that the situation has worsened in re-

WHAT THE PUBLIC EXPECTS FROM ITS CITY COUNCIL MEMBERS

1. To consider all sides of an issue.
2. To show genuine concern about municipal problems.
3. To refrain from taking a stand on an issue until all sides have been heard.
4. To think of yourself as a public servant, not as superior to your constituents.
5. To work hard in the public interest.
6. To grasp the central issues, not get side-tracked by minutiae.
7. To establish clear policies; to set goals for achieving those policies.
8. To be well-organized and efficient.
9. To be politically astute.
10. To be consistent in your positions.
11. To prevent private problems from affecting public job performance.
12. To be willing to surrender some privacy.
13. To admit mistakes and to correct them.
14. To be accessible to the public.
15. To value your office for itself, not as a stepping-stone to a more prestigious position.
16. To have a solid sense of yourself.
17. To have integrity.
18. To refrain from unfairly undermining the efforts of city council members with whom you do not agree.
19. To give citizens and employees credit for work well done.
20. To avoid making personal attacks.
21. To back up criticisms with facts, not make vague, general criticisms that cannot be answered or acted upon.
22. To make citizens feels secure about living in the city, by making the city as safe and well-administered as possible.
23. To make the city an enjoyable place to live.
24. To clean up deteriorating areas of town.
25. To plan for orderly growth and development as well as safeguard the environment.
26. To comply fully with open meeting laws and disclosure requirements, not evade the spirit of the law by seeking alternative ways to conduct closed meetings.
27. To communicate openly, honestly, and candidly about what is really going on.
28. To keep the media informed.
29. To be a good "ambassador" outside the city.
30. To assertively represent the city and defend its interest in county, state, and federal relations.

Source: *Handbook for Newly Elected City Officials* (Lexington, Ky.: Kentucky League of Cities and Department of Local Government, 1994), 33–34.

cent years. Officials tend to agree. As is noted later in the chapter, intense media scrutiny scares away potential candidates and prompts some council members to leave office voluntarily.

The issues that arise in a typical community vary widely: land use, availability of housing and services, tax policy and tax rates, service delivery (magnitude, delivery mechanisms, and fees), buildings and facilities, economic development, the environment, public safety, recreation, cultural opportunities, and more. Council members are expected by constituents and the media to be both generalists and specialists, a difficult task for anyone. This explains why the job is increasingly a full-time venture.

Constituents, Political Ambition, and Governing Style

The fervor with which council members tackle their job is not exclusively a product of various structures and position attributes. Constituent demands and concerns, along with a councilor's own priorities, governing style, and future political ambition, greatly affect what roles an elected official enjoys most. For example, a council member who has no ambition to run for higher office but who would like to be reelected to the city council may view constituency service and lawmaking as more interesting and important than executive oversight. Another, who plans to run for mayor some day, may put considerably more effort into executive and bureaucratic oversight. Sudden shifts in the nature and severity of problems confronting city councilors often cause them to alter both the roles they play and their political ambitions.

Problems Today's City Councils Must Address

The average city official today serves in an antigovernment, antitax environment. A growing portion of the public desires more and better services and facilities but wants to pay for them using yesterday's (or yesteryear's) tax rates. At the same time, the federal and state governments, each with its own fiscal and political difficulties, are reducing the amount of grants-in-aid they give to local governments while devolving more responsibility to them, which creates fiscal stress for many municipalities.

Social ills persist in many communities. Crime rates have risen, along with teenage pregnancies, homelessness, high-school drop-out rates, substance abuse, domestic violence, AIDS, racial tensions, and poverty. One of every five U.S. cities with more than 25,000 residents has a poverty rate greater than 20 percent. In fact, 42 percent of the nation's poor live in cities with populations greater than 25,000. Some feel there has also been a deterioration in the family and in the moral fiber and civility of our citizenry; who is to blame is the subject of intense debate. But one thing is certain — local officials have to address these problems, regardless of their origin.

TABLE 8.2. CITY OFFICIALS REPORTING WORSENING CONDITIONS IN THEIR
COMMUNITIES OVER A SINGLE YEAR, 1988–95 (IN PERCENTAGES)

Worsening Condition	1988	1989	1990	1991	1992	1993	1994	1995
Impacts of unfunded mandates	–	–	–	–	–	71	74	54
Gangs	–	–	–	–	–	49	51	50
Cable TV rates and service	–	–	–	–	57	48	49	47
Violent crime	45	37	33	38	41	43	41	27
Drugs	67	58	46	47	49	41	49	45
Teen pregnancy	–	–	–	–	–	37	46	45
Unemployment	18	8	37	51	54	31	19	16
Family stability	–	–	–	–	31	30	40	38
AIDS	36	13	38	45	40	29	37	38
Poverty	38	19	36	45	43	27	30	34
City fiscal condition	30	17	30	35	42	26	38	31
Housing affordability	51	42	42	35	36	25	–	–
Homelessness	43	18	36	41	35	24	29	34
Overall economic conditions	17	14	36	51	47	23	22	15
Quality of education	17	12	18	28	25	22	24	29
Race/ethnic relations	–	–	–	–	20	22	29	43
Low income housing availability	40	24	31	28	26	22	–	–
Infrastructure	–	–	–	–	–	17	27	24
Vitality of neighborhoods	–	–	–	–	21	17	19	16
High-school graduation rates	–	–	–	–	–	13	–	–
Health care	21	15	21	32	31	12	19	28
Solid-waste management	39	36	24	22	17	11	12	11
Police/community relations	–	–	–	–	–	9	14	12
Air quality	24	13	27	14	14	9	12	14
Immunization/preventive care	–	–	–	–	–	7	–	–
Water quality	–	–	–	–	–	6	6	8
Volunteerism/community service	–	–	–	–	–	6	8	9
Availability of quality, affordable housing	–	–	–	–	–	–	24	21
School violence	–	–	–	–	–	–	52	45
Youth crime	–	–	–	–	–	–	63	62

Source: Herbert L. Green Jr., *The State of America's Cities* (Washington, D.C.: National
League of Cities, January 1996), 10.

Note: – indicates the years a condition was not included for evaluation.

The National League of Cities conducts an annual survey of city
officials across the United States, asking these officials to identify the conditions in their communities that have worsened over the past year. Eight
years of results are shown in table 8.2. There is quite a bit of flux in these
figures, reflecting the highly dynamic nature of local politics.

In any community, there are those who argue that these problems could
be alleviated, or at least partially relieved, if only government would spend
more money addressing them. Others within the same community vehemently reject the notion that more government spending can eliminate these
formidable problems. Such polarized views of how to solve problems may
be held by a city's council members, especially if they are elected by districts
whose electoral constituency bases are radically different.

Pressures on a municipality's finances come from a variety of sources: population growth and decline, shifts in federal and/or state aid, new federal or state mandates, adverse court rulings, voter passage of taxing and spending referenda, changes in the vitality of the local economy and cost of living, and new or intensified demands to solve critical problems facing the community. These pressures differ from city-to-city because no two cities are identical in their population or socioeconomic and political profiles.

The functions for which cities are responsible also vary considerably. In some parts of the country, primarily the Northeast and older cities in the Midwest, municipalities have primary authority over, and major fiscal responsibility for, public schools, welfare, and public hospitals. In other parts of the country, schools are governed by school districts; welfare is the responsibility of counties or states; and hospitals are administered by a special authority, another type of local government, or by counties. These wide variations in functional responsibilities are yet another reason why the roles and responsibilities of city council members differ tremendously across the United States.

The taxing power in the hands of municipal officials, governed by state law, also varies. Some states allow their cities to impose local sales and income taxes, but most others prohibit it. All municipalities can, and do, rely on the property tax, although they differ with regard to maximum allowable rates, assessment practices, and exemptions they can grant to individuals and businesses.

The property tax has become very unpopular virtually everywhere ever since California passed Proposition 13 in 1978.[28] Consequently, city council members approve property-tax rate increases sparingly — and reluctantly. The more common revenue-raising approach in recent years has been to increase fees and service charges (see table 8.3, p. 184). But even fee increases can spark intense council debates in some cities. Council members representing poorer districts carefully scrutinize whether proposed fees are equitable or fair.

On the spending side, the most recent data available from the NLC (table 8.3) show that the largest cities have been the most aggressive in trying to put the brakes on spending, either by improving productivity levels, participating in intergovernmental cost-sharing agreements, contracting services from the private or nonprofit sectors, shrinking government payrolls, freezing hiring, or cutting back service levels. Many smaller cities also have attempted to cut spending.

Regardless of size, no city government (or private citizen for that matter) ever has all the resources it needs to meet everybody's demands. The bigger the revenue shortfall, the more intense the conflict over how to allocate existing funds or find new revenues. Many a challenger's run for city council has been prompted by a citizen's vehement disapproval of the way city monies were being raised and spent by incumbent council members.

TABLE 8.3. ACTIONS TAKEN BY CITIES TO RELIEVE FISCAL STRESS
(IN PERCENTAGES)

Action	All cities (n=338)	Small cities (10,000– 49,999)	Medium cities (50,000- 99,999)	Large cities (100,000– 299,999)	Largest cities (300,000 & over)
Expenditure actions					
Increased actual capital spending	55.6	54.3	55.6	66.2	65.2
Increased growth rate of operating spending	54.8	57.4	40.2	50.7	52.2
Increased size of city workforce	35.6	35.3	36.1	35.8	41.7
Increased city service levels	28.8	26.4	35.3	36.7	50.0
Increased contracting-out services	27.8	26.3	31.5	35.3	37.5
Improved productivity levels	23.7	20.3	30.9	34.0	63.2
Increased interlocal agreements	17.7	16.0	20.6	27.7	27.8
Reduced size of city workforce	16.3	15.5	19.4	19.4	16.7
Reduced actual capital spending	12.0	12.1	13.9	9.2	8.7
Reduced growth rate of operating spending	9.1	7.8	14.0	14.9	13.0
Reduced interlocal agreements	5.3	6.7	0.0	0.0	0.0
Reduced city service levels	4.0	4.6	1.2	4.1	0.0
Reduced productivity levels	1.4	1.4	0.0	4.3	0.0
Reduced contracting-out services	1.1	0.9	2.8	1.5	0.0
Revenue actions					
Increased level of fees/charges	32.5	32.8	27.4	25.0	66.7
Increased property tax rates	20.9	22.8	12.6	16.4	12.0
Increased number/level of impact or development fees	17.6	18.3	17.0	11.6	17.4
Increased number of other fees or charges	16.6	17.2	12.3	10.4	33.3
Reduced property tax rates	13.5	13.2	9.7	19.4	24.0
Increased innovative/ unconventional revenue-raising mechanisms	11.9	9.1	16.9	28.2	29.4
Increased tax base	7.8	8.0	7.4	5.8	8.7
Increased rates of other taxes	6.3	6.1	8.6	5.8	4.2
Increased sales tax rates	4.9	5.3	4.7	2.8	0.0
Reduced tax base	3.0	2.7	3.7	1.4	13.0
Reduced innovative/ unconventional revenue-raising mechanisms	2.6	1.5	0.0	0.0	0.0
Increased number of other taxes	2.5	2.6	1.9	2.9	0.0
Reduced rates of other taxes	1.2	0.9	1.0	4.3	4.2
Reduced number/level of impact or development fees	1.1	0.9	0.0	4.3	4.3
Increased income tax rates	0.8	0.9	1.0	0.0	0.0
Reduced income tax rates	0.8	0.9	0.0	0.0	4.0
Reduced sales tax rate	0.7	0.9	0.0	0.0	0.0
Reduced level of fees/charges	0.4	0.0	2.8	1.5	0.0
Reduced number of other fees or charges	0.4	0.0	2.8	1.5	0.0
Reduced number of other taxes	0.1	0.0	0.9	0.0	0.0

Source: Michael Pagano, *City Fiscal Conditions in 1997* (Washington, D.C.: National League of Cities, July 1997), 24.

TABLE 8.4. AGE AND MOTIVATION TO RUN FOR CITY COUNCIL
(IN PERCENTAGES)

Motivation	All Council Members (n=574)	Under 65 Years of Age (n=430)	65 & Older (n=144)
It's a way to get more involved in the community.	64.6	63.3	68.8
I can give something back to the community.	62.9	61.9	66.0
Friends and neighbors urged me to run.	59.9	57.2	68.1
Certain issues are being ignored.	52.6	52.8	52.1
I'm at a point in my life when I have time for it.	33.4	24.2	61.1
The kids are grown and I have resources to live on without the council salary.	19.7	15.1	33.3
I have always loved politics.	17.9	18.1	17.4
No one else was willing to do it.	10.1	10.5	9.0
It allows me to get experience before running for another office.	8.0	10.0	2.1
Meeting people helps my business/career.	5.4	6.3	2.8

Source: Mail survey of Florida city council members conducted July–August 1996, by the author.

Note: Respondents were asked: "Why did you personally decide to run for city council? (Check the major reasons.)"

Why People Run for City Council

Few Americans ever take the bold step of running for city council, although the formal qualifications for office are minimal. Most cities require that a candidate for council be a registered voter, a U.S. citizen, and a resident of the community for a certain period of time (usually a year or less). Persons convicted of a felony offense and those formally certified as mental incompetents generally are prohibited from running unless they petition to have their voting rights restored (most states have provisions for this).

One widely cited study by political scientist Timothy Bledsoe classifies council members along several dimensions, depending upon their stated reasons for running.[29] *Politicos* are those who say they ran because they enjoy politics and hope to move on to another office, but also because they see the business advantages of serving. *Self-regarders* are those who enter city politics intent on personal enrichment. *Community-regarders* run to serve the whole community and seek no personal gain. *Locals* run primarily to help friends and neighbors, not parties (*partisans*) or single-issue interest groups. *Particularists* run because of an overriding concern for a specific issue or issues; they tend to be outsiders — minorities or members of groups long underrepresented in government — and one-termers.

Motivations for running differ across age groups. A 1996 survey of city council members in Florida found that the number of senior citizens running for city council has increased over the past five years. Older persons, many of whom are retirees, report that they initially decided to run because they had the time and resources to do so (see table 8.4).

Who Wins?

Just a decade ago, a major study of city council members described the "typical" member as "a forty-seven-year-old white male, a lawyer or other professional by occupation, with an education beyond four years of college [and a] family income well above average in the over $45,000 per year category."[30] Today, that portrait is somewhat "out of focus," especially with regard to gender, race, and age.

Gender

Women are far better represented on city councils than in state legislatures or in Congress. The percentage of women increased substantially between 1976 and 1996 — from 9.7 percent to 21.3 percent — and it continues to rise (see table 8.1, p. 170). Women councilors are more prevalent in larger cities with racially and ethnically diverse, and more affluent and better-educated, populations.

Women (and men) who have been more active in civic and professional associations are more likely to get elected than those who have not. Winners of both sexes attribute at least part of their victory to this connection. Female city council candidates traditionally have received more support than have male candidates from neighborhood organizations, single-issue groups, and women's organizations. Male candidates still tend to get a marginally higher level of support from business groups, although this is changing, too.[31]

Some of the long-standing myths about the role of gender in city council elections have been refuted. We now know that when compared with male candidates, females win at the same rate; raise as much or more campaign money; are not disadvantaged by at-large elections, nonpartisan elections, run-off elections (second primaries), or newspaper or political party endorsements of male candidates; and are not deterred from running by steep filing fees. Media coverage of women candidates, relative to their male counterparts, has improved in frequency and content, although some still complain about it.[32] (In general, candidates never think that there is enough coverage or that what coverage there is is balanced.)

Age also is no longer much of a barrier. Formerly, younger and middle-aged professional women were the most likely to enter local politics, but that trend has changed considerably. Older women are running in record numbers, as the old notion that politics is "a male thing" has rapidly eroded.[33] By 1993 "only 6 percent of women and 5 percent of men were steadfast in the belief that women should stay out of politics."[34]

Black and Hispanic females do not run or win as often as do white females, even when they run against minority males. One study has concluded that these women's gender is a bigger barrier to their election to city councils than their race.[35]

Today, there are few city councils with no female members. And it is increasingly common for female candidates to end up running against other females for the same position — a marked change from the past. Women opposing women is simply one more piece of evidence that women are not a monolithic group. Gender actually is a fairly weak voting cue compared to age, race, education, income, or religion.[36]

In spite of the increasing numbers of female council members, women remain underrepresented relative to their proportion of the population in most cities, but this is primarily because fewer women run for office, not because they have a more difficult time than men once they declare their candidacy. Darcy et al. summarize the situation well: "We can be reasonably certain that, at least at the local level, when they become candidates, women do not have to jump large hurdles that men do not. The evidence indicates that their sources of support are just as firm and widespread as those of men."[37]

Race/Ethnicity

Minorities in most cities are more underrepresented than women. The available data show that blacks make up 5.5 percent of all city council members, Hispanics 2.4 percent, Asians 0.3 percent, and Native Americans 0.7 percent (see table 8.1, p. 170). But these figures (which include a lot of small cities without sizable minority populations) mask the strides minorities have made in larger cities. Minority candidates are most successful in larger cities, with sizable, concentrated, cohesive minority populations and better-educated, liberal white populations willing to vote for minority candidates.

There is little information about minority candidates' personal backgrounds. The bulk of the research on minority city councils members has focused on the degree to which various structures inhibit their electoral success, as noted earlier. However, we do know that minority males are considerably more likely to run and win than are minority females. And one study has found that Mexican-American city council members tend to be "somewhat younger, less well educated, and more conservative than their Anglo counterparts...and more likely than Anglos to view the city council as a stepping stone to higher political office."[38]

Interracial coalition-building is less critical to minority candidates running in cities where they make up a majority of the voting population. In 1990 fourteen U.S. cities with populations of 100,000 or more had black majorities, twelve had Hispanic majorities, and one had an Asian/Pacific Islander majority population. Interracial coalition-building is critical for minority candidates running in cities with less-than-majority-minority populations.[39] Across the United States, the trend is toward more racially pluralist cities, where no one racial group makes up a majority of the population.

Depending on the city, majority coalitions can be built by several minority groups joining together (e.g., blacks and Hispanics). In other cities, there may be open hostility between minority groups. In such places, it is more common to find a coalition between a portion of the Anglo population and one or more minority groups.

In general, the black community is more cohesive politically than other minority/ethnic groups, although it is gradually becoming less monolithic with the emergence of a sizable entrepreneurial sector. Hispanics differ considerably in their political preferences because the term encompasses a wide array of cultures including Cubans, Mexican Americans, Puerto Ricans, and identifiable clusters of groups from the Caribbean (Haitians and Dominicans), from Central America (Salvadorans, Guatemalans, and Nicaraguans), and other Latin nationalities.[40] The Asian/Pacific Islander category also includes some very diverse subpopulations (Chinese, Japanese, Koreans, Filipinos, Vietnamese, Asian Indians, Laotians, and Thais).[41]

There are some significant differences in campaigning across different minority groups. For example, African-American candidates routinely campaign in black churches, which have long played a major role in stimulating black turnout.[42] Mexican-American council candidates rely more on labor, business, and neighborhood groups.[43]

The degree to which a minority candidate emphasizes race in his or her campaign depends on the size of the minority population. A study by Metz and Tate concludes: "Most black candidates opt for the politically advantageous strategy. In cities with small black populations, black candidates most often turn to deracialized strategies. In cities where blacks near a majority of the population, black candidates favor more highly racial strategies."[44]

Minorities continue to be underrepresented on councils. But, as is the case for women candidates, structural arrangements increasingly fail to explain their underrepresentation. The impact of structures (including the electoral system) on representation is considerably weaker than minority population size, residential concentration, and cohesiveness or constituency income and education. The biggest barrier is a reluctance to run for office.

Age

America as a nation is aging. In 1970, 10 percent of the population was 65 years of age or older; by 1990 this age group was over 12 percent of the population. The "baby boomers" will begin hitting retirement age in 2010, and by the year 2030 over one-fifth of the population will be 65 or older. The aging trend is already noticeable in the age distributions of city council members. In 1981, 18.9 percent were 60 years of age or older; by 1996 that group was 23.8 percent (see table 8.1, p. 170). The growing tendency of older persons to jump into local politics has been prompted by the emergence of more age-segregated neighborhoods and communities, a higher level of interest in local politics among older voters, with more time to devote to them, and a dearth of younger persons interested in seeking local offices.

In the past, a city council seat has been seen as a "stepping stone" for persons seeking higher local, state, or national office. Those with higher ambitions were advised to "arrive on the council at a young age — before thirty-five — and move on to an intermediate office after one, or at most two four-year terms on the council."[45] New data show that fewer younger people are running for city council than in the past,[46] although their reasons for not running are very similar to those expressed by older Americans.

Why People *Don't* Run for City Council — Again or Ever!

Term limits aside, some council members choose not to run again after serving just a few terms, and the number is growing. There has been a sharp increase in the frustration levels of councilors, especially those serving in big cities. The greatest single source of frustration is conflict among council members, cited by 55 percent.[47] Conflict tends to be worse when councilors are elected from single-member districts with sharply divergent constituency profiles. Other sources of anxiety come from special-interest group pressures (46 percent), long hours (43 percent), time away from family (46 percent), amount of required reading (40 percent), and meeting frequency (35 percent). To these add low council salaries (43 percent), losses in private income (34 percent), media-related problems (36 percent), and rising campaign costs (49 percent), and it's a miracle anyone stays beyond a single term. It is not surprising, based on these figures (and term limits to a lesser degree), that the median length of service on city council is just five years.

Many Americans would never even consider running for city council. In their minds, council salaries are too low, citizen expectations are unrealistic, politicians are held in low regard, and the media scrutiny of candidates is too intense (see table 8.5, p. 190).

Communicating with the Electorate: As Candidate and Council Member

Council members operate in a political world dominated by television, public opinion surveys, electronic media-based campaigns, negative ads, and a highly cynical and disengaged public. Most constituents cannot even name their council member(s). This has sent councilors and candidates alike in search of new ways to get input from the electorate.

TABLE 8.5. DETERRENTS TO RUNNING FOR CITY COUNCIL
(IN PERCENTAGES)

Deterrent	All Council Members (n=567)	Under 65 Years of Age (n=425)	65 & Older (n=142)
Low salary relative to time involved.	56.3	55.1	59.9
Public expectations make the job thankless.	48.9	48.0	51.4
Low public esteem for politicians.	39.9	40.5	38.0
Intense media scrutiny.	38.1	40.7	30.3
Can't make a difference if elected.	36.3	37.4	33.1
Campaigning takes too much time.	35.1	35.3	34.5
Lack of knowledge about how to run.	24.9	23.1	30.3
Fund raising.	23.1	24.0	20.4
Campaign costs.	21.5	20.0	26.1
Too much pressure from special interest groups.	11.5	10.4	14.8
Professionalization of campaigns.	7.8	6.1	12.7
Too difficult to get on the ballot.	6.7	6.1	8.5
Fear for personal/family safety.	6.0	6.6	4.2
At-large elections (citywide).	4.2	4.2	4.2

Source: Mail survey of Florida city council members conducted July–August 1996, by the author.

Note: Respondents were asked: "In your personal opinion, what are the major reasons deterring more people in your community from running for council? (Check the major deterrents.)"

Telecommunication-Based Outreach Efforts

Many cities are putting information on-line about council meetings (dates, times, agenda items), tax and bill payment, court dockets, employment opportunities, parks and recreation activities, community "happenings," permit procedures and fees, and procurement (contractor certification requirements, Request For Proposal forms and procedures), to mention a few.[48]

A sizable number of communities use public-access television to allow residents to monitor council meetings and hearings without being in attendance. The public's opinions on various issues confronting the city often are solicited in requests for input via a designated telephone line that are flashed on the screen, giving those unable to attend a chance to express their views. Interactive approaches in general are more effective than more traditional approaches at reaching younger people. The primary drawback is that only a small proportion of the population, regardless of age, ever tunes in to public-access television.

Some cities have had success placing interactive informational centers in well-traveled shopping malls. These terminals connect back to government computers. From these mall-based centers, citizens can either request information or express their opinions on questions posed by council members or other government officials. This method of interactive communication is most popular among females and younger constituents.

Many city council members have recognized the growing importance of talk radio and talk television. More elected officials are agreeing to be guests on these interactive programs, although often with some reluctance. (This trend makes it even more imperative for today's city council members to have some media savvy.)

Traditional Means with New Twists

Citizen satisfaction surveys and public hearings remain popular and effective ways for council members to discover the public's concerns and priorities and to pinpoint the strengths and weaknesses of local government taxing, spending, and service-delivery efforts. They help to set priorities for current and future programs and projects, establish realistic political parameters (especially in the areas of taxation and infrastructure construction), and give guidance on better ways to communicate with the public at large, rather than with only a small group of community activists.[49] City councils are also trying to put more pizzazz into their public hearings. Council handbooks are filled with tips on how to make hearings more interesting, inclusive, and effective — all while keeping them relatively short. For example, the Virginia Municipal League's handbook[50] offers the following advice to councils:

- Hold hearings during the evening hours or on Saturday morning.

- Require registration prior to the public hearing in situations where many people will want to speak.

- Provide an informative opening statement.

- Clearly state the ground rules — time limits for each speaker and for a speaker representing a group; order of speakers; guidelines for format of remarks.

- Have experts present to answer questions or refute inaccurate information.

- Provide a summary at the end of the meeting.

- Limit comments and responses of council members until after the close of the public hearing.

When in Doubt, Toss the Ball Back to the Voters

Another trend in recent years has been for city councils to let voters make the final decision on highly explosive and divisive issues.[51] Councils in almost 90 percent of all cities have the authority to call special elections, or referendums. Fiscal issues (taxing, spending, and borrowing) and moral issues (e.g., abortion, gay rights, gambling) top the list of issues typically laid in the laps of city voters by nervous council members.

Some see the referendum device as an abdication of legislative responsibility in our representative democracy form of government. Others see the referendum as the purest form of democracy — direct democracy — which allows local citizens to speak for themselves rather than through an elected intermediary. The typical council member is likely to view the situation more pragmatically than philosophically: "Letting the voters decide a tough issue is often a safer political route than doing it yourself."

The Challenge of Serving on a City Council

City councils have changed considerably in recent years, moving from fairly homogeneous, consensual boards to very diverse, conflictual entities. In a relatively short time, more women and minorities have been elected, and structural barriers that once worked to the disadvantage of some women and minority candidates now affect their electoral success far less often than demographic, socioeconomic, and political factors. Age also is no longer a very strong deterrent to running.

The job of being a city council member has become much more difficult. Diversity within cities, especially those with district-based elections, often results in the election of city council members who have markedly different perspectives on how to deal with issues before the council. Consequently, the level of conflict among council members in the typical city has escalated, prompting many to serve only a short while. More city council members leave office voluntarily than get defeated at the ballot box.

The typical councilor must now be an expert on a wider variety of more technically complex issues than ever before. He or she is expected to come up with quick solutions to difficult problems that often have their origin outside government. Whatever a council member does or says, whether in a public or private setting, is likely to get intense scrutiny by the local press.

Constituents want council members to work magic with a city's finances — don't raise taxes, but *do* improve and expand city services. At the same time, it is getting harder for cities to generate revenues. Taxpayers are in a foul "no new taxes" mood. The federal and state governments, which used to be more generous in sharing revenues with localities, often have fiscal troubles of their own. Now they are more prone to reduce grants-in-aid to cities and to devolve service delivery responsibilities back to municipalities as a way of helping balance their own budgets.

It is not easy to communicate with a public that is less interested and less informed about politics, more distrustful of elected officials at all levels, and very mobile. City councilors are constantly expanding their telecommunications-based voter outreach efforts. They are televising council meetings on public-access channels, placing interactive terminals in high-traffic shopping malls, putting splashy home pages on the Internet, and stepping up the use of citizen satisfaction surveys (public opinion polls).

In spite of the difficulties facing today's city councils, a higher percentage of Americans continue to have far more faith and confidence in the capabilities and efficiencies of their local government than in either the state or federal government.

CHAPTER NINE
State and Local Parties in a Candidate-Centered Age
John F. Bibby

IN THE STATES, it is Republicans and Democrats who "make the major decisions regarding who pays and who receives."[1] Indeed, political parties permeate virtually every aspect of state government. Since 1950, only five individuals have been elected to a governorship as independents; state constitutional offices such as attorney general are controlled by Republicans and Democrats; and after the 1996 elections a mere .002 percent of the over 7,300 state legislators were not members of the two major parties (excluding the nonpartisan legislature of Nebraska).

In spite of the pervasiveness of parties in state politics, Americans from the first days of the republic have had misgivings about political parties. In *The Federalist,* the Founders warned of the calamities that a politics of factions would create, and in his Farewell Address, Washington admonished his fellow citizens to avoid a "spirit of party." The hostility of the American civic culture to political parties is reflected in polls showing that a majority of the voters believe that parties "do more to confuse issues than to provide a clear choice on them," and that "it would be better if we put no party labels on the ballot." In addition, state parties face stiff competition for influence from political action committees (PACs), political consultants, and candidates' personal organizations. Yet, despite a hostile cultural environment and potent challengers for influence over the electoral and governmental processes, state political parties have shown remarkable resiliency, adaptability, and durability.

Indeed, one of the most striking recent developments is the extent to which state parties have adapted to the increasingly *candidate-centered* nature of American politics by becoming professionalized service agencies for their candidates and local party affiliates.

The Changing Role of State Parties

State parties have gone through a series of transformations in this century in response, first, to changes in state policy toward parties espoused by progressive era reformers and, more recently, to more general shifts in the overall political environment.

State party organizations at the turn of the century were often hierarchically run operations that were closely linked to local machines, staffed with patronage workers, and frequently fueled and influenced by corporate interests. In many states, these traditional party organizations were capable of controlling nominations; providing money, manpower, and management for general election campaigns; and influencing the decisions of their party's elected officials.

Reflecting public distaste for such concentrations of power in the hands of party leaders, progressive reformers at the beginning of this century sought to undermine these party organizations by instituting the direct primary to reduce their control over nominations, civil service systems to limit party-based patronage, and corrupt practices laws to cut off some of the parties' sources of revenue.[2] These reforms had their intended impact, and by the 1920s the traditional state party machine had largely passed from the scene. The Republican and Democratic organizations that replaced them had significantly less influence over nominations and gradually lost their capacity to run statewide campaigns. The decline of the old-style state organizations was so pronounced that V.O. Key Jr., the leading student of state parties in the 1950s, observed that a common situation was "the almost complete absence of a functioning statewide organization" and that "the general impression that most of them are virtually dead is probably not far wrong."[3]

Most state party organizations today bear scant resemblance to either the traditional party organization of early in this century or the weak organizations that were so characteristic of the 1950s and early 1960s. The professionally staffed modern state party organization capable of providing campaign assistance to candidates and party-building help to local parties found in most of the states is a response to the electoral conditions that have emerged since the 1960s.

The Political Environment of the States in the 1990s

While there is great diversity among the states in terms of the strength of their political parties, the level of electoral competition, political cultures, and statutes regulating parties, there are common features in the electoral environment that have affected parties in all of the fifty states. These include the trend toward candidate-centered politics, the intensified use of sophisticated campaign techniques and professional consultants, an expanding role for PACs, greater competition between the parties in statewide elections and for control of state legislative chambers, and Supreme Court decisions that have cut severely into the remnants of patronage use to staff party organizations.

Candidate-Centered Politics

Since the primary election system for nominating candidates makes it unlikely that party organizations can guarantee favored candidates victory
in the primary elections, candidates are encouraged to rely upon their
own personal campaign organizations to win nominations. The direct
primary, which is used in all of the states to nominate state and congressional candidates, is a uniquely American institution. In most western-style
democracies, party organizations totally control nominations for public office. But in the United States, the direct primary makes party control over
the nomination process difficult to achieve. It is hard to overstate the party
weakening and fragmenting impact of the direct primary as it encourages
candidates to assume a posture of independence from their parties during campaigns and later while making policy decisions as governmental
officials.

The candidate-centered style of campaigning fostered by the direct primary carries over to the general election because the resources of the party
organizations are seldom adequate to ensure victory. In addition, most state
campaign finance laws put strict limits on the amount of money party organizations can spend in support of their parties' nominees. The Federal
Election Campaign Act also severely limits state party support to candidates
for federal offices. The candidates, therefore, are personally responsible for
raising the revenues necessary to run viable campaigns and for putting
together an effective campaign organization.

An important additional force driving the trend toward candidate-
centered state politics is an electoral environment in which voters have
weakened party loyalties. This causes them frequently to defect from their
party on election day and vote for candidates of the other party. Often voters split their ballots by voting for candidates of different parties. In 1994,
for example, 29 percent of voters voted for different parties' candidates
for governor and the U.S. House of Representatives.[4] Faced with a volatile
electorate, candidates increasingly stress their personal qualifications (many
no longer even put their party affiliations on their advertising!) rather than
party connections.

New Campaign Techniques and Professional Consultants

Gubernatorial, senatorial, congressional, and an expanding share of state
legislative elections increasingly use a variety of sophisticated campaign
techniques. State party organizations can provide some of these services
to their candidates, but no state party has the resources to provide a
full array of campaign services to all deserving candidates. Of necessity,
therefore, candidates hire their own professional campaign consultants to
provide them with the services they believe are required to win. These are

professionals skilled in such arts as campaign management, polling, media advertising, targeting direct mail messages, getting out the vote, and computerized analysis of electoral data.

The candidates' need for these so-called "hired guns" has spawned a whole industry — the professional campaign consulting firm. These firms tend to work exclusively either for Republican or Democratic candidates and are therefore an integral part of the party network of resources. Their involvement, however, does tend to reduce the party organization's role in campaigns and encourage the tendency toward candidate-centered politics.

The Rise of PACs

Just as PACs have become a major source of campaign funding for U.S. Senate and House campaigns, particularly the campaigns of incumbents, they are also a powerful force in state elections. In some states, PACs fuel legislative campaigns with over 50 percent of their funds. State level PACs generally follow a strategy of contributing to candidates, especially incumbents, rather than to parties. PACs are thus an additional force driving the tendency toward candidate-centered rather than party-centered politics. State parties have had to adapt to a political environment in which candidates now look to PACs for a significant share of their campaign war chests.

Competition for Control of State Government

In each of the fifty states, elections for major statewide offices such as the governorship are now highly competitive, with both parties capable of achieving victory.[5] The old bastions of one-partyism have crumbled. The once solidly Democratic South now regularly elects Republican governors and U.S. senators and representatives as well as state legislators. Similarly, in the old citadels of Republicanism such as Kansas, Maine, Nebraska, and Vermont, the Democrats now frequently win elective offices. There also are intense battles in the states for party control of legislative chambers. In these high-stakes contests, the shift of just a couple seats from one party to the other often can mean the difference between majority and minority status. Shifts in party control can carry with them major changes in the direction of state public policy. In this environment of electoral competition, an effective state party organization can make significant contributions to electoral success.

Decline of Patronage

In addition to such antipatronage forces as civil service laws and expanding public employee unions, the Supreme Court has added its considerable influence toward reducing party-based patronage. In a precedent-setting series of cases originating in once patronage-riddled Illinois, the Court has ruled that "party affiliations and support" are unconstitutional bases for filling the vast majority of public jobs. As a result, the state's Democratic chair has observed the "party no longer functions as an employment agency. More and more, we must rely on the spirit of volunteerism that moves so many other organizations."[6]

Even though patronage jobs no longer provide a basis for recruiting party workers and funds, other forms of political preferments continue to bring support to parties and officeholders. Gubernatorial appointments to commissions and boards controlling higher education, hospitals, state investments, environmental and recreational policy, and cultural activities are much sought after by individuals seeking influence, recognition, and material gain. Partisan considerations also can affect governmental decisions regarding bank deposits, purchase of legal and consulting services, state contracts, and economic development aid. These kinds of preferments, however, are significant primarily for fund-raising purposes; they do not provide campaign workers in the way that patronage did.

The Modern State Party Organization: A Service Agency

Most state party organizations have adapted to the current political environment by transforming themselves into service agencies capable of providing an array of essential services to candidates and local parties. These local parties are not capable of controlling nominations or running campaigns, as the old-style organizations did. Nonetheless, these organizations can be an important element in both state-level campaigns and the national party's electoral strategy. Evidence of the state parties' institutionalization as service agencies include permanent headquarters; professional leadership and staffs; substantial budgets; and programs to maintain the organization, support candidates and officeholders, and assist local affiliates.[7]

Permanent Headquarters

It was commonplace as late as the 1970s for state parties to lack permanent headquarters and to be run out of the offices and homes of the state chair. Such transitory and ad hoc operation has ceased. Virtually all state parties now have permanent headquarters in the state capital, and many of the parties conduct their business out of modern office buildings packed with hi-tech equipment. For example, in 1995 the Republican Party of Wisconsin opened a new three-story headquarters facility containing a telemarketing center capable of reaching 400,000 potential contributors in

a day, computers that link up to every media outlet in the state (with reporters' names listed by state senate, assembly, and congressional district),
a computer-based research facility, a finance center, and office space for
political operatives.[8]

Professional Staffing

Gone are the days of staffing party headquarters with either part-time help
and volunteers or a minimal staff consisting of a secretary and perhaps
an executive director. The tools of 1990s campaigning require specialized
skills and professionalism. Every state party today has a full-time chair or
executive director, and most have specialists for fund raising, communications, field operations, campaigns, and office administration. The turnover
of both state chairs and staff, however, is high. Tenure among state chairs
is rarely more than two years, since most of these party leaders do not view
politics as a principal vocation and few can afford to take more than a couple of years off from their regular occupations. Those state chairs who do
have higher political ambitions consider the chairmanship but a preparation for a campaign to achieve a major elective office. Staffers, too, have
short tenures. They normally stay in their positions for less than two years,
to learn their trade and make contacts before moving to more prestigious
or more lucrative positions with national party organizations, candidate
organizations, or political consulting firms.

Finances

Operating a headquarters that provides services to candidates and local
units, of course, requires substantial financing. Most state parties now operate sophisticated direct-mail and telemarketing systems, as well as more
traditional large-donor programs. State parties also have been the beneficiaries of fund transfers from national party organizations as the Republican
and Democratic Parties have sought to strengthen their infrastructures in
states deemed essential to national campaign strategies.

Although adverse electoral conditions can periodically cause fund-
raising dry spells that result in staff cutbacks at headquarters, state party
fund-raising programs are generally capable of sustaining a professionalized headquarters operation. For example, even without including monies
used exclusively for state and local campaigns, data compiled by the Federal Election Commission (FEC) reveal that a majority of state parties had
receipts in excess of $1 million during the 1991–92 election cycle; and four-
teen Democratic and nineteen GOP state parties had receipts in excess of $2
million, with the California Democrats leading with more than $12 million.
Because these data reflect only receipts reported in compliance with federal
campaign finance laws and, therefore, do not include money collected ex-

clusively for state and local campaigns, it is estimated that total state party receipts are at least 25 percent greater than those reported to the FEC.[9]

Programs of Party Building and Candidate Support

Since the 1960s most state parties have expanded their party-building programs through more regularized and sophisticated fund raising, voter identification and get-out-the-vote operations, polling, media advertising, newsletters, and research activities. The state parties have also developed programs that support their parties' candidates with money, fund-raising assistance (this includes helping channel PAC money to candidates), polling data, media consulting, and campaign seminars for candidates and their managers.[10]

Although today's state parties are organizationally stronger than in past decades and capable of providing essential services to their candidates, they can provide candidates with only selected professional services. They tend to concentrate their efforts on the expensive and labor-intensive voter identification/list management programs and get-out-the-vote drives (e.g., the Florida GOP operates a program to contact more than a million potential absentee voters).

State party chairs tend to avoid involvement in primary contests. A survey of state party chairs found that only sixteen of ninety-two state party organizations regularly supported candidates in primaries — an activity that old-style party operatives considered normal and essential for maintaining their clout. Many state chairs even abstain from discouraging candidates from running in an effort to avoid primary fights.[11] And the state parties no longer manage their nominees' general-election campaigns, though they do help train managers. It should be emphasized, therefore, that while the party organizations provide often critical assistance to candidates, the party's role in campaigns is selective and supplementary in character. This is, of course, a role that is consistent with the candidate-centered nature of politics in the 1990s.

Republican-Democratic Differences

Studies of state parties have generally shown the Republicans to be organizationally stronger than the Democrats — that is, they normally have greater financial resources and larger professional staffs capable of providing specialized services to candidates and local party units.[12] This interparty difference is also present at the national level.[13] It reflects a fundamental difference between the parties, meaning that Republican state organizations tend to be a more important campaign resource for their party's candidates than are Democratic state parties.

A party's organizational strength advantage over the opposition can provide it with additional increments of votes, but it does not guarantee electoral success. When parties build up sophisticated organizations, they do not automatically become more successful in winning elections. Thus, even though the Republicans had stronger party organizations than the Democrats in the South throughout the 1960s and 1970s, the GOP was unable to achieve electoral ascendancy in that period. A superior organization can help sustain a state party in power, however, as the Ohio Republicans and Minnesota Democrats have demonstrated. The relationship between party organizational strength and electoral success appears to be complex and often indirect. The importance of party organizational strength may be not so much its impact on any given election, but rather its role in providing an infrastructure for candidates and activists to continue to compete in the face of short-term defeats or even long-term minority status. Thus, the southern Republican state parties built up their organizations during the 1960s and 1970s and were then in a position to take advantage of a favorable electoral environment in the 1980s and 1990s.

The state Republican parties' frequent organizational strength advantage does not mean that Democratic candidates necessarily have fewer campaign resources than do Republicans. It does mean Democratic state organizations and their candidates rely more heavily for campaign assistance on allied nonparty organizations such as labor unions, especially teachers' unions, and social action groups. These organizations provide services (e.g., registration and get-out-the-vote drives, financial and in-kind contributions, and media advertising) that in the GOP would more likely be provided by the party organization.

The parties' use and even dependence on the services of allied groups demonstrates the need to view parties in a broad perspective that encompasses more than the regular, formally constituted organizations. In reality, the state party organization is a network that includes among its major participants the regular party organization, candidate organizations, allied groups, campaign consultants, and fund raisers.[14]

Party Organizational Strength and Electoral Success

Because state party activity is supplementary to that of the candidates' own personal organization, it is difficult to assess accurately the electoral impact of state party organizations. Clearly, the heavy emphasis that southern Republican parties placed on organization building in the 1960s and 1970s helped pave the way for their electoral successes of the 1980s and 1990s in a once one-party Democratic region. The party organization provided an infrastructure that was ready and in place when conditions were auspicious for Republican candidates. Similarly, the maintenance of an effective party organization has contributed to the continuing electoral success of the Minnesota and Michigan Democrats and the Ohio and Indiana Republicans.

On the other hand, having a state party organizational strength advantage is no guarantee of electoral dominance — witness the southern Republican parties' long period of wandering in the electoral wilderness, even after having built organizations stronger than those of their Democratic opponents. At most, a service-oriented state party can provide only a limited number of essential services that may enable a viable candidate to take advantage of such favorable electoral conditions as an incumbent's retirement, divisiveness within the opposition party, or a national shift of public sentiment away from the opposition.

The Governor-State Party Relations

Governors do not normally seek to direct the day-to-day operations of their state party organizations. Most play an advisory role, while providing support in fund raising and candidate recruitment. At the same time, a governor does not want the state headquarters operation to fall into the hands of intraparty rivals. Governors therefore frequently take an active role in designating the state chairs, and they normally have sufficient clout to make certain their choices are actually installed at the head of the state committees.

Even the most party-supportive governor, however, will look out first and foremost for his or her own political interests. As a result, governors cultivate personal followings that transcend partisanship and engage in extensive fund raising to maintain sophisticated personal campaign organizations. Such personal organization building, of course, can drain resources away from the state party.

Because the interests of the state party and the governor are seldom identical, it is not unusual for tensions to develop. For example, in 1991, Governor William Schaefer (D-Md.) sought to have the state party chair removed after they became embroiled in a dispute over legislative redistricting; and in 1992, the Virginia state Democratic committee forced Governor Douglas Wilder's appointee as state chair to share power with a steering committee after the chair was accused of placing the governor's presidential ambitions ahead of state party interests.[15]

Dramatic evidence of how ideological and policy conflicts can cause severe conflicts between the state party organization and its governor occurred in Minnesota's Republican gubernatorial primary in 1995. In this instance, the Republican state party convention endorsed a conservative allied with the religious right over the moderate Republican incumbent governor, Arne Carlson, who then went on to beat the organization's candidate handily in the primary.

That a popular governor would have such difficulties with his party organization illustrates an emerging and important feature of state parties. Although state party headquarters operations are being strengthened to provide services to candidates and are normally staffed by pragmatic professionals, the individuals who constitute the organizational base of the parties are simultaneously turning many party organizations into networks of issue activists. Evidence of this phenomenon is the fact that one could find almost no antiabortion delegates among the state delegations to the 1992 Democratic national convention, while the pro-choice minority at the Republican convention felt constrained to hide its preferences. This dramatic issue split between the two parties' activists attending national conventions occurred despite surveys that show that the abortion issue splits the mass voter base of each party almost identically.[16] To the extent that party organizations become networks of issue activists, elected official–party organization conflicts are likely to intensify. In addition, issue activist–dominated party organizations are likely to widen the policy differences between the parties.

The Emergence of Legislative Campaign Committees

Just as the congressional and senatorial campaign committees at the national level have developed into primary sources of party assistance to Senate and House candidates, legislative campaign committees at the state level have emerged as the principal party sources of support for legislative candidates. This reflects a division of labor among various elements of the party organization. State party committees concentrate on statewide races and working with local affiliates, while the legislative campaign committees focus on legislative races.

The legislative campaign committees are composed of incumbent legislators in both the upper and lower chambers, and they are normally led by the ranking party leaders in the chamber. These committees came about in response to intensified competition for party control of legislative chambers, the escalating costs of campaigns, the inability of state party committees to provide sufficient assistance to legislative candidates, and aggressive legislative leaders.[17] The development of legislative campaign committees is also linked in many of the states to a heightened level of professionalism — full-time legislators who are provided with adequate salaries, plus per diem allowances and fringe benefits, and backed up by ample staff. The professional legislator tends to place a high value on maintaining his/her seat. Fragile party majorities in legislative chambers dramatically increased legislators' stakes in elections because the outcomes could either bestow or deny the power and perquisites that go with majority status. Legislative leaders therefore created campaign committees to protect their own interests as well as those of their party colleagues. In addition, a professionalized legislature with its substantial staff resources provides essential ingredients for an effective campaign organization: virtually full-time leaders, party caucus staffs with proximity to the process, and computer and media resources.[18]

Legislative campaign committees began as mechanisms designed primarily to distribute money to candidates. Increasingly, however, they have become full-service operations for individual campaigns. For example, the Ohio Republican Senate Caucus provides its candidates with a "highly structured package of in-house polling, campaign managers, phone banks, media planning, issues research, and other campaign services" which can total as much as $3.5 million per election cycle.[19]

While the Republicans consistently have demonstrated a higher level of organization at the state headquarters level, there is no organizational strength advantage for the GOP when it comes to legislative campaign committees. Indeed, the long-time Democratic edge in controlling legislative chambers and the fund-raising benefits that attach to majority status have meant that, if anything, there has been a Democratic organizational strength advantage operating among legislative campaign committees.

A crucial aspect of legislative campaign committee activity is candidate recruitment. Recruitment activities affect the quality of a party's legislative candidates, which in turn affects the ability of the candidates to raise money, recruit campaign workers, establish credibility with the media, and make a competitive run for the legislative seat. State politics expert Alan Ehrenhalt stressed the importance of candidate recruitment after a national survey:

> Every other year, Democrats and Republicans battle for legislative control...
> in what is advertised as a debate about which party best reflects the views of
> the electorate. Within the corridors of the state capitol, however, the biennial
> legislative elections are recognized for what they really are: a competition to
> attract candidates who have the skills and energy to win and the desire and
> resourcefulness to stay in office.[20]

In a number of the states, the legislative party is also involved in legislative campaigns through PACs controlled and directed by party leaders. In Illinois during the 1991–92 election cycle, the Democratic Speaker's personal PAC spent more than $2.5 million, primarily on competitive, targeted races, and the House Republican Campaign Committee and minority leader's PAC laid out $1.9 million.[21]

Although PACs have normally been viewed as a threat to parties, it is interesting to observe that the rise of PACs coincides with the development of legislative campaign committees as full-service campaign organizations, as well as the strengthening of state party headquarters operations. Both the state committees, and especially the legislative campaign committees, have learned to adapt to a political environment in which PACs are big-time players. They have done this by working closely with the PACs to channel their money to races where additional funds hold the potential for affecting outcomes. The leaders of legislative campaign committees provide PACs with political intelligence about where their contributions will have maximum impact. Candidates also are assisted by the committees' mark of legitimacy — when campaign committee leaders identify them as good investments for PACs. As the president of the Maine senate observed, "for every one dollar we [the legislative campaign committee] raise, we direct two dollars of interest groups.[22] Legislative campaign committees tend to follow a strategy of concentrating their resources on close or competitive races, with an eye toward either gaining or maintaining control of a legislative chamber. Minority parties in the legislature, therefore, tend to focus their largess on challengers and open-seat candidates, while majority parties emphasize aid to endangered incumbents.

While legislative campaign committees are evidence of increased party organizational strength at the state level and constitute an important component of the party network within the states, it is important to note that these committees operate with a high level of autonomy. Upper and lower chamber legislative campaign committees of the same party have their own priorities, and both are separate and distinct from the regular state party committee. Friction is commonplace among these diverse elements of the party because of their differing priorities and competition for financial resources, not to mention the rivalries that inevitably develop among ambitious political leaders. Legislative campaign committees primarily serve the agendas and priorities of legislative partisans, and they are, therefore, largely insulated from pressures from other segments of their parties.[23] Integrated legislative campaign committee-state committee activity, therefore, is normally difficult to achieve.

Local Parties: Activity at the Grass Roots

The most common image of local party organizations is the much-written-about and romanticized urban party machine led by such legendary bosses as Chicago's Mayor Richard J. Daley and Mayor James Michael Curley of Boston. The latter's roguish escapades were captured in the best-selling novel *The Last Hurrah* and a film of the same name. While there are still some rare and struggling urban organizations that have survived into the 1990s, the hierarchical, patronage-based, and social service-dispensing organizations have little relevance to an understanding of contemporary local parties.

Most local parties are organized at the county level. Unlike their national and state counterparts, local parties are basically volunteer operations and, as such, rarely have attributes that require the accumulation and outlay of cash: paid staff, a year-round headquarters, or formal budgeting processes. This lack of structural development, however, does not represent a decline from some previous higher level of organizational development. Surveys of county leaders and legislative candidates reveal that, far from withering away, local parties are more active on the whole than in the past. They are involved in the campaigns of local candidates, particularly through such activities as distributing campaign literature, lawn signs, and posters; arranging campaign and fund-raising events; and organizing telephone campaigns.[24] County parties have also been shown to affect elections by running full slates of local candidates that create a "trickle up" effect by adding increments of voters to the party's total vote for offices higher up on the ballot.[25]

Despite the similarities, there is tremendous diversity among county parties, which range from those literally having no party organization to a few with paid staff, permanent headquarters, and computer facilities. Even parties with full-fledged organizational structures may be characterized by organizational slack. For example, Eldersveld's study of Wayne County (Detroit) led him to conclude that there is a "tendency for local activists to perform at a minimal level of efficiency, without too much system, in a rather hit-and-miss mode of operation."[26]

A force that could cause county parties to become more effective is the increased interest being demonstrated in them by the national party organizations. The Republican National Committee, for example, has embarked upon programs of cash grants and staff/technical assistance to its local affiliates. There is also evidence from the 1992 presidential campaigns that national party communications to local parties, attempts to integrate these units into national campaign efforts, and presidential candidate visits to a county stimulated high levels of local party campaign activity. Indeed, the authors of a nationwide study of county parties in the 1992 campaign concluded that "there is a vibrant party campaign at the grass roots."[27]

Just as the state committees' role is supplementary to that of the candidates, so too is that of the county parties. In state legislative races, for example, their principal function is grassroots outreach: recruiting volunteers and getting voters to the polls. In this candidate-centered age, the county party is not heavily involved in fund raising or campaign management.

Party Nationalization and the Integration of National and State Party Organizations

Until the 1970s, American political parties had a distinctly confederate character in which national party committees had only minimal influence over state organizations. Indeed, the national parties were so lacking in influence that a landmark study characterized them as "politics without power."[28] This description could not be farther from the truth in the 1990s. The Republican (RNC) and Democratic National Committees (DNC) have transformed themselves into well-financed, professional institutions capable of providing significant assistance to state and local parties and their candidates. In the process, they have acquired substantial influence over their state affiliates. The heightened influence of the national parties also has been accompanied by unprecedented integration and interdependence between the national and state parties.

National Party Rule Enforcement

Since 1968, the national Democratic Party has worked aggressively to use its rule-making authority to ensure the loyalty of state party organizations to the national ticket. Through a series of reform commissions, the party developed an elaborate set of rules governing national convention delegate selection procedures, which have been rigorously enforced upon state parties. With the backing of the Supreme Court, which has ruled that national party rules take precedence over state laws and state party rules in such matters as delegate selection, the DNC has acquired unprecedented legal power over its state affiliates, and it has not hesitated to use this authority to enforce compliance. For example, in 1984, Wisconsin Democrats were forced to abandon their traditional open presidential primary for selecting national convention delegates because the state's open primary violated a national party ban on open primaries. In 1974, the Democratic party also adopted a national charter that contains stipulations concerning the organization and operation of state parties.

Unlike the Democrats, the national GOP has not sought to use tough rule enforcement as a means to acquire increased leverage over its state units. Instead, it has continued to maintain a confederate legal structure and has been relatively permissive in permitting the state parties broad leeway in handling such matters as delegate selection. Strong nationalizing tendencies are operative in the Republican Party, however, albeit through quite different means than those used by the DNC.

Party Nationalization through Providing Services to State Parties

Because it started earlier and has been more effective in raising party money, especially through direct-mail solicitations, the RNC has been in a position to provide its state parties with a wide array of services: cash grants, professional staff, computer facilities, data processing, consulting on organizational development, fund raising, campaigning, media relations, and redistricting. A major priority has been voter list development and get-out-the-vote drives, which it has helped support with large-scale investments of money and professional personnel. In politics as in life, however, there is no free lunch. The RNC has tended to impose conditions in return for its grants of money and services to state parties. That is, the state parties were required to meet RNC requirements before they could receive services; for example, development of an RNC-approved campaign plan and hiring of qualified consultants. In the process, of course, the RNC has acquired substantial influence over the state parties that have been anxious to get an infusion of aid from the national party.

In the mid-1980s, the DNC began consciously to copy the RNC programs of assistance to state parties, although at a much reduced level. Like the RNC, the DNC also imposed conditions on state parties wishing to qualify for national party aid. For example, in 1986 state parties receiving a DNC-paid political operative and fund raiser were required to sign commitments pledging them to continue the DNC-sponsored programs and to cooperate with the DNC in presidential nominating procedures and the national campaigns.[29]

Integration of State Parties into the National Party Campaign Strategy

As the national Republican and Democratic Parties have refined their fundraising activities, they have reached a point where they can quite literally raise more money than they can legally spend on federal elections under terms of the Federal Election Campaign Act (FECA). As a result, they have adopted the strategy of transferring large amounts of money to state parties for "party-building activities" such as voter registration, voter list development, get-out-the-vote drives, general party (in contrast to candidate) advertising, and headquarters development. Under the FECA, state parties can spend without limit on these "party-building" (non-candidate-specific) activities. A major component of these national-to-state party fund transfers is "soft money," funds raised outside the restrictions of the FECA that cannot be used to support specific federal candidates but can be used for more general "party-building" activities.

In recent elections, both the national Republican and Democratic Parties have worked through their state parties to set up large-scale, state party-sponsored voter mobilization programs, often heavily funded with national party dollars. Frequently, the national party parachutes staff for these operations into the state party. In 1995 to 1996, the national parties' share of the cost of these programs was approximately $90 million; and, as in shown in table 9.1, the two national parties transferred over $162 million to their state parties during the 1995 to 1996 election cycle. On top of these expenditures, the national parties also made direct contributions of over $9.6 million to state and local candidates.

Because the FECA encourages the national party organizations to channel funds into their state affiliates in an effort to influence federal elections, the state party organizations have now become well integrated into the national campaign structure and play a significant role in presidential, sena-

TABLE 9.1. NATIONAL PARTY DISBURSEMENTS
INVOLVING STATE AND LOCAL PARTIES, 1995–96

Party organization	Transfers to state parties[a]	Contributions to state/local candidates[b]	Share of joint activity[c]
Republicans			
National committee	$66,296,989	$1,349,882	$40,325,732
Senatorial committee	2,038,024	3,015,370	7,668,704
Congressional committee	385,000	834,500	9,180,754
Total	$68,720,013	$5,199,753	$57,175,190
Democrats			
National committee	$74,348,612	$ 318,684	$27,592,503
Senatorial committee	10,515,560	3,049,918	2,385,324
Congressional committee	8,545,199	1,070,500	3,313,879
Total	$93,409,371	$4,439,102	$33,291,706

Source: Federal Election Commission press release, 19 March 1997.

a. Includes funds from both federal and nonfederal ("soft money") accounts.
b. Funds from national party organizations' nonfederal ("soft money") accounts.
c. Funds from national party organizations' nonfederal ("soft money") accounts. Joint activity includes such party-building activities as voter-registration drives, voter-list development, and get-out-the-vote drives.

torial, and congressional elections. The national parties' multimillion dollar programs to strengthen state parties and use them to achieve national party goals in federal elections have brought in their wake a major change in the relative power positions of state and national parties. Before the 1970s, the flow of intraparty money was from the state parties to the national parties; that is, the national parties were dependent upon their state affiliates. Today, however, the direction of flow has been reversed and this shift of direction has been accompanied by a change in the intraparty influence. Instead of being dependent upon the state parties, the RNC and DNC have gained substantial autonomy as well as increased leverage over their state units.

Massive national-to-state party fund transfers, joint national-state party campaign activities, provision of services to state parties by the national parties, and rule enforcement have meant that the two strata of party organization have achieved an unprecedented level of intraparty integration. This heightened level of party integration and nationalization of campaign efforts constitutes a change of major proportions in the American party system. It is no longer accurate to observe, as the leading parties scholar did in his 1960s text, that "no nationwide party organization exists.... Rather, each party consists of a working coalition of state and local parties."[30]

Because of the assistance provided to state parties by the national organizations and their use of state parties to implement national campaign strategies, the state parties have undergone a process of strengthening. At the same time, however, they have grown increasingly dependent upon the national party organizations and have lost a significant share of their traditional autonomy. State parties even run the risk of quite literally being taken over by national party operatives in presidential election years as staff are brought in to run campaign efforts. These campaign operatives and their supporting resources are normally pulled out as soon as the election is over. The state organization may not, therefore, derive much long-term benefit from its having been an integral cog in the national campaign effort. Nor is there much assurance of continuity in national party support. National resources flow in accord with national party strategies. Therefore, a state that is deemed important in one election cycle by the national party may not have a similar priority in the next election cycle and may find itself cut off from national party largess.

Strengthened State Parties in a Candidate-Centered Era

As voters' attachment to political parties declined in the 1970s and it appeared that parties were losing out to PACs and campaign consultants in the competition for a significant role in elections, at least one respected observer, the *Washington Post*'s David S. Broder, proclaimed *The Party's Over*,[31] while others foresaw the possibility of "partyless politics." Clearly, these apocalyptic visions of the parties' future were off the mark. They failed to acknowledge the remarkable qualities of resilience, adaptability, and durability that characterize Republican and Democratic state party organizations.

The current state parties, however, bear little similarity to the traditional party machines that were so common at the turn of the century. The party organizations of that period operated in an era of party-centered politics. The post-World War II era, however, is increasingly characterized not by party-centered, but by candidate-centered politics. In adapting to a candidate-oriented style of politics, state party organizations in most states have transformed themselves into service organizations to candidates and local parties. In so doing, they have assumed a role supplementary to that of the candidates' personal organizations. At the same time, the nationalizing forces of American politics have integrated the state and national party organizations to a degree that is unprecedented in this century. State parties are now an integral part of national campaigns.

In the political environment of the late 1990s and the new century, state political parties in their strengthened form have the potential to play an expanded role in state elections and to have a significant policymaking impact. Because a number of states have imposed term limits upon their state legislators, there will be fewer incumbents seeking reelection and more open seats being contested in the future. Since open seats tend to be the most competitive, state central committees and legislative campaign committees can be expected to pour expanded resources into these races. The outcome of these races is likely to have a major impact on the party battles to control legislative chambers. In an era when there are heightened policy differences between the parties, party control of legislative chambers can dramatically affect state policymaking. Indeed, because the stakes are so high, intensified struggles for party control of legislative chambers is a likely future scenario in state politics.

Adding to the significance of these battles for control of state legislative chambers and governorships has been the federal government's policy of devolving more responsibilities upon the states (e.g., the devolution of welfare to the states through the 1996 welfare reform act). The parties' role in contesting state elections and affecting who wins and loses thus takes on added significance for all Americans.

While state parties have the potential to play an expanded role in elections and policymaking, they also face significant forces that could limit their effectiveness. A comprehensive campaign finance law at the federal level that would severely limit or ban soft money, which is now routinely transferred in massive amounts to state parties by national party committees, could diminish the effectiveness of state party organizations. This would be especially true of the state parties' voter mobilization, get-out-the-vote programs. Similarly, antiparty and antipolitics sentiments among the public could result in tightened campaign finance laws at the state level that would limit state party involvement in campaigns. If the past is any guide, however, political parties can be expected to adapt to whatever changes and challenges the future holds.

CHAPTER TEN

The Opening Up of State and Local Election Processes

Charles S. Bullock III

SINCE 1960, ELECTIONS of state and local officials have become significantly more open to participation and influence. Change has been pursued along two tracks — efforts to make mass participation easier and structural changes intended to increase diversity in the ranks of officeholders. Civil rights legislation struck down barriers that had often impeded voter registration by racial or ethnic minorities, especially in the South. Subsequent interpretations of civil rights legislation, along with the implementation procedures of the U.S. Department of Justice, attacked structural requirements that were alleged to inhibit the likelihood of electing minorities to office, even after obstacles to registration and participation had been eliminated.

This chapter reviews the steps taken to remove barriers to political participation and examines a number of structural options that guide the conditions under which individuals run for state and local multimember bodies. The degree to which these structural options are related to the racial and gender makeup of collegial bodies is assessed. The chapter concludes with figures on the increase in minority and female officeholding in the states and localities.

Obstacles to Participation

Less than two generations ago, a number of prerequisites to voter registration often made minority registration difficult. Where these conditions were imposed in a discriminatory manner, minority registration became impossible.

A number of states, North and South, required literacy of prospective registrants. Particularly in rural southern counties these requirements were applied so that illiterate whites could make their mark in the registration book and vote, while literate African Americans were disqualified for trivial errors — or for no errors at all.[1] Where literacy was coupled with a requirement that applicants be able to explain any section of the federal or state constitution to the satisfaction of the local registrar, the position of minorities was particularly precarious. In Mississippi, voters also had to demonstrate their good character in order to get their names on the voters' rolls. Four southern states continued to collect a poll tax of a few dollars per year from anyone who would register to vote.

In many southern communities, particularly those in rural areas with large numbers of African Americans, the way might be barred by a hostile registrar, regardless of the qualifications of the potential black elector. Election officials bent on maintaining a white electorate in these communities would not only reject applications for trivial errors but would slow down the process so that only a handful of blacks could register on a given day. The registration office might be closed unexpectedly as the staff took long vacations and, when open, the personnel would make registration as difficult and unpleasant as possible. The efforts of officials might be reinforced by white supremacists who would harass prospective registrants and those leading the registration movement. In extreme cases, civil rights workers were murdered, and in many communities night riders fired shots into the homes of activists, burned churches used for registration rallies, and cut off credit to those who would exercise the franchise.

As evidence of the effectiveness of these techniques, prior to 1965 in six southern counties with sizable black populations (three had African-American majorities) only whites were on the registration rolls.[2] As table 10.1 on p. 214 shows, in Mississippi less than 10 percent of the potential black registrants could vote. While the Mississippi situation is extreme, table 10.1 reveals a substantial gap between potential and actual black registration in every southern state.

The limited space available here does not in any way do justice to the magnitude of the struggle needed to eradicate the discriminatory practices. The 1965 Voting Rights Act banned the use of all tests and devices prerequisite to registration in states in which participation in the 1964 presidential election fell below 50 percent of the voting-age population.[3] Any jurisdictions that met these conditions, known as the trigger mechanism, became subject to additional provisions of the legislation. For example, jurisdictions subject to the ban on registration tests could have their registration process supplanted by a federal official. Immediately after President Lyndon Johnson signed the legislation into law, federal registrars were sent into selected counties in five Deep South states and in three weeks enrolled more than 25,000 black voters. This graphic and rapid demonstration of the commitment of the federal government to eliminating procedural unfairness resulted in most other southern registration officials voluntarily coming into compliance.[4]

To help protect the rights of those newly registered to vote, the 1965 legislation also authorized the U.S. attorney general to send monitors into jurisdictions to watch over election-day activities. The federal monitors

TABLE 10.1. BLACK AND WHITE REGISTRATION RATES
BEFORE AND AFTER PASSAGE OF THE 1965 VOTING RIGHTS ACT
(IN PERCENTAGES OF THE VOTING AGE POPULATION)

State	Before		After		Percent Change	
	Black	White	Black	White	Black	White
Alabama	19.3	69.2	51.6	89.6	167.4	29.5
Arkansas	40.4	65.5	62.8	72.4	55.4	10.5
Florida	51.2	74.8	63.6	81.4	24.2	8.8
Georgia	27.4	62.6	52.6	80.3	92.0	28.3
Louisiana	31.6	80.5	58.9	93.1	86.4	15.7
Mississippi	6.7	69.9	59.8	91.5	792.5	30.9
North Carolina	46.8	96.8	51.3	83.0	9.6	−14.3
South Carolina	37.3	75.7	51.2	81.7	37.3	7.9
Tennessee	69.5	72.9	71.7	80.6	3.2	10.6
Texas	57.7	53.3	61.6	53.3	6.8	0.0
Virginia	38.3	61.6	55.6	63.4	45.2	3.8

Sources: All figures from U.S. Commission on Civil Rights, *Political Participation* (Washington, D.C.: Government Printing Office, 1968): 12–13, except the "Before" figures for Texas, which come from V.E.P. News 4 (January/February 1970): 3.

could not step in to correct possible intimidation, but their mere presence sufficed to cow some potential troublemakers.

The Twenty-Fourth Amendment to the Constitution invalidated poll taxes for federal elections. Shortly thereafter, the U.S. Supreme Court struck down collection of these taxes as a prerequisite to participation in state and local elections.

While techniques used to restrict the suffrage were under attack by Congress and in the courts, private efforts encouraged African Americans to register. The Voter Education Project and the Mississippi Freedom Summer were among the more extensive operations working out of storefronts and churches to prepare citizens who had long been denied the franchise to brave hostile registrars, taunts, and threats of violence.

As a result of the challenges across these multiple fronts, African-American registration rose rapidly. As the second column in table 10.1 demonstrates, in the immediate aftermath of the Voting Rights Act, substantial increases in black registration occurred in all southern states, with the most dramatic changes coming in those states where repression had been greatest only a few years earlier. In Mississippi, African-American registration increased almost 800 percent, reaching a level comparable with that of other southern states.

To guard against the possibility that southern officials might devise new barriers to participation, all changes in electoral laws in the states subject to the trigger mechanism had to obtain approval either from the attorney general or from the federal district court of the District of Columbia. Tens of thousands of proposed changes were scrutinized by federal officials, and all but a few of them were submitted to the attorney general because that process was quicker and less expensive.

The preclearance provision was so extraordinary that Congress approved it for only five years. Then, in 1970, Congress renewed this provision for another half decade and, at the same time, outlawed literacy tests nationwide. When the legislation came up for further consideration in 1975, Congress extended coverage to states with substantial minority-language populations, which had the effect of requiring Texas communities to submit changes in election laws for preclearance because of its substantial Spanish-speaking population.

Districting

Growth in the numbers of black officeholders did not keep pace with the spurt in black registration. Many people, especially those who wanted political careers of their own, were not content with conditions under which black votes could determine which whites would hold office. In assessing conditions that might account for the defeat of African-American candidates, several structural variables were identified. Of these, the one that has come under the most persistent and extended attack has been the use of at-large (AL) or multimember election districts (MMDs).

Until the mid-1960s, many states defined their legislative constituencies in terms of counties, with each county having one or more representatives in at least one chamber of the legislature. The apportionment rules provided for little difference in the numbers of seats given to more and less populous counties. Once the U.S. Supreme Court signaled the need for equipopulous districts, many states sought to continue to use counties as building blocks and gave more populous counties, or districts made up of multiple counties, several legislators, all of whom ran at-large. In urban areas it was not uncommon for counties having more than half-a-dozen representatives in the lower chamber to subdivide into two or more MMDs.

At the municipal level, the attraction of AL elections can be traced to good government reforms enacted in the early part of the twentieth century. Reformers concerned about the ability of political machines to control elections in selected city wards sought to dilute the influence of bosses by having some, if not all, council members run citywide.

Citywide elections also made sense for communities adopting the commission form of government. With each council member doubling as mayor or the head of an administrative unit, it did not make sense to have one ward elect the police commissioner while another elected the head of the waterworks and a third chose the mayor. With each commissioner having citywide responsibilities, it was appropriate to allow the entire electorate to participate in the selection. Thus, cities that followed Galveston, Texas, in embracing the promised business approach of commission government, as well as cities attracted to the expected efficiencies of a council-manager format, replaced wards with at-large elections. Some communities used a hybrid format — often referred to as a mixed system — with some councilors elected AL while others represented single-member districts (SMDs).

Beginning in the 1970s, attorneys representing civil rights groups challenged state legislative MMDs and AL systems in municipalities. Plaintiffs alleged that bloc voting by whites made it impossible for a minority to be elected if the bulk of the electorate were white. In cities or MMDs that had concentrations of minorities, switching to SMDs would permit the creation of district(s) in which minorities would be the dominant population, so that if they bloc-voted, they could elect one of their own.

Voting-rights plaintiffs who had enjoyed some success in challenging MMDs or AL systems during the 1970s were stunned when the Supreme Court required that a successful challenge to AL elections must demonstrate that the electoral system was adopted or maintained with an intent to discriminate. In *Mobile* v. *Bolden* the Supreme Court upheld AL elections to choose commissioners in Mobile, Alabama, even though no African American had been elected to the three-person governing body in the one-third black city.[5]

Bolden galvanized the civil rights community, which used the upcoming renewal of the preclearance provision of the 1965 Voting Rights Act as a vehicle for reversing the decision. Liberal Democrats spearheaded efforts to rewrite Section 2 of the legislation to permit finding discrimination whenever an electoral rule had the effect — regardless of intent — of minimizing minority political influence. Section 2 as amended in 1982 replaced the intent standard articulated in *Bolden* with a results or effects test. The amended section facilitated challenges to existing political structures which were not susceptible to attack under Section 5 since the latter dealt exclusively with proposed changes.

President Ronald Reagan and a number of Republican leaders opposed the substitution of a results test for an intent test, but as Abigail Thernstrom documented, they were outmaneuvered by the civil rights lobby.[6] The final sticking point evaporated when Democrats agreed to language demanded by Sen. Robert Dole (R-Kans.) stipulating that a mathematical demonstration that minorities filled a smaller share of the positions on a collegial body than their proportion of the population indicated would not suffice to prove vote dilution. The statute read, "*Provided*, that nothing in this section establishes a right to have members of a protected class elected in numbers equal to their proportion in the population." Critics did not see the Dole language as sufficient. Duke University professor Donald Horowitz warned that if an effects test were adopted, "what the courts are going to have to do is to look at the proportion of minority voters in a given locality and look at the proportion of minority representatives in a given locality. That is where they will begin their inquiry; that is very likely where they will end their inquiry."[7] In response to such warnings, Congress adopted a multipart standard, known as the totality-of-the-circumstances test, to help judges decide whether a challenged electoral system was dilutive. The following were factors identified in the Senate Judiciary Committee Report for the totality-of-the-circumstances test:

1. Previous elections of minority candidates

2. The extent of racially polarized voting

3. A history of discrimination that has affected the ability of minorities to register and vote

4. The degree to which minorities continue to show the effects of discrimination in terms of education, employment, and health care

5. Whether the jurisdiction has used unusually large electoral districts, runoff elections, anti-single shot provisions, or other procedures that might enhance the dilution of minority political influence

6. Whether racial appeals have been made in previous elections

7. Whether candidates have been chosen through a slating process from which minorities have been excluded

Also to be considered, although given less weight than the seven elements listed above, was whether the challenged procedure was supported by nothing more than a tenuous public policy and the degree of responsiveness accorded the minority community by policymakers.

Subsequent litigation demonstrated that the first two items above were the most significant. Jurisdictions that rarely elected minority members and in which whites generally did not vote for minority candidates faced near impossible odds when trying to defend AL elections. In *Thornburg v. Gingles,* the high court invalidated several North Carolina legislative MMDs even though most of these had elected African Americans.[8] The only MMD identified in the suit that survived was one in which blacks had consistently been elected at rates commensurate with their share of the population. *Thornburg* established three precondition tests for challenges to AL systems:

1. Is the minority group sufficiently large and geographically concentrated to constitute a majority in at least one SMD?

2. Is the minority group politically cohesive?

3. Does the candidate of choice of the minority group usually lose as a result of a white bloc vote?

Each of these questions must be answered in the affirmative before a court examines the totality-of-the-circumstances and allows the plaintiffs to demonstrate why they should prevail. In the wake of *Thornburg*, challenges to MMDs and AL elections were filed at an accelerated rate. Moreover, while Section 5 applied primarily to the South, Section 2 suits challenged jurisdictions across the nation with discrimination. Among the communities sued under Section 2 were Los Angeles, California; Anchorage, Alaska; Springfield, Illinois; Pittsburgh, Pennsylvania; and Niagara Falls, New York.

Relationship between Districting and Racial Makeup of Collegial Bodies

Key to challenges to MMD and AL plans have been claims that the electoral system is not as open to minorities as to whites. While litigation typically focuses on a single jurisdiction, a growing social science literature has explored comprehensively the relationship between districting and the presence of minorities on collegial bodies.

African Americans

Early research on this topic generally found blacks to be most equitably represented on city councils elected from SMDs, while AL elections were most likely to underrepresent African Americans.[9] Richard Engstrom and Michael McDonald, in an analysis of 239 cities having black populations below 50 percent, established the model for analysis used in subsequent studies of the relationship between the racial composition of the community and the presence of minorities on the governing body.[10] Rather than examining the difference between the percentage of minorities on the council and the percentage in the population or the ratio of minority percentage on the council to the minority percentage in the population, they examined the relationship between the percent minority on the council and the percent minority in the population using a statistical technique called regression. This technique generates estimates of the percentage of council seats filled by minorities for every level of minority concentration in the population. Different electoral systems (AL, SMD, mixed) can be compared in terms of how close their estimated values come to proportional representation at any given level of black population in a city.

Engstrom and McDonald's analysis of 1976 council membership found that African Americans came closest to having proportional representation in cities that chose all council members from SMDs. The disparity between the predicted values for AL and SMD cities increased among cities with higher black percentages in the population, suggesting that minorities were more underrepresented in AL cities in which they were more numerous.

Results similar to those of Engstrom and McDonald for different districting systems emerged from a 1981 data set of 1,420 cities with populations greater than 10,000.[11]

Following the 1982 amendment of the Voting Rights Act, many cities that elected AL but had no minorities on the council changed to a wholly or partially districted system. Jurisdictions that reduced the number of representatives chosen at-large almost always experienced an increase in minorities serving on the collegial body. Members of the local minority community had substantial input into crafting districting plans, and they demanded one or more districts likely to elect a minority. Cities that had a history of electing minorities at-large, such as Austin, Texas, managed to repel legal challenges.

As a result of the elimination of many at-large systems, by the mid-1980s differences in the rates at which minorities were elected in communities using different districting arrangements had largely been eliminated. Three separate analyses using data collected in the latter half of the 1980s found that blacks were no longer significantly more likely to be elected in cities that had SMD systems. Data collected in 1985 for cities with populations of 25,000 or more in which blacks constituted less than a majority generally did not find AL elections to be associated with significantly higher rates of black representation. After sorting cities in terms of whether elections were from SMDs, AL with a residency requirement, AL with a post requirement, pure AL with first-past-the-post winners, or a mixed AL and SMD combination, Bullock and MacManus noted that "only in the South are any types of AL elections associated with *lower* rates of black council membership. . . . In the Northeast, however, the slopes for the two interaction terms [percent black in the population multiplied by whether a city has a pure AL system and percent black times whether the city has a mixed electoral system] are *positive* and significant — just the opposite of the hypothesized relationship."[12]

Welch gathered data in 1988 on cities with at least 50,000 people and found the relationship between districting and black council representation to be much weaker than in the 1970s.[13] While a slight advantage for African Americans resulting from SMD elections persisted, once multivariate models were examined, there was no statistically significant difference among the AL, SMD, and mixed systems. Alozie reached similar conclusions after studying cities with populations greater than 100,000.[14]

Studies of African-American representation on councils in southern states that include many cities with small populations found that the level of black representation generally increased when 1970 was compared with the late 1980s.[15] The state-by-state studies typically found that African Americans are most equitably represented in SMD cities and underrepresented in AL cities. The continuing disparities echo what Bullock and MacManus found for larger southern cities.

A longitudinal study of Georgia county commissions found that in 1981 the strongest relationship occurred between the percentage of blacks among county registrants and the share of the county commission seats filled by African Americans in counties with mixed systems.[16] By the middle of the decade, after a number of previously AL counties had changed to SMDs, SMD counties elected black commissioners at rates comparable to those with mixed systems. Toward the end of the decade, use of SMDs was related to more African Americans being in office than in at-large counties, but there was no difference between SMDs and counties that combined SMD and AL elections.

With the districting format making less difference in the racial makeup of municipal and county governments, the primary determinant of whether African Americans are represented on local governments is the share of the population or electorate that is black. As a result of many communities changing districting arrangements in the wake of the amended Section 2 of the Voting Rights Act, various districting formats now have no more than a modest impact on the ethnicity of the local collegial bodies.

Latinos

The analyses examining the impact of districting on the election of Latinos have been fewer than those looking at African Americans. A study of Texas communities that had changed districting format concluded that Mexican Americans benefited from the use of SMDs, but the study failed to include a control group.[17] More comprehensive studies using data from the 1970s found that Latinos came closest to achieving proportional representation in mixed systems.[18]

Data collected in the 1980s continued to show Latinos holding far fewer council seats than their share of the population warranted. Another finding is that districting formats make relatively little difference in the incidence of Latino council presence.[19] Under a variety of districting formats, and for several sets of cities with populations in excess of 25,000, there is not a great deal of difference in the rate at which Latino population translates into Latino council members.[20] Cities using SMDs came closer to proportional representation than cities having other electoral designs when both majority Hispanic cities and those with very few Latinos (less than 5 percent) are excluded. In the Southwest, where cities with sizable Latino populations are concentrated, use of SMDs was not associated with higher levels of Latino council membership. An analysis of larger cities (50,000+) for 1988 found that, contrary to the work done in the 1970s, mixed systems were least hospitable for Latinos, while AL and SMD cities were equally likely to have Hispanic councilors.[21] A Texas study initially found that AL cities had slightly higher percentages of Mexican-American council members than comparable SMD cities; when only cities with high rates of residential segregation were examined, however, SMD cities were slightly more likely than AL cities to elect Mexican Americans, with the differences greatest in cities with larger Mexican-American populations.[22]

Women

Women, regardless of their race, tend to be represented in elective office at rates well below their share of the electorate.[23] The distribution of women, unlike African Americans, is not heavily concentrated in selected geographic areas. Consequently, there is little prospect for drawing SMDs that are predominantly female.

Some researchers have found that women are more likely to be elected in MMDs.[24] It has been suggested that the electorate is willing to choose a woman as one of its representatives when the district has multiple members on a collegial body but is less receptive to having a woman as its sole representative from an SMD. If MMDs do favor women, then the conditions that promote greater gender diversity may simultaneously impede racial and ethnic diversity.[25]

Just as more recent research questions whether African Americans are significantly advantaged by SMDs, the proposition that MMDs promote the election of women has also been challenged. Surveys from the latter half of the 1980s do not find districting format to be associated with the share of white females on county councils or on the councils of cities having populations in excess of 25,000.[26] Separate multivariate analyses of the incidence of Anglo, black, and Latina women on city councils concluded that "none of the election-type variables, including the interaction terms, are significantly related to representation of any of the women's groups."[27] An analysis of more than 4,800 cities of all sizes surveyed by the ICMA in 1991, however, found the incidence of councilwomen to be positively related to AL elections and negatively related to SMD elections, suggesting that constituency size may be an intervening factor.[28]

State Legislatures

By 1990 MMDs, once widespread, had almost been eliminated from the state legislative scene and were rare indeed in the South.[29] As was the case with the change from at-large elections at the local level, dividing legislative MMDs into SMDs usually produced new seats won by minorities. An examination of this transformation in five southern legislative chambers concluded that "the shift to SMDs was seemingly critical for the election of additional black legislators."[30] To the extent that new SMDs lacked an incumbent, the chances of minority candidates, ceteris paribus, improved, since white incumbents have often been able to hold on to districts with substantial minority populations but are much less likely to win an open seat in a heavily minority constituency.[31]

Adopting SMDs does not have as clear an impact on the election of women as it does for minorities. Pritchard concluded that the elimination of MMDs in the Florida General Assembly, coincident with the 1982 redistricting, promoted the election of women but could not be generalized to North or South Carolina when these states eliminated or reduced the usage of MMDs.[32] Bullock and Gaddie, however, did find a frequent relationship between the creation of SMDs that elected African Americans and neighboring ones that sent Republicans to the legislature. This symbiotic relationship between configuring predominantly black districts and Republicans thriving in nearby districts that have been drawn to preserve white majorities was exploited during the redistricting of the early 1990s.

Courts

As the number of cities, counties, and school boards where prospects for a successful challenge shrank, voting-rights attorneys set their sights on judicial circuits that elected multiple judges at-large. In 1991, the U.S. Supreme Court rejected the contention that the use of the word "representatives" in voting rights legislation did not preclude challenges to non-SMD courts.[33] In short order, some judicial circuits in Illinois, Louisiana, and Mississippi were subdivided so that some judges would be elected from heavily minority jurisdictions.

In opposition to the call for a judiciary that better reflected the diversity of those who appear in courtrooms is the observation that to treat judges as representatives may be the last thing one wants if the objective is fairness. The concern is that electing judges from small constituencies that lack racial or ethnic diversity may result in "home cooking," or bench favoritism, for local parties involved in litigation against "outsiders."

In 1994 the federal district court for the District of Columbia refused to order Georgia to subdivide its multijudge districts, each of which was made up of one or more whole counties. Specifically, the court precleared legislation that added judges to circuits that might have been subdivided so as to have at least one majority black SMD each. As part of its defense, Georgia pointed out that in some rural areas with black concentrations there were no African Americans qualified to sit as a judge. While anyone who meets the age threshold could be a candidate for a council or commission slot, to become a judge requires, at a minimum, legal training, and often one must have a specified level of experience. The Supreme Court has not resolved whether, or under what conditions, a jurisdiction is required to create SMDs likely to elect minority jurists.

Districting and Turnout

The switch from at-large or MMDs to SMDs may have consequences for participation rates. A study of several cities that changed from AL to SMD saw increased participation in the first election under the new rules. The authors, however, go on to note, "Even more striking is the consistency of decline in turnout, back to at-large levels, from the first to the second district election. This temporary surge may be due in part to the novelty of a new electoral system. But it is more likely to be strongly influenced by the sudden appearance of seats without incumbents, and thus with an unusual number of competitive elections."[34] To the extent that competition spurs participation, the long-range consequences of SMD elections may be less participation than in an AL system. Filling multiple positions from the same geographical unit in a single election heightens the probability of the electorate having choices. If, for example, five seats on a council are to be filled simultaneously, it is likely that at least one will attract opposition. If the election is at-large, then there would be at least one reason to vote, even if the other four posts went by default to unopposed candidates.

In contrast, in a SMD system, some districts will not have a hotly contested election in any given year. When an incumbent seeks another term and no one mounts a challenge, it would not be surprising if most voters in that district stayed at home. Of course, if the districted contest — or lack thereof — were paired with a jurisdictionwide election (such as for mayor), the electorate would still have an incentive to vote. But if no at-large contested offices are on the ballot, turnout may be abysmal in some districts but high in wards that have contested elections.

Alternative Electoral Structures

When a districting scheme has been found to dilute minority political influence, the typical remedy has been to draw SMDs. In some communities, however, the minority population is so dispersed that few if any SMDs likely to elect a minority can be drawn. The Supreme Court has ruled that a community has no obligation to enlarge the size of its governing body in order to draw one district in which the minority population would be a majority.[35] This underscores the first element of the *Thornburg* preconditions.

Inability to draw SMDs having high concentrations of minorities so that the number of SMDs in the community with minority majorities is roughly proportional to the minority share of the population has sparked interest in representational plans deviating from the traditional format that allows each voter to express a single preference for each position to be filled. Alternative voting systems, such as cumulative and limited voting, allow voters who share common interests to unite to elect their preference, thereby elevating interests over geographic proximity (the element that dominates SMDs).

For both cumulative and limited voting, one can compute a threshold of exclusion, which is the share of the electorate a group must constitute to be assured of electing its preference if it is united in its choice. Under both systems, a cohesive group can elect one of its own if its share of the electorate is at least equal to $1/(N+1)$ when N=numbers of seats to be filled in the election.

Limited Voting

One innovation limits voters to expressing fewer preferences than there are seats to be filled AL. In Granville County, North Carolina, African Americans constituted 44 percent of the population but it was impossible to draw three of the county's seven commission districts so that they would have a black majority. Frustrated that it could not provide a remedy under which blacks would likely attain proportional representation, the trial court imposed a limited voting arrangement under which commissioners would run at-large but voters could express preferences for no more than three of them. Even though this limited voting plan was invalidated on appeal, it demonstrated an advantage for minority candidates as three blacks won commission seats while the plan was in place.[36]

Cumulative Voting

Cumulative voting is a second type of alternative voting system proposed for facilitating the election of minorities. Under this procedure, candidates run at-large for multiple positions in a free-for-all, with the top-finishing N candidates winning office. In these contests of all-against-all, cumulative voting allows citizens to cast more than one vote for favored candidates. For example, if five posts are to be filled, each voter has five votes but can "plump" or cast all five ballots for one candidate. Other possible combinations give three votes to Candidate A and two to B, or give two to A, two to B, and one vote to C, or follow a conventional strategy and register one preference for each of five candidates.

A racial minority may be able to elect its candidate of choice by plumping for a single candidate. Or women may rally to the cause of female candidates by giving them multiple votes. The strategy requires a degree of organization and cohesion within the group, but might be used by gays, young voters, veterans, animal lovers, or any other segment of society that shares characteristics or policy preferences.

The most extended experiment with cumulative voting in the United States occurred in Illinois where, from 1870 until 1980, districts represented in the statehouse elected three members each. In most districts the minority party could win one seat if its supporters cast all their preferences for a single nominee; thus, a consequence of cumulative voting was to guarantee each party a solid base of support. In response, parties often curbed the numbers of nominations they made so that their supporters would not spread their votes so widely that the opposition could maximize its representation through greater cohesion. With cumulative voting in place, the parties' shares of statehouse seats closely approximated their shares of the statewide vote.[37] This voting format was eliminated following an unpopular legislative salary increase, which triggered an effort to reduce chamber size by one-third as a cost-cutting reform.

Recently, a handful of jurisdictions have turned to cumulative voting to resolve voting-rights challenges. The first community to make the switch, Alamogordo, New Mexico, used a combination of cumulative voting to fill AL seats along with SMDs for other council slots. The dispersion of the Latino community made drawing a district in which Hispanics would have been a majority difficult, but with cumulative voting, Alamogordo elected a Latina at-large.[38]

Cumulative voting subsequently has been adopted by several small Texas cities and school districts, and 80 percent of the jurisdictions currently using this voting scheme are in the Lone Star state.[39] A survey of sixteen of those communities in 1995 found that a necessary and sufficient condition for electing minority candidates was that the minority share of the voters equal or exceed the threshold of exclusion.[40] The technique has also been used to elect a Native American to the school board of Sisseton, South Dakota.[41] Voting-rights attorney Edward Still's analysis indicates that Alabama jurisdictions that have adopted cumulative voting have usually subsequently elected African Americans.[42] Alternative voting techniques have allowed blacks to win posts in jurisdictions where African Americans constituted barely 10 percent of the population. When blacks were not elected, it was typically because none ran. Given the size of the governing bodies and the distribution of the minority populations in these communities, it would be virtually impossible to create districts in which blacks would constitute a majority.

Assessments

The infrequency with which alternative voting systems are used has been matched by the paucity of research into consequences of these innovations other than a tendency to elect minorities. Exit polls in tiny Texas towns find that Latinos are more likely to plump their votes than are Anglos, and they thereby enhance the likelihood of electing a minority.[43] Drawing on data that are limited in time and scope, Still reports that cumulative and limited voting may stimulate higher turnover rates among officeholders.[44] It appears that the winners may come from opposite ends of the political spectrum: Republicans, by concentrating their votes on less than a full slate of candidates, also have succeeded in winning offices; thus, white Democrats have lost seats both to liberal black Democrats and to conservative Republicans. If collegial bodies come to be dominated by African Americans and Republicans, it may make for particularly explosive commission sessions. The ability to win by appealing only to a sliver of the electorate may create an environment that offers little incentive to build biracial coalitions or provide a broader ideological platform. Still concludes that, particularly with cumulative voting, a large share of the electorate will likely be able to elect a preferred candidate.

If cumulative voting has facilitated the election of minorities, then one might anticipate that the elimination of this electoral system in Illinois would presage a decline in minority and female representation. A review of electoral results for the 1980s from Illinois finds no evidence that African Americans' share of seats declined.[45] Instead, black and Latino representation increased once SMDs replaced cumulative voting. Blacks held approximately the same number of seats in the 1980s and 1970s, but since the size of the Illinois chamber was cut by a third with the elimination of cumulative voting, the percentage of seats held by African Americans rose by half. The share of seats held by women also increased in the 1980s.

Runoff Elections

Some jurisdictions establish a vote threshold for success. Failure to surpass this threshold necessitates a runoff election between the top two finishers in the initial election. Runoffs received much attention following Jesse Jackson's charge that requiring a majority for nomination discriminated against African Americans. Jackson compared the success of Harold Washington, who won Chicago's Democratic mayoral nomination in a three-person field with 36 percent of the vote, with a North Carolina congressional runoff. A North Carolina black legislator, Mickey Michaux, polled 44.5 percent of the initial vote, more than 12 percentage points better than his opponent, white legislator Tim Valentine. In the runoff, however, Valentine vaulted to a 54-percent victory. The juxtaposition of these events convinced Jackson that Michaux and other African Americans who lost Democratic runoffs in the South could win under a plurality rule. In Jackson's scenario, if one black competed against multiple whites, the white vote would fracture so that the African American could lead the pack in the first voting, while in the narrowed field of the runoff, the white vote would rally behind the surviving white candidate and swamp the African American. Some have seen a similar pattern in runoffs when one woman faces several males in a primary.

All eleven states of the old Confederacy except Louisiana, Tennessee, and Virginia have a vote minimum for partisan nomination. Alabama,

Arkansas, Florida, Georgia, Mississippi, South Carolina, and Texas specify a majority for nomination, while North Carolina requires 40 percent to avoid a runoff. The only nonsouthern state with a general runoff provision is Oklahoma, which mandates 50 percent plus one. In 1995, after a series of elections in which candidates for the governorship won plurality nominations, Kentucky implemented a majority vote for gubernatorial nominations. Georgia, in addition, has a vote threshold for general elections, which in 1995 was reduced from a majority to 45 percent for all but a few offices. Arizona briefly had a majority-vote provision for the gubernatorial general election, and in 1990, the one election year in which that statute was on the books, the state had a runoff.

Louisiana, which previously adhered to the same standard as most of its southern neighbors, switched to an all-parties ballot in 1975. Legendary Governor Edwin Edwards had fretted because in 1971 he had had to fight his way through a crowded Democratic primary and a runoff, while his Republican opponent, David Treen, had to compete only in the general election. To level the playing field, Edwards convinced the legislature to replace partisan primaries with a system in which all candidates face off against each other. Those who win a majority in this all-comers affair are elected; when no one manages a majority, the top two finishers compete in a runoff. Often the runoff competitors both are Democrats. In some contests, particularly for highly visible statewide posts, the second election is more like a general election with the field comprised of a Democrat and a Republican, as in the 1995 gubernatorial election. Occasionally, two Republicans advance to the final showdown, as in 1989, when David Duke won a seat in the state House.

Municipal Runoffs

While statewide runoff laws are found almost exclusively in the South, they are not so regionally concentrated at the municipal level. A major rationale for holding runoffs was to insure that, in one-party areas, those who governed had attracted a majority of the vote. Outside the South, the minority party usually had some potential for success, so bipartisan competition could ensure that if an extremist won one party's nomination by relying on a narrowly-based interest to get a plurality, that nominee might be defeated in the general election. The situation in many cities is analogous to the one-party South of old, in that if elections are nonpartisan, there is no potential for a general election to protect the polity from an extremist chosen by a plurality. To guard against that potential, many municipalities have a vote threshold, with a majority being the most popular though not the universal standard. One exception, New York City, has a 40-percent rule for mayoral nominations.

A 1985 survey of all cities with populations exceeding 25,000 in 1980 found that most had a vote threshold. Some cities use different vote thresholds for different offices. New York City has a vote minimum for mayoral nominations but not for council members, while the rule in Chicago is just the opposite.

Consequences

Empirical examinations of the Jackson proposition have uncovered, at best, mixed support. A study of biracial runoffs for Georgia county offices from 1970 to 1984 found that black primary leaders won runoffs only half the time, a rate of success substantially below the 71-percent win rate of all primary leaders, and even farther below the 84-percent win rate for whites who led primaries before facing an African American in the runoff.[46] The racial disparity, however, was due to outcomes between 1970 and 1977, when black primary leaders won nomination only 20 percent of the time. Between 1978 and 1984 African Americans converted primary leads to runoff victories 71 percent of the time. Moreover, African Americans who ran well in the primary, that is, who polled at least 40 percent of the vote and had a lead of at least 5 points, won more than three-fourths of their runoffs compared with barely a quarter of the blacks who had less impressive leads in the first round.

A study of runoffs for the Chicago city council — which requires a majority vote, while the nomination for mayor is by plurality — from 1975 to 1991 found no evidence that African Americans suffered.[47] Instead, in biracial contests, blacks had a net gain of five seats as they reversed second-place primary finishes while losing no runoffs after leading in primaries.

A different approach uncovered no evidence that runoffs discriminated against African Americans. Bullock and MacManus, who examined more than 900 cities with populations greater than 25,000, found that blacks were as likely to serve on city councils that had a majority-vote requirement as on councils elected by plurality.[48] The same authors reached a similar conclusion for the use of runoffs and the election of Latinos.[49]

The impact of runoffs on women has also been studied. Bullock and Johnson found that women who led males in primaries won nomination 72 percent of the time which, while in line with overall success rates for primary front-runners, was ten points lower than men who bested women in primaries.[50] The gender disparity was attributable to lower conversion rates for women who had insubstantial primary leads; women who had larger primary margins won nomination at rates almost identical to similarly situated males. Women facing males in the 1980s did better than their sisters had in the 1970s, and Democratic women converted primary pluralities more often than did their GOP counterparts.

A study of three Texas cities uncovered evidence that women primary

leaders had few problems surviving runoffs. Across a thirty-four-year period, female primary leaders won all but one of seven runoffs.[51] Overall,
women in Dallas, Fort Worth, and San Antonio won three more seats as a
result of the second chance provided by the runoff than they would have
gotten with a plurality rule.[52]

A comparison of the incidence of women councilors in 946 cities with
25,000 or more people found that only in the Midwest did women hold a
larger share of the seats in plurality than in runoff cities (23 versus 17 percent).[53] In other regions, rates of female presence were identical or slightly
greater in cities with vote thresholds.

Other findings from the runoff literature suggest that the belief that an
incumbent who cannot manage a majority is doomed to defeat is hyper-
bole. While Bullock and Johnson find that incumbents who lead a primary
less often win renomination than nonincumbents who finish first, many incumbents survive runoffs.[54] State legislators who placed first in primaries
won renomination almost two-thirds of the time, a success rate barely 5
percentage points less than that for all state legislative candidates.

Nor does the evidence support the proposition that candidates who
place second in a primary are destined to come from behind to win. While
not all primary leaders are ultimately successful, the tendency is for front-
runners to hold their positions, as about 70 percent of the plurality leaders
win runoffs. Runoffs constitute the most challenging obstacles to front-
runners for higher offices. Bullock and Johnson, who studied elections from
runoff states from 1970 to 1986, and Ewing, who looked at similar runoffs
from 1920 to 1948, agree that front-runner success is especially low — although in excess of 50 percent — in contests for governor and lieutenant
governor. In contests for the state legislature during both time periods
studied, candidates held their positions slightly more than 70 percent of
the time.

Easier Access to the Ballot

Eliminating prerequisites to voter registration, such as the literacy and good
character tests that had been used in the South, was intended to help
minorities overcome discriminatory obstacles. Despite removal of these
barriers and the presence of a better-educated electorate, however, voter
participation rates in the United States remain among the lowest in the developed world. Recent efforts to improve participation have attempted to
make the acts of registration and voting easier.

Motor Voter

In each election some voters become interested in a contest and would
like to participate but are denied that opportunity because the registra-

tion deadline for that election has passed. The longer the time between the closing of registration rolls and the election, the lower the turnout rate.[55] The potential for limiting the electorate through early registration deadlines was acknowledged as early as the Mississippi Constitution of 1890, which included among its components that were designed to remove and keep African Americans off the voters' lists a registration cutoff four months before the election.[56]

Registration requirements have been justified as necessary to prevent fraud; a few states, however, permit election-day registration. While the vast majority of states continue to have registration cutoffs early enough to prepare lists of eligible voters for distribution to polling places, recent federal law has made registration easier.

Beginning in 1995, federal law has demanded that states allow prospective voters to register at various public facilities or through the mail. New voters have been most likely to register where driver's licenses can be renewed, and for this reason the phenomenon has been dubbed "motor voter." Other possible registration sites include libraries and places where one signs up for food stamps, welfare, or other social services. Through the registration law's first eighteen months on the books, 8.8 million voters signed up when getting driver's licenses, while another 5 million registered through the mail.[57] In Georgia, two-thirds of new voters signed up at a driver's license office; approximately another 10 percent registered at a welfare agency.[58] In parts of the South, the Christian Coalition has spearheaded efforts to get church members on the voter rolls.

Motor voter seems to be another instance of the "law of unintended consequences" at work. At the time of passage, many people believed that easing registration requirements would benefit the Democratic Party, since the unregistered are disproportionately concentrated among the less educated and less affluent. But results for the statute's first two years show that, nationwide, the share of registered Democrats declined by 1 percentage point, the percent of Independents rose by a point, and GOP registration remained constant.[59] In the South, where the GOP has made some of its most impressive electoral gains, new voters have been more Republican than those already on the lists.[60] Turnout specialist Ruy Teixeira explains that "liberalizing registration is going to have the most effect on youth and in the South, and Republicans are kicking butt in the South."[61] Statistics compiled in Georgia, one of a handful of states that maintain registration records by race, show African Americans making greater use of relaxed registration rules than whites.

While registering to vote may have a symbolic value, it is of little political significance if the new registrants do not exercise the franchise. Kentucky is one of the few states that elected many of its officials in 1995, and results from the Bluegrass State were not encouraging for those who hoped motor voter would significantly increase participation. Only one of four new voters who registered during the first half of 1995 turned out in the general election.[62] Despite the strongest Republican bid for the governorship in a generation, among those who signed up when getting a driver's license fewer than 7 percent exercised their new right, and among voters enrolled at other offices, turnout hovered below 5 percent.

Comparable details for the 1996 national election are not available; nonetheless, it is obvious that easing registration did not promote greater participation. Even with millions of new eligible voters, the 1996 vote for president fell by more than 10 percent from the 1992 totals.

No-Wait Voting

In 1980 approximately a quarter of Americans who said that they did not vote even though they were registered attributed their absence from the polls to a lack of transportation, being away from home, or being unable to get away from work.[63] Another 17 percent identified illness or a family crisis as the obstacle to voting. Figures such as these suggest that turnout might rise if voting were made easier.

Two innovations intended to remove the hassle of voting are being tried in selected states. One of these is "no-fault" absentee voting. Unlike the typical absentee voting available to those who will be away from home on election day, the no-fault version is open to anyone who wants to avoid the lines at the polls. Early voting has become popular with a sizable chunk of the Texas electorate.

First tried in Monterey, California, in 1977, vote-by-mail was authorized by another fifteen states by 1995.[64] Mail election ballots are sent to the eligible electorate, which is given a certain number of days in which to register a preference. Many states that have vote-by-mail limit the process to special elections and/or ones in which only referendum items are decided, thereby foreclosing this option for choosing among candidates. In some states mail voting is permissible only in jurisdictions with few voters.

In a notable break with the general pattern, Oregon turned to vote-by-mail to conduct the 1995 election to fill the Senate vacancy caused by the resignation of Bob Packwood. Voters had almost three weeks in which to complete and return their ballots. Turnout in this special primary ran ahead of participation in the 1994 primaries and cost roughly half as much.[65]

The heightened voter turnout in Oregon parallels a general pattern in which far more people indicate that they would rather register preferences by mail than go to the polls on low-salience special elections to decide local issues. Participants' answers to questions posed in vote-by-mail elections signal that having the government pay return postage may stimulate greater participation.

While supporters of vote-by-mail boast that it saves money and spurs turnout, opponents raise other kinds of concerns. With voting going on for weeks, early voters will make choices without the advantage of late-breaking information. Revelation of a scandal or emergence of a new issue can have no impact on those who have already cast a ballot. In Louisiana, the officially endorsed Republican candidate withdrew from the contest just days before the 1990 U.S. Senate election in order to avoid splitting the vote and perhaps allowing David Duke to get into a runoff with the incumbent, Democratic Senator Bennett Johnston. Voters who cast absentee ballots for the GOP nominee not only lacked relevant information, their ballots were not counted, and Senator Johnston was reelected in the primary. Others see important symbolism associated with having the community go to the polls on a single day. Having a single day for voting may contribute to a growing interest in the outcome as activities and advertising mount to a crescendo.

Another consequence of mail balloting in contests that involve candidates may be an added boost to already spiraling campaign costs. When voters have weeks during which to file their ballots, candidates may be tempted to try to buy saturation television advertising for much of that period, rather than limiting that effort to the final days of a campaign. Only wealthy candidates, or those with expansive treasuries, would be able to maintain such a pace for long.

Officeholder Diversity

One manifestation of the growing openness of the political system at the state and local level is the growing diversity in the ranks of elected officials. In many communities these changes are so recent that some of "the firsts" are still in office and others remain politically active. For example, the first modern African American to serve in a southern state legislature, Leroy Johnson, who was elected to the Georgia Senate in 1963, continues to live in Atlanta although he is retired from politics. Andrew Young (D-Ga.), who, along with Barbara Jordan (D-Tex.), holds the distinction of being the first black elected to Congress during the twentieth century, was a key player in bringing the 1996 Olympics to Atlanta. Douglas Wilder of Virginia remains the only African American elected recently to govern a state.

Numerous "firsts" abound among women officials also. In 1994, Linda Schrenko, Georgia's state school superintendent, became that state's first nonjudicial officer elected statewide. In 1991, Gwen Margolis of Florida became the first woman to preside over a state senate anywhere in the nation. Mary Sue Terry, Virginia's first female attorney general, gave up her post for an unsuccessful bid for the governorship in 1993.

African Americans

Table 10.2 shows the growth in the number of African Americans serving in selected state and local offices. Since 1968, the number of black

TABLE 10.2. BLACK ELECTED OFFICIALS AT THE LOCAL LEVEL

Year	State Legislature	Other	County Commission	Other	City Mayor	Council	School Board
1968	168	1	64	11	48	552	362
1971	198	2	86	18	81	653	455
1972	206	4	132	29	86	780	657
1973	238	2	167	44	82	840	744
1974	236	3	200	42	108	1080	767
1975	276	5	267	38	135	1237	894
1976	276	5	315	40	152	1442	939
1977	294	4	334	47	162	1560	994
1978	294	4	358	52	170	1618	1086
1979	307	5	351	46	175	1696	1085
1980	317	6	394	57	182	1809	1149
1981	333	8	372	77	204	1818	1211
1982	330	6	392	73	223	1872	1203
1983	375	4	420	76	247	2030	1305
1984	385	4	447	71	255	2056	1300
1985	392	4	534	77	286	2189	1368
1986	396	4	596	85	289	2396	1437
1987	410	6	640	84	303	2483	1475
1988	406	7	656	86	301	2621	1476
1989	416	8	696	97	299	2882	1537
1990	415	8	710	100	313	2936	1577
1991	438	10	705	103	318	2977	1560
1992	475	9	745	112	338	2969	1550
1993	523	10	795	118	356	3161	1617
1994	539[a]		925[a]		3960[a]		1707[a]
1995	576[a]		912[a]		4042[a]		1853[a]
1996	578[a]		924[a]		4099[a]		1935[a]
1997	579	6	817	120	387	3375	1889

Sources: appropriate issues of *The National Roster of Black Elected Officials* (Washington, D.C.: Joint Center for Political and Economic Studies).

a. Combined figures for state, county, and municipal levels; school board figures include a few education officials other than school board members.

state legislators has more than tripled. Their numbers in other categories have grown even more impressively, with county commissioners and other county officials increasing more than tenfold. The number of African-American mayors has risen by a factor of eight, while city councilors have increased by almost 600 percent. School board membership has more than quintupled. The office most commonly held by blacks is that of city councilor. In many communities, the African-American presence on city councils is roughly proportionate to the black percentage of the population.

Within the past few decades, blacks have held the highest offices in all

TABLE 10.3. LATINO STATE AND LOCAL ELECTED OFFICE HOLDERS, 1984–94

Year	State Legislature	County	City	Judicial Law Enforcement	School Board	Total
1984	124	289	1,015	505	1,186	3,119
1985	119	291	1,025	517	1,185	3,137
1986	122	304	1,048	530	1,188	3,192
1987	127	314	1,098	568	1,199	3,306
1988	124	319	1,106	574	1,226	3,349
1989	133	338	1,178	575	1,340	3,773
1990	134	351	1,290	583	1,458	3,994
1991	140	378	1,314	596	1,489	4,092
1992	139	386	1,362	628	1,554	4,229
1993	163	406	1,474	633	1,582	4,403
1994	184	401	1,647	651	1,578	4,608

Source: The NALEO Educational Fund, *National Roster of Hispanic Elected Officials*, 1984–94.

of America's cities with populations of more than one million (except San Diego), and they have led such other major cities as Atlanta, Baltimore, Birmingham, Charlotte, Cincinnati, Cleveland, Denver, Kansas City, Memphis, Minneapolis, New Orleans, St. Louis, and Seattle. African Americans have won smaller shares of mayoral elections in towns and less populous communities.

Data collected in 1991 by the International City/Council Managers Association from more than 4,800 cities showed that blacks held almost 5 percent of the council seats, with their presence at its highest in larger cities.[66] African-American councilors also were more common in the South, in central cities, and in cities with larger councils.

Latinos

Latino elected officials have also become more numerous, their ranks swelling by approximately 50 percent over the decade ending in 1994.[67] As table 10.3 shows, this rate of increase is fairly constant across offices, with the exception of school boards and judicial positions, where the rate of growth has been slower. About two-thirds of all Latino officials serve on local collegial bodies — city councils or school boards. Until 1994, the latter always had slightly more Hispanics than did the former.

Approximately 97 percent of all Hispanic officials serve in nine states; the greatest number (2,215) are in Texas. California and New Mexico each had between 700 and 800 Hispanic officeholders in 1994. Almost a quarter of these officials were women, and they served disproportionately on school boards and were underrepresented in judicial/law enforcement positions.

Studies of the councils of larger cities do not reveal growth patterns like those in table 10.3, although Latinos have been mayors of Denver and San Antonio. In the early 1970s Mexican Americans were about one-third as likely to be council members as their numbers in the population would suggest; by the end of the decade their representation had grown to 44 percent.[68] Over the next decade there was, however, virtually no improvement in the representation ratio of Latinos.[69] These studies, the most recent of which gathered data in 1988, may have ended too soon to catch the growth during the 1990s that is reflected in table 10.3.

The disparity between the size of the Latino adult population and the component of that population holding U.S. citizenship creates an obstacle for increasing the ranks of Latino public officials. The differences tend to be greater near the Mexican border and in certain portions of cities and, when large, can result in districts in which Latinos constitute a sizable majority of the population yet remain a minority of the citizen voting-age population.[70] The Texas legislature sought to devise a Houston congressional district that would elect a Latino, but even though the grotesquely shaped district managed to snare a 54-percent Hispanic voting-age population, an Anglo eked out a majority in the decisive Democratic primary runoff.[71]

Women

In 1995 eighty-four women held statewide elective executive offices, including New Jersey's Governor Christine Todd Whitman and nineteen lieutenant governors.[72] A quarter of all the statewide executive posts filled by election had been won by women, exceeding the proportion of state legislative seats filled by women by 5 percentage points. Women held the largest shares of legislative seats in the West and New England but were least frequently elected in the South. In 1995 women constituted at least 30 percent of state legislators in Washington, Nevada, New Hampshire, Colorado, Arizona, and Vermont, with Washington leading the way with an almost 40-percent female composition.

San Diego was the largest city to have a female chief executive in 1995, making it one of the seventeen cities among the nation's one hundred most populous that were led by a woman. In recent years, women mayors have led such major cities as Chicago, Charlotte, Houston, Dallas, Minneapolis, San Antonio, San Francisco, and Washington, D.C. In cities with populations of at least 10,000, women held 20.9 percent of the mayor's offices and 21.9 percent of the council seats in 1994 (see table 10.4, p. 236). Thus, women hold slightly more than 40 percent of the share of the municipal positions they would be expected to occupy if the posts were filled at random. While still holding far fewer city offices than they would have if proportionately represented, there have been gains. In 1975 women held only 19 percent of the seats they would be expected to fill if councilors were selected randomly; three years later the figure had risen to 25 percent.[73] In the

TABLE 10.4. WOMEN IN ELECTIVE OFFICES (IN PERCENTAGES)

Year	Statewide elective	State legislature	County governing boards	Mayors and municipal councils
1975	10	8	3	4
1977	10	9	4	8
1979	11	10	5	10
1981	11	12	6	10
1983	11	13	8	NA
1985	14	15	8	14
1987	14	16	9	NA
1989	14	17	9	NA
1991	18	18	NA	NA
1993	22	21	NA	NA
1994	23	21	NA	21[a]
1995	26	21	NA	NA
1997	26	22	NA	NA

Source: "Women in Elective Politics," Center for the American Woman and Politics, Rutgers University.

NA=Not available.
a. Cities with populations greater than 10,000.

late 1970s, while all types of women were underrepresented, Anglo women fared far better than their African-American or Latina sisters.[74]

A survey sponsored by the International City/County Management Association (ICMA) in late 1991 found 634 women mayors in 4,860 cities that returned questionnaires.[75] Cities with populations between 250,000 and 499,999 were most likely to have female chief executives. The ICMA survey found female mayors most common at opposite ends of the country — in New England and along the Pacific Coast. Women generally held larger shares of the seats on the councils of more populous cities and in the West, although 70 percent of the cities nationwide had at least one female councilor. Twenty-six years earlier, only 40 percent of the cities had a woman on council.[76]

At the county level, the limited available research suggests that women are more likely to serve on school boards than on county commissions.[77] This finding is in keeping with the tendency for women to be active in shaping education and social programs. Women are relatively more numerous in county government in Florida, perhaps because of its urban nature.[78] In Georgia and South Carolina, women holding administrative positions are especially likely to serve as probate judges, tax commissioners, and clerks of court. They are infrequently found as sheriffs or prosecutors. Jobs that have a clerical component are more likely to be filled by women than posts that allow greater discretion.

Reasons for Increases

Two factors contribute mightily to growth in the numbers of public officials from groups long absent from the ranks of America's elected. Increases in the numbers of African Americans and Latinos serving on collegial bodies during the 1980s are partially — but not wholly — attributable to affirmative-action districting. Under the unblinking eye of the U.S. Department of Justice (DOJ), many southern jurisdictions and a few in other regions have been forced to concentrate minorities in districts in order to make probable the election of a minority-group member there. When districts for state legislators, city council members or county commissioners were designed with the intention that they elect a minority, it was surprising when the objective was not achieved.[79] The failure of heavily black state legislative districts to elect African Americans usually results from the presence of an entrenched white incumbent; once that individual retires, a black wins.[80]

Recently, districts drawn to be hospitable for minorities have come under attack if the predominant factor in their creation is race.[81] The U.S. Supreme Court has invalidated Georgia, Texas, and North Carolina congressional districts that ignored political boundaries (such as county lines), lacked compactness, and sometimes were alleged not to be contiguous, in order to make a racial minority the majority population. Lower courts have taken their cue from the high court and have reached similar conclusions in cases involving congressional districts in Louisiana, Florida, Virginia, New York, and South Carolina, and state legislative districts in Georgia and South Carolina.

The impetus for the DOJ demands for bringing together geographically disparate minorities to create districts in which these groups would constitute majorities was the belief that minorities should be able to elect candidates of their choice and that the only way to determine the preference of minorities was to present situations in which a minority candidate could win. The emphasis, then, was on descriptive or symbolic representation. With the 1982 amendment of Section 2 of the Voting Rights Act, having whites who would represent the policy preferences of minorities — a concept called substantive representation — ceased to be adequate. Among the items considered in determining whether minorities suffer discrimination, policy responsiveness was specifically demoted to secondary status, while the degree to which minorities have been elected in their jurisdictions became one of the two factors weighed most heavily by courts in challenges to the fairness of districting systems.

Increased tolerance among white voters has been a second major factor contributing to the growing ranks of minority elected officials. Early work on racial voting patterns found that white voter cohesion behind white candidates exceeded African-American unity for black candidates. While the general tendency is still for each race to prefer its own candidates, the share of the white vote attracted by black candidates typically exceeds the proportion of the black vote going to white candidates. For example, in winning Virginia's governorship, Douglas Wilder took 96 percent of the black vote and approximately 40 percent of the white vote.[82] Four years earlier, Wilder had won 44 percent of the white vote. In winning the New York City Democratic mayoral primary in 1989, David Dinkins got a third of the white vote along with 94 percent of the black vote and 57 percent of the Latino vote.[83] White candidate Mike Foster defeated African-American Cleo Fields for the governorship of Louisiana in 1995 by taking 84 percent of the white vote while getting only 6 percent of the black ballots.[84]

African-American candidates for mayor in major cities have been particularly successful in winning enough white votes to put together a successful biracial coalition. Among the predominantly white cities that have elected black mayors are Charlotte, Dallas, Denver, Minneapolis, Kansas City, Los Angeles, San Francisco, and Seattle. In almost 60 percent of the sixty-seven cities with populations in excess of 25,000 that had black mayors, the white population exceeded the African-American.[85]

Structural features have little relationship to the incidence of women officeholders, so multivariate models do poorly at explaining variance in the election of females. Bullock and MacManus come up with a five-variable model, four variables of which are statistically significant, but they can account for only 5 percent of the variance in female council membership.[86]

In recent years, a recurring theme has been that if more women are to be elected, more women must run. A 1975 survey of cities with populations greater than 25,000 led Karnig and Walter to observe that "the chief obstacle women encounter in achieving equitable council representation is apparently the shortfall of women candidates."[87]

SINCE THE 1960s, many barriers to registration and voting have been eliminated, yet turnout remains a problem. Racial barriers no longer impede those who would vote, and registration has been made almost painless, enabling citizens to get on the voter rolls at a number of government offices or through the mail. The American population is becoming better-educated and older, two correlates of higher levels of participation; nonetheless, turnout in 1996 sagged below the unimpressive 1992 rate. While part of the explanation for declining rates of participation may be growing cynicism about government and its leaders, a likely contributing factor is lack of competition. The replacement of multimember districts and at-large elections with single-member districts has heightened the potential that voters will avoid the polls because they find no choices on the ballot. Even though the courts have invalidated some of the more blatant instances in which affirmative-action districting separated white from minority voters, most of the SMD plans adopted during the past twenty years will endure.

The self-restricted electorate has, however, produced a cadre of officials that is more diverse than ever before. The numbers of women and racial and ethnic minorities have increased substantially across the range of offices. While some structural features have been identified as impediments to the political ambitions of these groups, the empirical evidence provides little support for many of these claims. The most often studied relationship has been that between districting and the election of African Americans. Even this linkage is weaker now than a generation ago, although in the South there remains a pattern of blacks winning larger shares of council offices in SMD cities. In part because political units that had not elected minorities at-large have been challenged in court and have had to change their electoral schemes, data gathered in the late 1980s showed little difference in the incidence of minorities on city councils across alternative districting arrangements.

Other techniques, such as minimum-vote thresholds and staggered terms, do not appear to impede the election of minorities or women. Given the hostility of the current Supreme Court, successful challenges to these approaches seem unlikely. The unwillingness of the high court to countenance districting that is primarily race-based may slow down the adoption of alternative voting procedures such as cumulative voting and limited voting. Courts lack the authority to impose these formats, and in the absence of an interpretation that requires the creation of majority-minority districts whenever possible, there may be little impetus to go beyond single-member districting as an alternative to AL or MMD elections. Some small communities that currently have SMDs may opt for cumulative or limited voting in order to avoid having to redraw their districts to achieve compliance with the one person, one vote requirement, or because creating districts with handfuls of voters may seem divisive or silly.

Barriers to the election of women are coming down. Women are becoming more numerous at all levels of government and dominate the ranks of some officeholders, such as county clerks of court in Georgia.[88] As more women come forward as candidates, their numbers in the ranks of public officials are likely to continue increasing. Latino officeholders also are likely to increase as the numbers of Spanish-surname citizens rise and as these citizens come to take a more active role in politics. The numbers of African-American officials will grow incrementally, although the jump in numbers registered following the redistricting of the early 1990s will not likely be duplicated.

States that have low rates of participation may try to improve their positions relative to other states by expanding the window of opportunity to vote by relaxing standards for absentee voting or permitting early voting.[89] Even in states where voting is more widespread, the electorate may favor options other than waiting in long lines to choose public officials. The cost savings and higher turnout rates coupled with the absence of evidence of widespread vote fraud in Oregon's use of a mail-out ballot to fill a U.S. Senate vacancy will likely induce other states to try using the postman when the alternative is to mobilize the full electoral machinery in order to choose one or a handful of officials. States that already permit voting by mail may lead the way by expanding the conditions under which this type of election can be held.

The disposal of reform proposals will, of course, be handled by partisan actors. To the extent that one party anticipates being disadvantaged by changing the rules governing elections, it will seek to delay, if not block, the modification. A majority party, particularly one that sees its grasp on power eroding, is the most likely source of reformist zeal. The scenario of a majority party in decline aptly characterizes the Democratic Party in a number of southern states, and some of these have already made changes, such as easing criteria for casting early votes in Texas. Vote-by-mail has been discussed in Georgia, but the necessary legislation has not been approved. Just as changing rules for registration has not enhanced turnout, modifying election laws also may prove ineffective in staving off Republican Party growth in the South.

CHAPTER ELEVEN

Interest Representation in the States

Virginia Gray and David Lowery

POLITICIANS, JOURNALISTS, AND CITIZENS routinely decry the power of special interests in government. Critics assert that such interests subvert democratic government with the corrupting influence of money. Votes in legislative chambers are bought with gifts or even outright bribes. Elections are rigged with campaign contributions. These charges are common because they play well in American politics. Their continuing power rests at least in part in how they resonate with the moralistic and populist traditions of American politics.

Traditions of political rhetoric alone, however, are not sufficient to account for why abusing lobbying organizations remains an American spectator sport. There must be enough real examples of corruption to make the rhetoric credible. And, unfortunately, the states have provided more than their fair share of examples. Historically, politics in a number of states was dominated by one or a few major interests: coal interests in Kentucky and West Virginia, the Southern Pacific Railroad in California, DuPont in Delaware, and oil in Texas.[1] While these examples are now in our past, charges of outright bribery of state legislators — most recently in South Carolina during the early 1990s and Louisiana in 1995 — still occur just frequently enough to give substance to our ingrained suspicions of special interests.

The venerable habit of demonizing special interests may blind us, however, from considering more broadly their role in state politics. A broader perspective is needed given that many of the attacks on lobbying organizations are at least in part disingenuous. For example, lobbying organizations are regularly assailed by elected politicians. Yet, they work closely — and often on quite friendly terms — with lobbyists in the legislative process and finance their elections with funds raised from members of lobbying organizations. The complaints of citizen critics can be disingenuous, too, although they are perhaps less often founded on blatant hypocrisy. Lobbying organizations supporting and opposing gun control, for example, vigorously attack each other as special interests while viewing their own lobbying as legitimate political expression by concerned citizens motivated solely by the public interest.

ile well aware of the potential dangers of organized interests, po-
cientists often cite their role in political representation.[2] Lobbying
organizations have a number of advantages compared to the other two
primary means democratic political systems use to aggregate and express
preferences: political parties and voting. Parties are broad coalitions that
often submerge policy differences in order to maintain voter support. And
individual voting can communicate only a preference for one candidate
over another. In contrast, lobbying organizations can provide highly detailed, nuanced signals about the specific problems citizens face, as well
as potential solutions. While organized interests cannot replace voting and
parties, neither can parties and voting replace lobbying organizations.

The real issue, then, must concern how well the interest systems of the
states are structured to both facilitate the positive contributions of organized interests and minimize their potential to corrupt politics or bias public
policy. This chapter examines how state interest systems are structured by
looking at four issues: the origins and maintenance of interest organizations,
how state interest communities are comprised, the lobbying and campaign
funding activities of organized interests, and their influence on government
and politics. In general, our conclusions are optimistic. The recent and
rapid expansion of state interest communities has reduced the power of
once-dominant interests in many states. This also means that the states have
become more like each other in recent decades, and that their interest systems
have become more similar to the interest community found in Washington.

Before beginning our review of state interest systems, however, we must
consider two issues: labeling and, more substantively, how best to peer
into the world of interest representation. First, we use the terms *interest
organization* or *lobbying organization* rather than the more familiar labels
interest group or *pressure group*. Quite simply, most lobbying organizations
have no members, but are institutions such as banks, industrial firms, universities, or hospitals.[3] Many other interest groups are associations. Their
membership is often comprised entirely of institutions: associations of businesses, university consortia, or federations of local governments. Indeed, we
will see that only a minority of state organized interests are organizations
with individual members deserving of the interest-group label.

The second issue concerns more than labels. That is, we might approach
the study of state interest systems from any of several different perspectives:
looking at distributions of interests within the states, at the lobbying organizations some of them sponsor, or at lobbyists themselves. Much of
the research reported in this chapter examines lobbying organizations —
organizations registered to lobby the legislatures of the fifty states. We do
not examine interests in society, because both the unorganized and organizations not engaged in lobbying are less likely to be important politically
than those engaged in lobbying. While we are confident about the general
validity of this assumption, we also realize that our focus will miss a number

of organizations that influence state politics in less direct ways than through lobbying.[4] Also, while we will frequently quote lobbyists, we do not focus on lobbyists as such. A large organization may employ several lobbyists, and a single lobbyist may represent several client organizations. More to the point, we are concerned about interest representation in the states — interests embedded within organizations and their membership — not in how many lobbyists a group hires or views of the lobbyists themselves.

The Origins and Maintenance of Interest Organizations

While we ultimately are concerned about the political behavior of organized interests, we must first consider a number of questions about organizations' internal operations. The most fundamental of these is how interest organizations come to exist in the first place. And once they exist, how do they maintain themselves? Much of the research on these questions has focused on national organizations. Therefore, in reviewing some of this work, we also will ask how it compares to research findings on state lobbying organizations. That is, we will try to determine if the origins and maintenance activities of state and national interest organizations differ.

The issue of the origins of interest organizations is framed by two of the most important books written about lobbying organizations in the last fifty years. The first is David Truman's *The Governmental Process,* first published in 1951.[5] Truman did not find the formation of interest organizations puzzling; he assumed that those with common interests naturally joined together. So when no organization emerged to articulate a particular position on public policy, he assumed that that position must be insufficiently compelling to energize support.

Truman's assumption was severely challenged by Mancur Olson in his 1965 book, *The Logic of Collective Action.*[6] It was not obvious to Olson that any but the smallest interest organizations, or those that could employ coercion, would emerge naturally. To understand Olson's point, consider the occupational regulation of barbers by the states. It is often thought that such regulation benefits barbers already in the profession by making it more difficult for new barbers to enter the market. But a practicing barber would benefit from regulation whether or not he joined the lobbying organization promoting it. He might take a "free ride," letting his fellow barbers do the work while he stayed home. Of course, since every barber is at least as smart as he, others might stay home too. The result is that a barber organization never forms, and occupational regulations are never adopted. Olson believed that the logic underlying this example makes it unlikely that many organizations will form naturally from shared interests.

The problem, of course, is that at least 1,100 occupations *are* regulated by one or more states.[7] And many organized interests lobby in state capitols. If such interests do not form naturally, why are there so many of them? The answer, suggested Olson, is that organizations use "selective benefits" to maintain membership. Our barber, for example, may be offered a special low-cost insurance policy upon joining a Barbers' Benevolent Society. Olson felt that organizations must rely on selective incentives to construct their memberships, not on the common "interests" of the members. This solution, however, poses problems for assessing the role of organized interests in democratic politics. If organizations are constructed via provision of selective incentives, then there may be only a weak connection between the concerns of members and their "interest" as represented through lobbying.

The research generated by the debate between Truman and Olson provides some support for both positions. On the one hand, it appears that organizations often form in the absence of very narrow selective incentives. Research by David King and Jack Walker examined a wide range of incentives that might lead members to join Washington interest organizations.[8] Surveys of the organizations' leaders asked whether they provided twelve different benefits to members.[9] The list included three selective or personal material benefits thought to be important by Olson — tours, insurance, and discounts on consumer goods — but it also included the professional benefits of conferences, professional contacts, and training; the purposive benefits of advocacy, government lobbying, and participation in public affairs; the solidary benefit of friendship; and the "other" benefits of publications and coordination with other interest organizations.

A similar study of state interest organizations was conducted in 1994.[10] King and Walker's findings for national interest organizations are presented, along with the state results, in figure 11.1. The first conclusion to draw from these findings is that only a minority of organized interests with members rely on the very narrow selective incentives of tours, insurance, and consumer discounts; less than 40 percent of both the state and national organizations offer these benefits. Instead, majorities of both samples rely on the kinds of solidary, professional, and purposive benefits that Truman would use to explain the formation of interest organizations. The second conclusion deserving note is that state and national interest organizations appear to be quite similar in the kinds of incentives they offer.

On the other hand, it has long been noted that the Washington interest community is dominated by narrow economic interests rather than mass membership organizations. Indeed, a majority of the lobbying organizations in Washington have no members per se, but instead are institutions, especially business corporations.[11] This would not surprise Olson, since corporations often have a large and direct stake in the decisions of government — contracts, tax breaks, and so on. Also, their hierarchical command structure means that they do not suffer from the "free rider" problem plaguing the formation of membership groups.

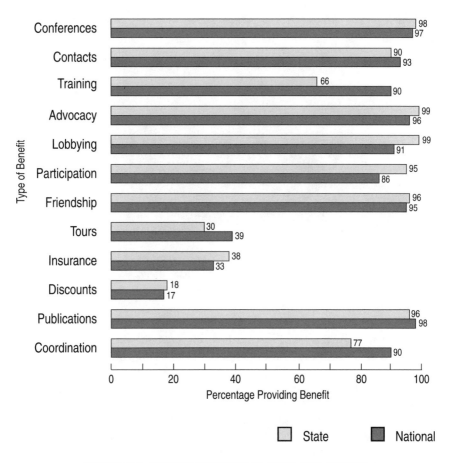

**FIGURE 11.1. BENEFITS PROVIDED BY STATE AND FEDERAL
LOBBYING ORGANIZATIONS**

Source: National results recalculated from David C. King and Jack L. Walker, "The Provision of Benefits by Interest Groups in the United States," *Journal of Politics* 54 (May 1992): 394–426. State data collected by authors.

Is this bias evident in the states too? We distinguish three types of organizations registered to lobby in the states: membership groups, associations, and institutions.[12] Membership groups have individuals as members and include labor unions, cause groups, and hobby groups. The members of associations, in contrast, are other organizations; these include federations of governments and businesses. Because both have members, associations and membership groups were included in the samples of organizations used to construct figure 11.1. The final set of organizations, institutions, have no members.

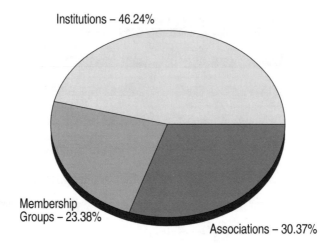

Institutions – 46.24%

Membership
Groups – 23.38%

Associations – 30.37%

**FIGURE 11.2. AVERAGE DISTRIBUTION OF STATE LOBBYING ORGANIZATIONS
BY TYPE OF ORGANIZATION, 1990**

Source: Data collected by authors.

As seen in figure 11.2, institutions, on average, accounted for 46.24 percent of all registered lobbying organizations in the states in 1990. Associations accounted for 30.37 percent, on average. And membership groups comprised, on average, only 23.38 percent of all interest organizations. There is, of course, variation in these proportions across the fifty states. Institutions, for example, are most strongly represented in Arizona (64.91 percent) and least dominant in Rhode Island (30.00 percent). Still, like the Washington interest community, state interest communities are dominated by institutions. And their dominance is increasing. A study of six states — Arkansas, South Dakota, North Carolina, Michigan, Minnesota, and Pennsylvania — compared the proportions of institutions within their lobbying communities in 1980 and 1990.[13] On average, the representation of institutions increased from 40.13 percent to 47.47 percent over the decade.

Therefore, the collective action problem identified by Olson does not inhibit interest organizations' forming in the absence of selective incentives. At the same time, though, the collective action problem probably biases the interest system toward organizations with large and direct material stakes in government policy.

Organizational Maintenance

Once lobbying organizations form, they must then work to survive. The issue of organizational maintenance is important, although many credit

lobbying organizations with substantial longevity. Indeed, studies of lobbying organizations in Washington suggest that very few disappear even
over several decades.[14] And many who criticize the influence of organized interests on government policy simply assume that, once established,
these organizations have the staying power of the Energizer Bunny.[15] Politicians may come and go, they argue, but organized interests are permanent
players in government policy.

Closer examination of state interest communities, however, points to
much greater fluidity. While some lobbying organizations are nearly permanent members of state interest communities, a study of lobby registration
rolls in six states from 1980 through 1990 found that many others do not
survive for long.[16] Fully 43.27 percent of North Carolina and 45.82 percent
of Michigan organizations registered to lobby in 1980 were not on their
1990 registration rolls. In South Dakota (50.79 percent) and Pennsylvania
(51.91 percent), a majority did not survive the 1980s. And in Arkansas and
Minnesota, a whopping 64.25 and 63.40 percent, respectively, of all 1980
interest organizations left their state's lobbying registration rolls by 1990.
So despite the seemingly permanent presence of organized interests in state
capitols, there is a great deal of coming and going.

What determines which organizations remain within state lobbying
communities and which do not? The answer seems to vary by type of
organized interest. A detailed follow-up of the Minnesota organizations
registered to lobby in 1980, but missing from the 1990 registration rolls,
found that 54.22 percent of the institutions that withdrew from lobbying continued to exist as organizations.[17] The remaining 45.78 percent,
however, disappeared as organizations, either dissolving or merging with
another entity. Still, for most of the institutions, withdrawing from lobbying did not signal their demise. This suggests that institutions, rather than
being permanent members, often enter and exit lobbying communities as
issues of direct concern to them — a particular regulation, tax issue, or
budget item — move on and off state policy agendas.

The fate of associations and membership groups is very different. The
Minnesota study found that 79.07 percent of the membership groups and
84.40 percent of the associations no longer registered in 1990 also no
longer existed as organizations. For these organizations, death of the lobbying function typically coincided with death of the organization supporting
it. Issues of organizational maintenance, therefore, are far from trivial for
associations and membership groups.

Niche Theory

The best explanation now available for why some organizations persist
while others perish is niche theory. James Q. Wilson noted the central
idea behind niche theory when he observed that "the easiest and most

prudent maintenance strategy is to develop *autonomy* — that is, a distinctive area of competence, a clearly demarcated and exclusively served clientele or membership, an undisputed jurisdiction over a function, service, goal, or cause."[18] That is, organized interests try to establish viable niches by securing exclusive access to the resources they need to survive as organizations.

There are two important implications of niche theory. First, the primary competitors of lobbying organizations are those organizations most like themselves. For example, while environmental interests and industrial firms will compete over policy, the most likely threat to the survival of environmental organizations is posed by other environmental organizations. This is because they are competitors for a common pool of members or funding sources. Second, much of this competition will not involve overt strife, but the partitioning of resources so that otherwise similar organizations avoid direct competition.[19] Thus, one environmental organization might specialize in recruiting middle-class adults, while another targets college students as members.

What are the most critical resources in establishing a viable niche? One study of associations and membership groups in six states (discussed earlier, p. 246) found strong evidence of partitioning — the hallmark of a critical resource — of membership and funding resources.[20] That is, these lobbying organizations placed high priority on developing a distinctive membership base and a secure source of funding, two resources that may be closely related. When respondents were asked to identify their sources of funding, the largest proportion cited member dues.[21] As seen in figure 11.3, the typical lobbying organization with members in the six states raised 60 percent of its funds from member dues.

Figure 11.3 also allows us to compare the sources of funding of state and national interest organizations by showing the results from the six-state study along with King and Walker's findings for national interest organizations with members.[22] Six funding sources are displayed: funds raised from dues, receipts from services (including publications, insurance, conference fees, and fees from other staff services), government contracts, contributions (funds — including gifts — from other associations, foundations, and individuals), interest revenue, and other revenue.[23] The national organizations rely somewhat less on dues (49 percent) and somewhat more on receipts, contracts, contributions, and interest than do their state counterparts. Still, the two patterns of revenue reliance are quite similar.

The lives of individual lobbying organizations in the states appear, then, to be quite similar to those of their counterparts lobbying the national government in Washington. In offering similar benefits to members, they implement common solutions to the collective action problem posed by Olson. State and national interest organizations typically rely on similar sources of funding. These commonalities should not be surprising. Some

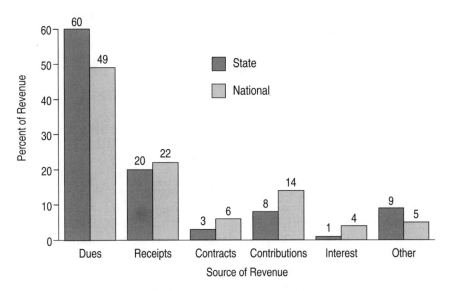

FIGURE 11.3. ESTIMATED SOURCES OF FINANCE OF STATE AND NATIONAL LOBBYING ORGANIZATIONS

Sources: National results recalculated from King and Walker, 1991. State data collected by authors.

organizations lobby in several states. For others, national umbrella organizations provide a forum for sharing information. And in the age of faxes and e-mail, news about successful strategies spreads rapidly.[24]

Interest Organization Communities

Individual interest organizations survive by developing a viable niche that provides the resources needed to maintain their operations. But not all interest organizations survive for long. It is important to note that the fate of these organizations may not depend solely on their own actions. That is, the six-state study from which we reported the mortality figures on lobbying organizations suggested that the nature of the interest community also matters.[25] That is, mortality rates — withdrawal from lobbying rolls from 1980 to 1990 — were found to be much higher in states with many organized interests relative to the size of their economies than in those with fewer registrations. This finding is consistent with niche theory. As interest communities become denser, it becomes more difficult to establish a viable niche. But this insight also suggests that interest communities not only are constituted by the patterns of survival of individual organizations, but that their survival patterns are influenced in turn by the composition of interest communities — by how many and what kinds of organizations already exist in the community.

Density

Community density is usually measured either by the number of organized interests registered to lobby or by the number of registered organizations relative to the size of a state's economy. These measures well illustrate our theme of variation across the states within an increasingly common pattern of interest representation. There certainly is variation in the numbers of lobbying registrations. In 1990, for example, Mississippi registered only 107 interest organizations, while Florida registered 2,969, more than double the number in California, the second densest interest community.[26]

This variation, however, masks powerful trends influencing most of the states. As seen in figure 11.4, the average number of organizations registered to lobby has increased markedly from 1975 through the period from 1980 to 1990. In the forty-four states for which we have complete data for 1975 and 1980, the average number of registrations increased from 195.57 to 342.36. By 1990, the average was 617.50 organizations in these same forty-four states and 587.04 for all fifty states. Thus, the interest communities of the states became more crowded, increasing in number threefold over a fifteen-year period. Indeed, Mississippi — with the least dense interest community in 1990 — was the only state reporting fewer registrations in 1990 than in 1980.

A study using the second measure of community density — the number of organized interests relative to the size of a state's economy — indicated that the rapid expansion of lobbying communities made the states more similar to each other by 1990 than they had been in 1975.[27] That is, the number of organizations registered to lobby relative to the size of the economy was found to increase as the size of state economies increased in all three years studied: 1975, 1980, and 1990. But the strength of this relationship increased sharply over time; the size of a state's economy was a better predictor of the size of its interest community in 1990 than it was in 1975 or 1980. This suggests that the interest communities of the states — especially their composition — now are responding to economic and political events far more uniformly than they used to.

What are the external events that seem to be so similarly shaping the densities of state interest communities? An analysis of six kinds of interests — agricultural, manufacturing, construction, environmental, local government, and welfare organizations — in all fifty states for 1990 suggested that three factors are critical.[28] The study examined how the densities of each of these six kinds of interest organizations varied across the states with (1) the number of potential members for each type of organization, (2) the amount of state government activity or potential activity in

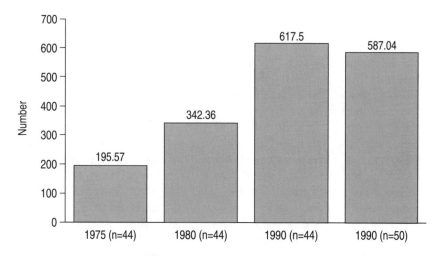

**FIGURE 11.4. AVERAGE NUMBER OF INTEREST ORGANIZATIONS
IN 1975, 1980, AND 1990**

Source: Data collected by authors.

Note: The 44-state bars exclude Alabama, Hawaii, Nevada, Rhode Island, Utah, and West Virginia because data for these states were not available for all years.

the area of interest to each, and (3) the likelihood that government policy would change in each area.

We can illustrate these findings by considering the results for construction interests. Not surprisingly, the number of construction lobbying registrations increased as the number of construction firms in a state grew. It was a surprise, however, to find that the rate of increase declined as the number of construction firms increased. Again, it seems that as more lobbying organizations represent a given interest, the difficulty of establishing a viable niche increases. The second factor was government activity or potential activity, measured for construction interests by the share of a state's budget devoted to such activities as road building. As state activity in construction increased, so did the number of construction lobbying organizations. Interests had more to lobby for. The final factor was the likelihood that government policy would change, measured by the level of party competition in each state. Numbers of construction interests increased as party competition increased. If competition between parties is intense, then the out-party stands a good chance of becoming the in-party with the next election. And because policies may change when new parties gain control of state government, uncertainty may lead to more lobbying activity as organized interests try to protect old benefits or jockey for new ones that might be provided.

These findings point to why the densities of state interest systems have increased so markedly over the last two decades. Over the same time period, the economies and political systems of the state have undergone considerable change. Not only are economies larger, they have become more diverse with the decline of older industries and the rapid growth of whole new industries. At the same time, the states have been doing more. Beginning with the Reagan election of 1980 and accelerating through the 1990s, national policy responsibilities have been shifted to the states. And political parties in the states have become more competitive, especially with the growing strength of the Republican Party in southern states. Therefore, we should not be surprised that the density of state interest communities has increased. All three factors have been pushing toward greater density.

Despite the fears of some scholars, however, this does not mean that interest organization communities will expand indefinitely.[29] Even if the forces promoting their expansion do not reverse as we move into the new century, we have seen that organized interests often leave lobbying communities, and such an exit is often associated with the death of the organization. Of equal importance, we have seen that exiting becomes more frequent as interest communities become denser. So there are very real limits to their size.

Diversity

The second major characteristic defining state interest communities is their diversity — the mix of different kinds of interests found on lobby registration rolls. It is important to remember, however, that the diversity and density of state interest communities are not determined separately. Rather, the diversity of an interest community is the cumulative outcome of the forces uniquely influencing the densities of the different types of organizations registered to lobby.[30] If a state has an unusually large number of construction firms and heavily funds construction activities, construction interests will be overrepresented in the lobbying community relative to the average state. But while the diversity of state interest communities is determined by the same forces that drive density, the political implications of which interests are represented before state governments makes the concept of diversity interesting in itself.

The diversity of interest organizations may be measured on a number of politically important dimensions, such as their distribution by geographic region or by economic class. But political scientists traditionally have looked at the mix of organizations from three perspectives. We have already examined the first: the distribution of interest organizational

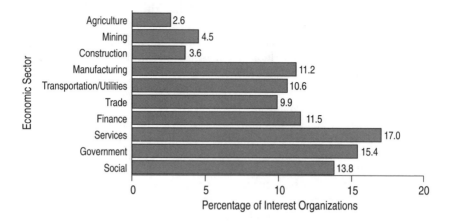

FIGURE 11.5. DISTRIBUTION OF AVERAGE STATE LOBBYING ORGANIZATIONS BY ECONOMIC SECTOR, 1990

Source: Data collected by authors.

types — institutions, associations, and membership groups — found in lobbying communities.

It is also common to examine the distribution of interests across the major sectors of economic activity found in the states. As seen in figure 11.5, for example, numbers of organized interests — as measured by 1990 lobbying registrations across eight profit-oriented economic sectors, government, and a residual category of "social" interests (clubs, cause groups, and so on) — are presented as proportions of the average or typical state interest community. Service industries, on average, generated the largest proportion of registered organizations, 17.0 percent, while the smallest proportion of lobbying registrations, only 2.6 percent, represented the mining industry.

Of course, the diversity of individual states varies from the "average" state reported in figure 11.5. But they do not vary by much, and all are quite diverse in terms of representation across major economic sectors. This can be understood most easily by examining Herfindahl index scores, which are summary measures for each state of distributions like those presented in figure 11.5. A Herfindahl index is created by summing the squared proportions of cases falling into a set of categories. If all organized interests fell into only a single category in figure 11.5 (such as the service sector), the index would have a value of one, indicating an extremely low level of diversity. If interest organizations were spread evenly across all ten categories in figure 11.5, the index value would be 0.10, a case of extreme diversity. The average index value for 1990 registrations for all fifty states was 0.130, very

close to the minimal value the index might take. The highest Herfindahl index score in 1990 was Colorado's (0.151), while the lowest was Idaho's
(0.110). Both index values representing the extremes in diversity now observed in the states fall near the low end of the distribution, which indicates
considerable diversity. In sum, the interest-organization communities of the
states are quite diverse in terms of representation across major economic
sectors.[31]

A third way we measure diversity is by assessing the representation of
the not-for-profit sectors of government and social interests relative to the
number of organizations arising from the eight profit-oriented economic
sectors reported in figure 11.5. This dimension especially intrigues political
scientists because it is often argued that private economic interests dominate interest systems to the exclusion of other interests.[32] While the "social"
category of interests in figure 11.5 certainly contains some profit-making
firms, we can gain a rough impression of the balance of profit and not-for-
profit organizations by combining the social and government proportions
reported therein. Their sum indicates that, on average, not-for-profit organizations comprised 29.16 percent of registered organizations in 1990.
There is, however, much more variation around this average than was reported for the Herfindahl index. Indeed, not-for-profit interests are heavily
represented in some states, with Colorado being the prime example with
44.21 percent of all registrations falling into the social and government sectors. At the other end of the distribution, Hawaii reported that only 16.84
percent of its registrations were from the government and social sectors.[33]

Combining our measures of density and diversity, figure 11.6 reports
the distribution of states by standardized scores of organization number
and the proportion of not-for-profit interests, excluding Florida given its
status as an outlier in terms of density. The states in the upper left have
relatively few registered interests and more not-for-profit interests. Except
for Rhode Island, these are smaller mountain and plains states. In the lower
right are those states with both relatively more organizations and a lower
proportion of not-for-profit interests. Except for Arizona and Washington,
these are all large industrial states: Massachusetts, New York, New Jersey, Michigan, Pennsylvania, and Texas. In the lower left are a number of
New England, southern, and border states. These states have smaller than
average interest populations, but lower than average proportions of not-
for-profit interests. Finally, the upper right quadrant includes states with
relatively large numbers of registered interests and more not-for-profit interests. This is our most heterogeneous mix of states, though all range from
mid- to large-size and have diverse economies.

Has this pattern changed over time? While numbers of registered interests have certainly increased, their diversity has not. The Herfindahl index
scores for the ten sectors in figure 11.5 in 1975 and 1980 were, respectively,
0.126 and 0.127. Because the index is an inverse measure of diversity, the

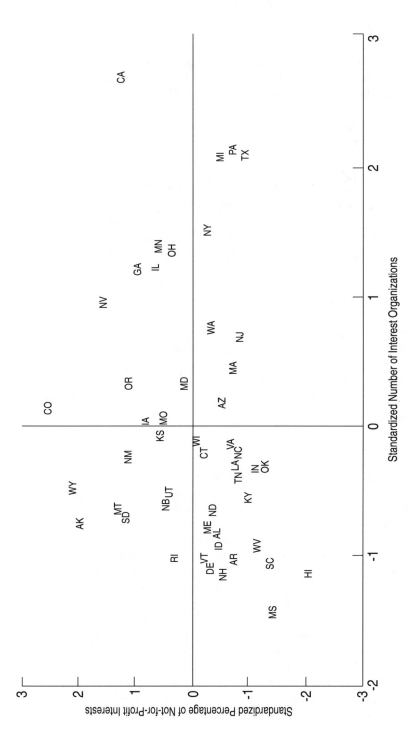

FIGURE 11.6. STATE INTEREST COMMUNITIES

Source: Virginia Gray and David Lowery, *The Population Ecology of Interest Representation: Lobbying Communities in the American States* (Ann Arbor: University of Michigan Press, 1996), 212

0.130 value for 1990 indicates that the diversity of state interest communities has actually declined, if ever so slightly, over the fifteen-year period. Nor has there been any great change in the proportion of not-for-profit interests registered to lobby. The 1990 proportion of 29.16 hardly differs from that observed for 1975 (28.20 percent) or 1980 (30.10 percent). Thus, while state interest communities have expanded greatly in size, their composition has not changed much at all.[34] In terms of the distribution in figure 11.6, then, the states have been moving sharply to the right.

The Work of Organized Interests

We are interested in the origins of lobbying organizations and in how interest communities are constituted because interest organizations are political actors. Representing the views of their constituents and/or their leaders, they try to influence the decisions of elected and unelected officials using a number of means. While some of these work indirectly by shaping public opinion about issues, the two most common means remain lobbying and campaign contributions.

Starting with Massachusetts in 1890, all fifty states now regulate lobbying.[35] In some states, this entails little more than registering an intent to lobby with a designated state official. Indeed, these registration lists provide directly or indirectly much of the data presented in this chapter. In most states, however, lobbyists must now provide detailed reports about their income, who they work for, and the expenditures they make to influence legislative actions.

Lobbying Regulations

While many states have increased the stringency of their lobbying regulations over recent decades, usually following scandals involving lobbyists,[36] there remains a great deal of variation in lobbying laws. Cynthia Opheim has conducted the most detailed study, and she ranks New Jersey, Washington, and Wisconsin as having the toughest regulations, while those of Arkansas are the weakest.[37] More generally, she found that the stringency of regulation is greatest among states with moralistic political cultures, professional legislatures, and weak political parties.[38] Only the last relationship seems surprising. But Opheim speculates that abuses by lobbyists — and thus the need for regulation — may be especially great in states where weak parties fail to organize support and opposition for major legislation.

How effective is lobbying regulation? The answer depends on the purposes for which the regulations are adopted. The most obvious of these is eliminating "inappropriate" forms of influence, such as gifts, favors, and other benefits perceived as corrupt. In this regard, regulation seems to have been effective. Interviews with long-time lobbyists during the mid-1990s[39] indicate that they believe their business is much "cleaner" now than in past decades. A Minnesota lobbyist, for example, reported that "there is more emphasis on technical information, less on socializing." Another Minnesotan added, "People used to sell themselves on being old boys, having relationships, being in a network. Now, we pride ourselves, sell ourselves on information and advocacy." A North Carolina lobbyist agreed, noting that "the good ole boy system is gone. Wining and dining is gone. Legislators are more sophisticated, [and] they want to know the issues." A Pennsylvania lobbyist observed that "[legislators] are less interested in whether you golfed with them than with the quality of your information." So the business of lobbying has changed over recent decades with increased regulation.

Lobbying regulation, however, has not greatly influenced the amount of lobbying done in state capitols. That is, stringency of regulation seems to have little impact on how many interest organizations or individual lobbyists register to lobby.[40] Nor has it seemed to reduce the influence of lobbyists. Most of the longtime lobbyists we have interviewed rate their collective influence as remaining about the same over several decades.[41] And an Arkansas lobbyist suggested that increased professionalism among both lobbyists and legislators has actually made the lobbyist's task easier: "They [the legislators] are more professional, have more staff. Agendas are prepared ahead of time. It makes our job easier, everything is more open." So lobbying regulations may have professionalized the influence game without having a concomitant impact on its outcome.

For most lobbying organizations, the bulk of the lobbying task probably remains much the same as ever. This entails simply monitoring state legislatures and executive agencies for signs that they are considering some policy, regulation, or law that touches on the concerns of the organized interest, as well as more actively promoting or opposing government actions. This does not mean, however, that the world of lobbying has been static over recent decades. There are now many more organizations engaged in monitoring government decisions. And, when mobilized, at least some of them have access to a greatly enhanced arsenal with which to influence public officials.

Contract Lobbying

The expansion of this arsenal is most evident in perhaps the single greatest change in lobbying in recent decades — the growing influence of contract lobbying firms in state capitols. These firms lobby not on their own behalf, but on behalf of clients. Long important in Washington, such firms now operate in nearly all of the states. Indeed, contract lobbyists are estimated to comprise from 15 to 20 percent of all state lobbyists.[42] Most organized interests still rely on in-house talent — a government relations officer or legislative liaison — for all of their lobbying. But many others now rely on in-house talent for day-to-day lobbying tasks but call on the professional services of contract lobbying firms when major issues arise. Interviews indicate that many firms now provide a diverse set of services, including organizing fund-raising activities, orchestrating hearings, setting up political action committees, organizing grassroots support for bills, and hiring polling firms.[43] So, like lobbying in Washington, lobbying in the fifty states has become more complex, specialized, and professional.

Political Action Committees

Another activity of interest organizations is making financial contributions to political campaigns through the political action committees (PACs) they sponsor. The states followed federal reforms of campaign finance in the 1970s by limiting some direct contributions to political campaigns by lobbying organizations. At the same time, the reforms provided for the establishment of separate organizations — political action committees. PACs may collect funds from the members of their parent interest organization and then contribute these funds to the political campaigns of elected officials.

There are an estimated 12,000 registered PACs in the states. But while most states follow federal practices in regulating PACs, there is still substantial variation in state rules.[44] Not all states prohibit direct corporate and union contributions, and still others prohibit direct contributions only from regulated industries. Some states place limits on PAC contributions while others do not. Some aggregate and publish PAC and other campaign finance data while others do not. And worst of all, some states do not distinguish among different types of PACs, including political party committees and individual candidate committees with multicandidate PACs. Finally, states vary in the quality of recording PAC activities. Clive S. Thomas and Ronald J. Hrebenar have sorted through these problems and report total numbers of PACs in thirty-eight states based on an array of sources.[45] Numbers of PACs ranged from highs of 1,500, 1,300, and 1,036 in California, Texas, and Pennsylvania, respectively, to lows of 38, 37, and 23 in, respectively, North Dakota, Arkansas, and New Hampshire. So there is still great diversity across the states in the use of PACs.

In considering the place of PACs in state politics, political scientists have been especially concerned with two issues. The first is whether PACs really represent a whole new approach to influencing legislation or are simply adjuncts of lobbying. Unlike traditional lobbying, which tries to influence the votes of sitting legislators, PACs might be used to affect who sits in legislatures. There have been few studies of state PACs, but research on federal PACs suggests that they are best viewed as adjuncts of traditional lobbying.[46] Richard Hall and Frank Wayman, especially, make a strong case that the returns from the electoral strategy — changing who the legislators are — are low.[47] An organization's investment is lost if its candidate loses. Therefore, it makes more sense, they argue, to use PAC contributions to influence those already in the legislature, that is, incumbents.

The second issue concerns PAC allocations — how campaign funds are used to influence legislation. Do PAC funds purchase the votes of legislators who otherwise would oppose the goals of an interest organization? Although, again, there is little research on this question at the state level, the answer seems to be no. That is, contributions typically go to legislators who already agree with the goals of the organization sponsoring the PAC.[48] What then are PAC contributions buying? Hall and Wayman suggest that they buy the attention, energy, and commitment of legislators who, while being inclined to support the interest organization's position, might otherwise use their time to promote or oppose other proposals.[49] This suggests that PAC contributions do not so much change votes as buy time and attention.

Analyses of state PACs supports at least one implication of this interpretation: if PAC contributions are used to buy the time and energy of busy legislators, then use of PACs by organized interests should be greater in states with dense interests communities than in those with few registered interests.[50] Competition for legislators' time should be especially great in the former states. As expected, surveys of interest-organization leaders in six states indicated that lobbying organizations were more likely to sponsor a PAC when they also reported facing competition from a similar organization. Also, an analysis of Thomas and Hrebenar's data on PACs from thirty-eight states indicated that sponsorship of PACs increases markedly as numbers of registered interest organizations increase. Rather than as an alternative to lobbying, then, PACs are best viewed as a response to the difficulties of lobbying within increasingly dense interest systems.

The goals of lobbying, then, have not changed as the interest communities of the states have evolved. Organized interests still seek to influence the votes of officials on issues of concern to them. But in the crowded communities of interests found in most states today, lobbying has become more professional, more often emphasizing the quality of information over connections. Lobbying also now entails using the services of specialists in contract lobbying firms, and it is integrated with campaign finance through the PACs sponsored by organized interests. In terms of the work done by their members, then, the fifty states' interest communities are becoming more similar to each other and more similar to the lobbying community in Washington.

The Influence of Organized Interests

Has this new professionalism increased the influence of organized interests? Are they more or less successful in directing state public policy than they were in the past? Are they more or less powerful? These questions are motivated by several sharply divergent perspectives on the role of interest organizations in democratic governance. In *The Governmental Process,* David Truman forcefully argued that interest organizations can have only a limited — and generally benign — impact on government because the influence of any one or few interests is checked by the influence of others. To Truman, "the activities of political interest groups imply controversy and conflict, the essence of politics."[51] And such conflict insures that no one interest will disproportionately influence public policy.

The pluralist school founded on Truman's analysis proved to be short-lived, however. By the 1960s, political scientists such as E.E. Schattschneider and Theodore Lowi began to challenge Truman's analysis. This new plural elitist school[52] argued that interest systems are only weakly organized for contention over policy, and that legislative committees organize the work of lawmaking in such a way that most interests are rewarded with specific benefits without competing with each other. Many economists who study lobbying organizations take the same position, suggesting that all special interests seek special advantages from government, and that most succeed. The result, they claim, is excessive government and a slowing of economic growth, as government policy is used to shield interests from market competition.[53]

More recently, though, a new view has emerged, resurrecting at least some of Truman's ideas. Jack Walker noted, for example, the dramatic expansion of the interest system and the emergence of sources of countervailing power in the form of new citizens' membership groups.[54] And at the same time, research by Heinz, Laumann, Nelson, and Salisbury suggested that conflict among organized interests in Washington was more extensive than plural elitists would expect.[55] While something less than Truman's benign pluralism, this neopluralist perspective at least allows for the possibility that interests may check interests. In Salisbury's words, "more groups, less clout."[56]

These very different perspectives on the influence of organized interests developed from studies of the Washington interest community. The fifty communities of the states provide us with many more interest systems to observe. Indeed, they provide historical examples fitting all three perspectives. Based on work in the 1960s and early 1970s, for example, Harmon Zeigler and Hendrik van Dalen identified five different types of interest systems.[57] Organized interests greatly influenced state politics in three of them: states with a single dominant interest (e.g., Anaconda Copper Company in Montana), an alliance of dominant interests (e.g., utilities, timber, and manufacturing in Maine), or conflict between two dominant interests (e.g., auto manufacturers and United Auto Workers in Michigan). In the remaining two types, there were either so many competing interests (e.g., California) or political parties were so powerful (e.g., Connecticut) that organized interests were not very influential. Thus, we can pick and choose among the states at different historic times to support all three perspectives on the role of organized interests in democratic governance.

Today, however, a strong case can be made that almost all of the states are moving toward the California model: the triumph of many interests. The explosion of lobbying registrations means that many more voices are clamoring to be heard within legislative chambers. And while all are not equal, the complexity of voices makes it much more difficult for one or a few interests to dominate.

While surely there are many cases where the actions of specific organized interests has been instrumental in the success or failure of specific legislative proposals, there is little evidence that the density or diversity of interest communities as a whole alters the direction of state government policy. Critics of the presumed influence of organized interests will be surprised by these findings. They argue that density leads inevitably to the adoption of policies shielding interests from competition. This, in turn, is expected to generate larger public sectors and slower rates of economic growth in the states.[58] But research has failed to find evidence that variations in the density and diversity of lobbying communities are related to rates of state economic growth, the size of their public sectors, or their rates of adopting occupational regulations or earmarked taxes.[59]

Conflicting Interests

The most likely reason for our failure to find such impacts is that the critics were wrong in assuming that interests do not compete with one another. Indeed, surveys of leaders of institutions, associations, and membership groups registered to lobby in six states in 1994 indicate that conflict is both intense and routine. As seen in figure 11.7A (p. 262), a majority of respondents of all three types of organizations indicated that the statement, "This policy area is marked by intense conflict and disagreement over fundamental policy goals," is sometimes true.[60] When combined with the always-true responses, two-thirds or more of the respondents view the policy arena as at least occasionally producing serious policy disagreements with competing interests. Nor is this conflict haphazard. As seen in figure 11.7B, a strong majority of the respondents indicated that the statement, "In making our case in this policy area, we repeatedly face the same opponents on each issue that comes up," is sometimes or always true. Indeed, a plurality of membership group leaders, and more than a third of the leaders of the other two sets of interest organizations, indicated that it was always true. Thus, the legislative process does not seem to segregate policy opponents so as to avoid policy confrontation.

Another indicator of conflict is one of its consequences: the difficulty of getting legislation introduced and passed. Controlling for a number of

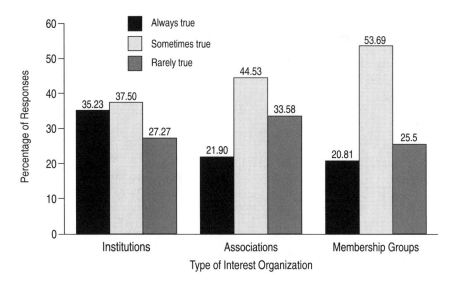

**FIGURE 11.7A. LOBBYING ORGANIZATION LEADERS' AGREEMENT
THAT POLICY AREA IS MARKED BY INTENSE CONFLICT**

Source: Data collected by authors.

Note: Total institutions=88; total associations=137; total membership groups=149.

other variables that might influence actions of state legislatures, a study of
forty-six states reported that many fewer bills were introduced and passed
into law during 1990 to 1991 in states with dense interest communities,
those in the lower half of figure 11.6 (p. 255).[61] This would not surprise neopluralists, given their emphasis on interests checking interests. As one Michigan lobbyist put it, "There is now much more intense competition over every
issue. It complicates the hell out of public policy. It is healthy for democracy,
having more points of view, but it makes life difficult for the policy-maker."[62]

Interest System Strength

While our analysis so far has emphasized the ways in which the power
of organized interests is constrained, there are variations in the strength
of interest systems across the states. Indeed, students of state politics —
including Belle Zeller in the 1950s and Sarah McCally Morehouse in the
early 1980s — have routinely ranked states by the strength of their interest systems.[63] Ronald J. Hrebenar and Clive S. Thomas have extended this
work over the last decade.[64] In addition to identifying which interests are
reputed to be the most influential in each state, these studies measure how

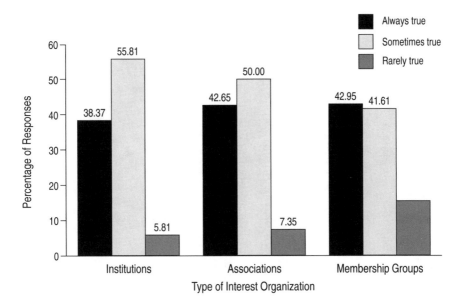

**FIGURE 11.7B. LOBBYING ORGANIZATION LEADERS' AGREEMENT
THAT OFTEN FACE SAME OPPONENT IN POLICY AREA**

Source: Data collected by authors.

Note: Total institutions=86; total associations=136; total membership groups=149.

powerful interest organizations overall are reputed to be relative to other
political actors.

Thomas and Hrebenar's latest ranking of the relative power of state interest systems is presented in table 11.1 (p. 264).[65] They identified five types
of interest systems, four that are observable and another type (e.g., subordinate) no longer found. The four observable types range from dominant,
through dominant/complementary and complementary, to complementary/
subordinate. Thomas and Hrebenar ranked seven states, most of them in
the South, as having extremely powerful or dominant interest systems,
with interests being relatively weak in Delaware, Minnesota, Rhode Island,
South Dakota, and Vermont. Fewer systems were rated as dominant than
in Morehouse's 1981 study or Thomas and Hrebenar's own analyses from
the 1980s, and more were rated as complementary/subordinate in influence.
Overall, then, states moved toward the weak end of the continuum where
the interest system as a whole has less impact.

Why are a few state interest systems reputed to be powerful and others
not? One possible explanation is that the "power" of interest communities may be related to their density and/or diversity. We have seen that
the plural elitist school argues that having more and more diverse organ-

TABLE 11.1. THOMAS AND HREBENAR CLASSIFICATION OF STATES
BY OVERALL IMPACT OF ORGANIZED INTERESTS

Dominant	Dominant/ Complementary	Complementary	Complementary/ Subordinate	Subordinate
Alabama	Arizona	Colorado	Delaware	
Florida	Arkansas	Connecticut	Minnesota	
Louisiana	Alaska	Indiana	Rhode Island	
New Mexico	California	Maine	South Dakota	
Nevada	Georgia	Maryland	Vermont	
South Carolina	Hawaii	Massachusetts		
West Virginia	Idaho	Michigan		
	Illinois	Missouri		
	Iowa	New Hampshire		
	Kansas	New Jersey		
	Kentucky	New York		
	Mississippi	North Carolina		
	Montana	North Dakota		
	Nebraska	Pennsylvania		
	Ohio	Utah		
	Oklahoma	Washington		
	Oregon	Wisconsin		
	Tennessee			
	Texas			
	Virginia			
	Wyoming			

Source: Clive S. Thomas and Ronald J. Hrebenar, "Interest Groups in the States," in *Politics in the American States*, 6th ed., ed. Virginia Gray and Herbert Jacob (Washington, D.C.: CQ Press, 1996), 152.

izations should increase the power of interest communities relative to the power of other political actors.[66] But neopluralists argue nearly the opposite, suggesting that greater density and diversity of interests should weaken interest systems overall, as the influence of any one or a few organizations is checked by others.[67] Indeed, Thomas and Hrebenar argued that the growing density and diversity of state interest communities has undermined at least some of the power of traditionally dominant interests, especially business.[68]

It appears, however, that both expectations are unwarranted. A study testing these competing hypotheses found no evidence that the Hrebenar and Thomas power ranking reported in table 11.1 is related to the density or diversity of state interest communities.[69] Having more and more diverse interest organizations does not seem to influence how powerful they are reputed to be relative to other political actors in the states. The most likely explanation for this null finding is that the power rankings indeed are tapping relative power, but not that of interest communities per se. That is, the interest communities of the states may now be sufficiently dense and diverse that differences on these dimensions contribute little to their overall reputations for power. If this is so, then it may be variations in the power of the other actors in the states — governors, legislators, and parties — that allow interest communities to exercise more or less influence. This suggests that, should organized interests be viewed as too powerful, the most effective way to control their influence is to strengthen the institutions of state government.

It might also be true that a reputation for power is tapping into something other than the characteristics of the interest community as a whole. Even in a state with dense and competitive interest systems, one, two, or a few organizations may be extremely influential across a broad array of issues. Even while acknowledging that states have been moving toward the weaker end of their power typology in recent years, Thomas and Hrebenar note that "a good case can be made that individual groups are more powerful than ever."[70] And while there is some variation across states and over time, the power rankings of Zeller, Morehouse, and Hrebenar and Thomas strike a common theme: the professions (school teachers, lawyers, and physicians) and general business organizations (chambers of commerce) have been, and remain, the most influential lobbying organizations in the states.

In explaining the professions' and business organizations' continuing status as the most effective members of interest communities, Thomas and Hrebenar point to a common array of strengths: "They all have extensive financial resources which they use to hire full-time political staffs and lobbyists, and in many cases they contribute to election campaigns. Their membership also tends to be spread geographically and is fairly politically cohesive. All this, plus the services they provide, makes public officials dependent on them to a high degree."[71] This account carries us full circle, back to our discussion of the origins of organized interests and their efforts to establish viable niches. These very strong organizations have established extremely viable niches in terms of both the resources needed to survive and those needed to project their influence outward to alter the decisions of elected and unelected officials.

Still, victory by even the strongest organized interests is by no means certain if elected officials and the public are mobilized. When Wiggins, Hamm, and Bell analyzed a sample of bills considered by three state legislatures, determining the positions of lobbyists, governors, and legislative party leaders on each bill, they found that broad interests represented within political parties generally win.[72] And even the contract lobbyists take a back seat when the public gets involved.[73] As one Arkansas lobbyist put it, "The tobacco lobby is one of the strongest lobbies; yet in the 1991 session the nursing home people got a cigarette tax slapped on. So the grassroots organization won over an embedded lobbying organization. All those little old ladies on their walkers was [sic] appealing." And a Michigan lobbyist added, "If the people are united on something, they get it. We have to get out of the way." So the power of even the strongest interests is limited if other players — elected officials and the public — get in the game.

How, THEN, shall we judge the role of organized interests in state government and politics? Earlier, we offered a standard by which to make such a summary assessment: whether the interest systems of the states are structured to facilitate the positive contributions of lobbying organizations and minimize their opportunities to corrupt politics or bias public policy. In the end, though, even this standard leads to something of a half-empty or half-full dilemma.

From the pluralist perspective developed by David Truman, which offers a benign view of interest organizations, there is much to worry about. While many lobbying organizations are founded on shared interests, many rely on selective incentives. Thus, there may be a gap between the real concerns of members and their "interest" as represented by the lobbying organizations to which they belong. Also, the collective action problem noted by Mancur Olson probably biases interest systems toward over-representation of institutions. At the same time, there are now many, many more interests clamoring for places on the public policy agendas of the states, with no change in the relative representation of not-for-profit interests. And with new tools of influence such as PACs and grassroots lobbying, the potential power of profit-oriented institutions may have increased over recent decades. Given a strong pluralist standard, then, the glass is clearly half-empty.

At the same time, however, we have reported a number of changes in state interest communities that point to a more optimistic conclusion. Shared interests seem to be the primary basis of organization for membership groups and associations. While state interest communities have undergone a population explosion, their growth is not unlimited; state interest systems are fluid, with many players disappearing from lobbying rolls. And while there has been no increase in the relative representation of not-for-profit interests, many more are now active in state capitols than in previous decades. We also have no evidence that PACs routinely buy legislative votes, or that contract lobbyists can overturn the preferences of political parties or the public when these preferences are strongly expressed. And perhaps most importantly of all, we have presented both direct and indirect evidence that organized interests compete with each other. Indeed, interest organizations face competition both from organizations most like themselves and from others with very different policy agendas. In sum, the direction of change in state interest systems over recent decades has been toward more openness and greater competition.

In the end, we believe that this half-full neopluralist evaluation is well founded on the evidence the fifty states provide us. There is, however, something ironic about the changes state interest communities have undergone.

That is, they have made the interest communities of the states more similar to each other and more similar to the interest system found in Washington. And the GOP majority which took control of Congress following the 1994 elections has begun shifting responsibilities for many public policies, particularly welfare reform, to the states. One reason offered for this dramatic change in federal relations is the desirability of moving domestic policy choices from the fevered environment of organized interests in Washington to the calmer, more practical settings of the states. We may discover, though, that the policy environments of the states are not so settled after all; we may be replacing one large hothouse with fifty smaller — but equally torrid — ones. Indeed, the proposed changes may further accelerate changes within state interest communities, changes that are already marching forward at a considerable pace. Therefore, it is unlikely that the future will leave us short of opportunities to exercise our traditional rhetoric decrying the power of special interests.

CHAPTER TWELVE
Policy Change in the American States
Evan J. Ringquist and James C. Garand

THE ADAGE THAT "change is inevitable" can be considered a truism when applied to public policy in the American states. Undoubtedly, the current policy environment in the American states bears little resemblance to that which existed at the end of World War II. In the late 1940s the public sector in each of the American states was very small, with an average of less than 5 percent of total personal income devoted to state government expenditures. This means that the ability of state governments to fund extensive programs to solve the problems confronting state populations was quite limited. Since that time the size of the public sector in the states has expanded considerably. Partly with the financial support of the federal government through a range of intergovernmental grant programs, partly at the behest of the federal government through the expansion of federal regulations and mandates, and partly at their own initiation, the governments of the American states are much more active in working to solve the social problems confronting their citizenries. Clearly, policy change has occurred in the American states in substantial proportions.[1]

The American states provide an excellent comparative laboratory for developing and testing theories that account for policy differences across states, patterns of policy change over time, and the consequences of different policy choices. Scholars have gradually taken advantage of the opportunities provided by these laboratories, and thus the academic study of public policy in the American states has shown considerable change over time. During the 1940s and 1950s many scholars of state politics focused their attention on basic descriptions of state politics, case studies of politics and policy in particular states, or analyses of political institutions and behavior within particular states. Arguably, so little was known about state politics and policy at the time that these (often prescientific) approaches were needed to provide scholars with the basic observational building blocks for the development of theories that would eventually have broader applicability across the states.

During the 1960s and 1970s, scholars began in earnest to study variation in public policy across states. In order to explain such variation, they used *cross-sectional research designs,* which involve the use of data collected for the fifty (or fewer) states at one point in time. While such designs are appropriate for understanding patterns of public policy across states at any given time, they are ill-suited to the task of understanding policy change within or across states over time. For example, cross-sectional designs are useful in understanding why some states spend more on welfare expenditures than other states, but are ineffective in understanding why welfare expenditures expand in any given state or why growth rates in welfare expenditures were higher in one state and lower in another.

Obviously, the idea of studying policy change requires introduction a temporal element into one's research. At the very least, the study of policy change necessitates the measurement of public policies or policy outputs at least two points in time; of course, more time points are even better. In recent years the development of new statistical technology and its widespread dissemination into the realm of political research has spawned a new era in the study of policy change in the American states. Some scholars have utilized *time-series designs,* which involve the collection of data in a given state political system for each year over a given time period and the use of such data to estimate the effects of various explanatory variables on public policies and their outputs over time. Such designs permit researchers to understand changes in public policy over time within a given state political system. More recently, other scholars have adopted *pooled cross-sectional time-series designs,* which involve the collection of data for each state and each year over a given time period. Pooled designs permit scholars to evaluate the causes of policy change across all states, and also allow for the development of explanations for why change occurs at one level for some states and at another level for others.

What all of this means is that the study of policy change in the American states has developed and begun to mature over the past two decades. The adoption of research methodologies that are explicitly oriented toward the study of change means that scholars have begun to better grasp the determinants and implications of policy change in the American states. With this newer technology, scholars have also begun to collect data over time *and* across states, and these data permit them to consider the determinants of policy change both within and across the American states. Most importantly, the development of statistical methods and data sets appropriate for the study of public policy change has allowed scholars both to test theories of policy change and to begin to be more serious about revising existing theory and developing new approaches.

In this chapter we discuss how and why public policy has changed in the American states in recent years. First, we address explicitly the causes of policy change in the American states, and develop a general framework that organizes those causal effects and that can be applied to a variety of policy areas. Second, we discuss how both the size of the public sector and the priorities of government spending have changed since the end of World War II. Finally, we explore the literature on patterns of state policy change in several policy areas, including welfare, environment, education, and economic development.

Causes of Policy Change in the States

Why does policy change occur in the states? Why has so much policy change occurred at the state level in recent years? Identifying the forces behind policy change gives us much more than an answer to the relatively uninteresting question "why do some states have different policies than do other states?" By identifying the determinants of state policy change, we address fundamental questions of federalism (do states have a sufficient degree of policy autonomy vis-à-vis the federal government?), state government responsiveness (do state governments respond to organized interests in policymaking?), accountability (to which groups do state governments respond?), and capacity (can state governments create new policies when they need to?). In this section we present the results of over three decades of research in political science, highlighting the most consistent findings with respect to what causes policy change at the state level. In general, these policy changes are produced by three broad sets of forces: internal state political factors, external political factors, and policy specific factors. As these factors change over time and across states, so does the probability of policy change.

Internal Political Factors

When a state adopts significant changes in public policy, most observers (citizens, journalists, and scholars) examine closely the internal characteristics of the state to see which of these characteristics may have precipitated the policy change. The most important internal state factors for policymaking are the politico-economic characteristics of the state, the diversity and density of organized interests in the state, and the characteristics of the state political system. These three sets of characteristics interact to produce many of the most important causes of policy change at the state level.

Politico-economic factors. The general political and economic characteristics of a state have a tremendous amount of influence over the kinds of policies that state will adopt. These characteristics go under different names in the policy literature; Hofferbert calls them "socioeconomic resources and conditions," while Salisbury dubs them "system resources."[2] Whatever they are called, characteristics regarding the level of wealth, economic development, and the general tenor of political ideology within a state form a milieu of needs and boundaries of acceptability out of which policy options develop.

Specifically, economic resources have an impact on public policy; wealth matters. Public programs cost money, so the wealth of a state can have some effect on the type of policies that a state adopts.[3] Contrary to the conclusions of early research in political science, however, wealth is not the only determinant of public policy at the state level. The levels of socioeconomic and industrial development also shape the type of policies adopted by states. Public policy is generally responsive, and a state will not adopt programs until the need for these programs exceeds a certain threshold. For example, California faces terrific pressures to create strong air-pollution-control regulations, reform the state welfare system, and re-form immigration policies because that state faces high levels of industrial air pollution, urban poverty, and illegal immigration. Since Wyoming faces none of these problems, it is unlikely that Wyoming will adopt policies sim-ilar to California's. Finally, the general ideological disposition of a state's citizens (i.e., public opinion) helps determine what sorts of policies are acceptable in a state. Thus conservative states are unlikely to be at the forefront in environmental protection. In fact, recent research by political scientists has demonstrated that citizens' political ideology is often the most important determinant of policy activity at the state level.[4]

Organized interest groups. While wealth, development, and political ide-ology may help set the "boundaries of possible action" within a particular state, these characteristics do not by themselves determine public policy.[5] Their combination naturally produces a number of different policy de-mands arising from advantaged and disadvantaged interests within society. These demands, however, must be articulated and pressed upon govern-ment. Organized interest groups in a state perform the crucial function of transforming the policy potential in a state into political influence, and any government purporting to be representative must respond to social interests represented through these organized groups.

Two characteristics of state interest-group systems are particularly rel-evant for public policy: density and diversity. Since 1970, there has been a remarkable increase in both the number and the resources of political interest groups at the state level (see the chapter by Lowery and Gray in this volume). There is no question, then, that interest groups are present to press for policy change in state capitals. The more relevant questions are (1) whether state interest group systems are *too* dense (i.e., whether the sheer numbers and power of these groups lead to less responsive state gov-ernments, overloaded government institutions, and diminished economic growth)[6] and (2) whether these state interest-group systems are diverse enough (i.e., are all relevant interests represented?).

With respect to the first question, it appears that state interest-group systems are to some degree self-regulated so that the number of groups does not become infinitely large.[7] State government institutions continue to op-erate, and the number of interest groups does not appear to affect state economic growth.[8] With respect to the second question, however, there is no doubt that the "heavenly chorus" of interest groups at the state level has an even greater bias that it does in Washington, D.C.[9] In fact, there is a good deal of evidence that the diversification of organized interests at the federal level has yet to reach the states.[10] In most states, groups representing dominant economic interests are by far the most numerous, and the most influential. Moreover, state governments in general are more susceptible to interest-group pressures than is the federal government.[11] Nevertheless, while industrial and economically advantaged interests may be more powerful, there is little evidence that state policy-making has been completely "captured" by these groups.[12] In short, as the strength of certain interest groups changes over time and across states, so does public policy.

    Political system characteristics. Economic and ideological concerns articulated by organized interests may press a state to adopt certain laws, but the characteristics of a state's political system determine the way in which these concerns affect public policy. Which "characteristics of the political system" are we talking about here? First of all, it is clear that parties in state government matter. In states with high levels of party competition, each party offers expanded government services in an attempt to attract voters.[13] In addition, Republican Party control of state government produces policy changes that reduce the scope of government, while Democratic Party control produces policy changes that expand the scope of government, all other things equal.[14] Second, the characteristics of the electorate matter: in states where the poor and working classes turn out to vote, state policies reflect the interests of these voters.[15] Third, certain unpopular policy changes (e.g., tax increases) are more likely to be made as far removed in time from state elections as possible.[16] Fourth, the institutions of state government matter as well. States that have more "professional" legislatures (e.g., full-time salaries, full-time professional staffs, extensive computer resources, etc.) and more "professional" administrative agencies (e.g., high numbers of employees with advanced degrees, well-developed civil service systems) appear better able to undertake aggressive and comprehensive policy changes than states whose political institutions lack these characteristics.[17] Finally, significant policy changes are often facilitated by state leaders who are willing to act as "policy entrepreneurs," gathering support for a particular change from different quarters and then shepherding it through the political process.[18]

External Political Factors

Internal characteristics are not the only determinants of policy change at the state level. Decision makers within each state must operate within a complicated intergovernmental environment where choices made by state officials are affected by changes in the national political environment, changes in national public policy, and policy choices made by neighboring and competing states. These forces influence state political environments, set the parameters within which state officials can exercise policy discretion (e.g., no state can legalize child labor without violating federal law), and can force state governments to take reactive or defensive policy stances vis-à-vis other states. In short, we cannot understand policy change without an appreciation for how each of these external factors can shape the policy actions of state decision makers.

National political environment. Many notable changes in the national political environment also affect policy decisions at the state level. For example, broad swings in national public opinion or changes in the "policy mood" of the American public cannot help but affect state public opinion as well.[19] Similarly, explosions in the number and diversity of interest groups, changes in party competition at the national level, and the force of "critical" or realigning elections on the national stage also affect the fortunes of political parties in the states.[20] Moreover, increases in interstate migration of citizens, interstate trade, and reliance on the national media have created an increasingly homogenous electorate and national political culture.[21] Thus, changes in the national political environment have had a larger impact on state political environments in the 1990s than was true in the 1960s.

National public policy. National public policies both limit the policy options available to state-level decision makers and force these same decision makers to enact more expansive or aggressive policy changes than they would otherwise choose to make. Three examples might help to clarify this point. First, the 1954 Supreme Court decision in *Brown* v. *Board of Education of Topeka, Kansas* required all states to dismantle their de jure segregated public school systems.[22] To speed the process of desegregation, the 1965 Elementary and Secondary Education Act (a program enacted at the national level) withheld federal aid from all segregated public schools. Many southern states resisted desegregation, claiming that as sovereign states they had the right to determine the structure of their own education systems. Faced with costly (and hopeless) legal battles and lost federal education assistance, however, de jure segregation became a thing of the past even in these obstructionist states. In this case, changes in national public policy forced policy change at the state level.

Second, most national regulations aimed at protecting human health and safety contain partial preemption provisions. While partial preemption allows states a great deal of flexibility in policymaking, it also clearly limits this flexibility: no state can administer a program that does not meet federal minimum standards. Hence, recent efforts by the state of Oregon to prioritize the medical procedures that could be paid for with Medicaid funds had to be approved by the federal government, since such a policy was at odds with federal guidelines. In this case the federal government did grant the necessary waivers, but Oregon and other states must still clear such innovations with the federal government before moving forward with their policies.

The final example of how changes in federal policy can affect changes in state policy deals with federal grants to the states. The vast increase of federal money to the states is one of the defining characteristics of intergovernmental relations since the 1930s. An important rationale for providing federal financial assistance is that these grants will entice states to do things they would not normally do. For example, in response to the energy crisis in the early 1970s, Congress passed legislation requiring states to adopt a 55–mile-per-hour speed limit as a precondition for receiving federal highway funds. States were free to maintain their sovereignty by adopting whatever speed limits they chose; however, the threat of losing valued federal highway funds meant that states were left with little choice but to comply with the federal strings attached to those funds. More recently, this "carrot" has been used effectively by the federal government in "encouraging" states to adopt a twenty-one-years-old minimum drinking age.

Federal money also provides states with an incentive to change their policy priorities. Left to their own devices, states generally will spend their money on what Paul Peterson calls developmental policies, or policies that enhance the potential for economic growth. Many federal grant programs, however, provide money for redistributive policies, those that benefit the disadvantaged.[23] To see if these federal grant monies do in fact alter state policy priorities, Frank Baumgartner and Bryan Jones aggregated federal and state spending data from the 1930s through the 1990s and found that, as federal grants to the states increased, so did the percentage of state budgets devoted to redistributional policies.[24] In short, a large flow of federal cash does indeed entice states to change their policy priorities.

In each of the three examples, then, we see how policy decisions made at the national level can affect state policy priorities (e.g., federal grants), simultaneously enhance and limit the flexibility of states in setting regulatory standards (e.g., federal partial preemption requirements), and in rare cases simply force states to make policy changes against their will (e.g., school desegregation).

Interstate influences. The final external political factor is the interstate environment within which state policy decisions are made. State governments often act as if they are in a zero-sum competition with other states when it comes to attracting economic and social "goods" and avoiding economic and social "bads." In this competition, state policymakers constantly keep one eye on potential opponents, and they often craft policies to counteract any perceived advantage enjoyed by a neighboring state.

We can clearly see the effect of the interstate environment in several policy areas. First, many states engage in an economic development strategy of "smokestack chasing," whereby they offer tax breaks, subsidized labor training, and the like to companies agreeing to relocate in the state.[25] When one state enacts these economic incentives, neighboring states are pressured to enact them as well in order to keep indigenous firms from relocating. Second, there is good evidence that states providing more generous welfare and Medicaid benefits act as "welfare magnets," attracting poor individuals from other states.[26] Thus, if state A offers welfare benefits that are substantially more generous than those provided by neighboring states, state A faces terrific pressure to lower welfare benefits to prevent an influx of welfare recipients from surrounding states.[27] Third, some scholars have identified the potential for a "Gresham's Law" of state regulation, whereby states compete with each other in a "race to the bottom" with regard to environmental and occupational health and safety regulation in an attempt to attract business.[28] Overall, this competition among states influences the adoption of nearly every type of policy imaginable.[29]

Policy-Specific Factors

The interplay of interstate, national, and internal state forces is often not enough to determine changes in state policy. Characteristics specific to the policy in question — some predictable, others not so predictable — provide the final piece of the state policymaking puzzle. The most important of these policy-specific factors are accumulated policy-relevant knowledge, focusing events, and issue redefinition.

Accumulated policy-relevant knowledge. Many different actors (e.g., elected officials, interest groups, policy experts, etc.) play important roles in policymaking. The constellation of actors involved in a particular policy area is often referred to as a *policy subsystem*.[30] Different actors within the same policy subsystem will have different policy preferences. For example, within the environmental policy subsystem, industry representatives will have a preference for less regulation, while environmental groups will have a preference for more regulation. Similar differences in policy preferences will be found among elected officials in this policy subsystem. Why do these actors hold the policy preferences they do? Without a doubt, material self-interest and political ideology play a large part in determining policy preferences. However, policy preferences are also strongly affected by each actor's understanding of the accumulated knowledge relevant to the policy in question. In other words, information matters, and over time, the accumulated policy-relevant knowledge can actually change the policy preferences of actors within a particular policy subsystem. A few examples will help to illustrate how the accumulation of policy-relevant knowledge has led to substantial changes in state policy.

Since the early 1970s, economists have argued that economic incentive approaches would, theoretically, provide more effective and efficient environmental protection than would traditional command and control regulations. Still, the dominant actors in the environmental policy subsystem rejected the economic incentive approach as unproven and risky. Over time, however, empirical studies by economists and other policy analysts, small national-level experiments with economic incentives, and European experiences with market mechanisms for pollution control all produced a body of evidence that these incentive approaches could in fact be more effective and efficient than traditional regulations. Over time, the accumulated policy-relevant knowledge changed, and this in turn altered the policy preferences of many members of the environmental policy subsystem. Many former opponents of these economic policy tools now support their use, and California recently enacted a wide variety of economic incentive approaches to controlling urban air pollution.

We find similar stories in other policy areas. In welfare policy, two decades of experience and study has demonstrated that certain elements of a welfare system that are supposed to end poverty actually have perpetuated the condition. This evidence has convinced both liberal and conservative participants in the welfare policy subsystem that policy change is needed. Many of the state innovations in welfare policy discussed later (e.g., income retention requirements and the provision of child care for welfare mothers who return to work) are due at least in part to the accumulated knowledge identifying these elements of welfare policy as important causes of a culture of poverty. Similarly, the accumulated empirical evidence that smokestack chasing does not do much to spur economic growth has caused many in the economic development policy subsystem to turn instead to investing in infrastructure and human capital as a strategy for economic growth.[31] On the other hand, where an accumulated body of policy-relevant knowledge does not exist (e.g., regarding the effectiveness of school choice), the policy preferences of subsystem participants are based largely upon ideology, and are thus difficult to change.

Focusing events. Changes in accumulated knowledge affect public policy over long periods of time. Changes in public policy can be brought about nearly overnight, however, by focusing events such as accidents, disasters, popular uprisings, and particularly influential research findings that, through widespread media attention, can dramatically affect the political system. Often the impact of a focusing event is so great that a social condition that was never before considered a problem suddenly becomes a top priority of state policymakers. Focusing events thus provide certain members of policy subsystems with a window of opportunity within which they can prod government officials to make substantial changes in public policy — even when objective conditions (i.e., the severity of the problem) have changed very little.[32]

For example, in 1978 California voters passed Proposition 13, an initiative that dramatically limited the ability of governments to tax property.

This event precipitated a rush in several other states to revise their property-tax structures as well, even though levels of property taxation had not changed appreciably in many of these states prior to the reforms. The string of unusually hot summers in the late 1980s and early 1990s, coupled with widely circulated conclusions from government scientists that "global warming" was a reality, stimulated many states to adopt their own global warming policies, even though actual average temperatures had changed very little.[33] Finally, the 1995 bombing of the federal building in Oklahoma City has caused many states to ratchet up their surveillance of radical right-wing antigovernment groups and independent state militias. In each of these cases, focusing events that the states had no control over precipitated substantial changes in public policy.

Issue redefinition. Very few citizens truly understand the complicated details of every policy issue. Most people, in fact, make sense of policy debates by using simplified "policy stories," or symbols that provide them with a general interpretation of these complex policy issues. Interest groups, legislators, and other members of policy subsystems reinforce this tendency by communicating to citizens via competing stories or by providing citizens with different definitions of a particular policy issue. A majority of the American public typically accepts one of these competing stories or issue definitions, and the proponents of this definition then go on to dominate the policy debate. Policy change occurs when the proponents of a different definition of the policy issue can change public perceptions and have their issue definition become the accepted definition among the public. Such a redefinition of an issue can occur due to changes in accumulated policy-relevant knowledge, because of focusing events, or because of a change in the venue within which policy decisions are made.

Baumgartner and Jones provide an excellent illustration of how issue redefinition took place in the area of nuclear power, and how it can radically change public policy. From the 1950s to the early 1970s, nuclear physicists and other proponents of nuclear power dominated the policy debate by defining the issue with visions of a safe, unlimited energy source providing electricity that would be "too cheap to meter." Over time, however, three things changed that redefined the issue of civilian nuclear power. First, accumulated knowledge regarding the true costs of nuclear power production and waste disposal dispelled the "too cheap to meter" myth. Second, opponents of nuclear power abandoned their attempts to influence Congress (where proponents of nuclear power were nearly invincible) and instead focused their attention on state siting laws and local zoning decisions; since no one wants a nuclear power plant in his or her backyard, participants at this level were much more receptive to opponents of nuclear power. Finally, the focusing events of the partial meltdown at Three Mile Island in 1979 and the Chernobyl accident in 1986 fundamentally changed the picture of nuclear power in the public's mind. Since that time, the vast majority of the American public has come to define nuclear power as too costly and/or too dangerous to pursue.[34]

Similar attempts to redefine issues are important in shaping state policy today. For example, in previous decades undocumented immigration from Mexico and other Latin American countries was either ignored or tacitly encouraged in many states. The accepted policy story during this period was that these workers provided a critical economic benefit to the states by providing cheap labor for the booming agricultural sector, and by taking jobs that American laborers were unwilling to accept. In the past ten years, however, the issue of undocumented immigration has been redefined, so that today illegal workers are seen as placing unacceptable demands on local schools and state welfare systems. In short, undocumented immigrants are now seen as an economic liability, rather than an economic asset. In response to this issue redefinition, border states (notably California and Florida) are in the process of amending state law to prevent these illegals from receiving a wide variety of state services.

Causes of State Policy Changes: A Recapitulation

To understand the causes of policy change at the state level, one must go beyond consideration of only state-level characteristics. There are three general sets of forces that help to determine policy change in the states: specific policy factors, external political factors, and internal state factors. All of these sets of policy-relevant factors, and the interactions among them, are represented in figure 12.1. As one can see, each of these sets of influences affects the others. Specific policy factors affect the national political environment by altering national public opinion, national public policy, and public policies in other states. Specific policy factors and external political factors affect forces internal to the states themselves, by altering the fortunes of political actors within the states, by affecting state economies, and by placing limits upon the discretion these states have in making policy changes. Moreover, the elements within the general sets of policy, national, and state factors also interact in sometimes complicated ways to influence public policy.

Patterns of Change in Expenditure Priorities

One area in which state policy has changed in the postwar era is that of expenditure levels and priorities. State governments are doing many more things today than they did in the late 1940s; they are spending more and drawing more resources from the private sector; and they are focusing attention on different spending priorities. These changes have had a profound effect on the role that state governments play in the lives of their citizens.

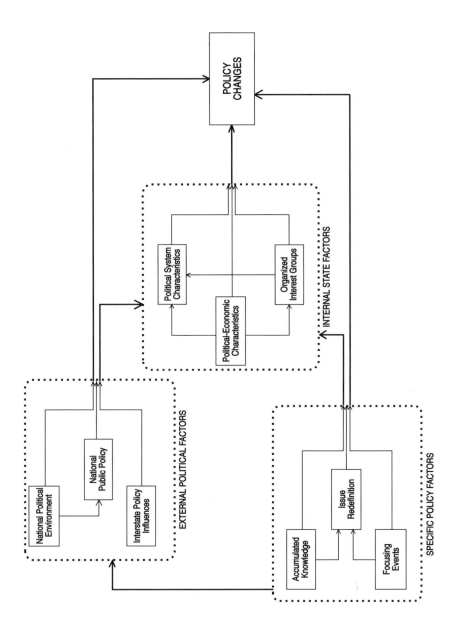

FIGURE 12.1. CAUSES OF STATE POLICY CHANGE

POLICY CHANGES

Political System Characteristics

Political-Economic Characteristics

Organized Interest Groups

INTERNAL STATE FACTORS

National Political Environment

National Public Policy

Interstate Policy Influences

EXTERNAL POLITICAL FACTORS

Accumulated Knowledge

Issue Redefinition

Focusing Events

SPECIFIC POLICY FACTORS

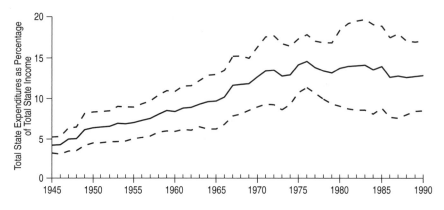

FIGURE 12.2. MEAN SIZE OF THE PUBLIC SECTOR IN THE STATES, 1945–90

Source: Compiled by the authors from *The Statistical Abstract of the United States* (various years) and various other U.S. Census documents.

Note: Public sector size is measured as total state expenditures as a percentage of total state personal income. The dashed lines represent one standard deviation above and one standard deviation below the mean for each year.

Government Size

The growth of the public sector in the American states has been well documented.[35] Figure 12.2 reflects the trend in the mean size of the public sector from 1945 to 1990; in order to depict the spread of states around these means, the dotted lines represent one standard deviation above and below the mean for each year. Following the convention established in the literature,[36] we measure the size of the public sector as total state government expenditures (including intergovernmental grants from the federal government) as a percentage of total state personal income. This measure represents the share of state personal income (representing roughly the size of the private-sector economy in a given state) devoted to the public sector.

As is readily apparent from figure 12.2, the average size of the public sector has increased fairly dramatically since the end of World War II. During the late 1940s, state governments, on average, devoted approximately 5 percent of the state personal income to the public sector. Since that time there has been a steady rise in the size of the public sector, with a pattern of sharper increases occurring during the decade from 1965 to 1975. Following the mid-1970s, state government growth leveled off at around 13 percent of state personal income. These data present a vivid picture of stable growth in the size of state public sectors during the period from 1945 to 1965, somewhat more rapid growth from 1965 to 1975, and then a leveling-off period through the 1980s.

What explains patterns of government growth and variation in the size of the public sector in the American states over time? Following the lead of scholars who have studied government growth at the federal level in the United States and other western democracies, James Garand has explored a number of explanations for variation in state government size over time.[37]

1. The *bureau voting* explanation posits that growth of the size of the public sector is due to the number of government employees in the state electorate; the reasoning is that since government employees are more supportive of government spending, more likely to vote, and more likely to support candidates who themselves support an expanded public sector, the relative number of public-sector employees in the electorate should be related positively to government size.[38]

2. The *intergovernmental grant* explanation suggests that the influx of grant funds from the federal government accounts for at least some of the increases in the public sector. Underlying this explanation is a simple argument: when states can pass the costs of increased spending to the federal government, they do so readily.

3. The *fiscal illusion* explanation suggests that growth in the size of government is due to the tendency of state governments to rely on sources of revenue (e.g., borrowed funds, income taxes collected through withholding provisions) that hide the costs of government. Such fiscal illusion leads citizens to underestimate the costs that they are paying for the services that they receive, and hence they demand more services than they would if the costs were more explicit.

4. The *party control* explanation depicts the size of the public sector as a function of the ideological dispositions of the political party controlling the governorship and state legislature; when state government is controlled by the more liberal Democrats, the size of the public sector should expand at a greater rate than if state government is controlled by the more conservative Republicans.[39]

5. *Wagner's Law* suggests that increases in the size of government are due to manifestations of increased industrialization that can only be addressed through an expanded public sector. For instance, industrialized societies often face policy problems (e.g., traffic congestion, pollution) that are not encountered by nonindustialized societies; since these problems are best solved through the public sector, scholars have speculated that industrialized states will have more extensive public sectors than less industrialized states.

6. The *political culture* explanation sees increases in the size of government as a function of the liberalism of state electorates; according to this argument, government should grow at a more rapid pace in states with liberal electorates that demand greater government participation in solving policy problems, but at a slower pace in states with more conservative electorates.

7. The *political need* explanation depicts government growth as a function of demands placed on state governments by those in the state population who are dependent upon government goods and services; hence, government

should grow more rapidly when state economic performance is poor (e.g., when unemployment is high), as well as in those states with populations with higher proportions of citizens (i.e., the elderly, racial minorities) who are more likely to be dependent on government goods and services.

Garand's findings suggest that the bureau voting and intergovernmental grant explanations come closest to describing patterns of government growth in the American states in the postwar era.[40] This suggests that the size of the public sector is greatest when government employees have the opportunity to play a more dominant role in electing state officials and state sources of revenue are supplemented with intergovernmental grants from the federal government. In more recent research covering a more limited time frame (1960 to 1984) necessitated by data availability, Garand confirms these earlier findings, and also points to the importance of partisan control of state government, state policy liberalism, and variables representing the political need explanation (in particular, economic conditions and minority populations) in shaping the size of the public sector. In particular, Garand finds that the size of the public sector increases when the Democratic Party controls state government, the state population has a higher proportion of citizens who identify themselves as liberal, economic conditions are on the decline, and the state population has a higher proportion of individuals (African Americans, the elderly) who are more dependent on government assistance.[41]

Expenditure Priorities

Given a fixed level of public-sector spending, states may allocate expenditures to a wide variety of alternative policy areas. The decisions to allocate more or less spending to one policy area and more or less to another reflect the spending *priorities* of state governments. For instance, with all else being equal, a state that allocates 20 percent of its budget to education spending might be thought of as giving a higher priority to education than another state that allocates only 10 percent of its budget to education. Spending allocations reflect state policy priorities — that is, the willingness to make choices among alternative spending options available to state decision makers.

Changes in spending priorities can be affected by a wide range of factors. First, the level of demand for specific types of public policies may shift over time, perhaps as a result of demographic changes or changes in the size of the clientele groups receiving state expenditures. For instance, an increase in the number of school-age children may necessitate an increase in budgetary allocations to education spending, even though the total budget is not increasing at a similar rate. Moreover, since crimes are more likely to be committed by adolescents, an increase in the teenage population may spur increased crime rates and resultant increases in budgets for

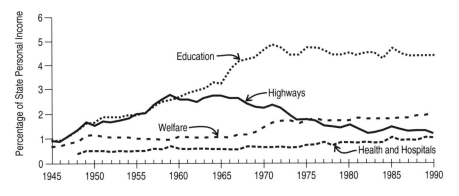

**FIGURE 12.3. STATE GOVERNMENT SPENDING PRIORITIES
AS A FUNCTION OF STATE PERSONAL INCOME, 1945–90**

Source: Compiled by the authors from *The Statistical Abstract of the United States* (various years) and various other U.S. Census documents.

Note: Spending priorities are measured as state expenditures in each spending area as a percentage of state personal income.

police, public safety, juvenile facilities, and prisons. Second, the supply of funding for specific government programs may shift over time, permitting state government officials to attach a greater priority to those programs. Such changes in funding may occur either as a result of increases in dedicated sources of revenue in a given state or because of changes in patterns of intergovernmental grants from the federal government. For example, increases in highway taxes, which often are dedicated to road improvements, might spur an increase in highway spending priorities, and increased intergovernmental grants in health-care spending may result in an strengthened priority for overall state health-care spending. Third, state electorates and, subsequently, state policymakers may change. States may increase spending priorities in a given policy area because citizens are willing to allocate higher amounts of spending to it, and these citizens may elect governors and state legislators who are willing to allocate more resources to that policy area.

Figures 12.3 and 12.4 present data on mean spending priorities in the policy areas of education, highways, welfare, and health and hospitals from 1945 to 1990. In figure 12.3 we define spending priorities as spending for a given policy area as a proportion of total personal income; this reflects the degree to which state policymakers are willing to devote funds from the private sector to each of these policy areas. On the other hand, in figure 12.4 we define spending priorities in terms of the proportion of total state government spending devoted to each of these spending areas; this reflects

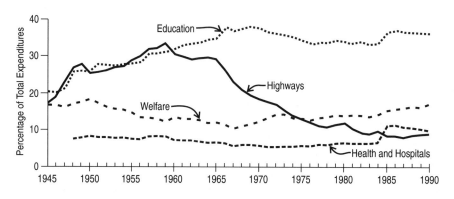

**FIGURE 12.4. STATE GOVERNMENT SPENDING PRIORITIES
AS A FUNCTION OF TOTAL EXPENDITURES, 1945–90**

Source: Compiled by the authors from *The Statistical Abstract of the United States* (various years) and various other U.S. Census documents.

Note: Spending priorities are measured as state expenditures in each spending area as a percentage of state personal income.

the degree to which state policymakers are willing to allocate public-sector funds to a given policy area.

As can be seen in figure 12.3, patterns of spending priorities have changed in the American states during the postwar era. Over the years, states have devoted a substantially greater share of state total personal income to education and welfare spending, a modestly higher share to health and hospital spending, and a substantially lower share to highway spending. At the beginning of this time period, education and highway priorities were at about the same level, and the upward trends in priorities for these two spending areas tracked each other closely until 1960. At that time, education spending priorities continued to increase steadily into the 1970s, by which time education was by far the highest priority for the average state. The pattern for highway spending priorities began to diverge from those of education when highway spending leveled off in the early 1960s and began a steady decline that lasted into the 1980s. By 1975 spending priorities for welfare had exceeded those for highways, and by the 1980s welfare spending priorities were discernibly and consistently greater than highways spending priorities.

A similar picture emerges when one redefines spending priorities in terms of percentages of total state expenditures. Here again, in the postwar era there has been a steady growth in the share of state expenditures dedicated to education spending, as well as a decline in the share devoted to highways. Moreover, the share of state expenditures devoted to welfare spending has been increasing since the mid-1960s, while expenditures dedicated to health and hospitals have increased only recently. For the most part, figures 12.3 and 12.4 paint a similar picture of changes in expenditure priorities in the American states since the end of World War II.

Obviously, state governments are doing different things today than they did in the late 1940s. As reflected in figure 12.2 (p. 280), they are taking on more than they did before, and figures 12.3 and 12.4 reveal that the mix of state government expenditures has changed since shortly after the end of World War II. At the simplest level, these data suggest that social spending (as represented by welfare, health and hospital expenditures, and, to some extent, educational spending) has emerged as a higher priority across the states, while spending on at least one type of infrastructure (highways) has begun to take a back seat when state governments determine their spending priorities.[42] These patterns may reflect a variety of forces, including the effects of the federal government (through regulatory mandates and intergovernmental grants), the growth of entitlements such as AFDC and Medicaid, a long-term shift in what state citizens value, and/or demands emanating from demographic changes experienced by many of the states.

Examples of Policy Change in the States

While the fifty state governments are often referred to as "laboratories of democracy," these laboratories went underutilized from the end of World War II until the mid-1970s, as policy responsibilities were centralized in Washington, D.C. Over the past two decades, however, the states have recaptured their role as centers of policy innovation and change in the American political system. At the beginning of the 1990s, the ability of states to create innovative policy solutions had developed to such a degree that one scholar could write:

> State governments have moved to the forefront in tackling the tough issues of toxic substances regulation, low-level radioactive waste disposal, gun control, comparable worth, AIDS, homelessness, surrogate motherhood, education for persons with disabilities, drug abuse, living wills, sexual harassment, rights for homosexuals, economic development, welfare reform — the list appears endless.[43]

Part of this flourishing of innovation in the American states may be due to inaction at the federal level; for example, the passage of the Family and Medical Leave Act in 1993 occurred only after the lack of a federal family-leave policy had prompted a number of states to establish their own mandated family-leave policies in the past decade.[44] For whatever reason, during the 1990s the states accelerated the pace and extended the reach of their efforts at policy reform. In the pages that follow, we look at some specific examples of state policy innovation and change in four highly salient policy areas: welfare reform, environmental protection, public education, and economic development.

Social Welfare Policy

The federal government funds and administers dozens of programs — from Social Security to unemployment compensation to public housing — that can be classified as social welfare policy. We focus here on three of the highest-profile programs targeted at aiding the poor: AFDC (now defunct following welfare reform legislation passed in 1996); food stamps; and Medicaid. These programs share many similarities. All three programs were created by the federal government but administered by the states. All three programs are "means tested" — family income must fall below a certain level before individuals are eligible for these benefits. AFDC was a cash benefit program (i.e., state governments sent checks to recipients), while both Medicaid and food stamps are in-kind benefit programs (i.e., the programs provide recipients with health care and food vouchers, respectively, instead of cash).

AFDC was the smallest of the three programs. In May 1997 roughly 11 million people received AFDC benefits (down 25 percent over four years), and these benefits totaled approximately $22 billion in 1996. The federal and state governments jointly funded AFDC, with the federal government paying between 50 and 80 percent of total program costs across the states. The food stamp program is slightly larger. In 1996 roughly 26 million individuals received food stamps at a total cost of about $26 billion. The federal government pays the full cost of food stamps and roughly half of each state's administrative costs. Medicaid is by far the largest of the three programs. In 1996 roughly 31 million people received Medicaid benefits, at a total cost of nearly $156 billion. The federal and state governments jointly fund Medicaid, with the federal government again covering between 50 and 80 percent of total costs.[45]

Opportunities for state flexibility. All three programs have provided the states with a great deal of flexibility. For example, states have determined eligibility requirements and benefit levels for all three programs, and the AFDC program itself was voluntary for states. This flexibility has produced some remarkable cross-state policy differences. In 1996, for instance, the maximum AFDC benefit for a family of three varied from $120 per month in Mississippi to $923 per month in Alaska (the next most generous state was New York at $703), with a national average of $377 per month. Similarly, differences in eligibility criteria mean that some states provide Medicaid benefits to only 20 percent of the poor, while other states cover nearly 90 percent. In addition to flexibility in determining eligibility and benefit levels, states can customize their social welfare programs by applying for a waiver of federal requirements under section 1115 of the Social Security Act, and an increasing number of states are doing just that. Finally, the 1988 Family Security Act made it significantly easier for states to depart from federal requirements in the administration of their antipoverty programs.

Why state reform activity? States have ample opportunity to reform their social welfare programs, but what about motive? These programs have been lightning rods for criticism. First, both liberals and conservatives agree that these programs are on the whole ineffective: liberals do not believe that they offer an effective hand up and out of poverty, while conservatives believe that they actually promote dependence on public assistance by producing a "culture of poverty."[46] Second, Medicaid costs in particular are skyrocketing and placing pressure on state treasuries. Third, substantial research suggests that cross-state differences in benefits turn some states into "welfare magnets" (i.e., poor individuals move there for the higher public assistance payments).[47] Finally, current ideological trends emphasize smaller government and increased reliance on individual responsibility. At the federal level, this change prompted President Clinton and the Republican Congress to enact sweeping welfare reform legislation (described in a later section). All of these conditions provide impetus for state reform of welfare policy.

An example of state welfare reform. Wisconsin is the national leader with respect to social welfare policy innovation. While the state has adopted over a dozen reforms and has created a permanent Office of Welfare Reform, most national attention has focused on the state's Learnfare program, which consists of two parts. First, student parents under the age of twenty are required to attend school (or a vocational education program) or risk losing their welfare benefits. Second, teenagers in families receiving cash benefits are placed on special state, county, and school attendance lists. If any student on this list has over three unexcused absences from school during any one month, his or her family will lose that child's portion of their welfare benefit. Child benefits are also lost if the student drops out of school or if the family refuses to provide necessary attendance and school information to the state. To help offset the burden imposed by these requirements, the state provides a number of support services for Learnfare participants, including day care services, transportation to school, alternative education programs for those in need, and a casework system for students in danger of being sanctioned. In cases where the student or his/her family believes that they were sanctioned unfairly by the state, there is a hearing process whereby these claims are adjudicated by a third party.

Roughly 30,000 students are subject to Learnfare guidelines each month in Wisconsin, and about 8 percent of these students are sanctioned. There is no doubt that Learnfare is costly. Program budgets average about $10 million per year, with the federal government paying half of these costs. Savings from the sanctioning process have equaled about $3 to $4 million per year, however, and this has helped offset a significant portion of program costs. Evidence regarding the effect of Learnfare on welfare caseloads, student grades, graduation rates, and employment prospects is mixed. Nevertheless, after surviving initial court challenges, the program's future appears secure, and the state is considering expanding the program to cover students aged six to twelve.[48]

Overall state efforts at welfare reform. While Wisconsin is a national leader, it is far from the only state to adopt important changes in social welfare policy. Through February of 1996, forty states had received over sixty policy waivers under section 1115 of the Social Security Act, with the pace of waiver proposals increasing dramatically during the Clinton administration.[49] Moreover, a number of state governments have proposed and/or enacted changes in welfare programs that do not require a federal waiver. The National Governors' Association (NGA) made a survey of state efforts at welfare reform, and the results of this survey are summarized in table 12.1.[50] Specifically, the NGA found that the majority of state welfare reform efforts can be placed into one of eight categories (the number of states that have proposed or implemented such reforms are listed in parentheses):

1. Rewarding work by reducing penalties placed on AFDC recipients who work or save money (42 states)

2. Requiring parents to support their children financially by providing child support, etc. (34 states)

3. Simplifying and improving the delivery of benefits through electronic transfer (35 states)

4. Supporting intact families by eliminating rules that prevent two-parent families from receiving benefits (34 states)

5. Improving access to health care and child care for parents who leave welfare for work (31 states)

6. Creating jobs for welfare recipients (30 states)

7. Linking benefits to school attendance and performance (27 states)

8. Imposing time limits on benefits (25 states)

In addition, fourteen states limit benefits for families having additional children while on welfare.[51]

National innovations in welfare policy. The Personal Responsibility and Work Opportunity Reconciliation Act of 1996 (PRWORA) produced the most far-reaching changes in welfare policy since the New Deal. This legislation eliminated the entitlement to cash welfare that had been part of national public assistance programs since the Social Security Act of 1935. In passing this act, both Congress and President Clinton made good their promises to "end welfare as we know it." In its place, PRWORA created two block grants: the Temporary Assistance to Needy Families (TANF) program provides cash assistance and other benefits to low-income families, while the Child Care and Development (CCD) block grant provides child and health care for low-income families.

TABLE 12.1. NUMBERS OF STATE INNOVATIONS IN WELFARE POLICY

State	Rank	Number of Innovations	State	Rank	Number of Innovations
Wisconsin	1	17	Pennsylvania	21	8
Michigan	2	16	Rhode Island	21	8
Illinois	3	13	Colorado	28	7
Vermont	3	13	Connecticut	28	7
Virginia	3	13	Maine	28	7
California	6	12	Mississippi	28	7
West Virginia	6	12	Massachusetts	32	6
Missouri	8	11	North Carolina	32	6
South Carolina	8	11	Oklahoma	32	6
Florida	10	10	Alabama	35	5
Iowa	10	10	Minnesota	35	5
Kansas	10	10	Nevada	35	5
Maryland	10	10	New Hampshire	35	5
New Jersey	10	10	Alaska	39	4
Ohio	10	10	Kentucky	39	4
Arizona	16	9	South Dakota	39	4
Delaware	16	9	Texas	39	4
Indiana	16	9	Wyoming	39	4
Nebraska	16	9	Arizona	44	3
Utah	16	9	Tennessee	44	3
Georgia	21	8	Washington	44	3
Montana	21	8	Hawaii	47	2
New York	21	8	Louisiana	48	0
North Dakota	21	8	Idaho	N/A	N/A
Oregon	21	8	New Mexico	N/A	N/A

Source: Compiled from Julie Strawn, Sheila Dacey, and Linda McCart, *Final Report: The National Governors' Association Survey of State Welfare Reforms* (Washington, D.C.: National Association of Governors, 1994).

Both of these programs provide states with fixed amounts of money for antipoverty programs, rather than the open-ended grants associated with AFDC. In addition, these grants place a number of new restrictions on benefit recipients. For example, all beneficiaries (except for mothers of very young children) must engage in community service after receiving benefits for two months, obtain work after receiving benefits for two years, and are limited to five years of receiving benefits. Moreover, teenage mothers are required to live at home or with a responsible adult, attend school, and establish the paternity of their children. Finally, PRWORA ends all but emergency welfare benefits for legal and illegal immigrants. (Observant readers might note that several of these requirements were pioneered by the states.)

States continue to exercise discretion under the new welfare law. For example, they still determine benefit levels. States can also transfer money across welfare block grant programs, save block grant money for use in future years, and borrow from a federal emergency fund. Finally, states have the option of continuing or ending their section 1115 waiver programs. In other areas, however, the new law reduces state discretion. For example, states are "encouraged" to rely upon charitable or religious organizations when implementing these programs. More importantly, states are penalized for failing to follow national guidelines for work requirement quotas, reductions in out-of-wedlock births, data-reporting requirements, eligibility criteria, and the like.[52]

Environmental Policy

The era of strong federal involvement in protecting environmental quality began in 1970 with the signing of the National Environmental Policy Act and the creation of the Environmental Protection Agency (EPA). Since that time, environmental protection has been one of the most active areas of policy change at the national level. In less than three decades, Congress has enacted the Clean Air Act, Clean Water Act, Safe Drinking Water Act, Resource Conservation and Recovery Act (regulating hazardous wastes), and over a dozen other major pieces of environmental protection legislation. In 1995, the EPA spent roughly $6 billion to implement these laws aimed at protecting and improving environmental quality, and environmental spending by other federal agencies nearly equaled this figure. The regulations and requirements of each of these pieces of legislation must be enforced in all states — a process that is overseen by one of EPA's ten regional offices.

Opportunities for state flexibility. Allowing for state flexibility in environmental protection makes a good deal of sense, because the character of environmental problems varies substantially across states. Each of the pieces of environmental legislation mentioned above provides states with a great deal of authority and flexibility with respect to the process of environmental regulation. Some laws, such as the Clean Water Act, have a primary role for the states written directly in the legislation. More importantly, nearly all federal environmental legislation contains a *partial preemption* provision. Under partial preemption — or "primacy" — the national government sets minimum standards for environmental protection. States are free to develop and administer their own environmental protection programs as long as these programs are at least as effective as the federal minimum standards. By 1993, forty-eight states had accepted primacy under the Clean Air Act, thirty-eight states had accepted primacy under the Clean Water Act, and forty-five states had accepted primacy under the Resource Conservation and Recovery Act. Moreover, nothing in federal legislation prevents states from creating programs that are stronger than federal minimum requirements, though some states, such as Colorado and North Carolina, have laws preventing this. Finally, nothing prevents states from adopting regulations in areas not addressed by federal legislation. For example, states were the first to regulate acid rain, nonpoint-source water pollution, toxic air pollutants, and the protection of groundwater. State governments have also played the lead role in exploring "takings" legislation that seeks to limit environmental regulation. In sum, states engage in setting goals and standards for environmental quality, they design and implement their own programs, they monitor and enforce these programs, and they fund these programs to a large degree.

An example of state environmental reform. California has always been at the forefront of environmental-protection policy. The Clean Air Act of 1970, for example, allowed California alone to set more stringent automobile exhaust standards than were required in the rest of the country. California has been ahead of the rest of the country in several other areas of environmental protection as well. Since 1986, Proposition 65 has required companies in California to disclose any public exposure to chemicals that pose a cancer risk or a threat to reproductive health. Proposition 65 also required the state to set safe exposure limits for a list of toxic chemicals (currently over 300) as recommended by a science advisory board. In 1989, the South Coast Air Quality Management District (SCAQMD) instituted the strongest set of air quality regulations in the nation — regulations that, at their extreme, could have outlawed fast-food drive-through restaurants, gasoline-powered lawn mowers, and outdoor barbecue grills. In 1993 the SCAQMD adopted the most extensive system of market-based incentives for air-pollution control found anywhere in the country. Under this plan, hundreds of major polluters will be able to buy and sell an ever-decreasing number of air-pollution allowances. Finally, California is a nationally recognized leader with respect to integrating the environmental permitting process.[53]

Overall state efforts at environmental policy reform. One estimate suggests that nearly 70 percent of the significant environmental regulations enacted by state governments have nothing to do with federal policy requirements.[54] These multiple opportunities for state innovation in environmental protection have created a situation where the strength of pollution control programs and the performance of states in environmental protection vary widely. Some states have created programs that go far beyond federal minimum requirements, but other states are prevented from exceeding these minimums.[55] While states spend a great deal of money on environmental protection (over $10 billion in 1991), per capita spending for environmental protection is up to five times higher in some states than in others.[56] Finally, enforcement of environmental regulations suffers in some states. For example, a 1993 EPA investigation found that 50 percent of all Clean Water Act permits issued by the states had expired, and

TABLE 12.2. NUMBERS OF STATE INNOVATIONS IN ENVIRONMENTAL POLICY

State	Rank	Number of Innovations	State	Rank	Number of Innovations
California	1	38	New Hampshire	23	19
Maine	2	33	Virginia	23	19
Oregon	2	33	Kansas	28	18
Connecticut	4	32	Texas	28	18
New York	4	32	Delaware	30	17
Minnesota	6	31	Georgia	31	16
New Jersey	6	31	Kentucky	31	16
Rhode Island	6	31	Nebraska	31	16
Wisconsin	9	29	Mississippi	34	15
Michigan	10	28	South Carolina	34	15
Vermont	10	28	New Mexico	36	14
Washington	10	28	Tennessee	36	14
Massachusetts	13	27	Arizona	38	13
Maryland	14	26	Idaho	38	13
Florida	15	25	Montana	38	13
North Carolina	16	24	Oklahoma	38	13
Ohio	16	24	Utah	38	13
Iowa	18	23	Wyoming	38	13
Illinois	19	22	Nevada	44	12
Missouri	19	22	North Dakota	44	12
Pennsylvania	21	21	West Virginia	46	11
Indiana	22	20	Alabama	47	10
Colorado	23	19	Alaska	48	9
Hawaii	23	19	Arkansas	48	9
Louisiana	23	19	South Dakota	50	5

Source: Adapted from Bob Hall and Mary Lee Kerr, eds., *1991-1992 Green Index* (Cavelo, Calif.: Island Press, 1991), 145.

this figure was as high as 94 percent in Virginia and 93 percent in New Mexico.[57]

The Institute for Southern Studies has completed the most comprehensive survey of state policy activity in environmental protection.[58] These researchers identified fifty important policy innovations in the areas of recycling, landfills, toxic waste, air pollution, water quality, agriculture, energy and transportation, growth management, and indoor pollution. Finally, these researchers tabulated which states had adopted which reforms, and ranked the states with respect to how many of these policy innovations they had adopted. The results of this study are summarized in table 12.2. As expected, California ranks as the most innovative state, and there is clearly great variation in the degree to which states have adopted innovative policy solutions in the area of environmental protection.

Education Policy

At least since the publication of *A Nation At Risk* in 1983, reform of public education has been an important item on the national political agenda.[59] The criticisms of public schools are several and familiar: dropping graduation rates; dropping standardized test scores; dilapidated school buildings that produce a debilitating educational atmosphere; horribly unequal school-funding formulas; poor U.S. student performance compared with their international peers; crime; drug abuse; and the like.[60] Solid empirical evidence suggests that some of these criticisms are overblown. For example, adjusted for student demographics, average SAT scores have actually risen over the past twenty years. Moreover, the United States has the world's highest percentage of high-school and college graduates.[61] Nevertheless, public education in this country does face some serious challenges that must be met by changes in public policy.

National-level political figures talk a great deal about reforming the educational system. Although the federal government does provide some money for elementary and secondary education, and federal laws prohibit de jure segregation in the schools, however, the government in Washington, D.C., has very little control over public education. According to Kevin Smith and Ken Meier,

> A national education system simply does not exist in this country. States constitute the largest aggregation of an educational "system" within the United States. Although the federal government has expanded its role in education during the past few decades, the states remain the highest level of government with extensive control over education standards and requirements and provide far more money and administrative support than does the federal government.[62]

For this reason, the context of educational policy reform is really a state context; nearly all major innovations in educational policy are made by state governments.

Educational policy reforms. Dozens of educational policy reforms have been offered for alleviating the public-school shortcomings identified earlier. Higher teacher salaries have been instituted by some states in an effort to attract higher-quality teachers. Teacher certification exams have been instituted by other states in an effort to ensure that all teachers have a minimum level of competence in their subject areas. Many states have established minimum graduation criteria, and in their larger school districts most states have created magnet schools that attract and concentrate students who are gifted in particular subject areas, such as science or the arts. Finally, school-funding formulas have faced court challenges in at least forty-one states, and at least ten states have been forced by their Supreme Courts to amend these formulas to create more equal funding for schools.[63]

Among the variety of education reforms undertaken by states, none has received more attention, or is more controversial, than school choice. The basic premise behind school choice is simple: education can and should be viewed as a market good. Given a choice, students (and their parents) will choose good schools over poor schools. Good schools will prosper, while poor schools will lose enrollments and either reinvent themselves to produce a higher-quality educational product or go out of business. Either way, more students receive a better education. Several varieties of school choice are discussed: open enrollment for all public schools in a single school district; open enrollment for all public schools across school districts; open enrollment for all schools, public and private, within or between school districts; and dollar-value vouchers that can be used to purchase educational services at either public or private schools. Choice advocates tout this reform as a panacea for whatever ails the nation's educational systems.[64] Critics of school choice, however, argue that experiments with choice have produced mixed results, that choice allows parents to pursue goals other than educational quality (e.g., religious training and racial segregation), and that choice undermines democratic control of educational institutions.[65]

Examples of state choice reforms. In 1987 Minnesota created the first and most extensive state-wide public school open-enrollment program. Under the Minnesota program, all elementary and secondary students may request transfers to public schools in other districts. State funds normally allocated to transferring students follow these students to their new schools in their new districts. No school district can prevent a student from leaving unless his or her departure would negatively affect desegregation guidelines, and no district can refuse an incoming transfer unless that transfer would cause overcrowding or negatively affect desegregation guidelines. Parents are responsible for transporting their transferring children to the border of the new school district.[66]

In 1990 the Wisconsin state legislature passed legislation creating the Milwaukee Parental Choice Program. Under this program, students in the Milwaukee public school system can choose to leave the public schools and attend private schools within the same school district. The money that the state typically would spend to educate this student in the public schools goes with the student and is paid to the private school in lieu of tuition. There are several restrictions in the Milwaukee public-private choice program. First, only low-income students are eligible for the program. Second, only nonsectarian private schools are eligible to participate in the program (to prevent state money from funding religious instruction). Finally, transfer students can make up no more than 49 percent of the enrollment of any private school, and the total number of student transfers is limited to 1 percent of the Milwaukee public schools' total enrollment.

Overall state experiments with school choice. While Minnesota and Wisconsin may provide the most developed examples of two varieties of school choice, they are far from the only states experimenting with this type of ed-

TABLE 12.3. STATE OPEN ENROLLMENT OR "SCHOOL CHOICE" PROGRAMS

State	Magnet Schools	Intra-District	Inter-District	Public-Private
Alabama	X	X	X	
Arizona		X	X	
Arkansas		X	X	
California		X		
Colorado		X	X	
Connecticut	X			
Florida	X			
Idaho		X	X	
Illinois	X	X		
Iowa		X	X	
Louisiana	X			
Maryland	X			
Massachusetts		X	X	
Michigan		X	X	
Minnesota	X	X	X	
Montana			X	
Nebraska		X	X	
New Jersey	X			
New Mexico			X	
New York	X		X	
Ohio			X	
Oregon		X	X	
Utah		X	X	
Virginia	X			
Washington		X	X	
Wisconsin	X			X

Source: Adapted from Jana Zinser, *Reinventing Education* (Cambridge, Mass.: National Conference of State Legislatures, 1994).

ucational reform. The National Conference of State Legislatures surveyed the states with respect to innovations in education policy, and the school choice aspects of this survey are summarized in table 12.3. While a large number of states are considering adopting some form of school choice at any one time, the information in table 12.3 deals only with school choice programs that were actually operational through the end of 1994.[67]

Economic Development Policy

Very much like education, the national government plays only a small role in economic development policy. Of course, certain federal policies may affect some state economies more than others (e.g., securing foreign grain sales benefits the economies of Midwestern states, while efforts to prevent the dumping of computer chips by foreign manufacturers may help domestic chip manufacturers in Texas, California, Massachusetts, and Oregon). Still, economic development is largely a state issue, and state officials are increasingly placing this issue at the top of the policy agenda. In fact, at least one scholar has argued that economic development has become so important that it transforms other policy debates in the states — that is, debates about education, environmental protection, and other policies take place within the context of what they will mean for economic development.[68]

While the federal government plays a small role in state economic development policy, for decades social scientists were unsure if even state governments could affect state economies. This skepticism had two sources. First, many observers believed that the national economy completely dominated individual state economies. In short, state economic fortunes would follow national economic trends, regardless of the efforts of state policymakers.[69] Second, other observers believed that state policy interventions aimed at stimulating economic growth would be ineffective at best and counterproductive at worst, because they would interfere with the natural economic growth produced by a free market.[70] Recent empirical evidence, however, demonstrates that state economies are becoming increasingly independent of the national economy, that state tax decisions can affect economic growth, and that state policy interventions can stimulate economic productivity.[71] State economic development policy does seem to matter.

Economic development policy reforms. State economic development efforts can be grouped into four general categories. First, states generally take great pains to project a positive business climate by minimizing corporate taxes, personal income taxes, and regulatory burdens. Second, states can invest in physical and human capital (e.g., well-designed and well-maintained transportation facilities, top-notch educational systems, cultural amenities) in an effort to attract industry. Third, states can engage in "smokestack chasing" (e.g., attempts to lure industries with promises of free land, free utilities, tax rebates, loan guarantees, and other financial incentives). Finally, states can engage in strategic planning and policy interventions: investing public seed money in high-technology industries, engaging in publicly financed research and development, creating public-private partnerships to seek out development opportunities, streamlining regulatory permitting processes, developing export markets, and the like.

Because states have adopted so many different approaches to promoting economic development, presenting detailed examples for one or two states would paint a highly misleading picture of policy activity in this area. Some states, such as Arizona and Texas, have taken a laissez faire approach to economic development (e.g., relying on low taxes, a hospitable business climate, and smokestack chasing), while New York, Michigan, and other states with longer histories of industrial development generally have pursued more

TABLE 12.4. NUMBERS OF STATE INNOVATIONS IN ECONOMIC DEVELOPMENT POLICY

State	Tax	R&D	Finance	State	Tax	R&D	Finance
Alabama	11	12	7	Montana	14	10	7
Alaska	7	12	7	Nebraska	10	12	8
Arizona	10	11	3	Nevada	7	12	4
Arkansas	10	12	7	New Hampshire	6	11	5
California	10	12	9	New Jersey	9	12	8
Colorado	8	12	8	New Mexico	8	12	6
Connecticut	12	12	10	New York	12	12	9
Delaware	13	12	7	North Carolina	6	11	0
Florida	14	12	6	North Dakota	9	11	7
Georgia	5	8	2	Ohio	12	12	9
Hawaii	12	12	7	Oklahoma	12	11	8
Idaho	10	11	0	Oregon	8	12	10
Illinois	11	12	8	Pennsylvania	11	12	8
Indiana	12	12	9	Rhode Island	12	12	9
Iowa	12	12	8	South Carolina	11	10	6
Kansas	12	9	3	South Dakota	8	12	6
Kentucky	9	11	8	Tennessee	8	11	3
Louisiana	13	10	9	Texas	5	12	10
Maine	11	12	8	Utah	7	12	2
Maryland	11	12	10	Vermont	7	10	8
Massachusetts	13	10	6	Virginia	10	12	6
Michigan	10	12	8	Washington	10	12	8
Minnesota	14	12	8	West Virginia	8	10	8
Mississippi	8	12	9	Wisconsin	9	11	6
Missouri	12	12	8	Wyoming	5	11	7

interventionist approaches (e.g., strategic policy interventions and investments in physical and human capital). The minimalist approaches seemed
to work better in the 1960s and 1970s, while the interventionist strategies
generally performed best during the 1980s.[72] During the 1990s, states have
used an increasingly broad array of economic development policy tools.

   Overall state efforts at economic development policy innovation. One of
the best collections of data on state economic development policy is found
in the journal *Site Selection.* Each year, the editors of this journal gather
information on which states have adopted any of nearly seventy policies
targeted at promoting economic development; in table 12.4 we summarize much of that information. Specifically, having identified fifteen taxation
policies (e.g., corporate income tax exemptions, tax credits for job creation), twelve research-and-development or training policies (e.g., programs
to promote research and development [R&D], retraining of industrial employees), and ten financial incentive policies (e.g., loan guarantees, aid for
plant expansion) that states may use to promote economic development,
we then provide a state-by-state breakdown of how many of these policies

each state had adopted by the end of 1993.[73] Most states have adopted all of the possible R&D and training policies, while the greatest variation is in the degree to which states have adopted explicit financial incentives for attracting industry. While we present data only for 1993, time series data show that, during the past two decades, all states have become more active in economic development policy, and states are becoming more alike in the types of policies they pursue.

THINGS CHANGE. This simple statement about life in general is particularly true when one considers patterns of public policy in the American states over time. Clearly, policy change is occurring, some of it rapid, and hence obvious, while other change is more incremental in nature, and hence less readily apparent. But all of these changes have important implications for the lives of citizens. Any effort to study American state politics without taking into account the changing nature of state policy fails to capture a dominant (dynamic) feature of policymaking at this level of government.

What kind of change has occurred during the past fifty years? Clearly, the American states are doing more today than at the end of World War II, and they also are providing a different mix of public policies. Moreover, these policy changes are not random. Empirical research has uncovered systematic patterns in the policy choices made by states, and the literature on state policy change is sufficiently well-developed that it is possible to draw from it a reasonably coherent general model of state policy change, as we have done in figure 12.1 (p. 279). We suggest that state policy change is a function of pressures from external political factors (such as the federal government and other states), internal state factors (such as socioeconomic characteristics and political institutions), and factors that are relevant to specific policy areas. These factors combine to form a context within which policy change can (and does) occur.

The large-scale devolution of policy responsibility to state governments has encouraged some scholars to look for even broader patterns of state policy activity. In particular, Paul Peterson suggests that the policy choices of states will (and should) differ depending upon whether the states are pursuing developmental policies (e.g., economic development and education) or redistributive policies (e.g., welfare). State governments face incentives to maximize activity with respect to the former (to attract businesses and satisfy political elites) and minimize activity with respect to the latter (since the poor make a lousy political constituency). According to Peterson, devolving responsibility for developmental policies to the states makes sense because interstate competition will force them to pursue these policies and match them to the needs of state citizens. Devolving responsibility for redistributive policies to the states, however, will likely encourage states to compete to provide the least costly social safety net (i.e., policy choices will be less likely to match state needs). Changes in federal-state relations over the past quarter century have largely followed Peterson's prescriptions. Most responsibilities devolved to the states were in the area of developmental policies, where state programs have diverged from previous national standards and made the entire federal system more efficient. The recent overhaul of the welfare system, however, suggests that patterns of federalism are changing in a less efficient direction. If Peterson is correct, placing responsibility for redistributive policy at a level of government less capable of handling such responsibilities may produce a "race to the bottom" where "the well-being of the most marginal members of society...will be adversely affected in serious ways."[74]

If the recent past is any indication, the future holds great promise for the study of state policy change. The development of relatively new research techniques appropriate for studying policy outcomes across states and across time promises to generate more rigorous tests of theories of state policy change, and to permit scholars eventually to develop a clear understanding of the causal processes that generate such change. As students of state politics collect more data across *both* states and time, and as they utilize the analytical tools made available to them in recent years, the potential for building on our understanding of state policy change is enhanced significantly.

CHAPTER THIRTEEN
Policy Change in American Cities and Counties
Elaine B. Sharp

THIS CHAPTER EXPLORES the topic of changing public policy at the local government level. Much of the research on urban policymaking adopts quite a different focus, emphasizing differences across local governments in the United States rather than change over time in subnational policymaking. There are good reasons for that focus, because the tremendous differences in the policies of the thousands of municipal and county governments in the United States may in some respects dwarf the concept of change in local policy over time. The magnitude, and perhaps the character, of New York City's policy response to homelessness would be expected to differ from that of Scranton, Pennsylvania because of the vast differences in the scope of the problem in each setting as well as in the institutional infrastructure and local political history. Similarly, we might expect substantial differences in the economic development policies of Detroit and Colorado Springs because of major contrasts in the economic outlooks for each region and important differences in the local political situations.

Furthermore, any effort to describe change in the public policy of local governments will confront the problem of generalizing across cities and counties that differ not only in their policy profile at a particular time point, but also in their policy dynamics. Indeed, much of the literature on policy innovation at the subnational level is organized around the attempt to explain why some governments adopt policy innovations while others do not, or why some governments adopt policy innovations so much sooner than others. This chapter attempts to accommodate both the comparative and dynamic perspectives by grounding the discussion of overall policy trends in an acknowledgment of dissimilarities across local governments that may stem from cities' being at different points in a policy innovation cycle.

Perspectives on Policy Change

Should we even expect to find change in the policies of American local governments? And if so, what kind of change? Existing theory and empirical research on agenda setting, policy dynamics, reform, and innovation point to four perspectives on the extent and shape of policy change: (1) an incrementalist perspective emphasizing the constraints on change, (2) a nonincrementalist perspective, (3) a cyclical change perspective, and (4) a "conditions for innovation" perspective.

An important strand of thinking suggests that an exploration of policy change in localities will discover little change, and that, to the extent that public policy does change, it does so only incrementally. In an important series of works, Charles Lindblom argued that policy change is incremental because of limits on policymakers' ability to get consensus for radical change and because of cognitive limits that make comprehensive policy change impossible.[1] Expanding on these insights, Michael Hayes explored the many institutional arrangements of American government — from the entrenched power of vested interests to the checks and balances of a system of separated powers to the complications of a federal system — that contribute to the difficulty of achieving consensus for comprehensive or radical change.[2] Because local governments share these characteristics, we might expect policy development in the localities to be heavily constrained. From this perspective, then, we might expect that initiatives for policy change at the local level would often be caught in institutional gridlock, that the policy status quo would seldom be seriously challenged, and that whatever policy change could be mustered would be limited to marginal, incremental adjustments.

Nevertheless, there are grounds for expecting that policy at the local level can and does change in dramatic, nonincremental fashion. This perspective is drawn largely from the work of theorists of agenda setting, who note the ways in which dramatic or focusing events can be the impetus for prompt attention to problems. Furthermore, when policy entrepreneurs take advantage of opportunities, and comprehensive solutions have been gestating within policy communities of attentive experts, nonincremental policy change can result.[3] Similarly, Bryan Jones demonstrated convincingly that the rapid change characteristic of a positive feedback system can occur in policymaking systems if entrepreneurs exploit issue redefinitions, awaken the attention of the media and the mass public, and thereby move decision-making out of the confines of policy subsystems and into more general and centralized policymaking venues.[4]

Yet a third perspective suggests that policy change in the United States tends to approximate a cyclical model — that is, a period of relatively dramatic change in one direction followed by a reactionary period of equally dramatic change in the other direction. Policy reversals stem from the fact that the enthusiasms of a reform period lead to unusually ambitious policy changes which inevitably carry their own contradictions, such that reactionary forces are set in motion by the dynamics of reform.[5] Alternatively, a cyclical pattern can result from the exhaustion and disappointment that follow periods of intense involvement with public affairs, leading to a collective turn toward a private-centered focus.[6] These and other theories suggest that policy change can be expected to follow a pattern of commitment and retrenchment, or policy extension and reversal.

Finally, the literature on the diffusion of policy innovations suggests that, because innovation involves risk and change, subnational governments are not equally positioned for innovation. States with ample economic resources to cushion political leaders from the consequences of failed innovations and states with political cultures more supportive of risk-taking, for example, are more likely prospects for early innovation; in other states, public officials are predisposed to hold back until innovative programs are "proven" elsewhere. Hence, a small number of innovation leaders will take the lead in adopting a new policy, and, through processes of communication and emulation, will influence those who have not yet adopted the change. The result is a cumulative pattern of policy innovation diffusion that approximates an S-shaped curve, with an initial phase in which only a few innovation leaders take up the change, followed by a take-off period in which many jurisdictions emulate the innovation leaders, and then a leveling-off phase in which there is no more uptake of the innovation because the only nonadopters left are jurisdictions with impenetrable barriers to policy change.[7] This diffusion-of-innovations perspective reminds us that several dimensions are at issue when we investigate the magnitude of policy change at the local level. Not only should we be concerned with whether or not policy change is radical, in the sense that dramatically different policy is exhibited by some local governments, but we should also note both the extent to which new policy approaches are manifested more broadly and the timing of this diffusion.

Figure 13.1 summarizes the four perspectives on policy change. It illustrates the possibility that the four models of policy change are not mutually exclusive, especially if assessments of a policy trend are being made "midstream" rather than from a historical vantage point. Thus, for example, the initial periods of both a cyclical change trend and a punctuated equilibrium model are similar. The policy reversal that is the crucial feature of a cyclical trend may emerge relatively quickly for some policies but require a much longer time frame for other policies. Similarly, the S-shaped pattern that is characteristic of the diffusion-of-innovations model is replicated in partial segments of the punctuated equilibrium model — that is, a punctuated equilibrium pattern could be viewed as a series of innovation diffusions. Despite these points of similarity and overlap, however, the four models are distinctive, particularly when used to assess long-term trends.

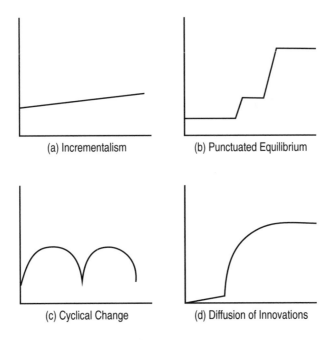

FIGURE 13.1. MODELS OF POLICY CHANGE

Spheres of Local Policymaking

Should our exploration of policy change in American localities be expected to provide definitive support for only one of these models? Once we acknowledge that local "policy" is not monolithic, the answer is clearly no. Which model of policy change we find likely will depend heavily on the particular type of policy that is explored. In particular, we might consider Peterson's influential categorization of urban governing activity into three types: developmental, allocational, and redistributional.[8] These types were derived from theoretical analysis of the consequences of different policies for higher-than-average taxpaying groups and, hence, for the city's capacity to remain competitive despite the potential mobility of those groups. Developmental policy involves local government efforts to build or sustain the economic vitality of the community through policies that make it attractive for private investment, and its efforts to balance the flow of benefits and costs of economic growth. The allocational policy sphere includes local government handling of an array of traditional distributional services, such that the ratio of benefits to burdens is as good for higher-than-average taxpaying groups as for any other. Redistributional policy involves programs and activities whose benefits are targeted toward the disadvantaged. Consistent with Peterson's analysis, we might expect that patterns of change in developmental policy, allocational policy, and redistributional policy would differ according to the institutional arrangements and political imperatives of each of these policy spheres.

For this reason, the discussion in this chapter focuses on specific policies exemplifying each of these three categories of local government activity. Within the developmental policy sphere, two trends in economic development policy are examined: the move to more entrepreneurial strategies for economic development and the emergence of "Type II" policies that make new demands on private-sector developers in exchange for land use approvals. The allocational policy sphere includes local government handling of an array of traditional services such as snow removal, trash collection, and street maintenance. This chapter focuses on the key policy trend in this sphere — privatization, including the use of contracting, in order to provide such services. Finally, the analysis turns to a prototypical redistributional policy: local governments' policy response to the homeless.

Economic Development Policy Change

Local governments cannot in any direct sense provide economic development, because they cannot *command* the private-sector investment that fuels economic activity in the community. Nevertheless, the consequences of private-sector investment, or lack thereof, are critical to the vitality of local communities. This situation inherently pits communities against one another in an ongoing competition to *induce* private-sector investment. This competition, coupled with the federal government's avoidance of any centralized development planning, means that city and county governments throughout the United States, in concert with their state governments, have been intensely involved in efforts to maximize opportunities for local economic growth and to overcome the reasons for private-sector disinvestment. A vast array of policies and programs are being undertaken in the name of economic development, including tax abatements and other financial inducements to private firms, land banking, industrial park development, other efforts to develop suitable sites for industrial location, promotional efforts, and many others. At the same time, many communities are grappling with the difficulties presented by growth, difficulties ranging from pollution, congestion, or other threats to "quality of life" in rapidly growing areas, to the equity issues raised when development does not necessarily carry benefits to disadvantaged segments of the community.

Two dimensions of policy change, therefore, are represented in the economic development sphere. First, there has been change in the approach that local governments have taken to meet the challenge of fostering economic growth. Second, there has been change in the extent to which local governments have acknowledged the problems that economic growth brings and enacted policies to address them. This section takes up each of these changes in turn.

Fostering Economic Growth: Demand-Side and Supply-Side Policies

In one of the most influential books on the topic, Peter Eisinger argued that the array of programs and activities that have traditionally characterized local economic development constitute a "supply-side" policy approach.[9] That approach is based on the assumption of a free market for local investment — a market in which investors' locational decisions are based on a straightforward calculus of minimizing the costs of doing business. From this perspective, the role of localities is to compete with other localities for such investment by providing various incentives to lure businesses — incentives presumed to be effective because they reduce the costs of doing business in a particular locality. Tax abatements, loan guarantees, the exemption of inventories or other categories of property from property taxes, and other financial inducements fit this characterization because they lower the costs of financing, and are offered either to firms in the community that are threatening to leave or firms elsewhere that might relocate to the community. Land banking, land write-downs, government-subsidized industrial parks, and other local governmental subsidies of infrastructure development fit the supply-side characterization of economic development policy as well, because they are designed to attract or retain existing industry by lowering the costs of land or other industrial infrastructure.

Eisinger also argued that a new array of very different economic development programs, constituting a "demand-side" policy approach, emerged in the 1980s. This policy approach is characterized by an emphasis on the search for new or expanded markets for existing products and support for the creation of wholly new products or enterprises — that is, encouraging economic expansion by fostering economic demand. Government's role in a demand-side approach to economic development policy is more entrepreneurial, in the sense that it bears substantial risks in exchange for potential benefits from innovative economic enterprises. Activities exemplifying the demand-side approach are export promotion (to open existing products to entirely new markets), venture capital financing (directed at economic enterprises too innovative to be candidates for start-up funds through conventional capital markets), and investment in high-technology enterprises (viewed as the locus for the greatest economic growth in the future).

Eisinger offered evidence of a strong movement toward demand-side policies in American cities and states in the 1980s, a trend that seems to epitomize the take-off phase of the diffusion of innovations model.[10] Similarly, Clarke and Gaile identified a policy shift toward demand-side economic development policy.[11] Based on a 1989 survey of the historical and contemporary economic development activities of cities above

100,000 in population, Clarke and Gaile reported a "shift away from conventional economic development orientations toward market-based, or entrepreneurial, approaches."[12] Local officials characterized their current approach to development policy as "oriented more toward risk taking, job growth, downtown development, job creation, local concerns, market feasibility, and aiding local firms, when compared with policies of 5 years ago."[13] This is reflected in changing policy tools. In the post-federal era (after 1980), at least a third of U.S. cities began to use demand-side policy tools such as trade missions abroad and business incubators; and some of these explored the possibility of still riskier and more entrepreneurially oriented economic development approaches, such as the establishment of public-private consortiums to generate equity pools, land banks, revolving loan funds, and venture capital funds.[14]

But if the 1980s represented the take-off period for demand-side policy innovation, there is also evidence that this trend has leveled off well short of a comprehensive spread throughout American subnational government. In fact, a recent investigation by Eisinger found evidence of some backing away from demand-side policy, such as a decline in the number of states running venture capital programs, the closing of trade offices overseas and the closing down of high-technology programs, along with evidence of a resurgence of the industrial recruitment activities that were presumably discredited elements of supply-side development policy.[15] Similarly, based upon a 1994 ICMA survey of cities and counties 2,500 population and over, Prager, Benowitz, and Schein found that efforts at attracting business continue to be a major element of local economic development efforts.[16]

Eisinger's assessment of the evidence does *not* support the wholesale rejection of demand-side approaches, as with a cyclical model of policy change. Instead, it suggests the sort of reassessment and evolution to be expected at the end of the initial, frenzied phase of any policy innovation. The majority of states responding to a 1993 survey indicated that they were equally committed to older, supply-side approaches and newer, demand-side approaches to economic development.[17] This combination strategy presumably allows even the most innovative states to hedge their bets while newer, demand-side programs are assessed and modified by experience. Eisinger suggests, however, that entrepreneurial retrenchment strategy is driven more by political imperatives than by a desire to learn from policy experimentation. Recent change is a function of economic pressures that force politicians into strategic pullbacks from longer-term, riskier approaches to economic development. Meanwhile, many communities still do not exhibit the fundamental capacity to engage in sophisticated demand-side activities. For example, Prager, Benowitz and Schein found a "relatively poor state of economic development planning at the local level."[18] Fewer than half the survey respondents indicated that they possess a formal written economic development plan to guide their efforts.

Fostering Economic Development: The Emergence of Type II Policies

Another important sea change in local development policy involves the emergence of what Goetz calls Type II policies, which are directed at the problems that economic growth brings, rather than the necessity of stimulating economic growth.[19] Unlike Type I policies, which involve unilateral local government support that is not contingent on private investment, Type II policies impose conditions or burdens that private-sector investors must meet in order to be granted development rights.[20] For example, developers may be required to provide all or part of the cost of streets, sewers, or other infrastructure needs created by growth, or they may be required to hire local residents or make contributions to the provision of affordable housing in the community.

The emergence of such Type II policies is important in two respects: (1) as a tool for managed, or controlled growth, such policy starkly contrasts with an earlier understanding of the inevitable power of progrowth elites;[21] and (2) because Type II policies can require developers to provide social services, contributions to affordable housing, assistance for community organizations, hiring and training of residents, and the like, they blur the distinction between economic development and redistributional policies. In other words, Type II policies represent an indirect way to steer local economic development policy toward a "human capital development" approach that traditionally has been eschewed because of the political risks and uncertainties involved.[22]

Attention to Type II policies is relatively recent, and broad-based surveys of the extent to which local governments have adopted such policies are even more recent. Hence, it is not possible to chart a trend or estimate the extent of policy change in any exact sense. The virtual absence of scholarly attention to the phenomenon, however, suggests that Type II policies were rare indeed prior to the 1980s. By 1990, however, some Type II policies were established in many locales, and a few locales were serving as innovation leaders for other Type II policies. Evidence of this comes from a late 1980s national-sample survey of cities and counties conducted by Goetz and a 1990 national-sample survey of cities conducted by Elkins.[23] Taken together, these two surveys show that a substantial majority of jurisdictions are demanding that developers make payments to help defray the cost of infrastructure and that a bare majority of jurisdictions are stipulating that developers train and hire local residents. While relatively few local governments have attempted Type II policies with strong redistributive features, such as mandates requiring developers to provide social services, other Type II policies with redistributional features are not particularly rare. For example, about one-quarter of the jurisdictions surveyed by Elkins reported that they require developers to contribute to low- and middle-income housing.

There is a certain irony in the juxtaposition of the two economic development trends outlined here. Localities have slowed the rush to demand-side development policies, presumably because they are too long-term and risky in an era of ever-heightening economic competition and demands that politicians deliver results; hence, the importance of efforts to woo existing business with supply-side policies that lower the cost of business. But, at the same time, Type II policies have been adopted, placing demands, sometimes costly ones, on developers. These two trends seem inconsistent; how can they be squared?

One possibility is that different kinds of cities are involved in each trend — that is, in declining central cities that are desperate for investment, one is least likely to find Type II policies and most likely to find the heaviest emphasis on supply-side policies, while faster-growing suburbs or other more prosperous cities are likely to sustain some innovative demand-side policies and to represent the cutting edge of Type II policies. This interpretation is consistent with earlier research suggesting that economically struggling communities are more likely to use supply-side development tools, despite their costs and questionable effectiveness;[24] and it is consistent with the logic that ties Type II policy viability to settings where population growth and consequent development profitability mean that policy demands on developers will not endanger economic growth. In exploring hypotheses such as these, however, Elkins finds no empirical data to support an economic-vitality explanation for the adoption of Type II policies and only limited support for an explanation attributing Type II policy adoption to the demand for land.[25] Nonetheless, political rather than economic characteristics of cities and their state partners are important predictors of the adoption of Type II policies. Type II development policies are more likely to be found in cities with potent neighborhood organizations and in states with high levels of interparty competition and highly mobilized interest groups.[26]

Service Delivery and Privatization: A Mature Innovation

In the area of basic city service delivery, or what Peterson would call the sphere of allocational politics, the most important policy trend in the 1980s was privatization of city services, especially in the form of contracting out.[27] In this respect, urban policymaking paralleled developments throughout the nation, where "privatization" reigned as the "single most influential concept of the decade."[28] In the context of basic city services, this means that many cities that once had city employees handling solid-waste collection, snow removal, street maintenance, and the like are now contracting with private firms for at least some of these services.

Characterizing the magnitude of this trend is complicated by different interpretations of the literature. While acknowledging the substantial evidence that the 1980s saw a broadening in the number of cities engaged in contracting out and in the types of services contracted for, Hirsch nevertheless suggested that the frenzy of scholarly and urban management interest in contracting out masks a relatively low level of actual conversion.[29] He pointed to the fact that Los Angeles County, which made major efforts to privatize in the 1980s, ultimately contracted out only 1.5 percent of its budget from 1987 to 1988.

Nonetheless, if no city is *intensively* involved in contracting, there is evidence of *extensive* use of this form of privatization. Contracting out is used at least to some extent by a large number of cities and counties, and a broad range of services is now subject to privatization. Data from two national sample surveys of cities and counties were reported by Miranda and Andersen, who noted that "contracting, which was once limited to specialized areas such as legal and insurance services, is now the most frequently used alternative service delivery approach."[30]

An examination of the data presented by Miranda and Andersen for 1982 and 1992 suggests that the diffusion of this innovation over the course of the decade has differed across services. Contracting with a for-profit company is now the predominant approach for services such as vehicle towing and commercial solid-waste collection — that is, the majority of cities and counties contract for these services. It is important to note, however, that these services were heavily contracted for by 1982. There was little change in contracting for these services during the 1980s, and such contracting appears to have run its course as an innovation diffusion. Similarly, services such as residential solid-waste collection and tree trimming or planting were handled by for-profit contracting in only about a third of cities and counties in 1982, and there has been little change since. The most dramatic increases in contracting out involve human services rather than physical services; cities increasingly have turned to both for-profit and nonprofit organizations for the delivery of these services. For example, day-care facility operation, already handled by for-profit organizations in one-third of local governments in 1982, was the subject of for-profit contracting by a little over half of local governments by 1992. Homeless shelters, which did not even appear as an item of inquiry on privatization surveys in 1982, were run by nonprofit organizations under contract with cities or counties in 54 percent of the jurisdictions surveyed in 1992. In 41 percent of city and county governments, cultural and arts programs currently are operated under contract with nonprofit organizations.

There are a variety of reasons for the growth in privatization of city services. The key reason is cost savings, and most of the literature suggests that city and county governments have realized such savings.[31] These savings are derived largely from differences in the labor practices of the private and public sectors, particularly in the use of part-time labor and the scope of fringe benefits provided. Further motivation derives from the efforts to minimize municipal liability and to escape the constraints that unions and civil service systems impose. Finally, the nation's special reliance on nonprofits to deliver government-funded human services — which Salamon calls "non-profit federalism"[32] — has meant an increase in contracting with nonprofits by local governments dealing with emergent social problems, such as homelessness, in the 1980s.

In short, privatization through contracting out appears to be a maturing innovation trend. Growth in contracting for those services that were the subject of the earliest attention for privatization is no longer substantial, and the diffusion of contracting for other services has leveled off without ever taking hold in large numbers of jurisdictions. But other services, especially human services, have recently been the focus for explosive growth in contracting.

The privatization trend is being extended in another sense as well. While straightforward yet limited versions of privatization, such as municipal contracting, have now matured as innovations, complex versions of privatization may be in an explosive stage of growth. In particular, it is instructive to note the rise in residential homeowner associations (RHAs), such as planned developments, stock cooperatives, condominiums, or community apartments, which function as virtually full-scope "private governments."[33] They are based on the mandatory, dues-paying membership of all property owners, they manage commonly owned property, they can contract for basic urban services such as snow removal and fire protection, and they regulate the use of privately owned property through deed restrictions. In short, they have the private-sector equivalents of taxing power, land-use planning and management authority, service-delivery responsibility, and order maintenance. Growth in these private governments has been long-standing and substantial, and it shows no sign of abating. "There were fewer than five hundred such homeowner associations in 1964. By 1970 there were 10,000 homeowner associations; by 1975 there were 20,000; by 1980, 55,000; by 1990, 130,000; and by 1992, there were 150,000 associations private governing an estimated 32 million Americans."[34]

In short, private delivery of allocational services probably best fits the pattern of a punctuated equilibrium, with periods of rapid expansion of privatization (e.g., contracting for physical services), followed by a relatively short-lived "equilibrium," followed by yet another period of rapid expansion into another version of privatization (e.g., contracting with nonprofits for human services, or creation of residential community organizations). Stated another way, privatization among local governments may fit the pattern of a punctuated equilibrium because privatization really involves a family of different policies. Each of these may exhibit the classic S-shaped curve in diffusion of innovations, but each particular mode of privatization has occurred on a somewhat different cycle. The overlay of these various cycles gives the overall privatization movement the appearance of a revolution in progress.

Policies for the Homeless: Short-Term Cyclical Change

Homelessness appeared on the municipal and national agenda in the 1980s. While there were then, and continue to be, fundamental disagreements about the magnitude of the problem, the demands on overburdened shelters in times of severe weather, the emergence of homeless encampments and squatter settlements in a number of cities, and the increased visibility of homeless individuals in public spaces across the United States made the existence of the problem undeniable. Debates about the reasons for the emergence of a substantial homelessness problem abound as well. There have always been some individuals who are homeless "by choice" — that is, they opt for the "hobo" life because they do not want to, or do not believe they can, fit the constraints and obligations of "normal" society. But the emergence of substantial numbers of homeless individuals in the 1980s focused attention on a variety of structural explanations for homelessness. One such explanation cites economic trends that have dislocated workers, changed the composition of work opportunities in the United States, and eroded the middle class. Other explanations point to market trends that have disrupted the supply of affordable housing, including federal funding reductions for housing programs and ongoing processes of "gentrification" as formerly low-income neighborhoods are converted for the use of high-income populations.[35] The deinstitutionalization movement of the late 1970s, which moved large numbers of mentally ill individuals out of large state institutions in favor of community-based care, also contributed to the problem in places where community-based care turned out to be inadequate. Other social problems, such as spouse abuse, divorce, and other forms of family breakdown, can contribute to the problem of homelessness, and, in particular, may account for an increased number of emergency, short-term cases of homelessness involving women and children.

The problem of homelessness is thus multifaceted, involving many kinds of individuals who have become homeless for a variety of reasons. There is evidence in a number of cities and counties of nonincremental policy change in response to the problem of homelessness. As documented by Blau, there has been an explosive expansion of existing shelter facilities.[36] In Los Angeles, for example, the number of shelter beds grew by 231 percent from 1984 to 1988. In San Francisco, which made a limited response to the homeless during Mayor Dianne Feinstein's administration (1980 to 1988), a dramatic policy response occurred during the subsequent Agnos administration, with shelter facility capacity increasing 52 percent by 1991, along with the purchase and renovation of hotels suitable for single-room occupancy and the designation of a homeless coordinator for the city. In 1985 St. Louis committed itself to a plan to produce more emergency beds and permanent housing units for the homeless, as well as a crisis reception center, transportation, and day care services. Between 1984 and 1988 Philadelphia increased its shelter capacity by 491 percent and passed a city ordinance guaranteeing a right to shelter. A similar "right to shelter" ordinance was established by ballot proposition in Washington, D.C., in 1984.[37]

This explosion of urban policy for the homeless cannot be attributed solely to the autonomous action of city and county officials. Nonprofit organizations played important roles in developing shelter systems in many cities, and the federal government's passage of the McKinney Act provided some funding for local government responses to the homelessness problem. But the magnitude of the problem has exceeded the capacities of the nonprofit sector in many cities, and McKinney Act funding has been insufficient to compensate for the federal government's pullback from programmatic efforts to increase the supply of affordable housing. As a result, the problem of the visible homeless has been left at the doorstep of sometimes unwilling local governments. In some cities, for example, dramatic policy commitments on behalf of the homeless occurred only in response to legal action by homelessness activists. This was the case in St. Louis, for example, where the city's package of policy commitments was agreed to only days before a lawsuit, filed by proponents for the homeless, was scheduled to go to trial.[38] Nevertheless, whether influenced by pressures from local businesses concerned about the impact of homeless populations on their business activity or prompted by progressive political cultures, local governments also have acted in the absence of litigation and devoted funds more discretionary than those provided by the McKinney Act to the needs of the homeless. Community Development Block Grant funds have been used for this purpose, for example, and Seattle established itself as a policy innovator in this field early on by applying local tax funds to low-income housing.[39]

The important point is that the 1980s witnessed an interesting example of nonincremental policy change in urban America as cities responded to homelessness. New programs, explosive growth in existing shelter efforts, and the institutionalization of new entitlements in city ordinances are evidence, *in some cities,* of this phase of nonincremental policy change.

In other cities, however, including ones with substantial homelessness problems, no such nonincremental change occurred. Many local governments chose to continue policies of minimal responsiveness, relying instead either on neighboring jurisdictions' facilities or on nonprofit organizations, but with no genuine public-private partnership. In their study of the responses of Los Angeles metropolitan area communities to homelessness, Wolch and Dear found that "more than half of all municipalities spent no local or nonlocal funds on homeless programs. Homeless individuals were typically referred to local nonprofit providers or to shelters and services in nearby jurisdictions."[40] Blau also identified cities that relied primarily on the nonprofit sector to handle the homeless, with little or no support from the public sector.[41]

In short, the arrival of the homelessness issue on urban agendas in the 1980s elicited a minimalist response from some local governments and dramatic, innovative policy responses from others, leading to striking differences in policy approaches to the problem. This pattern may be consistent with research on the diffusion of innovations, which suggests that, in the early phase of the innovation process, a small number of diffusion leaders show the way, followed by a takeoff phase in which substantial numbers of jurisdictions follow the lead of the early innovators.[42] But it is *not* a pattern that might have been expected for a redistributional policy area such as homelessness services. Expanded redistributional policy commitments presumably are not only particularly sensitive to fiscal capacity, but are also constrained by fears of the "welfare magnet" dynamic.[43] That is, localities are not willing to stand out by offering distinctively generous or effective social services because they fear that needy individuals will be drawn in large numbers to the community. Theory thus suggests that innovation leaders will not be found in the realm of redistributional policies such as aid to the homeless, despite important variations in need.

But if the explosion of new policy commitments for the homeless in the 1980s was contrary to theory, it was a brief contradiction, soon to be undone by new policy developments. By the 1990s another policy shift occurred — emphasizing and extending the control-oriented, law enforcement–focused measures that local governments have long maintained as part of their repertoire for dealing with vagrants and other "undesirable" elements. Many of the same cities that had pioneered in providing substantial shelter services for the homeless turned, in the 1990s, to sometimes quite punitive and hostile control-oriented policies. Ordinances that in various ways prohibit "aggressive solicitation" were adopted in San Francisco, San Diego, Anaheim, Cincinnati, Atlanta, Santa Monica, Dallas, and Beverly Hills. In Memphis, beggars are required first to obtain a city permit, and those caught begging without it are subject to arrest; in addition, panhandling is not allowed on buses or at trolley stops and is restricted to daylight hours. In 1993 Washington, D.C., toughened its existing antibegging ordinance with provisions defining aggressive begging in terms of the subjective perceptions of those being panhandled and banning begging near automatic teller machines and at public transportation stops.[44] Similarly, Santa Cruz enacted an ordinance designed to keep beggars away from bank teller machines, bus stops, and public benches.[45] New York has focused its new antibegging policy on begging, even of the most passive sort, in the subway system; and Chicago police have been cleared to enforce aggressively the portion of the city code that bans solicitation of funds on public ways.[46]

In addition to antibegging ordinances, localities have adopted other measures that effectively criminalize the homeless. For example, in 1994 Seattle approved an ordinance designed to control the homeless by prohibiting individuals from lying or sitting on public pavements from 7 am to 9 pm.[47] In 1993 San Francisco unveiled a new policy of arresting and ticketing people for sleeping, camping, or urinating in public, and in the 1992 to 1993 period eight cities in Southern California adopted policies banning sleeping or camping in public places. Other cities that already had such laws on the books adopted policy changes in the form of new commitments to enforce the long-neglected ordinances.[48] Many city governments, basing their action on these types of ordinances, have instituted a policy of aggressive arrest sweeps directed at the homeless.[49]

The reactionary period of homeless policy thus is largely an overlay of punitive, regulatory policies on top of the expanded redistributive services that emerged in the 1980s, although there also is some evidence of a retraction of the service commitments made in the 1980s, such as Washington, D.C.'s revocation of its policy statement establishing a right to shelter.[50] Discussions of this reactionary period emphasize society-centered explanations, such as popular hostility to the homeless and "compassion fatigue."[51] But it is not really necessary to explain the policy reversal described here in terms of a mass-based, reactionary movement. Instead, the reversal may be viewed as a short-term correction in what was otherwise an anomalous situation. Some localities, either in response to court action, or because expansive resources allowed for a ready response to unique need, or because they had special competence in seeking McKinney Act funds, had established themselves as innovation leaders in providing helping services for the homeless; in order to avoid the role of "magnet" for the homeless, however, such communities coupled their expansive shelter programs with more punitive, control-oriented policies. And such control-oriented policies appear to be growing apace, in formerly generous and formerly laissez-faire localities alike, because such approaches are not subject to the problems generated by leadership in innovative redistributive programs.

FOR THOSE WHO are concerned about the adaptive capacities of the public sector and the ability of local government leaders to move beyond the status quo, this chapter offers some reassurance. Local governments in the United States have demonstrated substantial policy change in several different areas. Such policy change is, in some cases, intensive but not extensive — that is, it involves dramatic change but in a limited number of settings — as in the uptake of programs for the homeless and the adoption of Type II economic development policies in a relatively limited number of localities. In other cases, policy change is extensive but not intensive, as in the relatively widespread involvement of cities that employ service contracting, though for only a limited number of services in any given community. While policy change sometimes is quite sustained and evolutionary, as has been the case with the trend toward privatization, it nevertheless appears substantial enough to warrant a characterization other than incrementalism.

In contrast, the example of homelessness policy suggests that what initially appears to be dramatic policy change along the lines of a punctuated equilibrium may well resolve into a cyclical model of dramatic policy response followed by reversal and reaction. The political logic of redistributive policymaking may make it especially susceptible to such short-term cycles, because localities presumably cannot afford for very long to be welfare magnets in their region. In other policy areas, change cycles appear to be longer, if they exist at all. In the development policy realm, for example, there is some evidence that the trend toward demand-side policies has stalled; whether policy in this field moves to a cyclical change pattern depends upon whether localities over the next decade choose to abandon wholesale the riskier, more entrepreneurial development policies that have been adopted by the innovation leaders.

The privatization trend that has dominated the allocational policy domain shows no sign of reversal. To find evidence of cyclical change in the allocational policy domain, one would have to examine policies specific to particular services. For example, in recent years there has been a surge of interest in, and adoption of, "community policing" programs. These programs incorporate decentralization of police administration, enhancement of police-community relations, and a broader view of crime fighting that involves officers in helping with community problems such as abandoned buildings and graffiti.[52] These programs are by no means new, however. They are a reincarnation of a policy innovation in policing that occurred in the 1970s under the label of team policing. Indeed, the history of policing in America seems to exhibit a repeated cycling back and forth between the principles of decentralization and community responsiveness on the one hand and centralized professionalism on the other.

Whether cyclical or sustained, the policy changes discussed in this chapter involve important alterations in resource allocation, creation (and/or abandonment) of programs, reprioritization of tasks, and adaptations in institutional arrangements. These are not the phenomena that spring to mind if one is characterizing a flabby monopoly, an entrenched bureaucracy, or any of the other stereotypes that are often applied to government.

What, then, are the sources of such discontinuities in policy? The substantial institutional changes discussed earlier in this volume surely are implicated. Transformation in governmental and nongovernmental institutions is of interest, in large part because of the potential that it carries for consequent policy change. Changes in the economic, social, and national political environment within which local governments operate are clearly implicated as well. The rise of entrepreneurial development policies, for example, was at least partly the result of global competition for capital and the clear message from Washington that cities were on their own in that global competition. And new developments in homeless policy initially were a response both to the sudden emergence of visible numbers of homeless individuals and the availability of federal funds for homeless programming.

Last but not least, policy changes are a function of "policy learning," *as filtered through the imperatives of local politics.* Local governments do emulate each other, adopting new approaches, such as privatization, whenever the successes of other communities, as communicated personally or reified in the professional literature, suggest that it is wise to do so. Whether or not a community privatizes, and which services it chooses to contract out, however, are political as well as analytical matters, incorporating factors such as the power of labor unions and the accountability concerns of public officials.[53] Similarly, we have seen in this chapter that subnational governments in the United States began a major turn toward entrepreneurial development policies, but that trend has stalled in recent years. This may partly be a response to reservations accumulated through experience with export promotion, high-technology programs, and other entrepreneurial initiatives. But, as Eisinger argued, political considerations, such as the politicians' need for more immediate successes, are perhaps even more important.[54]

Notes

CHAPTER ONE

1. On the events that led up to the framing of the Constitution, and the intentions of the Framers and the ratifying state bodies generally, see Gordon S. Wood, *The Creation of the American Republic 1776–1787* (Chapel Hill: University of North Carolina Press, 1969).

2. For an illuminating discussion of the checks-and-balances structure of the Constitution and its implementation of the notion of dual sovereignty, an excellent source is the contemporary exposition by three of the Framers, James Madison, Alexander Hamilton, and John Jay, *The Federalist Papers*, ed. Isaac Kramnick (Harmondsworth, England: Penguin Books, 1987; originally published 1787–88).

3. "Federal Grants: Design Improvements Could Help Federal Resources Go Further," GAO/AIMD-97-7 (letter report, 18 December 1996).

4. David B. Walker, *The Rebirth of Federalism* (Chatham, N.J.: Chatham House, 1995), 132.

5. Ibid.

6. Robert Pear, "Governors Helping to Set National Agenda Like Never Before," *New York Times*, 30 January 1995.

7. Ibid.

8. *Gregory v. Ashcroft*, 501 U.S. 452 (1991).

9. *New York v. United States*, 505 U.S. 144 (1992).

10. *United States v. Lopez*, 514 U.S. 549 (1995).

11. *Printz v. United States*, 138L Ed 2d 914, 117 S.Ct. 2376 (1997).

12. *City of Boerne, Texas v. Flores* 117 S.Ct. 2157 (1997), 73 F.3d 1352, reversed.

13. Paul Peterson, *The Work of Federalism* (Washington, D.C.: Brookings Institution, 1995).

14. See, for example, B. Dan Wood, "Federalism and Policy Responsiveness: The Clean Air Case," *Journal of Politics* 53 (August 1991): 851–59.

15. Joseph Schlesinger, *Ambition and Politics* (Chicago: Rand-McNally, 1966); Michael B. Berkman, *The State Roots of National Politics* (Pittsburgh: University of Pittsburgh Press, 1993).

16. James K. Conant, "Reorganization and the Bottom Line," *Public Administration Review* 46 (January/February 1986): 48–56.

17. The discussions of state spending and revenue actions draw heavily on *The Fiscal Survey of States* (Washington, D.C.: National Governors' Association and National Association of Budget Officers, December 1997).

18. See National Conference of State Legislatures, *State Tax Actions 1998*, http://www.ncsl. org/programs/fiscal/sta98sum.htm.

19. See "State Governments, Federal Agencies Graded on How Well They Run," *PA Times* 22 (March 1999): 1–2.

20. Paul Brace, *State Government and Economic Performance* (Baltimore, Md.: Johns Hopkins University Press, 1993).

21. These examples of bidding wars are taken from Paul Brace, "Taxes and Economic Development in the American States: Persistent Issues and Notes for a Model," in *Significant Issues in Urban Economic Development*, ed. Richard D. Bingham and Robert Mier (Thousand Oaks, Calif.: Sage, 1997).

22. See Brace, *State Government and Economic Performance.*

CHAPTER TWO

1. Keith Watson and Steven D. Gold, *The Other Side of Devolution: Shifting Relationships between State and Local Governments* (Washington, D.C.: Urban Institute, 1997), 1.
2. Timothy Conlan, *From New Federalism to Devolution* (Washington, D.C.: Brookings Institution, 1998), 224–27.
3. Watson and Gold, *Other Side of Devolution,* 1.
4. Ibid.
5. Richard P. Nathan, "The Newest New Federalism for Welfare," *Rockefeller Institute Bulletin* 3 (1997): 4–11.
6. Watson and Gold, *Other Side of Devolution.*
7. Two other sources of market failure are natural monopolies and asymmetries of information. Corrections for both can involve government regulation. The unit and level of government responsible for regulation is determined by the scope of benefits and costs associated with the good or service (i.e., its externalities). See David L. Weimer and Aidan L. Vining, *Policy Analysis: Concepts and Practices* (Englewood Cliffs, N.J.: Prentice Hall, 1989) for a further discussion of government responses to market failures.
8. Richard Musgrave, "The Voluntary Exchange Theory of Public Economy," *Quarterly Journal of Economics* 52 (February 1938): 213–17; P.A. Samuelson, "The Pure Theory of Public Expenditure," *Review of Economics and Statistics* 40 (May 1958): 332–38.
9. Elections are the main way in which public preferences are revealed to government officials. Voting is a voluntary behavior that is performed by less than a majority of all eligible voters. For these reasons, elections are not considered to be efficient means for revealing public preferences for publicly provided goods and services.
10. Charles Tiebout, "A Pure Theory of Local Expenditures," *Journal of Political Economy* 64 (October 1956): 416–24.
11. Ibid.; James Buchanan, "The Principles of Urban Fiscal Strategy," *Public Choice* 4 (1971): 1–16; Paul Peterson, *City Limits* (Chicago: University of Chicago Press, 1981); Gary Miller, *Cities by Contract* (Cambridge, Mass.: MIT Press, 1981).
12. Compare Keith Dowding, Peter John, and Stephen Biggs, "Tiebout: A Survey of the Empirical Literature," *Urban Studies* 31 (May 1994): 767–97.
13. Buchanan, "Principles of Urban Fiscal Strategy"; Peterson, *City Limits;* Miller, *Cities By Contract.*
14. Peterson, *City Limits,* 4.
15. Ibid.; Paul Peterson, *The Limits of Federalism* (Washington, D.C.: Brookings Institution, 1995).
16. Paul Brace, *State Government and Economic Performance* (Baltimore: Johns Hopkins University Press, 1993).
17. Ibid., 118.
18. Edward M. Gramlich and Daniel L. Rubinfeld, "Micro Estimates of Public Spending Demand Functions and Tests of the Tiebout and Median-Voter Hypotheses," *Journal of Political Economy* 90 (June 1982): 536–59.
19. Ibid., 536.
20. Miller, *Cities By Contract.*
21. Ibid., 83.
22. Harry Long, "Poverty Status and Receipt of Welfare among Migrants and Nonmigrants in Large Cities," *American Sociological Review* 39 (February 1974): 48.
23. R. Blank, "The Effect of Welfare and Wage Levels on the Location Decisions of Female-Headed Households," *Journal of Urban Economics* 24 (September 1988): 186–211; Edward Gramlich and Deborah Lauren, "Migration and Income Redistribution Responsibilities," *Journal of Human Resources* 9 (Fall 1984): 489–511.
24. Paul Peterson and Mark Rom, "American Federalism, Welfare Policy, and Residential Choices," *American Political Science Review* 83 (September 1989): 711.
25. Robert M. Stein, *Urban Alternatives: Public and Private Markets in the Provision of Local Services* (Pittsburgh: University of Pittsburgh Press, 1990).
26. Peterson, *City Limits.*

27. Joseph Zimmerman, *Participatory Democracy: Populism Revived* (New York: Praeger, 1970); William Anderson and Edwin Weidner, *American City Government*, rev. ed. (New York: Henry Holt, 1960).

28. Anderson and Weidner, *American City Government*, 609–10.

29. Vincent Ostrom, Robert Bish, and Elinor Ostrom, *Local Government in the United States* (San Francisco: Institute for Contemporary Studies, 1988); Geoffrey Brennen and James Buchanan, *The Power to Tax* (New York: Cambridge University Press, 1980); Robert Bish, *The Public Economy of Metropolitan Areas* (Chicago: Markham, 1971); idem, *Local Government in British Columbia,* (Vancouver: University of British Columbia, 1987); William Niskanen, *Bureaucracy and Representative Government* (Chicago: Aldine, 1971); Gordon Tullock, "Entry Barriers to Politics," *American Economic Review, Papers and Proceedings*, 1965, 458–66.

30. Wallace E. Oates, *Fiscal Federalism* (New York: Harcourt Brace Jovanovich, 1972); idem, "Searching for Leviathan: An Empirical Study," *American Economic Review* 75 (1985): 748–57.

31. M.A. Nelson, "Searching for Leviathan: Comment and Extension," *American Economic Review* 77 (March 1987): 198–204.

32. Michael Marlow, "Fiscal Decentralization and Government Size," *Public Choice* 56 (March 1988): 259–69; Henry J. Raimondo, "Leviathan and Federalism in the United States," *Public Finance Quarterly* 17 (April 1989): 204–15.

33. Jeffrey Zax, "Is There a Leviathan in Your Neighborhood?" *American Economic Review* 79 (1989): 560–67; Kevin Forbes and Ernest M. Zampelli, *American Economic Review* 79 (1989): 569–77.

34. Nancy Burns, *The Formation of American Local Governments* (New York: Oxford University Press, 1994).

35. Tiebout, "A Pure Theory"; Peterson, *City Limits;* idem, *Limits of Federalism;* Vincent Ostrom, Charles M. Tiebout, and Robert Warren, "The Organization of Governments in Metropolitan Areas: A Theoretical Inquiry," *American Political Science Review* 55 (December 1961): 831–42.

36. William N. Grubb, "The Dynamic Implications of the Tiebout Model — The Changing Composition of Boston Communities, 1960–1970," *Public Finance Quarterly* 10 (January 1982): 17–38; Miller, *Cities By Contract;* Janet Pack and Howard Pack, "Metropolitan Fragmentation and Suburban Homogeneity," *Urban Studies* 14 (June 1977): 191–201.

37. Robert M. Stein, "Tiebout's Sorting Hypothesis," *Urban Affairs Quarterly* 22 (September 1987): 199–225.

38. Compare Dowding, John, and Biggs, "Tiebout: A Survey."

39. R.J. Cebula, "A Survey of the Literature on the Migration Impact of State and Local Government Policies," *Public Finance* 34 (1970): 69–84; R.J. Cebula, "Local Government Policies and Migration: An Analysis According to Race, Sex and Age," *Journal of the American Statistical Association* 69 (December 1974): 876–79; idem, "An Empirical Note on the Tiebout-Tullock Hypothesis," *Quarterly Journal of Economics* 92 (November 1978): 705–11; R.J. Cebula and R.M. Kohn, "Public Policies and Migration Patterns in the United States," *Public Finance* 30 (1975): 186–96; M. Schneider and J. Logan, "The Effects of Local Government Finances on Community Growth Rates," *Urban Affairs Quarterly* 18 (September 1982): 95–105; K.E. Mills, M.B. Percy, and L.S. Wilson, "The Influence of Fiscal Incentives on Interregional Migration — Canada, 1961–1978," *Canadian Journal of Regional Science* 6 (1983): 207–29; R. Ellson, "Fiscal Impacts on Intrametropolitan Residential Location: Further Insights on the Tiebout Hypothesis," *Public Finance Quarterly* 8 (April 1980): 189–212; Peterson and Rom, "American Federalism"; B.J. Cushing, "The Effect of the Social Welfare System on Metropolitan Migration in the U.S. by Income Group, Gender, and Family Structure," *Urban Studies* 30 (March 1993): 325–38; R.M. Day, "Interprovincial Migration and Local Public Goods," *Canadian Journal of Economics* 25 (February 1992): 123–44.

40. D. Lowery and W. Lyons, "The Impact of Jurisdictional Boundaries: An Individual-Level Test of the Tiebout Model," *Journal of Politics* 51 (February 1989): 73–97; W. Lyons, D. Lowery, and R. DeHoog, *The Politics of Dissatisfaction: Citizens, Services, and*

Urban Institutions (Armonk, N.Y.: M.E. Sharpe, 1992). See also Stephen L. Percy and Brett W. Hawkins, "Further Tests of Individual-Level Propositions from the Tiebout Model," *Journal of Politics* 54 (November 1992): 1149–57; John Orbell and Toru Uno, "A Theory of Neighborhood Problem Solving: Political Action vs. Residential Mobility," *American Political Science Review* 66 (June 1972): 471–86; Elaine Sharp, "Exit, Voice, Loyalty in the Context of Local Government Problems," *Western Political Quarterly* 38 (March 1984): 67–83; idem, *Citizen Demand-Making in the Urban Context* (University: University of Alabama Press, 1986).

41. M. Schneider, Paul Teske, and Michael Mintrom, *Public Entrepreneurs: Agents for Change in American Government* (Princeton, N.J.: Princeton University Press, 1995).

42. Compare Clarence N. Stone and Heywood T. Sanders, *The Politics of Urban Development* (Lawrence: University Press of Kansas, 1987), 17.

43. Ibid.

44. Charles M. Tidmarch, Lisa J. Hyman, and Jill E. Sorkin, "Press Issue Agenda in the 1982 Congressional and Gubernatorial Election Campaigns," *Journal of Politics* 46 (November 1984): 1239.

45. John Chubb, "Institutions, the Economy, and the Dynamics of State Elections," *American Political Science Review* 82 (March 1988): 133–54.

46. Robert M. Stein, "Economic Voting for Governor and U.S. Senator: The Consequences of Federalism," *Journal of Politics* 52 (February 1990): 29–54.

47. Chubb, "Institutions"; Stein, "Economic Voting."

48. Susan E. Howell and James E. Vanderleeuw, "Economic Effects on State Governors," *American Politics Quarterly* 18 (April 1990): 158–68; Paul Brace, "The Changing Context of State Political Economy," *Journal of Politics* 53 (May 1991): 297–317; Richard G. Niemi, Harold W. Stanley, and Ronald J. Vogel, "State Economies and State Taxes: Do Voters Hold Governors Accountable?" *American Journal of Political Science* 39 (November 1995): 936–57; Lonna Rae Atkeson and Randall W. Partin, "Economic and Referendum Voting: A Comparison of Gubernatorial and Senate Elections," *American Political Science Review* 89 (March 1995): 99–107; Thomas Carsey and Gerald Wright, "State and National Factors in Gubernatorial and Senatorial Elections," *American Journal of Political Science* 42 (July 1998): 994–1002.

49. *Roe v. Wade*, 410 U.S. 113 (1973).

50. Maris A. Vinovskis, "Abortion and the Presidential Election of 1976: A Multivariate Analysis of Voting Behavior," in *The Law and Politics of Abortion,* ed. Carl E. Schneider and Maris A. Vinovskis (Lexington, Mass.: Lexington Books, 1980), 184–205; John E. Jackson and Maris A. Vinovskis, "Public Opinion, Elections, and the Single Issue 'Issue,'" in *The Abortion Debate and the American System,* ed. Gilbert Stein (Washington, D.C.: Brookings Institution, 1980), 64–81; Michael Traugott and Maris A. Vinovskis, "Abortion and the 1978 Congressional Elections," *Family Planning Perspective* 12 (September/October 1980): 238–46; Donald Granberg and James Burlison, "The Abortion Issue in the 1980 Elections," *Family Planning Perspectives* 15 (September/October 1983): 231–38.

51. See, for example, David Garrow, *Liberty and Sexuality: The Right to Privacy and the Making of Roe v. Wade* (New York: Macmillan International, 1994), 673.

52. Susan E. Howell and Robert T. Sims, "Abortion Attitudes and the Louisiana Governor's Election," *American Politics Quarterly* 21 (January 1993): 54–64.

53. This section draws on Kenneth N. Bickers and Robert M. Stein, "The Micro Foundations of the Tiebout Model," paper presented at the annual meeting of the Midwest Political Science Association, Chicago, 1995.

54. For example, Lowery and Lyons, "Impact of Jurisdictional Boundaries"; Lyons, Lowery, and DeHoog, *Politics of Dissatisfaction.*

55. James Q. Wilson, *Thinking About Crime* (New York: Basic Books, 1983).

56. Arthur Lupia and Matthew McCubbins, *The Democratic Dilemmas: Can Citizens Learn What They Need to Know?* (Cambridge, England: Cambridge University Press, 1997).

57. See, for example, Lowery and Lyons, "Impact of Jurisdictional Boundaries"; Schneider et al., *Public Entrepreneurs.*

CHAPTER THREE

1. Coleman B. Ransone Jr., *The Office of the Governor in the United States* (University: University of Alabama Press, 1956).

2. F. Ted Hebert, Jeffrey Brudney, and Deil S. Wright, "Gubernatorial Influence and State Bureaucracy," *American Politics Quarterly* 11 (April 1983): 243–64.

3. Thomas Dye, "Executive Power and Public Policy in the States," *Western Political Quarterly* 27 (December 1969): 926–39.

4. Dennis O. Grady, "Gubernatorial Behavior in State-Federal Relations," *Western Political Quarterly* 40 (June 1987): 305–18.

5. National Governors' Association, "The Governor's Powers," *State Government* 55 (Autumn 1982); Nelson C. Dometrius, "Measuring Gubernatorial Power," *Journal of Politics* 41 (May 1979): 589–610.

6. E. Lee Bernick, "Gubernatorial Tools: Formal vs. Informal," *Journal of Politics* 41 (May 1979): 656–64; Lee Sigelman and Nelson Dometrius, "Governors as Chief Administrators: The Linkage between Formal Powers and Informal Influence," *American Politics Quarterly* 16 (April 1988): 157–70.

7. Leslie Lipson, *The American Governor: From Figurehead to Leader* (Chicago: University of Chicago Press, 1939), 14.

8. Larry Sabato, *Good-bye to Good-time Charlie: The American Governorship Transformed*, 2d ed. (Washington, D.C.: CQ Press, 1983), 4.

9. Joseph A. Schlesinger, "The Politics of the Executive," in *Politics in the American States: A Comparative Analysis*, 2d ed., ed. Herbert Jacob and Kenneth Vines (Boston: Little, Brown, 1971), 210–37.

10. Eric B. Herzik and Charles W. Wiggins, "Governors vs. Legislatures: Vetoes, Overrides, and Policymaking in the American States," *Policy Studies Journal* 17 (Summer 1989): 841–62.

11. Nelson Dometrius, "Measuring Gubernatorial Power: The Measure vs. the Reality," *Western Political Quarterly* 40 (June 1988): 319–34.

12. These figures are estimated from data provided in Morris Fiorina, David Rohde, and Peter Wissel, "Historical Change in House Turnover," in *Congress in Change*, ed. Norman J. Ornstein (New York: Praeger, 1975), 37.

13. Given the attempts in some southern states to maintain the exclusion of former slaves from full political and economic participation, some Reconstruction policies may have been justified. Our point here is not to examine their merit, or lack of merit, but to describe the experiences of many of the citizens of southern states that led them to later adopt particular governing arrangements.

14. Terry Sanford, *Storm Over the States* (New York: McGraw-Hill, 1967), 29.

15. Governors were not necessarily better people, less prone to corruption than state legislators, they were just easier to change. Changing one person in the governor's chair from a promachine politician to an antimachine one was a simpler prospect than changing fifty or more legislators to achieve the same purpose.

16. Sabato, *Good-bye to Good-time Charlie*, 6.

17. Ira Sharkansky, "Agency Requests, Gubernatorial Support, and Budget Success in State Legislatures," *American Political Science Review* 62 (December 1968): 1220–31.

18. Glenn Abney and Thomas P. Lauth, "The Line Item Veto in the States," *Public Administration Review* 45 (May-June 1985): 372–77.

19. See James J. Gosling, "Wisconsin Item-Veto Lessons," *Public Administration Review* 46 (July/August 1986): 292–300; and Glenn Abney and Thomas P. Lauth, "The Governor as Chief Administrator," *Public Administration Review* 43 (January/February 1983): 40–49.

20. Sabato, *Good-bye to Good-time Charlie*, 1983.

21. D. Sevener, "The Amendatory Veto: To Be or Not to Be So Powerful?" *Illinois Issues* 11 (February 1985): 14–17.

22. Eric Herzik, "Governors and Issues: A Typology of Concerns," *State Government* 56 (Spring 1983): 58–64.

23. Thad L. Beyle, "Issues Facing the State and Governors," *State Government* 56 (Spring 1983): 65–69.

24. Glenn Brooks, *When Governors Convene: The Governor's Conference and national Politics* (Baltimore: Johns Hopkins University Press, 1961).

25. Lynn R. Muchmore, *Organization and Staffing Patterns in the Governor's Office* (Washington, D.C.: National Governors' Association, 1988).

26. National Governors' Association, *Governing the American States* (Washington, D.C.: NGA, 1988).

27. Many details of this case were drawn from Marshall Kaplan and Sue O'Brien, *The Governors and the New Federalism* (Boulder, Colo.: Westview, 1991).

28. Robert Johnston and Dan Durning, "The Arkansas Governor's Role in the Policy Process, 1955–79," *Arkansas Political Science Journal* 2, no. 1 (1981): 16–39; Diane Blair, *Arkansas Politics and Government* (Lincoln: University of Nebraska Press, 1988).

29. The Texas governor has no veto power, except an item veto of appropriation bills.

30. Many details of this case were drawn from Dan Durning, "Education Reform in Arkansas: The Governor's Role in Policymaking," in *Gubernatorial Leadership and State Policy,* ed. Eric B. Herzik and Brent W. Brown (New York: Greenwood Press, 1991).

31. Donald H. Haider, *When Governments Come to Washington* (New York: Free Press, 1974).

32. Deil S. Wright, Mary Wagner, and Richard McAnaw, "State Administrators: Their Changing Characteristics," *State Government* 49 (Summer 1977): 152–59; "The Other Revolutions," *U.S. News & World Report,* 23 January 1995, 26–29.

33. Randall R. Bovbjerg, *Medicaid in the Reagan Era: Federal Policy and State Choices* (Washington, D.C.: Urban Institute, 1982).

34. "As Clinton Inches toward Reform, Governors Tiptoe around the Issue," *Congressional Quarterly Weekly Report,* 9 October 1993, 2736–37.

35. "Governors' Groups Sidelined in Welfare Debate," *Congressional Quarterly Weekly Report,* 20 May 1995, 1424.

36. "Putting on the Brakes," *U.S. News & World Report,* 28 November 1994, 51, 53.

37. "The Other Revolutions," *U.S. News & World Report,* 23 January 1995, 26.

38. Kaplan and O'Brien, *Governors and the New Federalism.*

39. Saundra K. Schneider, "Governors and Health Care Policy in the American States," *Policy Studies Journal* 17 (Summer 1989): 909.

40. Jerry F. Medler, "Governors and Environmental Policy," *Policy Studies Journal* 17 (Summer 1989): 895–908.

41. Ann O'M. Bowman and Richard C. Kearney, *The Resurgence of the States* (Englewood Cliffs, N.J.: Prentice Hall, 1986).

42. Ibid., 238–39.

43. Marilyn K. Dantico and Alvin H. Mushkatel, "Governors and Nuclear Waste: Showdown in the Rockies," in Herzik and Brown, *Gubernatorial Leadership,* 173–90.

44. Dennis O. Grady, "Governors and Economic Development Policy: The Perception of Their Role and the Reality of Their Influence," *Policy Studies Journal* 17 (Summer 1989): 880.

45. Dennis O. Grady, "State Economic Development Incentives: Why Do States Compete?" *State and Local Government Review* 19 (Fall 1987): 86–94; Melvin Dubnick, "American States in the Industrial Policy Debate," *Policy Studies Review* 4 (August 1984): 22–27.

46. Grady, "Governors and Economic Development Policy," 887.

47. Ibid., 884.

48. William M. Berry and William A. Mussen, *Export Development and Foreign Investment: The Role of the States and its Linkage to Federal Action* (Washington, D.C.: National Governors' Association, 1980).

49. Glen Abney and Thomas P. Lauth, "The Executive Budget in the States: Normative Idea and Empirical Observation," *Policy Studies Journal* 17 (Summer 1989): 829.

50. Lipson, *American Governor.*

51. Sabato, *Good-bye to Good-time Charlie.*

52. Alan Rosenthal, *Governors and Legislatures* (Washington, D.C.: CQ Press, 1993); Robert S. Erikson, Gerald Wright, and John McIver, *Statehouse Democracy* (New York: Cambridge University Press, 1993).

53. Thad Beyle, "The Executive Branch: Organization and Issues, 1990–91," *The Book of the States*, 1992–93 ed. (Lexington, Ky.: Council of State Governments, 1992), 57.
54. Don F. Hadwiger, "State Governors and American Indian Casino Gaming: Defining State-Tribal Relationships," *Spectrum* 69 (Fall 1996): 16–25.
55. Charles Mahtesian, "Ganging Up on the Governors," *Governing* 11 (August 1997): 23–25.
56. Jeffrey L. Katz, "Governors Group Sidelined in Welfare Debate," *Congressional Quarterly*, 20 May 1995, 1423–25.
57. Kaplan and O'Brien, *Governors and the New Federalism*, 9.
58. Bowman and Kearney, *Resurgence of the States*, 31–40.
59. Kim Fridkin Kahn, "The Distorted Mirror: Press Coverage of Women Candidates for Statewide Office," *Journal of Politics* 56 (February 1994): 161.
60. There were earlier black governors during the Reconstruction era, but they were essentially appointed by the North. L. Douglas Wilder was the first truly elected black governor.
61. Eric B. Herzik, Brent W. Brown, and Alvin H. Mushkatel, "State Policymaking under Duress: The Governorship of Evan Mecham," *Policy Studies Journal* 17 (Summer 1989): 927–40.

CHAPTER FOUR

We are indebted to Michael Berkman of Pennsylvania State University for generously sharing data used in this chapter. Stephanie Post provided valuable research assistance.

1. Alan Ehrenhalt, "An Embattled Institution," *Governing*, January 1992, 30.
2. Nelson Polsby, "The Institutionalization of the U.S. House of Representatives," *American Political Science Review* 62 (March 1968): 145–53.
3. H. Douglas Price, "Congress and the Evolution of Legislative 'Professionalism,' " in *Congress and Change*, ed. Norman Ornstein (Westport, Conn.: Greenwood, 1975); "Careers and Committees in the American Congress: The Problem of Structural Change," in *The History of Parliamentary Behavior*, ed. William O. Aydelotte (Princeton: Princeton University Press, 1977).
4. Christopher Z. Mooney, "Measuring U.S. State Legislative Professionalism: An Evaluation of Five Indices," *State and Local Government Review* 26 (Spring 1994): 70–71.
5. Ann Bowman and Richard C. Kearney, "Dimensions of State Government Capability," *Western Political Quarterly* 41 (June 1988): 341–62; Peverill Squire, "The Theory of Legislative Institutionalization and the California Assembly," *Journal of Politics* 54 (November 1992): 1026–54.
6. Peverill Squire, "Professionalization and Public Opinion of State Legislatures," *Journal of Politics* 55 (May 1993): 479–91.
7. Joel A. Thompson, "State Legislative Reform: Another Look, One More Time, Again," *Polity* 19 (Fall 1986): 27–41.
8. Peverill Squire, "Legislative Professionalization and Membership Diversity in State Legislatures," *Legislative Studies Quarterly* 17 (February 1992): 69–80.
9. Ibid.
10. Morris Fiorina, "Divided Government in the American States: A Byproduct of Legislative Professionalism?" *American Political Science Review* 88 (June 1994): 304–16.
11. Data on legislative composition, turnover, and compensation were compiled by Michael Berkman from the *Book of the States* (Lexington, Ky.: Council of State Governments, various years). Legislative operating budgets were computed by the authors using *State Government Finances in (year)* and *Government Finances in (year)* (Washington, D.C.: Government Printing Office). To compute relative compensation, per capita personal income was obtained from the *U.S. Statistical Abstract* (Washington, D.C.: Government Printing Office, various years). All dollar figures were converted to constant (1982–84) from current values using the Consumer Price Index as a deflator.
12. Paul Brace and Daniel S. Ward, "The Transformation of the American Statehouse: A Study of Legislative Institutionalization," paper presented at the annual meeting

of the Midwest Political Science Association, Chicago, 1989; Bowman and Kearney, "Dimensions of State Government Capability."

13. Polsby, "Institutionalization of the U.S. House"; Mooney, "Measuring U.S. State Legislative Professionalism."

14. Polsby, "Institutionalization of the U.S. House"; Price, "Congress and the Evolution of Legislative 'Professionalism' "; Price, "Careers and Committees."

15. Joseph Schlesinger, *Ambition and Politics* (Chicago: Rand McNally, 1966); David Mayhew, *Congress: The Electoral Connection* (New Haven, Conn.: Yale University Press, 1974).

16. Mayhew, *Congress,* 7.

17. Ibid., 81.

18. Richard Fenno, *Congressmen in Committees* (Boston: Little, Brown, 1973).

19. Fiorina, "Divided Government," 306.

20. *U.S. Statistical Abstract.*

21. For a detailed discussion of the committee system in state legislatures, see Wayne L. Francis, *The Legislative Committee Game: A Comparative Analysis of Fifty States* (Columbus: Ohio State University Press, 1989).

22. Gary F. Moncrief and Joel A. Thompson, eds., *Changing Patterns in State Legislative Careers* (Ann Arbor: University of Michigan Press, 1992).

23. David Breaux and Malcolm Jewell, "Winning Big: The Incumbency Advantage in State Legislative Races," in Moncrief and Thompson, *Changing Patterns.*

24. Ronald E. Weber, Harvey J. Tucker, and Paul Brace, "Vanishing Marginals in State Legislative Elections," *Legislative Studies Quarterly* (February 1991): 29–47.

25. Ehrenhalt, "Embattled Institution," 28.

26. Mark P. Petracca, "The Poison of Professional Politics," Cato Institute Policy Analysis, no. 151; John H. Fund, "Term Limitation: An Idea Whose Time Has Come," in *Limiting Legislative Terms,* ed. Gerald Benjamin and Michael J. Malbin (Washington D.C.: CQ Press, 1992).

27. George F. Will, *Restoration: Congress, Term Limits, and the Recovery of Deliberative Democracy* (New York: Free Press, 1992).

28. Cleta Deatherage Mitchell, "Limit Terms? Yes!" in *Extensions* (Norman, Okla.: Carl Albert Research Center, Spring 1991).

29. Nelson Polsby, "Some Arguments against Congressional Term Limitations," *Harvard Journal of Law and Public Policy* 16 (1992): 1515–26.

30. Rebekah Herrick, Michael K. Moore, and John R. Hibbing, "Unfastening the Electoral Connection: The Behavior of U.S. Representatives when Reelection Is No Longer a Factor," *Journal of Politics* 56 (February 1994): 214–27.

31. Alan Rosenthal, "The Effects of Term Limits on Legislatures: A Comment," in *Limiting Legislative Terms,* ed. Gerald Benjamin and Michael J. Malbin (Washington D.C.: CQ Press, 1992).

32. Arlene Levinson, "So Much to Do, So Little Time," *State Legislatures* (July/August 1995): 36.

33. Ibid.

34. Rob Gurwitt, "California, Here We Come: The Professional Legislature and its Discontents," *Governing* 4 (August 1991): 65.

35. Charles Mahtesian, "When the Voters Freeze Your Pay," *Governing* 7 (December 1993): 35.

36. Robert S. McCord, "Revival in the Arkansas House," *State Legislatures* 21 (July/August 1995): 40–45; Rob Gurwitt, "Reform in the Unlikeliest Places," *Governing* 7 (January 1994): 36–41.

37. Brian Weberg, "Change Ahead for Legislative Staffs," *State Legislatures* 19 (February 1993): 22.

38. Levinson, "So Much to Do," 37.

39. Drew Leatherby, *Report on Term Limits* (Lexington, Ky.: Council of State Governments, 1998).

40. The Council of State Governments survey obtained responses from only 56 legislators in Maine and 18 in California.

41. Gary Moncrief, Joel Thompson, Michael Haddon, and Krobert Hoyer, "For Whom the Bell Tolls: Term Limits and State Legislatures," *Legislative Studies Quarterly* 17 (February 1992): 37–47.

42. David M. Hedge, *Governance and the Changing American States* (Boulder, Colo.: Westview, 1998).

43. V.O. Key Jr., *Southern Politics in State and Nation* (New York: Knopf, 1949).

CHAPTER FIVE

1. V.O. Key Jr., *American State Politics* (New York: Knopf, 1956), 278.

2. See, for example, Gordon Tullock, *Private Wants, Public Means* (New York: Basic Books, 1970).

3. Theodore Lowi, *The End of Liberalism* (New York: Norton, 1970).

4. See, for example, Anthony Downs, *Inside Bureaucracy* (Boston: Little, Brown, 1967). For a review of models of the implications of one party's having more information than another in political decisionmaking, see Terry Moe, "The New Economics of Organization," *American Journal of Political Science* 28 (November 1984).

5. Michael Lipsky, *Street Level Bureaucracy* (New York: Russell Sage Foundation, 1982).

6. *Publius* (Alexander Hamilton), *The Federalist Papers*, No. 68 (New York: Mentor Books, 1961), 411–15.

7. See James Garnett, *Reorganizing State Government: The Executive Branch* (Boulder, Colo.: Westview, 1980).

8. Woodrow Wilson, "The Study of Administration," *Political Science Quarterly* 2 (June 1887); reprinted in *Classics of Public Administration*, ed. Jay Shafritz and Albert Hyde (Chicago: Dorsey, 1987), 10–25.

9. Paul Van Riper, *History of the United States Civil Service* (Evanston, Ill.: Row, Peterson, 1958).

10. Norton Long, "Power and Administration," *Public Administration Review* 9 (Autumn 1949): 257–64.

11. See J. Leiper Freeman, *The Political Process* (New York: Random House, 1955); John W. Kingdon, *Agendas, Alternatives, and Public Policies* (Boston: Little, Brown, 1984).

12. John Kingdon, *Agendas, Alternatives*, esp. chap. 6.

13. Glenn Abney and Thomas Lauth, *The Politics of State and City Administration* (Albany:State University of New York Press, 1986), esp. chaps. 2–6.

14. Richard Elling, *Public Management in the States* (Westport, Conn.: Praeger, 1992), chap. 6.

15. Robert Erikson, Gerald Wright, and John McIver, *Statehouse Democracy* (New York: Cambridge, 1993).

16. Charles Barrilleaux and Mark Miller, "The Political Economy of Medicaid," *American Political Science Review* 82 (December 1988); Saundra Schneider, "Intergovernmental Influences in Medicaid Program Expenditures," *Public Administration Review* 4 (July/August 1988): 756–63; Charles Barrilleaux, Paul Brace, and Bruce Dangremond, "The Sources of State Health Reform," paper presented at the annual meeting of the American Political Science Association, New York, September 1994; Paul Brace and Charles Barrilleaux, "A Unified Model of State Policy Reform," paper presented at the annual meeting of the American Political Science Association, Chicago, September 1995.

17. Meredith De Hart, "Government Employment in 1992," *The Book of the States, 30 (1994–1995)* (Lexington, Ky.: Council of State Governments, 1994), 435–48.

18. State employees are often the target of derogatory remarks. In Florida, state employees are known as "lardbricks," a term attributed to former GOP Governor Robert Martinez (1987–91). In New York, it is often said that state employees do not spend their mornings looking out their windows because that would leave them nothing to do all afternoon.

19. These data do not reflect the size of either sector relative to changes in state population, the implication being that social insurance administration employment may have seen a decline when viewed as a ratio of state population.

20. Lee Sigelman, "The Quality of State Administration," *Administration and Society* 8 (January 1976): 107–44.

21. Ibid., 110.

22. Charles Barrilleaux, Richard Feiock, and Robert Crew Jr., "Measuring and Comparing American States' Administrative Characteristics," *State and Local Government Review* 24 (Winter 1992): 12–18.

23. Charles Barrilleaux and Frances Berry, "Measuring the Scope, Efficiency, and Professionalism of American States' Public Sectors, 1969–1994," paper presented at the annual meeting of the American Political Science Association, San Francisco, September 1996.

24. Barrilleaux and Berry, "Measuring the Scope," 3–4.

25. *Managerial efficiency* refers to the process of doing some prescribed task in the "best" way possible, including consideration of equity. *Economic efficiency* refers simply to using resources in the best way possible, that is, so that the greatest gain is received from a given input irrespective of equity. There are often conflicts between managerial and economic efficiency. For a discussion of these problems, see, for example., David L. Weimer and Aidan R. Vining, *Policy Analysis,* 2d ed. (Englewood Cliffs, N.J.: Prentice Hall, 1992), 16–19.

26. Debates over school choice, privatization of prisons and other historically public services, and the like are part of the government reinvention debate.

27. See Downs, *Inside Bureaucracy,* for a discussion of the life cycle of bureaus. A theoretically better-developed perspective on the relations between organizational and individual behavior is provided in James March and Johann Olson, *Rediscovering Institutions* (New York: Free Press, 1989).

28. A clientele group is one with a direct interest in the substance of an agency's work. For example, an agency responsible for regulating the licensure of barbers would count barbers among its clientele.

29. See James K. Conant, "Reorganization and the Bottom Line," *Public Administration Review* 46 (January 1986): 48–56; James K. Conant, "In the Shadow of Wilson and Brownlow: Executive Branch Reorganization in the States, 1965 to 1987," *Public Administration Review* 48 (November 1988): 892–902; Garnett, *Reorganizing State Government;* Kenneth J. Meier, "Executive Reorganization of State Government: Impact on Employment and Expenditure," *American Journal of Political Science* 24 (May 1980): 396–412.

30. The "blue ribbon" panel, called the National Commission on State and Local Public Service, was chaired by former Mississippi Governor William Winters and directed by Frank Thompson of the State University of New York at Albany's Nelson A. Rockefeller Institute of Government. An overview of the commission's findings is provided in The National Commission on the State and Local Public Service, *Hard Truths/Tough Choices: An Agenda for State and Local Reform* (Albany, N.Y.: Nelson A. Rockefeller Institute of Government, 1993).

31. Ibid., 21.

32. Ibid., 23–24.

33. Ibid., 25.

34. Council of State Governments, *Book of the States.*

35. See National Commission on the State and Local Public Service, *Hard Truths,* 25–38.

36. Paul Brace and Charles Barrilleaux, "A Model of State Policy Reform," paper presented at the annual meeting of the American Political Science Association, San Francisco, September 1996.

37. See Charles Lindblom, *The Policymaking Process* (Englewood Cliffs, N.J.: Prentice Hall, 1968) for a concise statement about the gradual nature of change in American politics. For a less concise statement, see Charles Lindblom, *Inquiry and Change* (New Haven, Conn.: Yale University Press, 1992).

38. Frances Stokes Berry, Richard Chackerian, and Barton Wechsler, "Reinventing Government: Lessons from a State Capital," paper presented at the 3d National Public Management Research Conference, Lawrence, Kans., 5–7 October 1995.

39. Ibid., 6–7.

40. See Anthony Downs, "Up and Down with Ecology: The Issue Attention Cycle," *The Public Interest* 28 (Summer 1972): 38–50.

CHAPTER SIX

1. Philip L. Dubois, *From Ballot to Bench: Judicial Elections and the Quest for Accountability* (Austin: University of Texas Press), 2.

2. See, for example, Henry R. Glick and Craig Emmert, "Selection Systems and Judicial Characteristics: The Recruitment of State Supreme Court Justices," *Judicature* 70 (December-January 1987): 228–35. The consolidation of state trial courts has had the effect of reducing the proportion of judges who are not lawyers. Harry P. Stumpf and John H. Culver, *The Politics of State Courts* (New York: Longman, 1992).

3. *United States* v. *Lopez,* 514 U.S. 549 (1995).

4. For a more complete discussion of the importance of state courts, see Melinda Gann Hall, "The Wisconsin Judiciary," in *Wisconsin Government and Politics,* ed. Ronald E. Weber (New York: McGraw Hill, 1996). This chapter draws on that discussion.

5. Henry R. Glick, *Courts, Politics, and Justice* (New York: McGraw Hill, 1993).

6. William Brennan, "State Supreme Court Judge versus United States Supreme Court Justice: A Change in Function and Perspective," *University of Florida Law Review* 29 (1966): 225–37.

7. See, for example, Charles A. Johnson, "Lower Court Reactions to Supreme Court Decisions: A Quantitative Examination," *American Journal of Political Science* 23 (November 1979): 792–804; Thomas R. Marshall, "Policymaking and the Modern Court: When Do Supreme Court Rulings Prevail?" *Western Political Quarterly* 42 (December 1989): 493–507.

8. Lawrence Baum, "Making Judicial Policies in the Political Arena," in *The State of States,* ed. Carl E. Van Horn (Washington, D.C.: CQ Press, 1993); also see G. Alan Tarr and Mary Cornelia Porter, *Supreme Courts in State and Nation* (New Haven, Conn.: Yale University Press, 1988).

9. Steven W. Hays, *Court Reform: Ideal or Illusion?* (Lexington, Mass.: D.C. Heath, 1978), 106.

10. Philip L. Dubois, ed., *The Analysis of Judicial Reform* (Lexington, Mass.: D.C. Heath, 1982).

11. Glick, *Courts, Politics, and Justice.*

12. Henry R. Glick and Kenneth N. Vines, *State Court Systems* (Englewood Cliffs, N.J.: Prentice Hall, 1973).

13. Ibid., 25.

14. Hays, *Court Reform,* 1, and Glick and Vines, *State Court Systems,* provide excellent discussions of the political implications of court congestion and delay.

15. Glick, *Courts, Politics, and Justice.*

16. Ibid.

17. See, for example, Carl Baar and Thomas A. Henderson, "Alternative Models for the Organization of State Court Systems," in Dubois, *Analysis of Judicial Reform.*

18. Council of State Governments, *Book of the States* (Lexington, Ky.: CSG, 1980–81), 143.

19. The Arkansas Courts of Common Pleas and the Justice of the Peace Courts have decided very few cases in recent years.

20. Delaware, Georgia, Indiana, Mississippi, New York, Ohio, Oregon, and South Carolina.

21. National Center for State Courts, *State Court Caseload Statistics, 1993* (Williamsburg, Va.: NCSC, 1995). As a second example, New York operates the following limited-jurisdiction trial courts: Civil Court of the City of New York, Court of Claims, Criminal Court of the City of New York, District and City Courts, Family Courts, Surrogates' Courts, and Town and Village Justice Courts.

22. Council of State Governments, *Book of the States* (Lexington, Ky.: CSG, 1984–85).

23. Alabama, Alaska, Colorado, Connecticut, Delaware, Hawaii, Indiana, Iowa, Kansas, Kentucky, Maine, Maryland, Massachusetts, Michigan, Missouri, Nebraska, New Hampshire, New Mexico, New York, North Carolina, North Dakota, Oklahoma, Oregon, Rhode Island, South Dakota, Vermont, Virginia, West Virginia, and Wyoming had committed to centralization by 1983; Arkansas, Georgia, Louisiana, New Jersey, Washington, and Wisconsin were considering similar arrangements.

24. Stumpf and Culver, *Politics of State Courts.*

25. Council of State Governments, *Book of the States* (Lexington, Ky.: CSG, 1961–62). The states were Alaska, Colorado, Connecticut, Hawaii, Illinois, Iowa, Kentucky, Louisiana,

Maryland, Massachusetts, Michigan, Missouri, New Jersey, New Mexico, New York, North Carolina, North Dakota, Ohio, Oregon, Rhode Island, Virginia, and Washington.

26. State courts of last resort are referred to as supreme courts in this chapter, because this is the most common label assigned to these courts. However, courts of last resort have a variety of formal names, including Supreme Court of Appeals (West Virginia), Supreme Judicial Court (Maine, Massachusetts), and Court of Appeals (Maryland, New York). Oklahoma and Texas each have two courts of last resort. These states divide the civil and criminal jurisdiction into separate institutions: Supreme Courts, which have final review of civil matters, and Courts of Criminal Appeals, which have final authority over criminal cases.

27. The number of judges serving in each state court of last resort currently ranges from five to nine. In most (twenty-six) states, supreme courts have seven members. Council of State Governments, *Book of the States* (Lexington, Ky.: CSG, 1996–97).

28. Many other alternatives were advocated to assist appellate courts in managing their caseloads. Thomas B. Marvell, "State Appellate Court Responses to Caseload Growth," *Judicature* 72 (February-March 1989): 282–91, presents a comprehensive discussion of these proposals, including internal operating changes such as limiting oral argument and deciding cases without formal opinion.

29. Intermediate appellate courts have a variety of names. Most states call these courts the Court of Appeals, while other states have labeled them the Appeals Court or Appellate Court (Connecticut, Illinois, Massachusetts), District Courts of Appeals (Florida), Intermediate Court of Appeals (Hawaii), and Superior Court (Pennsylvania).

30. States without intermediate appellate courts are Delaware, Maine, Mississippi, Montana, Nevada, New Hampshire, North Dakota, Rhode Island, South Dakota, Vermont, West Virginia, and Wyoming. However, since the 1990–91 volume, the Council of State Government's *Book of the States* lists North Dakota as operating an intermediate appellate court on a temporary basis. The states operating a single-tiered appellate structure are those where litigation rates have not been so threatening as to cause the need for major structural change.

31. Marlin O. Osthus, *Intermediate Appellate Courts* (Chicago: American Judicature Society, 1976) provides a detailed description of the structural variations in intermediate appellate courts through 1976.

32. There may be limited categories of cases that courts with otherwise discretionary dockets are required by statute to review (e.g., cases where lower courts have declared laws unconstitutional). Also, there may be options to allow supreme courts to bypass intermediate appellate courts, either in certain types of cases defined by statute (e.g., cases in which defendants have been sentenced to death) or at the prerogative of the supreme court. Additionally, state supreme courts have original jurisdiction in some cases, typically disciplinary cases pertaining to members of the bar and a variety of other matters crucial to state government. Supreme courts decide relatively few of these cases annually.

33. See, for example, James A. Gazell and Howard M. Rieger, *The Politics of Judicial Reform* (Berkeley, Calif.: California Book Company, 1969); Glick, *Courts, Politics, and Justice*; Marvell, "State Appellate Court"; Osthus, *Intermediate Appellate Courts*; John A. Stookey, "Creating an Intermediate Appellate Court of Appeals: Work Load and Policymaking Consequences," in Dubois, *Analysis of Judicial Reform*.

34. Marvell, "State Appellate Court."

35. National Center for State Courts, *State Courseload Statistics, 1993*. This is not to say that caseload problems in state supreme courts have been solved. Even with discretionary dockets, for instance, supreme courts must rule on petitions requesting review, a very demanding task.

36. Glick, *Courts, Politics, and Justice*, 45–46.

37. Discussing the decision-making propensities of state courts is surprisingly difficult. Information about the decisions actually rendered by state judicial institutions is gathered only infrequently, usually by political scientists conducting case studies of a single state or handful of states. Therefore, it is not possible at this point to compare state courts comprehensively along the lines of who wins and loses the cases, what kinds of sentences or monetary awards are being handed down, how often trial courts

are overturned by appellate courts, or how individual judges decide cases. Nonetheless, some data have been gathered that allow comparisons on several interesting dimensions related to decision making in these courts.

38. Craig F. Emmert, "Judicial Review in State Supreme Courts: Opportunity and Activism," paper presented at the annual meeting of the Midwest Political Science Association, Chicago, 1988.

39. Ibid.

40. See, for example, Steven A. Peterson, "Dissent in American Courts," *Journal of Politics* 43 (May 1981): 412–34; Paul Brace and Melinda Gann Hall, "Neo-Institutionalism and Dissent in State Supreme Courts," *Journal of Politics* 52 (February 1990): 54–70; idem, "Integrated Model of Judicial Dissent," *Journal of Politics* 55 (November 1993): 914–35; Henry R. Glick and George W. Pruet Jr., "Dissent in State Supreme Courts: Patterns and Correlates of Conflict," in *Judicial Conflict and Consensus: Behavioral Studies of American Appellate Courts,* ed. Sheldon Goldman and Charles Lamb (Lexington, Ky.: University Press of Kentucky, 1986).

41. Glick and Pruet, "Dissent in State Supreme Courts."

42. See, for example, David W. Rhode and Harold J. Spaeth, *Supreme Court Decision Making* (San Francisco: W.H. Freeman, 1976); Jeffrey A. Segal and Harold J. Spaeth, *The Supreme Court and the Attitudinal Model* (New York: Cambridge University Press, 1993).

43. John T. Wold and Greg A. Caldeira, "Perceptions of 'Routine' Decision Making in Five California Courts of Appeal," *Polity* 13 (Winter 1980): 338.

44. Ibid., 346.

45. Dubois, *From Ballot to Bench.*

46. Kenneth N. Vines and Herbert Jacob, "State Courts," in *Politics in the American States: A Comparative Analysis,* ed. Herbert Jacob and Kenneth N. Vines (Boston: Little, Brown, 1971).

47. New Mexico has one of the most unusual judicial selection systems: justices are nominated by the governor based on recommendations by a nominating commission, but they must be approved by voters in partisan, contested elections. After this initial election, justices then appear before voters in retention elections rather than in partisan races.

48. A number of states use several methods of selection, depending upon the type of court being staffed. For instance, some states utilize partisan or nonpartisan elections for choosing trial court judges and the Missouri Plan for the court of last resort.

49. In table 6.4, states are classified as gubernatorial appointment states if the justices are nominated by the governor, with or without the participation of judicial nomination commissions, but are not required to appear in retention elections.

50. In practice, election systems, like Missouri Plan schemes, are quite varied. For example, judges in some states (Illinois, Louisiana, Mississippi, Kentucky, Maryland, Nebraska, Oklahoma, South Dakota) are elected from districts, while judges in other states are elected statewide. Terms of office also vary significantly, from six to twelve years in supreme courts, from four to twelve years in intermediate appellate courts, and from four to fifteen years in general-jurisdiction trial courts.

51. James Herndon, "Appointment as a Means of Initial Accession to Elective State Courts of Last Resort," *North Dakota Law Review* 38 (1962): 60–73.

52. Dubois, *From Ballot to Bench.*

53. Mary L. Volcansek, "The Effects of Judicial Selection Reform: What We Know and What We Do Not," in Dubois, *Analysis of Judicial Reform,* presents a comprehensive review of judicial selection research published through 1981.

54. Every state has formal qualifications for serving on the state bench. These requirements are minimal, however, usually stipulating that candidates for judgeships be members of the state bar for some specified minimum period. In twenty states, judicial candidates must meet a minimum age requirement. Other than these basic qualifications, the states do not attempt to define the credentials of judicial candidates.

55. Glick and Emmert, "Selection Systems and Judicial Characteristics."

56. See, for example, Bradley C. Canon, "The Impact of Formal Selection Processes on the

Characteristics of Judges — Reconsidered," *Law and Society Review* 6 (May 1972): 579–93.

57. Who becomes a supreme court justice? Like other political elites in the United States, justices are disproportionately male, white, and Protestant. Additionally, most justices are connected to the states in which they serve by birth or education; they are "home-born and home-raised." Kenneth N. Vines, "The Selection of Judges in Louisiana," *Studies in Judicial Politics* 8 (1962): 105; Glick and Emmert, "Selection Systems and Judicial Characteristics."

58. State court judges can be removed by a wide variety of methods other than simply being voted out of office at the completion of their terms, including impeachment (44 states), legislative address (14 states), recall (6 states), and removal by the supreme court upon conviction of a felony, recommendation of a judicial disciplinary committee, or retirement for a disability (48 states). Council of State Governments, *Book of the States* (Lexington, Ky.: CSG, 1994–95). The likelihood of a sitting judge being ousted from office by any of these alternative means, however, is quite remote.

59. These patterns are not unique to judicial elections. As Dubois (*From Ballot to Bench*) noted, incumbency advantage and low voter turnout characterize elections to other national and state-level offices.

60. Dubois, *From Ballot to Bench*.

61. Ibid.

62. Richard A. Watson and Rondal G. Downing, *The Politics of the Bench and the Bar* (New York: John Wiley, 1969).

63. William K. Hall and Larry T. Aspin, "What Twenty Years of Judicial Retention Elections Have Told Us," *Judicate* 70 (April-May 1987): 340–47.

64. Melinda Gann Hall, "Constituent Influence in State Supreme Courts: Conceptual Notes and a Case Study," *Journal of Politics* 49 (November 1987): 1117–24; idem, "Electoral Politics and Strategic Voting in State Supreme Courts," *Journal of Politics* 54 (May 1992): 427–46; idem, "Justices as Representatives: Elections and Judicial Politics in the American States," *American Politics Quarterly* 23 (October 1995): 485–503. The extent to which elected justices respond to their constituencies on all other matters of public policy, especially issues not very salient to voters, remains unknown.

65. Hall, "Constituent Influence," "Electoral Parties," "Justices as Representatives."

66. John D. Felice and John C. Kilwein, "Strike One, Strike Two...: The History of and Prospect for Judicial Reform in Ohio," *Judicature* 75 (December-January 1992): 193–200.

67. Arkansas Judiciary Annual Report, 1991–1992, Office of the Chief Justice, Little Rock, Ark.

CHAPTER SEVEN

1. This view and the counterargument that follows are summarized in Douglas Yates, *The Ungovernable City* (Cambridge, Mass.: MIT Press, 1977).

2. A third possible approach is the commission form. The commission is a plural executive, in that each of a small number of commissioners (usually five) has the authority to direct a department of city government. Together the commissioners meet as the legislative body to make policy. The commission form tends to be weak in coordination, with no focal point of political leadership and no single executive to pull separate activities together. Each commissioner is inclined to ignore problems in other departments in return for freedom to run his or her own. According to *The Municipal Yearbook 1997* (Washington: International City Management Association, 1997), xi, only 2 percent of cities over 2,500 now use the commission form. The largest is Portland, Oregon.

3. International City Management Association, *Who's Who 1995–96* (Washington, D.C.: International City Management Association, 1995). The regions are standard in the Northeast, Southeast, and Midwest; Mountain-Plains includes Arizona, Arkansas, Colorado, Idaho, Kansas, Montana, Nebraska, New Mexico, North Dakota, Oklahoma, South Dakota, Texas, Utah, and Wyoming; and West Coast includes Nevada, Alaska, and Hawaii in addition to the three coastal states.

4. An alternative to the strong mayor form, the so-called weak mayor-council form

disperses authority more widely and does not assign a full-range of executive powers to the mayor. The city council or other boards or commissions make other appointments and directly supervise the work of certain departments and may share in the authority to formulate the budget. Certain department heads, such as the controller, and members of some boards or commissions may be directly elected. These practices contribute to fragmentation of authority — no one has comprehensive administrative authority — and weaken the powers of the mayor. This form is most commonly found in small cities. The weak mayor-council government found in very small towns is essentially government by committee, in which the mayor is first among equals. These towns have limited staff, and the mayor and council members supervise the work of staff and perform some administrative tasks themselves.

5. Estimate based on data provided by the National League of Cities, 1996. Other titles may be used, such as vice-mayor.

6. James B. Hogan, *The Chief Administrative Officer* (Tucson: University of Arizona Press, 1976).

7. This was a survey conducted by the author of all city managers and CAOs in cities with populations of 50,000 and over, and a one-quarter sample of those in cities between 2,500 and 49,999 in population. See James H. Svara, "U.S. City Managers and Administrators in a Global Perspective," *Municipal Yearbook 1999* (Washington, D.C.: International City Management Association, 1999).

8. See James H. Svara, *Official Leadership in the City: Patterns of Conflict and Cooperation* (New York: Oxford University Press, 1990), chap. 2.

9. Veto and election and veto statistics from Charles R. Adrian, "Forms of City Government in American History," *Municipal Yearbook, 1982* (Washington, D.C.: International City Management Association, 1982), 10.

10. Chester A. Newland, "Council-Manager Governance: Positive Alternative to Separation of Powers," *Public Management* 67 (July 1985): 8.

11. James H. Svara, "Roles and Relationships in Council-Manager Cities: Perspectives from Recent Research," in *Partnerships in Local Government* (Washington, D.C.: International City Management Association, 1989), 11.

12. Craig Wheeland, "Council Evaluation of the City Manager's Performance," *Municipal Year Book, 1995* (Washington, D.C.: International City Management Association, 1995), 13.

13. This is different from mayors who believe that the council-manager form should be replaced by the mayor-council form to give themselves access to executive leadership. This situation is discussed later in the chapter.

14. James H. Svara, "Key Leadership Issues," in Svara et al., *Facilitative Leadership in Local Government: Lessons from Successful Mayors and Chairpersons* (San Francisco: Jossey-Bass, 1994), 236–37.

15. Barbara Ferman, *Governing the Ungovernable City* (Philadelphia: Temple University Press, 1985), 120.

16. Voters in Los Angeles rejected expanded control over administrators protected by civil service in June 1993, as they had in 1983 and 1984. See Marc Lacey, "Civil Service Protections Are Upheld," *Los Angeles Times,* 9 June 1993, A-3.

17. Richard D. Bingham et al., *Managing Local Government* (Newbury Park, Calif.: Sage, 1991), 79–80.

18. Tari Renner and Victor DeSantis, "Contemporary Patterns and Trends in Municipal Government Structures," *Municipal Year Book 1993* (Washington, D.C.: International City/County Management Association, 1993), 57–69.

19. James H. Svara, *A Survey of America's City Councils* (Washington, D.C.: National League of Cities, 1991), 81.

20. National Commission on the State and Local Public Service, *Hard Truths/Tough Choices* (Albany, N.Y.: Nelson A. Rockefeller Institute of Government, 1993), 15.

21. Carl B. Stokes, *Promises of Power* (New York: Simon and Schuster, 1973), 132.

22. Edward C. Banfield, *Political Influence* (New York: Free Press, 1961).

23. Robert A. Dahl, *Who Governs?* (New Haven, Conn.: Yale University Press, 1961).

24. Alan Ehrenhalt, *The United States of Ambition* (New York: Random House 1991).

25. John J. Harrigan, *Political Change in the Metropolis*, 5th ed. (New York: HarperCollins, 1993), 230.

26. William D. Eggers and John O'Leary, *Revolution at the Roots* (New York: Free Press, 1995), 155.

27. Ferman, *Governing the Ungovernable City*, 202-5.

28. National Commission on the State and Local Public Service, *Hard Truths/Tough Choices*, 15.

29. Svara, "Key Leadership Issues," 219-27.

30. James H. Svara, "The Structural Reform Impulse in Local Government," *National Civic Review* 83 (Summer-Fall 1994): 323-47.

31. See Svara, "The Dichotomy Model as Aberration," *Public Administration Review* 58 (January/February 1998): 51-58.

32. John Nalbandian, "Reflections of a 'Pracademic' on the Logic of Politics and Administration," *Public Administration Review* 54 (November/December 1994): 531-36.

33. Svara, *Survey of America's City Councils*, 81.

34. John Nalbandian, *Professionalism in Local Government* (San Francisco: Jossey-Bass, 1991).

35. For example, should the new recreation center go into the neighborhood that has organized to pressure officials to select that area, or into the neighborhood where the need is greatest?

36. David Osborne and Ted A. Gaebler, *Reinventing Government* (Reading, Mass.: Addison-Wesley, 1992).

37. For an explanation of the conservative agenda for local government, see Eggers and O'Leary, *Revolution at the Roots*.

38. Gordon P. Whitaker and Kurt Jenne, "Improving City Managers' Leadership," *State and Local Government Review* 27 (Winter 1995): 90-91.

CHAPTER EIGHT

1. Tari Renner and Victor S. DeSantis, "Contemporary Patterns and Trends in Municipal Government Structures," in *The Municipal Year Book 1993* (Washington, D.C.: International City/County Management Association, 1993), 57-69.

2. Susan A. MacManus and Charles S. Bullock III, "Women and Racial/Ethnic Minorities in Mayoral and Council Positions," in *The Municipal Year Book 1993* (Washington, D.C.: International City/County Management Association, 1993), 70-84.

3. Susan Welch and Albert K. Karnig, "Correlates of Female Office-Holding in City Politics," *Journal of Politics* 41 (May 1979): 478-91.

4. Susan A. MacManus and Charles S. Bullock III, "Second Best? Women Mayors and Council Members: A New Test of the Desirability Hypothesis," in *Women in Politics: Outsiders or Insiders?* 2d ed., ed. Lois Lovelace Duke (Englewood Cliffs, N.J.: Prentice Hall, 1996).

5. Susan Welch and Timothy Bledsoe, *Urban Reform and Its Consequences* (Chicago: University of Chicago Press, 1988).

6. Peggy Heilig and Robert J. Mundt, *Your Voice at City Hall* (Albany: State University of New York Press, 1984); Charles S. Bullock III, "Turnout in Municipal Elections," *Policy Studies Review* 9 (Spring 1990): 539-50.

7. Robert Darcy, Susan Welch, and Janet Clark, *Women, Elections, and Representation*, 2d ed. (New York: Longman, 1994).

8. Susan A. MacManus and Charles S. Bullock III, "Electing Women to Local Office," in *Gender in Urban Research*, ed. Judith A. Garber and Robyne S. Turner (Thousand Oaks, Calif.: Sage, 1995), 155-77.

9. Compare Richard Engstrom and Michael McDonald, "The Election of Blacks to City Councils," *American Political Science Review* 75 (June 1981): 344-55; Susan Welch, "The Impact of At-large Elections on the Representation of Blacks and Hispanics," *Journal of Politics* 52 (November 1990): 1050-76.

10. MacManus and Bullock, "Women and Racial/Ethnic Minorities," 80.

11. See Susan A. MacManus and Lawrence Morehouse, "Redistricting in the Multi-Racial 21st Century: Changing Demographic and Socioeconomic Conditions Pose Important New Challenges," in *Race and Representation: National Political Science Review* 6, ed. Georgia A. Persons (1997): 116–36.

12. For an excellent overview of the birth of the Reform movement, see Richard Hofstadter, *The Age of Reform* (New York: Knopf, 1955); Edward C. Banfield and James Q. Wilson, *City Politics* (New York: Vintage, 1963); Samuel P. Hayes, "The Politics of Reform in Municipal Government in the Reform Era," *Pacific Northwest Quarterly* 55 (October 1964): 157–89.

13. Victor S. DeSantis and Tari Renner, "Term Limits and Turnover among Local Officials," *The Municipal Year Book 1994* (Washington, D.C.: International City/County Management Association, 1994), 36–42.

14. MacManus and Bullock, "Women and Racial/Ethnic Minorities," 81.

15. Other elements of the municipal reform movement were civil service systems for hiring public employees; competitive bidding among firms for government contracts; fair-election practices to prevent voting fraud; the Australian (secret) ballot; short ballots with fewer offices on which to vote; and initiative-and-referendum measures. Renner and DeSantis, "Contemporary Patterns," 57–58.

16. Carol A. Cassel, "Social Background Characteristics of Nonpartisan City Council Members: A Research Note," *Western Political Quarterly,* September 1985, 495–501; Welch and Bledsoe, *Urban Reform and Its Consequences.*

17. David R. Morgan and Robert E. England, *Managing Urban America,* 4th ed. (Chatham, N.J.: Chatham House, 1996), 44.

18. James Svara, *A Survey of America's City Councils* (Washington, D.C.: National League of Cities, 1991).

19. Victor DeSantis, Janay Pollock, and Kimberly Moore, *Use of Council Committees in Local Government,* Baseline Data Report, vol. 24, no. 3 (Washington, D.C.: International City/County Management Association, 1993).

20. Judith Meyers and John E. Kyle, *Critical Needs, Critical Choices: A Survey on Children and Families in America's Cities* (Washington, D.C.: National League of Cities, 1996).

21. DeSantis, Pollock, and Moore, *Use of Council Committees,* 9.

22. James H. Svara, *Official Leadership in the City: Patterns of Conflict and Cooperation* (New York: Oxford University Press, 1990), 122.

23. Another 4.7 percent, mostly smaller municipalities in New England, have a town meeting form, wherein all citizens of a town meet to approve the budget, select personnel, etc. Some 0.5 percent of small towns in New England rely on a representative town meeting format. All figures are from 1996. Tari Renner and Victor DeSantis, "Municipal Forms of Government: Issues and Trends," *The Municipal Year Book 1998* (Washington, D.C.: International City/County Management Association, 1998), 30–41.

24. Virginia Gray and Peter Eisinger, *American States and Cities* (New York: HarperCollins, 1991), 193.

25. Compare International City/County Management Association, *Elected Officials Handbooks,* 4th ed. (Washington, D.C.: ICMA, 1994), Book 1: *Setting Goals for Action;* Book 2: *Building a Policy-Making Team;* Book 3: *Setting Policies for Service Delivery;* Book 4: *Setting Policies for Internal Management;* Book 5: *Pursuing Personal Effectiveness.*

26. Kentucky League of Cities and Department of Local Government, *Handbook For Newly Elected City Officials, 1994 Edition* (Lexington, Ky., 1994), 3–4.

27. John Wade, *Dealing Effectively with the Media: What Local Government Officials Need to Know about Print, Radio, and Television Interviews* (Washington, D.C.: National League of Cities, 1993), 15.

28. Compare Arthur O'Sullivan, T.A. Sexton, and S.M. Sheffrin, *Property Taxes and Tax Revolts: The Legacy of Proposition 13* (New York: Cambridge University Press, 1995).

29. Timothy Bledsoe, *Careers in City Politics: The Case for Urban Democracy* (Pittsburgh: University of Pittsburgh Press, 1993).

30. Welch and Bledsoe, *Urban Reform,* 22.

31. Darcy, Welch, and Clark, *Women, Elections, and Representation.*

32. Lois Lovelace Duke, "Women and Sex Stereotypes: Cultural Reflections in the Mass Media," in Duke, *Women in Politics,* 229–39.

33. Susan A. MacManus, "It's Never Too Late to Run — and Win! The Graying of Women in Local Politics," *National Civic Review* 80 (Summer 1991): 294–306.

34. Linda L.M. Bennett and Stephen E. Bennett, "Changing Views About Gender Equality in Politics: Gradual Change and Lingering Doubts," in Duke, *Women in Politics,* 38.

35. Darcy, Welch, and Clark, *Women, Elections, and Representation,* 35.

36. Cal Clark and Janet Clark, "Whither the Gender Gap? Converging and Conflicting Attitudes among Women," in Duke, *Women in Politics,* 78–99.

37. Darcy, Welch, and Clark, *Women, Elections, and Representation,* 44.

38. J.L. Polinard, Robert D. Wrinkle, Tomas Longoria, and Norman E. Binder, *Electoral Structure and Urban Policy: The Impact on Mexican American Communities* (Armonk, N.Y.: M.E. Sharpe, 1994), 167.

39. Compare James Jennings, ed., *Blacks, Latinos, and Asians in Urban America* (Westport, Conn.: Praeger, 1994); Rufus P. Browning, Dale R. Marshall, and David H. Tabb, *Protest Is Not Enough: Struggle of Blacks and Hispanics for Equality in Urban Politics* (Berkeley: University of California Press, 1984); David Ian Lublin and Katherine Tate, "Racial Group Competition in Urban Elections," in *Classifying by Race,* ed. Paul E. Peterson (Washington, D.C.: Brookings Institution, 1995), 245–61; David Haywood Metz and Katherine Tate, "The Color of Urban Campaigns," in Peterson, *Classifying by Race,* 262–77; Paula D. McClain and Joseph Stewart Jr., *"Can We All Get Along?" Racial and Ethnic Politics in American Politics* (Boulder, Colo.: Westview, 1995); Katherine Tate, *From Protest to Politics: The New Black Voters in American Elections* (New York: Russell Sage Foundation, 1993); Rufus P. Browning, Dale Rogers Marshall, and David H. Tabb, *Racial Politics in American Cities,* 2d ed. (New York: Longman, 1997); Grace Yun, *Intergroup Cooperation in Cities: African, Asian, and Hispanic American Communities* (New York: Asian-American Federation of New York, 1993).

40. Rodolfo O. de la Garza, Louis DeSipio, F. Chris Garcia, John Garcia, and Angelo Falcon, *Latino Voices: Mexican, Puerto Rican, and Cuban Perspectives on American Politics* (Boulder, Colo.: Westview, 1992); Rodney Hero, *Latinos and the U.S. Political System* (Philadelphia: Temple University Press, 1992); Barry A. Kosmin and Ariela Keysar, "Party Political Preferences of U.S. Hispanics: The Varying Impact of Religion, Social Class, and Demographic Factors," *Ethnic and Racial Studies* 18 (April 1995): 336–47.

41. Herbert Barringer, Robert W. Gardner, and Michael J. Levin, *Asians and Pacific Islanders in the United States* (New York: Russell Sage Foundation, 1993).

42. Frederick C. Harris, "Religious Institutions and African American Political Mobilization," in Peterson, *Classifying by Race,* 278–313; Tate, *From Protest to Politics.*

43. Polinard et al., *Electoral Structure and Urban Policy,* 73.

44. Metz and Tate, "Color of Urban Campaigns," 272–73.

45. Bledsoe, *Careers in City Politics,* 49.

46. Susan A. MacManus, *Young v. Old: Generational Combat in the 21st Century* (Boulder, Colo.: Westview, 1996).

47. Svara, *Survey of America's City Councils.*

48. Evelina R. Moulder and Lisa A. Huffman, "Connecting to the Future: Governments On Line," *The Municipal Year Book 1996* (Washington, D.C.: International City/County Management Association, 1996), 24–30.

49. Mark A. Glaser and John W. Bardo, "A Five-Stage Approach for Improved Use of Citizen Surveys in Public Investment Decisions," *State and Local Government Review* 26 (Fall 1994): 161–72.

50. Virginia Municipal League, *Public Meetings/Public Hearings: Local Democracy in Action: Practical Help for Local Government Leaders* (Richmond, Va., February 1995), 4.

51. Thomas E. Cronin, *Direct Democracy: The Politics of Initiative, Referendum, and Recall* (Cambridge, Mass.: Harvard University Press, 1989).

CHAPTER NINE

1. Sarah McCally Morehouse, *State Politics, Parties, and Policy* (New York: Holt, Rinehart, and Winston, 1981), 29.
2. David R. Mayhew, *Placing Parties in American Politics* (Princeton, N.J.: Princeton University Press, 1986), 212–17.
3. V.O. Key Jr., *American State Politics: An Introduction* (New York: Knopf, 1956), 271, 287.
4. *The Public Perspective,* October/November 1995, 53.
5. John F. Bibby and Thomas M. Holbrook, "Parties and Elections," in *Politics in the American States: A Comparative Analysis,* 6th ed., ed. Virginia Gray and Herbert Jacob (Washington, D.C.: CQ Press, 1996), 103–9.
6. A. James Reichley, *The Life of the Parties: A History of American Political Parties* (New York: Free Press, 1992), 385.
7. Ibid., 386–91; Cornelius P. Cotter, James L. Gibson, John F. Bibby, and Robert J. Huckshorn, *Party Organizations in American Politics* (New York: Praeger, 1984), 13–39.
8. Mike Flaherty, "State GOP Steps Up Telemarketing as It Settles into New Headquarters," *Wisconsin State Journal,* 11 May 1995, 1B.
9. Robert Biersack, "Hard Facts and Soft Money: State Party Finance in the 1992 Federal Elections," in *The State of the Parties: the Changing Role of Contemporary Parties,* ed. Daniel M. Shea and John C. Green (Lanham, Md.: Rowman and Littlefield, 1994), 117–22.
10. Advisory Commission on Intergovernmental Relations, *The Transformation of American Politics: Implications for Federalism* (Washington, D.C.: Government Printing Office, 1986), 115; Reichley, *Life of the Parties,* 389–90.
11. Reichley, *Life of the Parties,* 390.
12. Ibid., 387–91; Cotter et al., *Party Organizations;* ACIR, *Transformation of American Politics.*
13. Paul S. Herrnson, "The Revitalization of National Party Organizations," in *The Parties Respond: Changes in the American Party System,* 2d ed., ed. L. Sandy Maisel (Boulder, Colo.: Westview, 1994), 45–68.
14. Mildred Schwartz, *The Party Network: the Robust Organization of the Illinois Republicans* (Madison: University of Wisconsin Press, 1990).
15. Donald P. Baker, "Va. Democratic Chief Survives Bid to Oust Him," *Washington Post,* 10 June 1992, D1.
16. Byron E. Shafer, *Postwar Politics in the G-7: Eras and Orders in Comparative Perspective* (Madison: University of Wisconsin Press, 1996), 32.
17. Anthony Gierzynski, *Legislative Party Campaign Committees in the American States* (Lexington: University of Kentucky Press, 1992), 11–14; Daniel M. Shea, *Transforming Democracy: Legislative Campaign Committees and the Political Parties* (Albany: State University of New York Press, 1995), 31–46; Cindy Simon Rosenthal, "New Party or Campaign Bank Account? Explaining the Rise of State Legislative Campaign Committees," *Legislative Studies Quarterly* 20 (May 1995): 249–68.
18. Rosenthal, "New Party or Campaign Bank Account?" 252.
19. "Guru in Ohio," *Congressional Quarterly Weekly Report,* 4 November 1989, 2977.
20. Alan Ehrenhalt, "How a Party of Enthusiasts Keeps Its Hammerlock on a State Legislature," *Governing,* June 1989, 28–33.
21. Kent D. Redfield, "Candidates, Campaigns and Cash," *Comparative State Politics* 14 (1993): 17–25.
22. Gierzynski, *Legislative Party Campaign Committees,* 55.
23. Frank J. Sorauf, *Inside Campaign Finance: Myths and Realities* (New Haven, Conn.: Yale University Press, 1992), 120; Shea, *Transforming Democracy.*
24. John P. Frendreis, Alan R. Gitelson, Gregory Flemming, and Anne Lyzell, "Local Parties and Legislative Races in 1992," in Shea and Green, *State of the Parties,* 140.
25. John P. Frendreis, James L.Gibson, and Laura L. Vertz, "The Electoral Relevance of Local Party Organizations," *American Political Science Review* 84 (March 1990): 226–35.

26. Samuel J. Eldersveld, *Political Parties in American Society* (New York: Basic Books, 1982), 145.

27. Paul Allen Beck, Audrey Haynes, Russell Dalton, and Robert Huckfeldt, "Party Effort at the Grass Roots: Local Parties Campaigning in 1992," paper presented at the annual meeting of the Midwest Political Science Association, Chicago, 14–16 April 1994.

28. Cornelius P. Cotter and Bernard Hennessy, *Politics without Power: National Party Committees* (New York: Atherton, 1964).

29. David S. Broder, "The Force," *Washington Post,* 2 April 1986, A23.

30. V.O. Key Jr., *Politics, Parties, and Pressure Groups,* 5th ed. (New York: Crowell, 1964), 315.

31. David S. Broder, *The Party's Over: The Failure of American Politics* (New York: Harper and Row, 1971).

CHAPTER TEN

1. Harrell R. Rodgers Jr. and Charles S. Bullock III, *Law and Social Change: Civil Rights Laws and Their Consequences* (New York: McGraw-Hill, 1972), 21–22; *Report of the U.S. Commission on Civil Rights, 1959* (Washington, D.C.: Government Printing Office, 1959): 80; U.S. Commission on Civil Rights, *Voting, 1961* (Washington, D.C.: Government Printing Office, 1961): passim.

2. Registration figures by race for many southern counties are reported in U.S. Civil Rights Commission, *Political Participation* (Washington, D.C.: Government Printing Office, 1968), 224–56.

3. The "trigger mechanism" of the 1965 Voting Rights Act specified that if less than 50 percent of the voting-age population registered or voted in 1964 and the jurisdiction had a registration test or device in place, the prerequisite could not be used and the jurisdiction would be subject to other restrictions.

4. Rodgers and Bullock, *Law and Social Change,* 33–34.

5. *City of Mobile* v. *Bolden,* 446 U.S. 55 (1980).

6. Abigail M. Thernstrom, *Whose Votes Count?* (Cambridge, Mass.: Harvard University Press, 1987), esp. chaps. 5 and 6.

7. Testimony of Donald L. Horowitz before the Senate Subcommittee on the Constitution, Committee on the Judiciary, on the Voting Rights Act (Washington, D.C.: Government Printing Office, 1982), 1312.

8. *Thornburg* v. *Gingles,* 478 U.S. 30 (1986).

9. As examples of this extensive literature, see Theodore Robinson and Thomas Dye, "Reformism and Representation on City Councils," *Social Science Quarterly* 59 (June 1978): 133–41; and Albert Karnig and Susan Welch, "Electoral Structure and Black Representation on City Councils," *Social Science Quarterly,* March 1982, 99–114. A dissent from this view is represented by Susan A. MacManus, "City Council Election Procedures and Minority Representation," *Social Science Quarterly* 59 (June 1978): 153–61.

10. Richard Engstrom and Michael McDonald, "The Election of Blacks to City Councils: Clarifying the Impact of Electoral Arrangements on the Seats/Population Relationship," *American Political Science Review* 75 (June 1981): 344–54.

11. Jeffrey S. Zax, "Election Methods, Black and Hispanic City Council Membership," *Social Science Quarterly* 71 (June 1990): 339–55.

12. Charles S. Bullock III and Susan A. MacManus, "Testing Assumptions of the Totality-of-the-Circumstances Test: An Analysis of the Impact of Structures on Black Descriptive Representation," *American Politics Quarterly* 21 (July 1993): 297.

13. Susan Welch, "The Impact of At-Large Elections on the Representation of Blacks and Hispanics," *Journal of Politics* 52 (November 1990): 1051–76.

14. Nicholas O. Alozie, "Socioeconomic Factors and Black Electoral Gains: Black Resources and White Middle-Class Expansion," paper presented at the annual meeting of the Southwestern Political Science Association, Fort Worth, Tex., 28–31 March 1990.

15. Chandler Davidson and Bernard Grofman, eds., *Quiet Revolution in the South* (Princeton, N.J.: Princeton University Press, 1994), include chapters prepared by local

academics and attorneys for the eight southern states largely or wholly covered by Section 5 of the Voting Rights Act.

16. Charles S. Bullock III, "Section 2 of the Voting Rights Act, Districting Formats, and the Election of African-Americans," *Journal of Politics* 56 (November 1994): 1098–1105.

17. Chandler Davidson and George Korbel, "At-Large Elections and Minority Group Representation: A Re-Examination of Historical and Contemporary Evidence," *Journal of Politics* 43 (November 1981): 982–1005.

18. MacManus, "City Council Election Procedures and Minority Representation," 153–61; Delbert A. Taebel, "Minority Representation on City Councils," *Social Science Quarterly* 59 (June 1979): 142–52.

19. Zax, "Election Methods," 351.

20. Charles S. Bullock III and Susan A. MacManus, "Structural Features of Municipalities and the Incidence of Hispanic Councilmembers," *Social Science Quarterly* 71 (December 1990): 665–81.

21. Welch, "Impact of At-Large Elections," 1070.

22. J.L. Polinard, Robert D. Wrinkle, Tomas Longoria, and Norman E. Binder, *Electoral Structure and Urban Policy: The Impact on Mexican American Communities* (Armonk, N.Y.: M.E. Sharpe, 1994), 59–60.

23. See, for example, Michelle A. Saint-Germain, "Patterns of Legislative Opportunity in Arizona: Sex, Race, and Ethnicity," in *United States Electoral Systems: Their Impact on Women and Minorities,* ed. Wilma Rule and Joseph F. Zimmerman (New York: Greenwood, 1992), 119–28.

24. Robert Darcy, Susan Welch, and Janet Clark, "Women Candidates in Single- and Multi-Member Districts," *Social Science Quarterly* 66 (December 1985): 945–53; Susan Welch and Donley Studlar, "The Impact of Multi-Member Districts on the Representation of Women in Britain and the United States," *Journal of Politics* 52 (May 1990): 391–412; M. Margaret Conway, "Creative Multimember Redistricting and Representation of Women and Minorities in the Maryland Legislature," in Rule and Zimmerman, *United States Electoral Systems,* 91–109.

25. Conway, "Creative Multimember Redistricting," notes that conditions in Maryland result in MMDs not disadvantaging minorities while simultaneously promoting the numbers of female legislators.

26. Victor DeSantis and Tari Renner, "Minority and Gender Representation in American County Legislatures: The Effect of Election Systems," in Rule and Zimmerman, *United States Electoral Systems,* 150–51.

27. Susan Welch and Rebekah Herrick, "The Impact of At-Large Elections on the Representation of Minority Women," in Rule and Zimmerman, *United States Electoral Systems,* 161.

28. Susan A. MacManus and Charles S. Bullock III, "Second Best? Women Mayors and Council Members: A New Test of the Desirability Thesis," in *Women in Politics: Outsiders or Insiders?* ed. Lois L. Duke (Englewood Cliffs, N.J.: Prentice Hall, 1995), 122.

29. On the incidence of MMDs well before they were challenged as diluting the influence of racial minorities, see Maurice Klain, "A New Look at the Constituencies: The Need for a Recount and a Reappraisal," *American Political Science Review* 49 (December 1955): 1105–19. For a relatively current enumeration of where MMDs are used, see Richard G. Niemi, Simon Jackman, and Laura R. Winsky, "Candidacies and Competitiveness in Multi-member Districts," *Legislative Studies Quarterly* 10 (November 1991): 91–109.

30. Charles S. Bullock III and Ronald Keith Gaddie, "Changing from Multimember to Single-Member Districts: Partisan, Racial, and Gender Consequences," *State and Local Government Review* 25 (Fall 1993): 162.

31. Charles S. Bullock III, "Minorities in State Legislatures," in *Changing Patterns in State Legislative Careers,* ed. Gary F. Moncrief and Joel A. Thompson (Ann Arbor: University of Michigan Press, 1992), 54–55.

32. On Florida, see Anita Pritchard, "Changes in Electoral Structure and the Success of Women Candidates: The Case of Florida," *Social Science Quarterly* 73 (March 1992): 60–70. Florida and the Carolinas are examined in Bullock and Gaddie, "Changing from Multimember to Single-member Districts."

33. *Chisom v. Roemer,* 111 S.Ct. 2354 (1991).
34. Peggy Heilig and Robert J. Mundt, *Your Voice at City Hall: The Politics, Procedures and Policies of District Representation* (Albany: State University of New York Press, 1984), 77.
35. *Holder v. Hall,* 512 U.S. 874; 129 L.Ed.2d 687 (1994).
36. In *McGhee v. Granville County,* 860 F.2d 110 (1988), the Fourth Circuit Court of Appeals held that the only remedy that a trial court could impose was SMDs, even though no such plan could produce three districts in which African Americans would be the majority population.
37. David H. Everson, "The Effect of the 'Cutback' on the Representation of Women and Minorities in the Illinois General Assembly," in Rule and Zimmerman, *United States Electoral Systems,* 112.
38. Richard L. Cole, Delbert A. Taebel, and Richard L. Engstrom, "Cumulative Voting in a Municipal Election: A Note on Voter Reactions and Electoral Consequences," *Western Political Quarterly* 43 (March 1990): 191–99.
39. Robert R. Brischetto and Richard L. Engstrom, "Cumulative Voting and Latino Representation: Exit Surveys in Fifteen Texas Communities," *Social Science Quarterly* 78 (December 1997): 973–91.
40. Robert Brischetto, "Cumulative Voting as an Alternative to Districting," *National Civic Review* 84 (Fall-Winter 1995): 347–54.
41. Richard L. Engstrom and Charles J. Barrilleaux, "Native-Americans and Cumulative Voting: The Sisseton-Wahpeton Sioux," *Social Science Quarterly* 73 (June 1991): 388–93.
42. Edward Still, "Cumulative Voting and Limited Voting in Alabama," in Rule and Zimmerman, *United States Electoral Systems,* 183–96.
43. Brischetto and Engstrom, "Cumulative Voting and Latino Representation," 980.
44. Still, "Cumulative Voting and Limited Voting in Alabama," 184–91, is relied on for many of the ideas in this paragraph.
45. Everson, "Effect of the 'Cutback,'" 115–17.
46. Charles S. Bullock III and A. Brock Smith, "Black Success in Local Runoff Elections," *Journal of Politics* 52 (November 1990): 1205–22.
47. Charles S. Bullock III and Ronald Keith Gaddie, "Runoffs in Jesse Jackson's Backyard," *Social Science Quarterly* 75 (June 1994): 446–54.
48. Bullock and MacManus, "Testing Assumptions," 297.
49. Bullock and MacManus, "Structural Features of Municipalities," 675–76.
50. Charles S. Bullock III and Loch K. Johnson, *Runoff Elections in the United States* (Chapel Hill: University of North Carolina Press, 1992), 64–70.
51. Arnold Fleischmann and Lana Stein, "Minority and Female Success in Municipal Runoff Elections," *Social Science Quarterly* 68 (June 1987): 378–85.
52. Comparisons of the number of successes under a runoff rule with those under a plurality rule assume that the numbers of candidates and the distribution of votes would have been quite similar even with a different electoral rule. Such assumptions may, of course, be erroneous.
53. Bullock and MacManus, "Municipal Electoral Structure," 76–89.
54. The next two paragraphs draw on Bullock and Johnson, *Runoff Primaries in the United States,* although the source for the earlier material is Cortez A.M. Ewing, *Primary Elections in the South: A Study in Uniparty Politics* (Norman: University of Oklahoma Press, 1953).
55. Raymond E. Wolfinger and Steven J. Rosenstone, *Who Votes* (New Haven, Conn.: Yale University Press, 1980), 71–76.
56. V.O. Key Jr., *Southern Politics in State and Nation* (New York: Knopf, 1949), 538.
57. "20 Million 'Motor Voters,'" *New York Times,* 16 October 1996, A13.
58. Data provided by Norma Lyons of the Elections Division of Georgia's Office of the Secretary of State. Similar nationwide figures are reported in "Motor Voter: Newest Method of Voter Registration Motivating Those with a Mission," *Athens Banner-Herald,* 1 October 1996, 22. In Pasco County, Florida, reports from the driver's license bureau were that most people signed up to vote, while at the food stamp offices very few

did. John Harwood, "In a Surprise for Everyone, Motor-Voter Law Is Providing a Boost for GOP, Not Democrats," *Wall Street Journal,* 11 June 1996, A16.

59. "Study: 9 Million Register Via Motor Voter," *Atlanta Journal,* 15 October 1996, A6.

60. Harwood, "In a Surprise for Everyone."

61. Alan Greenblatt, "Court Rejects 'Motor Voter' Case, but the Battle Isn't Over," *Congressional Quarterly* 54 (27 January 1996): 233.

62. Drummond Ayres Jr., "Motor Voter Law Doesn't Boost Election Turnout," *Atlanta Journal-Constitution,* 9 December 1995, A7.

63. Calculated from data in U.S. Bureau of the Census, Current Population Reports, Series P-20, No. 370, *Voting and Registration in the Election of November 1980* (Washington, D.C: Government Printing Office, 1982), 80.

64. Extensive source material on vote-by-mail can be found in Margaret Rosenfield, *All-Mail-Ballot Elections* (Washington, D.C.: National Clearinghouse on Election Administration, 1995), and this source is drawn on heavily in this section.

65. "More Voters Turn Out at Mailbox," *Atlanta Journal,* 6 December 1995, A4.

66. Susan A. MacManus and Charles S. Bullock III, "Women and Racial/Ethnic Minorities in Mayoral and Council Positions," *Municipal Year Book 1993* (Washington, D.C.: International City/County Management Association, 1993), 70–84.

67. Figures on the growth in the number of Hispanic elected officials from 1984 to 1994 come from *1994 National Roster of Hispanic Elected Officials* (Los Angeles: NALEO Educational Fund, 1994).

68. Albert A. Karnig and Susan Welch, "Sex and Ethnic Differences in Municipal Representation," *Social Science Quarterly* 60 (December 1979): 467.

69. Welch, "Impact of At-Large Elections," 1067.

70. William A.V. Clark and Peter A. Morrison, "Demographic Paradoxes in the Los Angeles Voting Rights Case," *Evaluation Review* 15 (December 1991): 716–18.

71. Douglas D. Abel and Bruce I. Oppenheimer, "Candidate Emergence in a Majority Hispanic District: The 29th District in Texas," in *Who Runs for Congress: Ambition, Context, and Candidate Emergence,* ed. Thomas A. Kazee (Washington, D.C.: CQ Press, 1994), 45–66.

72. Data on numbers of female officeholders come from "Women in Elective Office 1995," Center for the American Woman and Politics, Eagleton Institute of Politics, Rutgers University, 1995.

73. Karnig and Walter, "Election of Women to City Councils," 607; Susan Welch and Albert Karnig, "Correlates of Female Officeholding in City Politics," *Journal of Politics* 41 (May 1979): 484.

74. Karnig and Welch, "Sex and Ethnic Differences," 469.

75. MacManus and Bullock, "Women and Racial/Ethnic Minorities," 70–84.

76. Karnig and Walter, "Election of Women to City Councils," 607.

77. Charles S. Bullock III, "Women Candidates and Success at the County Level," paper presented at the annual meeting of the Southern Political Science Association, Atlanta, 8–10 November 1990, provides data on Georgia and South Carolina.

78. On Florida, see Susan A. MacManus, "Representation at the Local Level in Florida: County Commissions, School Boards, and City Councils," in *Reapportionment and Representation in Florida: A Historical Collection,* ed. Susan A. MacManus (Tampa: University of South Florida, Intrabay Innovation Institute, 1991): 493–538.

79. See, for example, Davidson and Korbel, "At-Large Elections and Minority-Group Representation," 982–1005; Davidson and Grofman, *Quiet Revolution in the South.*

80. Bullock, "Effects of Redistricting on Black Representation"; idem, "Racial Composition of District Population and the Election of African-American Legislators," *Southeastern Political Review* 24 (December 1996): 611–28.

81. *Miller v. Johnson,* 515 U.S. 900 (1995).

82. Margaret Edds, *Claiming the Dream* (Chapel Hill, N.C.: Algonquin Books, 1990), 240.

83. John Hull Mollenkopf, *A Phoenix in the Ashes: The Rise and Fall of the Koch Coalition in New York City Politics* (Princeton, N.J.: Princeton University Press, 1992): 178.

84. *Evans-Novak Political Report* 29 (28 November 1995): 7.

85. Stephan Thernstrom and Abigail Thernstrom, *American in Black and White: One Nation, Indivisible* (New York: Simon and Schuster, 1997), 295.

86. Bullock and MacManus, "Municipal Electoral Structure and the Election of Councilwomen," 85.
87. Karnig and Walter, "Elections of Women to City Councils," 611.
88. Bullock, "Women Candidates and Success at the County Level."
89. See, for example, a report produced in Georgia, a state that invariably falls near the bottom of the list in turnout: Georgia Vote Commission, *Proposals for Increased Voter Participation and Ballot Security* (Atlanta: Office of the Secretary of State, 1997).

CHAPTER ELEVEN

1. For thorough reviews of the interest systems of many of the states, see the collections edited by Ronald J. Hrebenar and Clive S. Thomas: *Interest Group Politics in the American West* (Salt Lake City: University of Utah Press, 1987); *Interest Group Politics in the Southern States* (Tuscaloosa: University of Alabama Press, 1992); *Interest Group Politics in the Northeastern States* (University Park: Pennsylvania State University Press, 1993); *Interest Group Politics in the Midwest States* (Ames: Iowa State University Press, 1993).
2. For works emphasizing the dangers of organized interests, see Theodore Lowi, *The End of Liberalism* (New York: Norton, 1969); Grant McConnell, *Private Power and American Democracy* (New York: Knopf, 1966); Kay Lehman Schlozman and John T. Tierney, *Organized Interests and American Democracy* (New York: Harper and Row, 1986). For a more positive view, see David Truman, *The Governmental Process* (New York: Knopf, 1951).
3. Robert Salisbury, "Interest Representation: The Dominance of Institutions," *American Political Science Review* 78 (March 1984): 64–76.
4. For an excellent discussion of these kinds of organizations, see Clive S. Thomas and Ronald J. Hrebenar, "Interest Groups in the States," in *Politics in the American States,* 6th ed., ed. Virginia Gray and Herbert Jacob (Washington, D.C.: CQ Press, 1996), 122–58. A good example of such organizations, long active in Washington and now appearing in the states, are think tanks. For an interesting discussion of state think tanks, see Charles M. Lane and Glen A. Halva-Neubauer, "Selling Ideas: Assessing the Impact of State-Level Conservative Think Tanks on Southern Legislatures," paper presented at the annual meeting of the Midwest Political Science Association, Chicago, April 1995.
5. Truman, *Governmental Process.*
6. Mancur Olson Jr., *The Logic of Collective Action* (Cambridge, Mass.: Harvard University Press, 1965).
7. Pamela L. Brinegar and Kara L. Schmit, "State Occupational Professional Licensure," *Book of the States, 1992–93*, vol. 29 (Lexington, Ky.: Council of State Governments, 1992), 567–72.
8. David C. King and Jack L. Walker, "The Provision of Benefits by Interest Groups in the United States," *Journal of Politics* 54 (May 1992): 394–426. For a general review of this literature, see Allan J. Cigler, "Interest Groups: A Subfield in Search of an Identity," in *Political Science: Looking to the Future,* vol. 4, ed. William Crotty (Evanston, Ill.: Northwestern University Press, 1991), 99–135.
9. They actually asked about 16, but we are able to compare the results for these 12 to similar results for state interests.
10. David Lowery and Virginia Gray, "How Similar are State and National Interest Organizations?" *Comparative State Politics* 18, no. 1 (February 1996): 1–16.
11. Schlozman and Tierney, *Organized Interests and American Democracy;* Salisbury, "Interest Representation."
12. Given our focus on interest organizations, we excluded individual lobbyists and state agencies from the lobbying registration lists used to construct these and other data reported in this chapter. For a general description of our data sources, see Virginia Gray and David Lowery, *The Population Ecology of Interest Representation: Lobbying Communities in the American States* (Ann Arbor: University of Michigan Press, 1996).
13. Virginia Gray and David Lowery, "The Demography of Interest Organization Communities: Institutions, Associations, and Membership Groups," *American Politics Quarterly* 23 (January 1995): 3–32.

14. Schlozman and Tierney, *Organized Interests and American Democracy;* Howard E. Aldrich, Udo Staber, Catherine Zimmer, and John J. Beggs, "Minimalism and Organizational Mortality: Patterns of Disbanding Among U.S. Trade Associations, 1900–1983," in *Organizational Evolution: New Directions,* ed. Jitendra V. Singh (Newbury Park, Calif.: Sage, 1990), 21–52.

15. Mancur Olson Jr., *The Rise and Decline of Nations* (New Haven, Conn.: Yale University Press, 1982).

16. Gray and Lowery, "Demography of Interest Organization Communities."

17. Ibid.

18. James Q. Wilson, *Political Organizations* (New York: Basic Books, 1973), 263.

19. For a discussion of niche theory, see Virginia Gray and David Lowery, "A Niche Theory of Interest Representation," *Journal of Politics* 59 (March 1996): 91–111. For an excellent example of competition via partitioning, see Michael G. Bath, "Think Tanks, Patrons, and Funding Niches: Noncompetitive Methods of Competition," paper presented at the annual meeting of the Midwest Political Science Association, Chicago, April 1995.

20. Gray and Lowery, "Niche Theory of Interest Representation."

21. Lowery and Gray, "How Similar are State and National Interest Organizations?"

22. David C. King and Jack L. Walker Jr., "The Origins and Maintenance of Groups in America," in *Mobilizing Interest Groups in America: Patrons, Professionals, and Social Movements,* ed. Jack L. Walker Jr. (Ann Arbor: University of Michigan Press), 81.

23. In order to compare the state and federal surveys, King and Walker's categories were collapsed somewhat. These and other measurement choices are discussed in Lowery and Gray, "How Alike are State and National Interest Organizations?"

24. Clive S. Thomas and Ronald J. Hrebenar, "Nationalization of Interest Groups and Lobbying in the States," in *Interest Group Politics,* 3d ed., ed. Allan J. Cigler and Burdett A. Loomis (Washington, D.C.: CQ Press, 1991).

25. Gray and Lowery, "Demography of Interest Organization Communities."

26. Gray and Lowery, *Population Ecology of Interest Representation.*

27. David Lowery and Virginia Gray, "The Nationalization of State Interest Group System Density and Diversity," *Social Science Quarterly* 75 (June 1994): 368–77.

28. David Lowery and Virginia Gray, "The Population Ecology of Gucci Gulch, or the Natural Regulation of Interest Group Numbers in the American States," *American Journal of Political Science* 39 (February 1995): 1–29.

29. Olson, *Rise and Decline of Nations.*

30. Virginia Gray and David Lowery, "Environmental Limits on the Diversity of State Interest Group Systems: A Population Ecology Simulation," *Political Research Quarterly* 76 (March 1996): 103–18.

31. Gray and Lowery, *Population Ecology of Interest Representation.*

32. E.E. Schattschneider, *The Semisovereign People* (New York: Holt, Rinehart, and Winston, 1960); Kay Lehman Schlozman, "What Accent the Heavenly Chorus? Political Equality and the American Pressure System," *Journal of Politics* 46 (November 1984): 1006–32.

33. Gray and Lowery, *Population Ecology of Interest Representation.*

34. Ibid.

35. Cynthia Opheim, "Explaining the Differences in State Lobbying Regulation," *Western Political Quarterly* 44 (June 1991): 405.

36. Clive S. Thomas and Ronald J. Hrebenar, "The Regulation of Interest Groups and Lobbying in the Fifty States: Some Preliminary Findings," paper presented at the annual meeting of the Midwest Political Science Association, Chicago, April 1991.

37. Opheim, "Explaining the Differences," 409.

38. Ibid., 418.

39. Results from these interviews — carried out in the spring and summer of 1994 — are presented in Gray and Lowery, *Population Ecology of Interest Representation,* and in Virginia Gray and David Lowery, "The World of Contract Lobbying," *Comparative State Politics* 17, no. 5 (1996): 31–40.

40. David Lowery and Virginia Gray, "Do Lobbying Regulations Influence Lobbying Registrations?" *Social Science Quarterly* 75 (June 1994): 382–84; Kennith G. Hunter,

Laura Ann Wilson, and Gregory G. Brunk, "Social Complexity and Interest-Group Lobbying in the American States," *Journal of Politics* 53 (May 1991): 488–503. But for an alternative view, see Keith E. Hamm, Andrew R. Weber, and R. Bruce Anderson, "The Impact of Lobbying Laws and Their Enforcement: A Contrasting View," *Social Science Quarterly* 75 (June 1994): 378–81.

41. Gray and Lowery, "World of Contract Lobbying."

42. Thomas and Hrebenar, "Interest Groups in the States," 142; Gray and Lowery, "World of Contract Lobbying."

43. Gray and Lowery, "World of Contract Lobbying."

44. Clive S. Thomas and Ronald J. Hrebenar, "Political Action Committees in the American States: Some Preliminary Findings," paper presented at the annual meeting of the American Political Science Association, Washington, D.C., 29 August–1 September 1991.

45. Thomas and Hrebenar, "Political Action Committees."

46. Ann B. Matasar, *Corporate PACs and Federal Campaign Laws: Use or Abuse of Power* (New York: Quorum Books, 1986), 52; Larry J. Sabato, *PAC Power: Inside the World of Political Action Committees* (New York: Norton, 1984), 124; Frank J. Sorauf, *What Price PACs?* (New York: Twentieth Century Fund, 1984), 73.

47. Richard D. Hall and Frank W. Wayman, "Buying Time: Moneyed Interests and the Mobilization of Bias in Congressional Committees," *American Political Science Review* 84 (September 1990): 797–820.

48. Ibid., 803–4; John R. Wright, "PAC Contributions, Lobbying, and Representation," *Journal of Politics* 51 (August 1989): 725–26; James F. Herndon, "Access, Record, and Competition as Influences on Interest Group Contributions to Congressional Campaigns," *Journal of Politics* 44 (November 1982): 1001.

49. Hall and Wayman, "Buying Time."

50. Virginia Gray and David Lowery, "Reconceptualizing PAC Formation; It's Not a Collective Action Problem, and It May Be an Arms Race," *American Politics Quarterly* 25 (October 1997); 319–46.

51. Truman, *Governmental Process,* 502–3.

52. Lowi, *End of Liberalism;* McConnell, *Private Power and American Democracy;* Schattschneider, *Semisovereign People.*

53. For a review of this literature, see William C. Mitchell and Michael C. Munger, "Economic Models of Interest Groups," *American Journal of Political Science* 35 (May 1991): 512–46.

54. Jack L. Walker, *Mobilizing Interest Groups in America: Patrons, Professionals, and Social Movements* (Ann Arbor: University of Michigan Press, 1991).

55. John P. Heinz, Edward O. Laumann, Robert L. Nelson, and Robert Salisbury, *The Hollow Core* (Cambridge, Mass.: Harvard University Press, 1993).

56. Robert Salisbury, "The Paradox of Interest Groups in Washington: More Groups, Less Clout," in *The New American Political System,* 2d ed., ed. Anthony King (Washington, D.C.: American Enterprise Institute, 1990), 203–30.

57. Harmon L. Zeigler and Hendrik van Dalen, "Interest Groups in State Politics," in *Politics in the American States,* 3d ed., ed. Herbert Jacob and Kenneth Vines (Boston: Little, Brown, 1976), 93–136.

58. This train of logic can be followed through George Stigler, "The Theory of Economic Regulation," *Bell Journal of Economics and Management Science* 2 (Spring 1971): 3–21; Sam Pelzman, "Towards a More General Theory of Regulation," *Journal of Law and Economics* 19 (August 1976): 211–40; Peter J. Coughlin, Dennis C. Mueller, and Peter Murrell, "Electoral Politics, Interest Groups, and the Size of Government," *Economic Inquiry* 28 (October 1990): 682–705; Dennis G. Mueller and Peter Murrell, "Interest Groups and the Size of Government," *Public Choice* 48, no. 1 (1986): 125–45; and Olson, *Rise and Decline of Nations.*

59. Gray and Lowery, *Population Ecology of Interest Representation.*

60. Figures 11.7A and 11,7B are reprinted by permission of the University of Texas Press from Gray and Lowery, "Niche Theory of Interest Representation."

61. Virginia Gray and David Lowery, "Interest Representation and Democratic Gridlock," *Legislative Studies Quarterly* 20 (November 1995): 531–52.

62. See note 39.
63. Belle Zeller, *American State Legislatures*, 2d ed. (New York: Crowell, 1954); Sarah McCally Morehouse, *State Politics, Parties, and Policy* (New York: Holt, Rinehart and Winston, 1981).
64. Hrebenar and Thomas, *Interest Group Politics in the American West; Interest Group Politics in the Southern States; Interest Group Politics in the Northeastern States; Interest Group Politics in the Midwest States.*
65. Reprinted by permission of CQ Press from Thomas and Hrebenar, "Interest Groups in the States," 152.
66. Olson, *Rise and Decline of Nations.*
67. Salisbury, "Paradox of Interest Groups."
68. Thomas and Hrebenar, "Interest Groups in the States," 155.
69. Gray and Lowery, *Population Ecology of Interest Representation.*
70. Thomas and Hrebenar, "Interest Groups in the States," 155.
71. Ibid., 150.
72. Charles W. Wiggins, Keith E. Hamm, and Charles G. Bell, "Interest-Group and Party Influence Agents in the Legislative Process: A Comparative State Analysis," *Journal of Politics* 54 (February 1994): 82–100.
73. Gray and Lowery, "World of Contract Lobbying."

CHAPTER TWELVE

1. James C. Garand, "New Perspectives on the Size of Government in the American States: A Pooled Analysis, 1945–1984," paper presented at the Conference on State Economic Development, Chicago, May 1993; Paul Peterson, *The Price of Federalism* (Washington, D.C.: Brookings Institution, 1995).
2. Richard Hofferbert, *The Study of Public Policy* (Indianapolis: Bobbs-Merrill, 1974); Robert Salisbury, "The Analysis of Public Policy: A Search for Theories and Roles," in *Political Science and Public Policy,* ed. Austin Ranney (Chicago: Markham, 1968).
3. Thomas Dye, *Politics, Economics, and the Public* (Chicago: Rand McNally, 1966).
4. Robert Erikson, Gerald Wright Jr., and John McIver, *Statehouse Democracy* (Cambridge, England: Cambridge University Press, 1993).
5. Heinz Eulau and Kenneth Prewitt, *Labyrinths of Democracy* (Indianapolis: Bobbs-Merrill, 1973).
6. Theodore Lowi, *The End of Liberalism: The Second Republic of the United States* (New York: Norton, 1979); Jeffrey Berry, *The Interest Group Society* (Boston: Little, Brown, 1984); Mancur Olson, *The Rise and Decline of Nations* (New Haven, Conn.: Yale University Press, 1982).
7. Virginia Gray and David Lowery, "The Diversity of State Interest Group Systems," *Political Research Quarterly* 46 (March 1993): 81–98; David Lowery and Virginia Gray, "The Nationalization of State Interest Group Diversity and Density," *Social Science Quarterly* 75 (June 1994): 368–77; idem, "The Population Ecology of Gucci Gulch, or the Natural Regulation of Interest Group Numbers in the American States," *American Journal of Political Science* 39 (February 1995): 1–29.
8. David Lowery and Virginia Gray, "The Compensatory Impact of State Industrial Policy: An Empirical Assessment," *Social Science Quarterly* 76 (June 1995): 438–46; Allen B. Breirly and Richard Feiock, "Accounting for State Economic Growth: A Production Function Approach," *Political Research Quarterly* 46 (1993): 657–70. See also Olson, *Rise and Decline of Nations,* and James C. Garand, "Changing Patterns of Relative State Economic Growth over Time: Limitations on Cross-Sectional Tests of Olson's Thesis," *Western Political Quarterly* 45 (June 1992): 469–83.
9. E.E. Schattschneider, *The Semi-Sovereign People: A Realist's View of Democracy in America* (New York: Holt, Rinehart, and Winston, 1960); Kay Lehman Schlozman and John Tierney, *Organized Interests and American Democracy* (New York: Harper and Row, 1986).
10. Gray and Lowery, "Diversity of State Interest Group Systems."
11. Harmon Ziegler and Henrik van Dahlen, "Interest Groups in State Politics," in *Politics in the American States,* ed. Herbert Jacobs and Kenneth Vines (Boston: Little, Brown,

1976), 93–138; Clive Thomas and Ronald Hrebenar, "Nationalization of Interest Groups and Lobbying in the American States," in *Interest Group Politics*, ed. Allan Cigler and Burdett Loomis (Washington, D.C.: Congressional Quarterly, 1983), chap. 3.

12. Kenneth J. Meier, *The Political Economy of Regulation: The Case of Insurance* (Albany: State University of New York Press, 1987); Evan J. Ringquist, *Environmental Protection at the State Level: Politics and Progress in Controlling Pollution* (Armonk, N.Y.: M.E. Sharpe, 1993).

13. V.O. Key Jr., *Southern Politics in State and Nation* (New York: Knopf, 1949); Thomas Holbrook and Emily van Dunk, "Electoral Competition in the American States," *American Political Science Review* 87 (December 1993): 955–62.

14. Charles Barrilleaux and Paul Brace, "A Model of Policy Reform in the American States," paper presented at the annual meeting of the American Political Science Association, Chicago, 1995. See also Garand, "New Perspectives," and idem, "Partisan Change and Shifting Expenditure Priorities in the American States, 1945–1978," *American Politics Quarterly* 13 (October 1985): 355–91.

15. Kim Quaile Hill and Jan Leighley, "The Policy Consequences of Class Bias in State Electorates," *American Journal of Political Science* 36 (1992): 351–65; Kim Quaile Hill, Jan Leighley, and Angela Hinton-Andersson, "Lower Class Mobilization and Policy Linkage in the U.S. States," *American Journal of Political Science* 39 (May 1995): 75–86.

16. Frances Stokes Berry and William Berry, "State Lottery Adoptions as Policy Innovations: An Event History Analysis," *American Political Science Review* 84 (June 1990): 395–415; idem, "Tax Innovation in the States: Capitalizing on Political Opportunity," *American Journal of Political Science* 36 (May 1992): 715–42.

17. Ann O'M. Bowman and Richard Kearney, "The Dimensions of State Government Capability," *Western Political Quarterly* 41 (June 1988): 341–62; Jeff Brudney and F. Ted Hebert, "State Agencies and Their Environments: Examining the Influence of Important External Actors," *Journal of Politics* 49 (February 1987): 189–206; Edward Carmines, "The Mediating Influence of State Legislatures on the Linkage between Interparty Competition and Welfare Policies," *American Political Science Review* 68 (September 1974): 1118–24; J. Grumm,"The Effects of Legislative Structure on Legislative Performance," in *State and Urban Politics,* ed. Richard Hofferbert and Ira Sharkansky (Boston: Little, Brown, 1971).

18. John Kingdon, *Agendas, Alternatives, and Public Policies* (Boston: Little, Brown, 1984).

19. James Stimson, *Public Opinion in America: Moods, Cycles, and Swings* (Boulder, Colo.: Westview, 1991).

20. Berry, *Interest Group Society;* Walter Dean Burnham, *Critical Elections and the Mainsprings of American Electoral Politics* (New York: Norton, 1970).

21. John Chubb, "Institutions, the Economy, and the Dynamics of State Elections," *American Political Science Review* 82 (March 1988): 133–54.

22. *Brown v. Board of Education of Topeka, Kansas,* 347 U.S. 483 (1954).

23. Paul Peterson, *City Limits* (Chicago: University of Chicago Press, 1981).

24. Frank Baumgartner and Bryan Jones, *Agendas and Instability in American Politics* (Chicago: University of Chicago Press, 1993).

25. Paul Brace, *State Government and Economic Performance* (Baltimore: Johns Hopkins University Press, 1993).

26. Paul Peterson and Mark Rom, "American Federalism, Welfare Policy, and Residential Choices," *American Political Science Review* 83 (September 1989): 711–28; idem, *Welfare Magnets: A New Case for a National Standard* (Washington, D.C.: Brookings Institution, 1990).

27. In an effort to reduce the state's attractiveness as a "welfare magnet," the governor of Wisconsin proposed a two-tiered welfare system whereby welfare recipients who had recently moved to Wisconsin from another state would receive welfare benefits equal to those paid in that state. The state legislature refused to enact such a system.

28. L.K. Rowland and Roger Marz, "Gresham's Law: The Regulatory Analogy," *Policy Studies Review* 1, no. 3 (1982): 572–80; Brace, *State Government.*

29. Jack Walker, "The Diffusion of Innovation among the American States," *American Political Science Review* 63 (September 1969): 880–99; Virginia Gray, "Innovation in

the States: A Diffusion Study," *American Political Science Review* 67 (1974):1174–85; Brace, *State Government.*

30. Paul Sabatier and Hank Jenkins-Smith, *Policy Change and Learning: An Advocacy Coalition Approach* (Boulder, Colo.: Westview, 1993).

31. Brace, *State Government;* Lowery and Gray, "Compensatory Impact"; Brierly and Feiock, "Accounting for State Economic Growth"; Margery Ambrosius, "The Effectiveness of State Economic Development Policies: A Time Series Analysis," *Western Political Quarterly* 42 (September 1989): 283–300.

32. Kingdon, *Agendas.*

33. Bradford Jones, "State Responses to Global Climate Change," *Policy Studies Journal* 19 (1991):73–82.

34. Baumgartner and Jones, *Agendas and Instability.* For issue redefinition in pesticide policy, see Chris Bosso, *Pesticides and Politics: The Lifecycle of a Public Issue* (Pittsburgh: University of Pittsburgh Press, 1987). For a further illustration of public disenchantment with nuclear energy, see Joseph Morone and Edward Woodhouse, *The Demise of Nuclear Energy? Lessons for Democratic Control of Technology* (New Haven, Conn.: Yale University Press, 1989).

35. James C. Garand, "Explaining Government Growth in the U.S. States," *American Political Science Review* 82 (March 1988): 837–49; idem, "New Perspectives."

36. Garand, "Explaining Government Growth"; William Berry and David Lowery, *Understanding United States Government Growth: An Empirical Analysis of the Postwar Era* (New York: Praeger, 1987); David Lowery and William Berry, "The Growth of Government in the United States: An Empirical Assessment of Competing Explanations," *American Journal of Political Science* 27 (November 1983): 664–94; Michael Lewis-Beck and Tom Rice, "Government Growth in the United States," *Journal of Politics* 47 (1985): 2–30.

37. Garand, "Explaining Government Growth"; idem, "New Perspectives."

38. William Niskanen, *Bureaucracy and Representative Government* (Chicago: Aldine, 1971); James C. Garand, Catherine Parkhurst, and Rusanne Jourdan Seoud, "Bureaucrats, Policy Attitudes, and Political Behavior: An Extension of the Bureau Voting Model of Government Growth," *Journal of Public Administration Research and Theory* 1 (1991): 177–212.

39. James C. Garand, "Partisan Change"; André Blais, Donald E. Blake, and Stephane Dion, "Do Parties Make a Difference? Parties and the Size of Government in Liberal Democracies," *American Journal of Political Science* 37 (February 1993): 40–62.

40. Garand, "Explaining Government Growth."

41. Garand, "New Perspectives."

42. The decline in highway spending priorities may reflect changes in intergovernmental grants available for highway construction. During the 1950s and 1960s, the federal government invested substantial resources in highway construction, particularly in the interstate highway system. The declining spending priorities for highways may reflect an artificially high level of spending during the 1950s and 1960s rather than a real decline in highway spending priorities.

43. Ringquist, *Environmental Protection,* 66.

44. James C. Garand and Pamela A. Monroe, "Family Leave Legislation in the American States: Toward a Model of State Policy Adoption," *Journal of Family and Economic Issues* 16 (1995): 341–63.

45. U.S. Department of Health and Human Services, *The 1996 Green Book* (Washington, D.C.: Government Printing Office, 1996).

46. Theodore Marmor, Jerry Mashaw, and Philip Harvey, *America's Misunderstood Welfare State* (New York: Basic Books, 1990); Charles Murray, *Losing Ground* (New York: Basic Books, 1984).

47. Peterson and Rom, "American Federalism."

48. Jeffrey Worsham and Evan Ringquist, "The Diffusion of Policy Innovation in the States: The Case of Learnfare," paper delivered at the annual meeting of the American Political Science Association, Washington, D.C., 1991.

49. DHHS, *1996 Green Book.*

50. Julie Strawn, Sheila Dacey, and Linda McCart, *Final Report: The National Governors' Association Survey of State Welfare Reforms* (Washington, D.C.: National Governors' Association, 1994).

51. DHSS, *1996 Green Book.*

52. Ibid.

53. Barry Rabe, "Power to the States: The Promise and Pitfalls of Decentralization," in *Environmental Policy in the 1990s*, 3d ed., ed. Norman Vig and Michael Kraft (Washington, D.C.: CQ Press, 1997); Ringquist, *Environmental Protection.*

54. R. Steven Brown et al., *Resource Guide to State Environmental Management*, 3d ed. (Lexington, Ky.: Council of State Governments, 1993).

55. Ringquist, *Environmental Protection.*

56. Rabe, "Power to the States."

57. "Expired Permits," *Detroit Free Press*, 20 February 1995, 6A.

58. Bob Hall and Mary Kay Kerr, *The Green Index* (Washington, D.C.: Institute for Southern Studies, 1991).

59. National Commission on Excellence in Education, *A Nation At Risk* (Washington, D.C.: U.S. Department of Education, 1983).

60. John Chubb and Terry Moe, *Politics, Markets, and America's Schools* (Washington, D.C.: Brookings Institution, 1990); Jonathan Kozol, *Savage Inequalities* (New York: Crown, 1991); National Commission on Excellence in Education, *A Nation at Risk.*

61. Sandia National Laboratories, "Perspectives on Education in America: An Annotated Briefing," *Journal of Educational Research* 93 (1993): 259–310; Jeffrey Henig, *Rethinking School Choice* (Princeton, N.J.: Princeton University Press, 1994).

62. Kevin Smith and Kenneth Meier, *The Case against School Choice: Politics, Markets, and Fools* (Armonk, N.Y.: M.E. Sharpe, 1995).

63. Alan Hickrod, Edward Hines, Gregory Anthony, John Dively, and Gwen Pruyne, "The Effect of Constitutional Litigation on Education Finance: A Preliminary Analysis," *Journal of Education Finance* 18 (1992): 180–210.

64. Chubb and Moe, *Politics, Markets.*

65. Smith and Meier, *Case Against School Choice*; Henig, *Rethinking School Choice*; John Witte, "Private School versus Public School Achievement: Are There Findings That Should Affect the Educational Choice Debate?" *Economics of Education Review* 11 (1992): 371–94.

66. Henig, *Rethinking School Choice.*

67. Jana Zinser, *Reinventing Education* (Cambridge, Mass.: National Conference of State Legislatures, 1994).

68. Russell Hanson, "The Development of Development Policy in the American States," in *State Policy Problems*, ed. Fred Meyer Jr. and Ralph Baker (Chicago: Nelson Hall, 1993).

69. Brace, *State Government*; Rebecca M. Hendrick and James C. Garand, "Variation in State Economic Growth: Decomposing State, Regional, and National Effects," *Journal of Politics* 53 (November 1991): 1093–1110.

70. F.A. Hayek, *The Road to Serfdom* (Chicago: University of Chicago Press, 1957); Milton Friedman, *Capitalism and Freedom* (Chicago: University of Chicago Press, 1962).

71. Brace, *State Government*; Thomas Dye and Richard Feiock, "State Income Tax Adoption and Economic Growth," *Social Science Quarterly* 76 (September 1995): 648–54; Thomas Plaut and Joseph Pluta, "Business Climate, Taxes and Expenditures, and State Industrial Growth in the U.S.," *Southern Economic Journal* 50 (July 1983): 99–119.

72. Brace, *State Government.*

73. We gratefully acknowledge the contributions of Laura Langer at Florida State University and Sharon Fox at the University of Illinois-Chicago in collecting and coding these economic development policy data, and the assistance of Philip J. Ardoin at Louisiana State University in collecting and coding data on state expenditures.

74. Paul Peterson, *The Price of Federalism* (Washington, D.C.: Brookings, 1996).

CHAPTER THIRTEEN

1. Charles Lindblom, "The Science of Muddling Through," *Public Administration Review* 19 (1959): 77–88; idem, *The Intelligence of Democracy* (New York: Free Press, 1965); David Braybrooke and Charles E. Lindblom, *A Strategy of Decision* (New York: Free Press, 1963).
2. Michael Hayes, *Incrementalism and Public Policy* (New York: Longman, 1992).
3. John Kingdon, *Agendas, Alternatives, and Public Policy* (Boston: Little, Brown, 1984).
4. Bryan D. Jones, *Reconceiving Decision-Making in Democratic Politics* (Chicago: University of Chicago Press, 1994).
5. Arthur F. Schlesinger Jr., *The Cycles of American History* (Boston: Houghton Mifflin, 1986).
6. Albert O. Hirschman, *Shifting Involvements* (Princeton, N.J.: Princeton University Press, 1982).
7. Virginia Gray, "Innovation in the States: A Diffusion Study," *American Political Science Review* 67 (December 1973): 1174–85.
8. Paul Peterson, *City Limits* (Chicago: University of Chicago Press, 1981).
9. Peter Eisinger, *The Rise of the Entrepreneurial State* (Madison: University of Wisconsin Press, 1988).
10. Ibid.
11. Susan E. Clarke and Gary L. Gaile, "The Next Wave: Postfederal Local Economic Development Strategies," in *Exploring Urban America*, ed. Roger W. Caves (Thousand Oaks, Calif.: Sage, 1995), 154–69.
12. Ibid., 157.
13. Ibid., 158–59.
14. Ibid., 161.
15. Peter Eisinger, "State Economic Development in the 1990s: Politics and Policy Learning," *Economic Development Quarterly* 9 (May 1995): 148, 151.
16. Adam J. Prager, Philip Benowitz, and Robert Schein, "Local Economic Development: Trends and Prospects," *The Municipal Yearbook 1995* (Washington, D.C.: International City Management Association, 1995), 21–35.
17. Eisinger, "State Economic Development," 152.
18. Prager, Benowitz, and Schein, "Local Economic Development," 35.
19. E.G. Goetz, "Type II Policy and Mandated Benefits in Economic Development," *Urban Affairs Quarterly* 26 (December 1990): 170–90.
20. Goetz, "Type II Policy."
21. David Elkins, "Testing Competing Explanations for the Adoption of Type II Policies," *Urban Affairs Review* 30 (July 1995): 809–39.
22. Charles J. Spindler and John P. Forrester, "Economic Development Policy: Explaining Policy Preferences among Competing Models," *Urban Affairs Quarterly* 29 (1993): 28–53.
23. Goetz, "Type II Policy"; Elkins, "Testing Competing Explanations."
24. Irene Rubin and Herbert Rubin, "Economic Development Incentives: The Poor (Cities) Pay More," *Urban Affairs Quarterly* 23 (September 1987): 37–61.
25. Elkins, "Testing Competing Explanations."
26. Goetz, "Type II Policy"; Elkins, "Testing Competing Explanations."; David R. Berman and Lawrence L. Martin, "The New Approach to Economic Development: An Analysis of Innovativeness in the States," *Policy Studies Journal* 20, no. 1 (1992): 10–21.
27. Peterson, *City Limits*.
28. Werner Z. Hirsch, "Contracting Out by Urban Governments: A Review," *Urban Affairs Review* 30 (January 1995): 458.
29. Ibid., 470.
30. Rowan Miranda and Karlyn Andersen, "Alternative Service Delivery in Local Government," *The Municipal Year Book 1994* (Washington, D.C.: International City Management Association, 1994), 26–35.
31. Elaine Sharp, *Urban Politics and Administration* (White Plains, N.Y.: Longman, 1990), 108–9. For a contrasting view, see Hirsch, "Contracting Out."
32. Lester M. Salamon, *Partners in Public Service* (Baltimore: Johns Hopkins University Press, 1995).

33. Evan McKenzie, *Privatopia* (New Haven, Conn.: Yale University Press, 1994).
34. Ibid., 126.
35. Susan Yeich, *The Politics of Ending Homelessness* (Lanham, Md.: University Press of America, 1994).
36. Joel Blau, *The Visible Poor: Homelessness in the United States* (New York: Oxford University Press, 1992), 121–28.
37. Jeffrey Henig, "To Know Them Is To . . . ? Proximity to Shelters and Support for the Homeless," *Social Science Quarterly* 75 (December 1994): 741–53.
38. Blau, *Visible Poor,* 126.
39. Ibid., 127.
40. Jennifer Wolch and Michael Dear, *Malign Neglect* (San Francisco: Jossey-Bass, 1993), 159.
41. Blau, *Visible Poor.*
42. Gray, "Innovation in the States."
43. Peterson, *City Limits,* 48; Paul Peterson, *Welfare Magnets: A New Care for a National Standard* (Washington, D.C.: Brookings Institution, 1990).
44. Madeleine Stoner, *The Civil Rights of Homeless People* (New York: Aldine de Gruyter, 1995), 139–41.
45. "No Spare Change," *The Economist,* 26 February 1994, 27–28.
46. Stoner, *Civil Rights,* 140–41.
47. "No Spare Change."
48. Stoner, *Civil Rights,* 150–53.
49. Ibid., 163–66.
50. Henig, "To Know Them."
51. Stoner, *Civil Rights,* 149.
52. D.P. Rosenbaum and A.J. Lurigio, "An Inside Look at Community Policing Reform: Definitions, Organizational Changes, and Evaluation Findings," *Crime & Delinquency* 40 (July 1994): 301–2.
53. Robert Stein, *Urban Alternatives* (Pittsburgh: University of Pittsburgh Press, 1990).
54. Eisinger, "State Economic Development."

About the Contributors

Charles Barrilleaux is Associate Professor of Political Science and faculty director of the DeVoe Moore Center Survey Research Laboratory at Florida State University. His research focuses on state politics and policymaking and has been published in several journals, including the *American Political Science Review* and the *American Journal of Political Science,* as well as in edited volumes.

John F. Bibby is Professor of Political Science at the University of Wisconsin-Milwaukee. A specialist in American political parties, he is the author of *Politics, Parties, and Elections in America,* 3d ed.; and coauthor of *Two Parties — Or More? The American Party System* and *Party Organizations in American Politics.* He has also held leadership positions in national and state party organizations.

Paul Brace is the Clarence L. Carter Chair in Legal Studies in the Department of Political Science at Rice University. His research interests include the presidency, Congress, state and local politics, and judicial politics and processes. He is the author of *State Government and Economic Performance* and coauthor (with Barbara Hinckley) of *Follow the Leader: Opinion Polls and the Modern Presidency,* winner of the Neustadt Prize. He is coeditor (with Gary King and Christine Harrington) of *The Presidency in American Politics.* His published research has appeared in the *American Political Science Review, The Journal of Politics, Political Research Quarterly, Polity, Social Science Quarterly, Legislative Studies Quarterly, American Politics Quarterly, Judicature,* and in several edited volumes.

Charles S. Bullock III is Richard B. Russell Professor of Political Science at the University of Georgia. A specialist in legislative politics and southern politics, he recently coedited *The New Politics of the Old South* and coauthored *Runoff Elections in the United States.* The latter volume won the V.O. Key Award from the Southern Political Science Association. His research has also been published in numerous journals and edited volumes. He is a past president of the Southern Political Science Association and the American Political Science Association's organized section on Legislative Studies.

Nelson C. Dometrius is Professor of Political Science and past chair of the department at Texas Tech University. He is the author of *Social Statistics Using SPSS* and coeditor of *Politics and Policy: U.S. and Texas.* His research on governors, state policies, and research methods has been published in the *American Journal of Political Science, The Journal of Politics, Political Research Quarterly, Social Science Quarterly, American Politics Quarterly, Public Administration Review,* and other journals.

James C. Garand is Professor of Political Science at Louisiana State University. His research on American politics has been published in a wide range of scholarly journals, including the *American Political Science Review, The Journal of Politics, American Journal of Political Science, Political Research Quarterly, Legislative Studies Quarterly, American Politics Quarterly,* and the *British Journal of Political Science.* He is former editor of the *American Politics Quarterly* and is also coeditor (with James Campbell) of *Before the Vote: Forecasting the 1996 American National Elections.*

Virginia Gray is Professor of Political Science at the University of Minnesota. She has published widely on numerous topics in state politics and public policy, including interest groups, economic development, and policy innovations. Her most recent books are *The Population Ecology of Interest Representation,* written with David Lowery, and *American States and Cities,* 2d ed., written with Peter Eisinger.

Melinda Gann Hall is Professor of Political Science at Michigan State University. Her research on judicial politics and behavior has appeared in *The Journal of Politics, Political Research Quarterly, Social Science Quarterly, American Politics Quarterly, Judicature,* and a variety of other scholarly journals and edited volumes. She also serves as co-principal investigator on the State Supreme Court Data Base, a fifty-state data collection project sponsored by the National Science Foundation.

David Lowery is Thomas J. Pearsall Professor of State and Local Government in the Department of Political Science at the University of North Carolina-Chapel Hill where he has served on the faculty since 1986. His research and teaching interests include the politics of state interest groups, urban politics, and tax and spending policy. He has published extensively on these topics in such journals as the *American Political Science Review,* the *American Journal of Political Science,* and *The Journal of Politics.* He is currently editor of *The Journal of Politics.*

Susan A. MacManus is Professor of Public Administration and Political Science at the University of South Florida-Tampa and has written extensively on urban issues. Her two most recent books are *Doing Business with the Government* and *Young v. Old: Generational Combat in the 21st Century.* Each examines the changing roles, responsibilities, and configurations of local governments across the United States. She is past president of the Urban Politics organized section of the American Political Science Association, the Southern Political Science Association, and the Florida Political Science Association. She received the University of South Florida's Outstanding Research Scholar Award in 1991 and the University's Phi Kappa Phi Artist-Scholar Award in 1997.

Evan J. Ringquist is Associate Professor of Political Science at Florida State University, where he specializes in environmental public policy, state politics, and bureaucratic politics. He holds an M.A. and Ph.D. in Political Science and M.S. in Land Resources from the University of Wisconsin. He is the author of *Environmental Protection at the State Level, Contemporary Regulatory Policy,* and numerous journal articles and book chapters.

Elaine B. Sharp is Professor of Political Science at the University of Kansas and a past president of American Political Science Association's organized section on Urban Politics. Her published work includes four books: *Urban Politics and Administration, Citizen Demand-Making in the Urban Context, Culture Wars and Urban Politics,* and *The Dilemma of Drug Policy,* along with numerous articles and chapters on economic development, citizen participation, and social policy in cities.

Robert M. Stein is the Lena Gohlman Fox Professor of Political Science and Dean of the School of Social Sciences at Rice University. He has written on urban politics and intergovernmental relations. He is the author (with Kenneth Bickers) of *Perpetuating the Pork Barrel* and *Urban Alternatives.*

James H. Svara is Professor and Head of Political Science and Public Administration at North Carolina State University. He specializes in local government politics and management and has a special interest in the roles of officials — mayors, council members, and administrators in local governments. He is the author of *Official Leadership in the City* and *Facilitative Leadership in Local Government.* Recent journal publications include "Complementarity of Politics and Administration as a Legitimate Alternative to the Dichotomy Model," which appeared in *Administration and Society,* and "The Shifting Boundary Between Elected Officials and City Managers in Large Council-Manager Cities," which appeared in *Public Administration Review.*

Daniel S. Ward is vice-president of Gelb Consulting Group in Houston, Texas. He has a Ph.D. in Political Science from New York University and has published in the areas of legislative politics and political party organization. His work has appeared in *The Journal of Politics, Legislative Studies Quarterly, Comparative Politics, Party Politics, Electoral Studies,* and *State and Local Government Review,* in addition to numerous book chapters. He is coeditor of *State Party Profiles,* published by Congressional Quarterly Books.

Ronald E. Weber is Wilder Crane Professor of Government in the Department of Political Science, University of Wisconsin-Milwaukee, former coeditor of *The Journal of Politics,* and a past president of the Southern Political Science Association. His research interests include representation, legislative systems, and state and local politics and policymaking. He is the coauthor (with Eric M. Uslaner) of *Patterns of Decision-Making in State Legislatures* and editor of *Wisconsin Government and Politics,* 6th ed. His published research has appeared in the *American Political Science Review, The Journal of Politics, Midwest Journal of Political Science, Polity, Public Opinion Quarterly, Legislative Studies Quarterly, American Politics Quarterly, Judicature, Political Methodology,* and in several edited volumes.

Index